COMPLETE GI

MW00745474

CREDIT AND COLLECTION LAW

SECOND EDITION

2002 SUPPLEMENT

ARTHUR WINSTON
JAY WINSTON

PRENTICE HALL

Library of Congress Cataloging-in-Publication Data

Winston, Arthur
   Complete guide to credit and collection law / Arthur Winston, Jay Winston.—2nd ed.
     p. cm.
   ISBN 0-13-042315-7
     1. Debtor and creditor—United States.   2. Executions (Law)—United States.   3.
   Bankruptcy—United States.   4. Credit—Law and legislation—United States.   5. Collection
   laws—United States.   I. Winston, Jay.   II. Title.
   KF1501 .W56 2002
   346.7307'7—dc21

                                                                        02-089707

Printed in the United States of America.

10 9 8 7 6 5 4 3 2 1

ISBN 0-13-042315-7

This publication is designed to provide accurate and authoritative information in regard
to the subject matter covered. It is sold with the understanding that the publisher is not
engaged in rendering legal, accounting, or other professional service. If legal advice or
other expert assistance is required, the services of a competent professional person should
be sought.

. . From the Declaration of Principles jointly adopted by a Committee of the American Bar
Association and a Committee of Publishers and Associations.

ATTENTION: CORPORATIONS AND SCHOOLS
Prentice Hall books are available at quantity discounts with bulk purchase for
educational, business, or sales promotional use. For information, please write to:
Prentice Hall Special Sales, 240 Frisch Court, Paramus, NJ 07652. Please supply:
title of book, ISBN, quantity, how the book will be used, date needed.

PRENTICE HALL
www.phdirect.com

*To Audrey
and
Liz*

ACKNOWLEDGMENTS

I wish to specifically thank the following persons and law firms for some of the appendix material appearing in the book.

- Don Maurice, Bridgewater, New Jersey, Counsel to Winston & Winston, P.C., for the in-depth article entitled "Assignee Liability for Truth in Lending Act Violations."

- Joseph D. Looney of Hudson Cook LLP, Crofton, Maryland for the table entitled, "Post Repossession Requirements for Motor Vehicles."

- Grant Mitchell of Reed Smith LLP for his article on Internet Lending and RESPA. The use of this article is gratefully acknowledged to the Quarterly Report of the Consumer Finance Law Conference, Oklahoma City, University of Law where this material was first published.

- Dan L. Nicewander of Gardere Winne Sewell LLP, Dallas, Texas for his article entitled "Summarizing the UCC Article 9 Revisions."

- Markus B. Heyder and Ann P. Forteney of Lovells, Washington, D.C. for their article entitled "Privacy Issues Update," covering the financial privacy regulations promulgated by the FTC pursuant to the Gramm-Leach Bliley Act.

- The National Conference of Commissioners on Uniform State Laws for allowing us to reprint the "Uniform Electronics Transaction Act."

- The National Association of Credit Management for "State Laws Controlling Assignment of Wages." (This table was prepared in 1996 and is furnished for guidelines and information. Significant and material changes may have been enacted since 1996.)

- Collections and Credit Risk magazine for the table, "Who's Who in Skiptracing Services."

- American Collectors Association for the table on "Special State Text Requirements for Dunning Notices."

HOW THIS SUPPLEMENT WILL HELP YOU

The purpose of this *Supplement* is to furnish users of the *Complete Guide to Credit and Collection Law* with key recent developments in the field. The information furnished in this *Supplement* has been developed by reason of the authors' subscribing to a number of credit and collection publications and attending several credit and collection conferences during the year. We are also members of several trade associations, including The National Association of Retail Collection Attorneys (NARCA), Commercial Law League, and the Map Attorney Program of the American Collector's Association. In addition, our firm, Winston & Winston, P.C., New York, NY, is actively engaged in the credit and collection industry, maintaining our own network of attorneys (WAMN) across the country for the collection of commercial and consumer debts. During the year, these attorneys often furnish us with information about new cases and changes in the law as well as new developments in the credit and collection industry.

While the crash in prices of the technology stocks may have discouraged some in the technology industry, the future is still electronic technology, websites, Internet, and e-mail. In the last few years, lawmakers have been struggling to effectively regulate this new means of communication and many of these laws directly affect the credit and collection industry. As a result, we have added a new chapter (E-Commerce Technology) which will address the problems of this information technology universe as it affects the industry.

The Gramm-Leach-Bliley Bill and the Health Insurance Portability and Accountability Act are treated, as well as revised Section 9 of the Uniform Commercial Code. Only now are some court decisions being rendered interpreting the provisions of revised Section 9 which took effect in 46 states on July 1, 2000.

The following are some of the highlights of this *Supplement*:

- Regarding the use of letters of credit, we discuss the Uniform Customs and Practices for Documentary Credits and furnish the information as to where the complete set of rules may be obtained. Almost every bank will require that a letter of credit be subject to the Uniform Customs and Practices (Chapter 2).

- The continued use of arbitration clauses by financial institutions is reviewed, including some suggestions on the drafting of a proper arbitration clause (Chapter 4).

- The impact of revised UCC 9 is covered in an informative article by Dan L. Nicewander in the Appendix to Chapter 10.

- A discussion on the issue of Stripping Liens in a bankruptcy proceeding is offered in Chapter 5.

- Chapter 9 on privacy covers the Health Insurance Portability and Accountability Act. The Appendix to Chapter 9 provides excerpts from the Gramm-Leach-Bliley Act and a review of the privacy issues being confronted by the financial institutions who during the year send out a multitude of privacy notices to their customers.

- Prescreening is a common procedure in the direct mail industry; a summary of the provisions of this section on the Fair Credit Reporting Act is provided in Chapter 14.

- The unique application of the "Offer of Judgment" in Class Actions under the Fair Debt Collection Practices Act is covered in Chapter 11.

- An excellent presentation on the Liabilities of Assignees under the Truth in Lending Act is presented by Don Maurice, of counsel to our firm, in the Appendix to Chapter 12.

- A review of lending procedures through the Internet is covered in an in-depth article by Grant Mitchell in Chapter 10.

The material in this *Supplement* is arranged to substantially correspond with the chapters in the main volume.

NOTE

No attempt has been made here to review, include, or comment upon all the relevant laws and statutes. The major federal laws mentioned in the text or set forth in the Appendices must be considered in light of the laws passed by each of the fifty states. Some states have passed separate laws which directly subject creditors to regulations. Other states have passed more oppressive or burdensome mirror images of the federal law.

Most of the general statements presented are representative of the laws in the majority of states, but some states have passed laws that modify or change the legal consequences of the general statement. Exceptions exist to every general statement. Therefore, a general statement should not be used to fit a particular set of circumstances until after a thorough examination of the facts and laws plus a review of the decisions of the court of the appropriate state.

Laws and statutes are continually amended, revised, and repealed and court decisions may be reversed or rendered obsolete by more recent decisions or decisions of higher courts. The limited material presented here reflects what generally existed at the time this book was written. By the time this second edition reaches the reader, the reader must be aware that there may have been changes in the statutes and that more recent cases may have affected the contents. The author recommends that a review of all the state laws and federal laws as well as the court decisions of the federal courts and the state courts should be done before any decision is made with regard to any legal problem involved with the credit or collection effort and consultation with an attorney is always recommended before proceeding.

While we attempt to cover all the major amendments to laws as well as the major decisions that affect the industry, we know that it is impossible to be comprehensive and complete. There are certainly many changes in the laws of the various states as well as decisions that we have not addressed, either because we are not aware of them or because of the limited space available.

The tables offered were probably prepared months or much longer prior to publication, and thus the information should be verified.

We welcome any reader to bring to our attention any state law or court decision which significantly affects the credit and collection industry. Please forward any material to: Winston and Winston P.C., 18 East 41st Street, New York, NY 10017, Attn: Arthur Winston.

This book is not intended to be a substitute for consultation with an attorney. Consultation is not only recommended, but encouraged. We hope that this volume provides you with additional compliance guidance in your credit and collection efforts.

CONTENTS

Chapter 8   REPOSSESSION OF PROPERTY   163

Chapter 9   HARASSMENT, INTIMIDATION, AND INVASION OF PRIVACY   169

CHAPTER 1

An Explanation
of Legal Terminology
in a Collection Case

SURETYSHIP

A contract of suretyship is a promise made by a third person to be responsible for the debtor's obligation with some benefit to the party becoming the surety (an insurance contract). A surety in the strict sense is primarily liable for the debt of the principal. The creditor need not exhaust all remedies against the principal debtor before holding the surety responsible. Moreover, a surety agreement that benefits the surety does not have to be in writing to be enforceable, whereas a contract of guarantee, where someone promises to answer for the debt of another, does have to be in writing and may be of no benefit to the guarantor. With a guarantee, the guarantor is secondarily liable. The guarantor can only be required to pay the obligation after the principal defaults, the surety is primarily liable.

A surety may be known as a co-maker or an endorser or an accommodation party. A surety includes all types of guarantors. If the creditor received collateral from the debtor, the surety could be discharged to the extent of the impairment of said collateral. If the creditor repossessed an auto and was negligent in storing the vehicle before the auction sale, and the car was damaged, the surety may be discharged to the extent of the damage of the collateral.

PAROLE EVIDENCE RULE

Parole evidence is a rule of evidence that bestows a preferred status on final written agreements. The rule is designed to provide stability in business transactions. The rule protects the agreement from the risk of perjured testimony and the risk of uncertain testimony of a party with a "slippery" and "self-serving" memory. At trial, the rule excludes earlier oral agreements or any contemporaneous oral agreements. The basis of the rule is that these earlier agreements were not intended to survive, but to be merged into the final agreement.

The Parole Evidence Rule holds that where an agreement has been reduced to writing and is intended to be the final and complete expression of the agreement between the parties, any evidence of earlier oral or written agreements or any contemporaneous oral agreements are not admissible in a court of law to vary, add to, or contradict the terms of the written agreement.

When Does the Parole Evidence Apply? There are two key issues: First, one must determine whether the parties intended the writing to be the final written agreement. Second, one must determine whether there is partial or total integration of the prior oral or written agreements. If a court determines that only partial integration exists, the agreement may be supplemented by additional terms. Seems simple, right? Well, five different tests have been developed to apply this rule.

Four Corners Rule—In applying the first test, the trial judge actually examines only the written agreement and makes a determination if the agreement represents the final intent of the parties. This test is not widely accepted due to the limited information provided. The drafter of the agreement is subject to the subjective interpretation of the judge hearing the case. This test usually favors the drafter of the agreement unless the agreement is too specific or too vague. If the agreement is poorly drafted, the drafter of the agreement suffers, especially if this interpretation is beneficial to the other party. Although many creditors desire the courts to apply this test, it rarely occurs, especially in consumer credit transactions.

Any Relevant Evidence Test—The second test directs the court to seek out the actual intention of the parties to determine if the document was partially or totally integrated. Under this test, a judge would admit evidence of all relevant prior negotiations and treat the document as partially integrated. This test is increasingly applied by judges, because it permits the court wide latitude in making its determination to admit evidence, since anything may be relevant.

Collateral Contract Rule—This test is subject to two interpretations. Under one version, (A) all written agreements are deemed to be partially integrated. Additional terms in prior or contemporaneous agreements that do not contradict the writing are admissible. The key point is that the additional terms may not contradict the terms in the main agreement. Additional writings explaining the original writing would be admissible.

(B) if the additional terms are covered in the original written agreement, the evidence is excluded. However, if the additional terms are not covered by the original agreement, the document is treated as partially integrated, and the additional terms are considered by the court. The test is applied only by a few courts and is open to subjective interpretation.

The Modern Test—This test holds that if the written agreement includes a merger clause, expressly and conspicuously stating that this writing is intended to be the final and complete version of the agreement, the agreement is held to be completely integrated. Only if it is obvious that the agreement is incomplete, or that the merger clause was included as a result of fraud or mistake, will a court consider additional evidence. In the absence of the merger clause, the court will examine the writing. Additional terms may be provided if the writing is obviously incomplete, or if the additional terms are of the type that would naturally appear in a separate writing.

U.C.C. Test—The fifth test is set forth in Section 2-202 of the Uniform Commercial Code, which applies to contracts for the sale of goods. Section 2-202 states:

> Terms with respect to which the confirmatory memoranda of the parties agree or which are otherwise set forth in the writing intended by the parties as a final expression of the agreement with respect to such terms as are included therein may not be contradicted by evidence of any prior agreement or of a contemporaneous oral agreement, but may be explained or supplemented
>
> (a) by course of dealing or usage of trade... or by course of performance...; and
>
> (b) by evidence of consistent terms unless the court finds the writing to have been intended also as a complete and exclusive statement of the terms of agreement.

The U.C.C. test is a liberal test because evidence of a separate agreement is admissible unless the matters covered in the alleged agreement "certainly would have been included" in the writing.

Depending on which test is used, a different result may occur. Judges usually consider fairness, equity, and who benefits from the interpretation of the agreement. For example, a liberal judge is more likely to use a test that favors a consumer against a large corporation. However, in a situation between two corporations, the same test might lead to a different outcome.

This rule only prohibits the allegations from being offered into evidence. If the allegations are not in evidence, the trier of fact (jury) will never hear the evidence. In a trial by a judge, the judge makes the ruling of admissibility as well as being the trier of fact. Once the document is offered, and the judge has seen the document, the issue of admissibility may no longer be relevant.

Even if the allegedly damaging allegations are admitted into evidence, what weight the trier of the fact (judge or jury) assesses to the prior negotiations is another story. Many judges believe that the evidence should be excluded. To prevent being overturned on appeal, the judge, nevertheless, admits the documents into evidence, but then assesses little credibility to the evidence when rendering a decision. Appellate courts have discretion to determine if evidence was excluded, but rarely overrule a judge or jury on assessing the credibility of the evidence.

EXEMPLIFIED JUDGMENT/TRIPLE SEAL JUDGMENT

If a creditor obtains a judgment in one state and the debtor travels to another state, in most instances the full faith and credit provisions follow the debtor to enforce collection of the judgment. The courts of one state must afford full faith and credit to the judgments of another state. In order that one state will recognize the judgment of another state, the courts will usually require that the creditor obtain a triple seal or exemplified copy of the judgment which can be obtained from the County Clerk or the Judgment Clerk where the particular judgment was entered. The clerk will certify in writing, affixing a corporate seal or some form of a stamp, that the particular judgment was entered and will list the name of the judgment creditor, the name of the judgment debtor, the amount of the judgment, the date the judgment was entered, and the court and index number under which the judgment was entered. The creditor files this instrument in the state and county where the debtor now resides and under most statutes is entitled to enforce the judgment in the same manner as the judgment entered in the state where the debtor formerly resided.

One exception are judgments that are obtained on default where the debtor has neither answered the complaint nor appeared in the action. Some states (New York, Connecticut, Massachusetts) rely on the position that a judgment of this nature should not be recognized since the debtor has neither answered nor appeared in the action and therefore has not submitted to the jurisdiction of the court. Under these circumstances, the creditor will have to institute a separate suit on the judgment against the debtor. In these states, the courts frown on default judgments based on long-arm jurisdiction and will often vacate these judgments. It is strongly recommended that counsel for the creditor sue not only on the judgment but also sue the debtor on the underlying debt in the states that do not permit enforcement of a foreign judgment where the judgment was obtained by default.

CHAPTER 2

Legal Concepts of Business

LETTER OF CREDIT

When a person first encounters the transaction of a letter of credit, or arranges for the issuance of the letter of credit, or is the recipient of the letter of credit, the transaction surrounding the letter of credit may seem somewhat complex. We will attempt to furnish a basic explanation.

First, the letter of credit is a direct agreement between the issuing bank and the beneficiary (selling party) of the credit. Basically, the beneficiary of the credit is the party who is to receive payment and the bank is the party who is to issue payment to the beneficiary (seller).

Second, a separate agreement lies between the account party (buyer) and the issuing bank. The account party (purchasing party) is a debtor and owes the bank money in the event that a letter of credit is exercised. The account party has a separate agreement with the bank, and under the terms of this agreement must pay the bank in advance or reimburse the bank for any monies paid under the letter of credit, i.e., for any monies that the bank pays to the beneficiary. This agreement between the issuing bank and the account party is totally separate and distinct from the actual letter of credit, which is a separate agreement between the issuing bank and the beneficiary (seller).

Distinct and apart from the above two contracts, a separate contract exists between the beneficiary (seller) and the account party (buyer), which is the contract for the sale of the goods and the terms and conditions of payment for the goods by a letter of credit.

Therefore, three contracts exist:

(1) a contract between the issuing bank and the beneficiary (the selling party) of the credit;

(2) a contract between the issuing bank and the account party (the purchasing party) who is obligated to advance or to reimburse the bank for any monies paid out by the bank; and

(3) the contract between the beneficiary (the selling party) and the account party (the purchasing party) who arranges for the issuance of the letter of credit.

One of the results of the above contractual relationships is that in a bankruptcy proceeding of the account party, the selling party is still entitled to enforce the letter of credit because the account party is not involved in nor has any connection with the agreement between the beneficiary and the issuing bank.

The concept that each contract is separate and distinct from the other contract is most important to understand in the letter of credit transaction. Each contract is independent and can be enforced by the parties to the contract regardless of the other two contracts.

Where a seller delivers defective goods to a buyer, the buyer attempts to persuade the bank not to pay the letter of credit. Because of the separateness of the contracts, the bank is under a direct obligation to fulfill the letter of credit if the seller presents the proper documents of title to the bank. The failure of the bank to honor the said letter of credit will expose the bank to a lawsuit directly by the seller. After the bank pays the seller, the buyer may institute suit for a breach of contract or a breach of warranty (or whatever other remedies are available against the seller) for the seller's failure to deliver the merchandise as it was ordered.

On the other hand, situations arise where a bank may choose to dishonor a letter of credit even on presentation of proper documents or titles. If the buyer can produce a clear evidence of fraud in the underlying contract that was entered into between the buyer and seller, the bank may have a right to refuse to honor the letter of credit in a fraudulent situation.

The buyer must produce convincing evidence that the entire transaction was a total fraud, e.g., the shipment consists of empty cartons with no furniture in the cartons. What is more likely to happen is that the buyer would retain counsel, make an application to court, and have the court issue an injunction directing the bank not to make payment under its obligation to the seller.

If the bank does honor the letter of credit and pays the seller, the buyer may now sue the seller to recover all or part of the letter of credit proceeds from the seller. The seller cannot avail itself of the defense that a separate contract existed between the seller and the bank to defend itself against the buyer's suit, because the theory of independence is not applicable once the payment by the bank has been made. Whereas the separate contract guarantees that the money will reach the seller upon presentation of the proper documents of title, the independence theory does not affect the contract between the seller and the buyer after payment has been made by the bank. A buyer may sue the seller for a breach of contract.

In a situation where the bank honors its obligation to the seller, but the buyer does not reimburse the bank, the bank may immediately commence suit against the buyer for reimbursement. The bank also may claim to be subjugated to the seller's rights against the buyer. Accordingly, the bank would have two claims against the buyer. The first claim would be under its contract with the buyer to reimburse, and the second claim would be under the seller's contract with the buyer to be paid for the monies that the bank paid to the seller.

Types of Letters of Credit—Commercial and Standby

There are two types of letters of credit. The first is the commercial letter of credit facilitating the sale of goods and protecting a third party against the customer's default in the underlying obligation. The buyer arranges for a bank to issue a letter of credit for the benefit of the seller. The buyer is the applicant, the seller is the beneficiary, and the bank is the issuer. The letter is an undertaking by the bank to honor all drafts drawn by the seller for the purchase price as long as the drafts are accompanied by the necessary documents in the letter such as the invoice, a bill of lading, or an inspection certificate. The risk of the buyer's insolvency is shifted to the bank, as is the risk of the buyer trying to renege on the agreement. The seller receives the benefit of the bank's undertaking upon the seller complying with the documentary requirements.

The second type of letter of credit is the standby letter of credit. The standby letter of credit guarantees that the bank will honor its customer's performance of obligations in a variety of situations. For example, instead of a performance bond from a surety, an owner of real estate may require the contractor to procure a letter of credit obligating its bank to pay the owner upon presentment of a certificate of default accompanied by a draft demanding payment. The letter of credit was a standby letter of credit, which is common in the construction industry.

A letter of credit may state that it is governed by the "Uniform Customs and Practices for Commercial Documentary Credit." Unfortunately, the Uniform Customs and Practices for Documentary Credit has no provisions that cover fraud. The Uniform Customs does not specifically prohibit the defense of fraud in a transaction; but being silent on the subject, the court may use the Uniform Commercial Code. The Uniform Commercial Code allows the dishonor of a draft on a letter of credit when fraud is in the transaction.[1]

UCC Section 5-114 states:

(1) issuer must honor a draft or demand for payment that complies with the terms of the relevant credit regardless of whether the goods or documents conform to the underlying contract for sale or other contract between the customer and the beneficiary...

(2) unless otherwise agreed when documents appear on the face to comply with the terms of credit but...there is fraud in the transaction:

Subdivision B...an issuer acting in good faith may honor the draft or demand for payment despite notification from the customer of fraud, forgery, or other defect not apparent on the face of the document, but a court of appropriate jurisdiction may enjoin such honor.

A commercial letter of credit is made up of three independent contracts: one between the customer (buyer) and the issuer, one between the issuer and the beneficiary (seller), and one between the beneficiary and the customer. A standby letter of credit involves the customer (construction firm), the issuer (the bank), and the insurer beneficiary (the bonding company). Each contract is independent of the other contract, and for this reason, the courts interpret the contracts on a strict basis. Nevertheless, the UCC states that the bank may honor a letter of credit in the case of fraud despite notification from the customer, and the courts interpret this to

---

[1]*Prairie State Bank v. Universal Bonding Ins. Co.*, 953 P.2d 1047 (C.A. Kan. 1998).

mean that the bank may also decide not to honor the letter of credit. The option is with the issuer of the letter of credit.

The fraud in the transaction must stem from the conduct of the beneficiary against the customer, not by the customer against the issuer of the letter of credit. The purpose of the letter of credit is to allow the beneficiary to rely thereon. Fraud in this connection is defined as "of such an egregious nature as to vitiate the entire transaction."

A bank may dishonor a sight draft drawn on a letter of credit valid on its face and made in compliance with the terms of the letter of credit if it determines fraud was committed. The fraud must be of a serious nature to outweigh the public policy consideration requiring issuing banks to pay upon demand under the letter of credit if the documents submitted comply with the terms of the letter of credit. Where there is a blatant fraud being practiced, and evidence of the fraud is present, a bank can refuse to pay the letter of credit.

To what extent the customer would have to indemnify the bank is an open question since banks recognize that if they do not pay a letter of credit when the sight draft complies strictly with the requirements of the letter of credit, a suit will be instituted and a claim may be made upon the bank not only for the funds that it refuses to pay, but for consequential damages flowing from the failure to honor the letter of credit and even punitive damage. It is a rare situation, even with fraud, that a bank will refuse to honor a letter of credit. What is more likely is that the customer obtains a court order expressly enjoining the bank from paying the letter of credit. Consult with experienced counsel.

Letters of Credit—Strict Interpretation

The strict interpretation that courts apply to letters of credit has produced significant litigation over the years. Many courts in other nations use their own national law as the United States would apply the appropriate sections of the Uniform Commercial Code. On the other hand, many domestic letters of credit incorporate the rules set forth by the Uniform Customs and Practices for Documentary Credit, which is used internationally. Most international letters of credit are controlled by the Uniform Customs and Practices for Documentary Credit and the application of the UCP to the letter of credit is recited in the letters of credit itself.

A case in New York analyzed problems in two irrevocable letters of credit. The purchaser placed an order for clothing with the plaintiff; the plaintiff (seller) would ship the clothing to the purchaser and would submit to the bank that issued the letter of credit whatever documents of the shipment the irrevocable letter of credit required. The bank that issued the letter of credit on behalf of the purchaser would pay the balance under the irrevocable letter of credit. This is the simple triparty transaction where there are three separate contracts: one between the purchaser and the plaintiff seller, one between the plaintiff and the bank, and one between the seller and the bank.

The UCP Article 14 addresses the issues of banks' and beneficiaries' rights when the beneficiary's documents contain discrepancies in a payment demand. The standard of strict compliance applies to the beneficiary's duty to provide the documentation that the letter of credit requires, which means that even slight discrepancies in compliance with the terms of the letter of credit justify refusal to pay. The courts have carved a narrow exception to the standard of strict compliance for variations in documents so insignificant that said variations do not relieve the issuing bank of its obligation to pay, including a situation where a word in the document is unmistakably clear despite an obvious typographical error, or where the customer provides only five copies of the documents instead of six.

When documents containing discrepancies are presented to an issuing bank, the issuing bank must provide notice of the refusal decision within seven days, stating exactly what the discrepancies are and why the bank is refusing the documents. If the bank doesn't provide such notice, it is precluded from claiming that the documents are not in compliance with the terms and conditions of the letter of credit. The bank must explain which discrepancies are the basis for its refusal to accept the letter of credit. Merely listing discrepancies and not distinguishing which are immaterial and which are significant is insufficient. The notice must set forth in clear language the exact grounds for refusal to accept the letter of credit. A letter listing all the discrepancies, both the material and the immaterial, would not be an adequate notice, and the issuer of the letter of credit may be liable if the documents submitted were rejected.[2]

Letter of Credit—Red Clause

A "red clause" allows a beneficiary under a letter of credit to receive advances, even before shipping the merchandise, upon presenting certain documents, including an undertaking that it would later present the normal papers (a red clause is so called because it is often printed in red). The

---

[2]*Creaciones Con Idea, S.A. de C.V. v. MashreqBank PSC,* 51 F. Supp.2d 423 (S.D.N.Y.), dismissed by 75 F. Supp.2d 279 (S.D.N.Y. 1999); *Trifinery v. Banque Paribas,* 762 F. Supp. 1119 (S.D.N.Y. 1991).

reason a red clause is printed in red is that it is a deviation from the normal letter of credit and it may create a dangerous problem when a party receives advances but has not produced the product ready for delivery. Red clauses are often present where there is collusion, fraud, or gross negligence between the bank and the seller, because advancing the money before shipping opens up a world of opportunity for the seller to defraud the purchaser.

Letter of Credit—Silent Confirmation

The independence principle is a cornerstone of the letter of credit bank. Many courts have stated that the confirming or nominating bank (agent bank of issuing bank) owes a statutory duty only to the issuing bank and not to the issuing bank's customer. Often the customer of the issuing bank wishes to proceed against the nominating or confirming bank and the courts have held that there is no privity between the customer and the nominating or confirming bank and will not permit the beneficiary to proceed against said bank.

A silent confirmation occurs when a bank agrees to confirm a letter of credit but the agreement to do so does not appear on the face of the letter of credit. Silent confirmations often happen when a bank is authorized but not obligated by the issuing bank to make advances against the letter of credit. Under the new UCC, effective after January, 1998, subrogation is allowed so that a customer may stand in the place of the bank and proceed against a nominating or confirming bank, but prior thereto the UCC did not provide for this right of subrogation.[3]

Letter of Credit—Waiver of Discrepancies

Under the "independence rule" applied to letters of credit that set forth three separate contracts among the three parties, the law is well established that a bank is entitled to refuse to honor a letter of credit. Strict compliance with the terms and conditions as set forth in the letter of credit must be met.

The independence principle supports the concept that an issuing bank is not bound to accept an applicant's waiver of discrepancies. The letter of credit is a contract between the beneficiary and the issuing bank. The issuing bank will honor its payment obligations if the beneficiary strictly complies with the letter of credit. If the beneficiary's documents do

---

[3]*Leonard A. Feinberg, Inc. v. Central Asia Capital Corp.*, 974 F. Supp. 822 (E.D. Pa. 1997); *Tokyo Kyogo Boeki Shokai v. United States Nat'l Bank of Oregon*, 126 F.3d 1135 (9th Cir. 1997).

not comply, the issuing bank at that point has an option to ask the buyer (who paid for the letter of credit) whether the buyer wishes to waive the discrepancies in the terms and conditions of the letter of credit. The issuing bank runs the risk that the buyer may forthwith file a bankruptcy petition, but the issuing bank would still be liable under the letter of credit. Thus, the contract between the buyer and the bank will have no effect between the bank and the seller as to the question of compliance with the letter of credit.

While the established law seems to be that the bank still has the right to insist on strict compliance notwithstanding the waiver, over the years some cases have determined that the bank must comply with a waiver of discrepancies communicated to it by the buyer.

We now have another case where an issuing bank had sought and received a waiver of discrepancies. The court felt there "would be no reason for the bank to seek this waiver unless it had first determined that it would not insist upon whatever right it had to demand strict compliance." Perhaps if the bank did not seek the waiver and received the waiver voluntarily from the buyer, the court might have held differently. This decision may produce future cases attacking the concept that the bank can always refuse to honor the letter of credit because of discrepancies, notwithstanding a waiver.[4]

The International Chamber of Commerce publishes a booklet entitled "ICC Uniform Customs and Practices for Documentary Credits" (UCP). (This booklet can be obtained from the ICC Publishing, Inc. in New York.) It is common in international letters of credit and in domestic letters of credit that the letter of credit issued is subject to the provisions of the Uniform Customs and Practices.

Article 14(c) of the UCP provides that if the issuing bank determines that the documents appear on their face not to be in compliance with the terms and conditions of the credit, the bank in its sole discretion may approach the applicant for a waiver of the discrepancy. The UCP does not expressly make any statement whether the bank must accept the waiver of discrepancies by the buyer. The position of most of the courts is that the bank has no obligation to accept a waiver of discrepancy and may refuse to honor the credit notwithstanding the communication of a written waiver by the buyer to the bank.

The request for a waiver does not extend the period of time set forth in Article 13(b). The bank has seven days to examine the documents and

---

[4]*Lectrodryer v. Seoul Bank,* 77 Cal. App. 4th 723 (Cal. App. 2 Dist. 2000).

determine whether to accept or refuse the documents and to inform the party from whom it received the documents.

> **Credit & Collection Tip:** *A business utilizing letters of credit should obtain the Uniform Customs and Practices for Documentary Credits. Almost all letters of credit issued by the banks, both domestic and foreign, are issued under the provisions of the UCP. Counsel for the banks are familiar with the provisions and you should also be familiar with the provisions of the UCP before you undertake the use of letters of credit.*

Letter of Credit—Confirming Bank

Typically, a standby letter of credit transaction consists of three independent contracts between the three parties. The buyer of the product (applicant) contracts with the bank (the issuer) to reimburse the bank, either before or at the time the bank pays the letter of credit; the issuing bank contracts with the seller who is paid upon performance; and the applicant contracts with the seller for the actual purchase.

The principle of independent contracts in a letter of credit transaction is set forth in the Uniform Customs and Practices, Article 3(a) and (b) ("Credit v. Contracts"), which states that each of the contracts is separate and distinct from the others. When a confirming bank is brought into the transaction, the issuing bank creates a contract between them wherein the issuing bank will reimburse the confirming bank for any payments that the confirming makes to the seller. This contract is separate and distinct from the other three contracts. The confirming bank also creates a separate obligation to the seller.

Should the confirming bank not perform its contract with the seller, the buyer, who does not have a separate independent contract with the confirming bank, would have difficulty asserting a claim against the confirming bank.

Letters of Credit—Third-Party Beneficiary

The undertaking of a letter of credit is sometimes called a contract, but most prefer to refer to it only as a letter of credit or as an "undertaking" and not as a contract. The courts wish to avoid contract inferences primarily because of the third-party beneficiary status of others. In any event, the letter of credit is a unilateral undertaking with no promise by anyone other than the bank.

A third-party beneficiary is one for whose benefit a promise is made in a contract between two parties, but who is not one of the two parties to the contract. A classic example is an insurance policy where a husband obtains life insurance from the insurance company. The wife is the beneficiary and can enforce the terms of the contract against the insurance company if the insurance company fails to pay, but she was not a party to the contract between the husband and the insurance company. A prime requisite to the status of a third-party beneficiary is that the two parties to the contract must have intended to benefit the third party, which intent must be something more than a mere incidental intention. The third party would have the right to institute suit against either one of the parties to the contract in the event that the particular party failed to perform the terms of the contract, which is not the case in a letter of credit.[5]

BILL OF LADING

Similar to a letter of credit, a bill of lading is a contract that is strictly construed. Absent a valid agreement to the contrary, the carrier (the issuer of the bill of lading) is responsible for releasing the cargo only to the party who presents the original bill of lading. If instead of insisting upon the production and surrender of the bill of lading, the carrier chooses to deliver to the wrong party, the carrier is then liable for conversion and must indemnify the shipper for any loss that results.

In a recent case in New York, the carrier delivered the goods without obtaining surrender of the bill of lading. The party to whom the goods were delivered did not have a bill of lading and thus the carrier misdelivered the goods. Unless this misdelivery of the goods was caused or induced by the shipper, the carrier is liable to the shipper for conversion since delivery was made without obtaining a surrender of the bill of lading. This is a different situation where the carrier delivered the goods without obtaining a bill of lading, but the recipient did have possession of the bill of lading.

Although this may seem like plain and simple common sense, the Federal Court in the 2nd Circuit cited a case in 1985 that stated "absent a valid agreement to the contrary, the carrier, the issuer of the bill of lading, is responsible for releasing the cargo only to the party who presents the original bill of lading....If the carrier delivers the goods to one other than

---

[5]*Pere Marquette Ry. Co. v. J. F. French & Co.*, 254 U.S. 538, 41 S.Ct. 195, 65 L.Ed. 391 (1921).

the authorized holder of the bill of lading, the carrier is liable for misde-livery".[6]

OFFERS AND ACCEPTANCE DO NOT AGREE

UCC Section 2-207 was an attempt to clarify the situation where a buyer submitted a written purchase order to purchase goods (with printed terms on the reverse side) and the seller then confirms the offer to purchase in writing. If the seller merely confirms the order and accepts the order on the terms submitted by the buyer, no problem would exist. What often happens is that the seller sends additional terms either separately or with the product itself (such as in the carton) and these additional terms do not match the terms of the purchase order under which the buyer intended to purchase the goods.

Under traditional contract law, an offer had to be identical for the acceptance to be effective. If any discrepancy existed between the terms of the written offer and the written acceptance, it would be treated as a rejection of the contract and there would be no contract. The additional terms would constitute another offer. If there was no contract and the additional offer was not on identical terms, the parties did not have a contract and were not obligated under any contract.

If the parties perform the contract by having one party ship the goods and the buyer accepts the goods and utilizes the goods, under the common law, the act of performance was an acceptance of the original offer made by the purchaser. If there was no performance but the purchaser needed the goods and the seller refused to perform, the attitude of the courts was that no contract existed since there was no acceptance. If there was performance as we described above on the terms of the original offer, and a dispute arose after the performance, the general perception was that a contract existed on the terms of the original offer.

Simply put, most merchants understood under the law prior to the Uniform Commercial Code that an offer had to be accepted. If the offer was not accepted under the terms of the offer, the best that could be said is that there was a counter offer and it was now up to the other party to accept the counter offer. That was the law until the Uniform Commercial

[6]*Datas Industries Ltd v. OEC Freight (HK), Ltd.*, 2000 WL 1597843 (S.D.N.Y. Oct. 25, 2000); *Allied Chemical Intern. Corp. v. Companhia de Navegacao Lloyd Brasileiro*, 775 F.2d 476 (2nd Cir. 1985)

Code and particularly Section 2-207 was adopted. The section was designed to promote trade between merchants and was further designed to eliminate litigation over the type of terms that would not impact a transaction. Unfortunately, rather than clarify and make trading more simple, in many instances Section 2-207 has made things complicated and created more litigation. We will try to put this section in simple terms, although we doubt we will be successful.

2-207. Additional Terms in Acceptance or Confirmation.

(1) A definite and seasonable expression of acceptance or a written confirmation that is sent within a reasonable time operates as an acceptance even though it states terms additional to or different from those offered or agreed upon, unless acceptance is expressly made conditional on assent to the additional or different terms.

(2) The additional terms are to be construed as proposals for addition to the contract. Between merchants, such terms become part of the contract unless:

(a) the offer expressly limits acceptance to the terms of the offer;

(b) they materially alter it; or

(c) notification of objection to them has already been given or is given within a reasonable time after notice of them is received.

(3) Conduct by both parties that recognizes the existence of a contract is sufficient to establish a contract for sale although the writings of the parties do not otherwise establish a contract. In such case, the terms of the particular contract consist of those terms on which the writings of the parties agree, together with any supplementary terms incorporated under any other provisions of this Act.

Section 1 states that acceptance or confirmation (sent within a reasonable time) operates as an acceptance of an offer even though it states terms additional to or different from those offered or agreed upon. The section provides for one exception where the offer expressly states that acceptance is totally conditional on agreeing to the additional or different terms. In summary, additional or different terms in the acceptance still creates an acceptance unless the original offer expressly sets forth in writing that no additional or different terms will be tolerated.

The drafters understood that there were additional problems with Subdivision 1 and attempted to clarify these problems in Subdivision 2. When a contract is entered into between the parties by reason of Subdivision 1 (additional or different terms), one must now read Subdivision 2 to understand what are the terms of the contract. The additional terms are to be construed as proposals for additions to the contract in all situations unless the contract is between merchants. Thus, if the contract is between two individuals or the contract is between a merchant and an individual, the additional terms are to be construed as proposals. Nevertheless, between merchants, such terms become part of the contract (a) unless the offer expressly limits acceptance to the terms of the offer (and this refers to the last lines of Subdivision 1), (b) unless the additional or different terms materially alter the contract, or (c) unless notification of objection to them has already been given or is given within a reasonable time after notice of them is received.

Unless two merchants are involved, any additional or different terms are merely a proposal and do not become part of the contract unless expressly accepted by the other party to the contract. The reasoning is simple. The additional terms probably were inserted solely for the benefit of the party inserting them. It is for this reason that the contract between the parties is based on the offer as it was originally submitted without any additional terms and the acceptance deals with the terms of the original offer.

The issue of whether a consumer is subject to the terms of click wrap or shrink wrap is another issue. In these situations, the consumer breaks the seal on a software tape or a CD tape, and terms and conditions are set forth therein, or a consumer uses the Internet and when he clicks onto a website, certain terms and conditions are set forth on the website. The small print usually prohibits the users from making unauthorized copies or reverse engineering the programs in the software, disclaims any warranties, and limits the liability of the operator of the website.

The courts seem to treat these contracts as offers by the seller to purchase their goods and the buyer is accepting the offer when they break the seal on the software program or on the CD. Normally, the license flashes onto the screen of the computer and, at that point, the individual buyer has a right to refuse the purchase if the terms are not acceptable and return the software. If the individual purchaser inspects the package and tries the software and then learns of the license, and thus had an opportunity to return the goods and did not return the goods, the court treats this as an acceptance of the contract terms. The same thing would apply to the shrink wrap for a CD-Rom.

Between merchants, the additional terms become effective unless three contingencies happen. The first contingency is that the additional terms will not become part of the contract if the offer expressly limits acceptance to the terms of the offer. The offer must expressly state that there will be no contract unless you accept all the terms or the specific terms set forth in this contract. It must be spelled out in the contract.

Secondly, the new proposals do not become part of the contract if they are material. The official comment to this section sets forth certain examples of typical clauses that materially alter the contract and result in surprise or hardship if incorporated without express awareness by the other party. The examples are a clause negating such standard warranties as that of merchantability or fitness for a particular purpose, a clause requiring a guarantee of 90% or 100% deliveries where the usage of the trade allows greater leeway, a clause reserving to the seller the power to cancel upon the buyer's failure to meet any invoice when due, a clause requiring that complaints be made in a time materially shorter than customary or reasonable, or inclusion of an arbitration clause. No attempt will be made to define what is and what is not a material clause. Suffice it to say that judges will go different ways on the same set of facts. Nevertheless, between two merchants, an additional term that is not customarily used in the industry and causes some kind of hardship or burden on the other party may well be considered a material term.

The third exception is where the additional terms do not become part of the contract between merchants when notification of objection has already been given or is given within a reasonable time after notice of them is received. The purchaser would therefore have a reasonable time to object to the additional terms.

As to different terms, Section 2-207 presents significant questions. An examination of Subdivision 1 of UCC 2-207 reveals a reference to both additional and different terms. Unfortunately, a reference to Subdivision 2 of UCC 2-207 only deals with additional terms and makes no reference at all to different terms. When there are different terms in the offer and in the acceptance that covered the same subject matter, the two sets of different terms cancel themselves out and the contract is deemed silent on the issue. Revised Article 2 of the Uniform Commercial Code was recently submitted for approval before the National Conference of Commissioners on Uniform State Laws in 1999; significant changes have been made in Sections 2-207 and 2-204.

What the difference is between a different term and an additional term is also a fine question of law. What some courts consider a different term, other courts will consider an additional term. The general thesis is that a different term contradicts a term from the other contract. An additional term that may not affect the exact subject area may still be an additional term as well as a different term.

There will probably be considerable material published on these two sections of what is known as the "battle of the forms" both in legal publications and in legal decisions. In any event, for the purposes of this book, to educate the credit and collection managers, I hope that I have at least clarified (although not solved) what the problems are when you are dealing with additional or different terms—although I may have added to the confusion.[7]

BATTLE OF FORMS

We have often seen the following type of disclaimer in various contracts:

> "It is expressly agreed that no warranty of merchantability or fitness for use, nor any other warranty express or implied, is made by seller herein. This paragraph states the seller's entire and exclusive liability and buyer's exclusive and sole remedy for any damages in connection with the sale of the products hereunder. Seller will in no event be liable for any special or consequential damages whatsoever."

Industrial purchased steel castings for six years from Wakesha, and on sixty different occasions, Wakesha shipped the steel castings to Industrial. In each case, Industrial placed an order via the telephone and thereafter, Industrial faxed a confirming purchase order to Wakesha. Wakesha claims that following its receipt of each purchase order, it sent Industrial an acknowledgment form confirming the order that contained the above terms and conditions of sale. Industrial stated that Wakesha did not issue acknowledgment forms and its president affirmed under oath that he denied ever receiving any acknowledgment forms. On the other hand, Wakesha enclosed with every shipment of castings a packing slip that contained the same terms and conditions of sale referenced above and followed each shipment with an invoice that also included these terms and conditions.

Once the existence of a contract is established, the court stated that it must refer to UCC Section 2-207(2) to determine which, if any, additional terms contained in subsequent written confirmations become part of the agreement. The court referred to Section 2-207 as the determining factor in solving this problem and stated there are three circumstances that preclude the incorporation of additional terms contained in a written confir-

---

[7]*Ionics, Inc. v. Elwood Sensors,* 110 F.3d 184 (1st Cir. 1997)

mation in a contract of sale. The second of the three circumstances was relevant to this situation, i.e., whether the additional terms "materially alter" the contract. Warranty disclaimer and limitations of remedies are deemed to be material alterations. It seems that Industrial consented to the terms and conditions contained in more than 400 packing slips and invoices it received over the six-year period due to acquiescence.

The fact that Industrial did not receive acknowledgments of 60 orders seems unusual, but Industrial did receive the shipments and returned defective castings for replacement by requesting credit. The court took judicial notice of the fact that Industrial had financial difficulties and was now claiming that it knew nothing of the terms and conditions in the course of performance under the 60 contracts of sale. Industrial also had many opportunities to clarify or memoralize its objections to any of the contract terms. The court finally concluded that Industrial should not be able to foist its own financial difficulties onto Wakesha by now claiming that it knew nothing about the terms and conditions.[8]

In another case involving a shipment of highland fleece, contained in the acknowledgment forms were certain limited and liquidated damage clauses. The highland fleece fabric apparently had potential flammability and accordingly, Suzy Phillips, who purchased the highland fleece, wanted to return a substantial amount of merchandise. The court again engaged in a discussion of the battle of the forms as to whether they were additional or different terms, material or immaterial terms.

In this instance, Suzy Phillips did not deny receiving the particular acknowledgment forms and never objected to or proposed additional terms to the forms. The fact that Suzy Phillips never signed the forms was not relevant. The course of performance was the equivalent of assent to these terms.

Under UCC 2-207, if no answer is received within a reasonable time after additional terms are proposed, it is both fair and commercially sound to assume that the other party had assented to their inclusion. The only exception to this rule is where the additional terms materially alter a contract. Such terms do not become part of the contract unless the other party specifically assented. An alteration is material if consent to it cannot be presumed.

In this instance, the court referred to the Official Commentary 4 to the UCC Section 2-207 which provides examples of clauses that materially alter a contract, all of which have in common that they significantly alter standard industry practice and thus could surprise a buyer who would

---

[8]*Wakesha Foundry, Inc. v. Industrial Engineering, Inc.*, 91 F. 3d 1002 (7th Cir. 1996).

not have expected to be operating under such terms. Clauses that are not material are mentioned in Comment 5, which are alterations that limit a remedy in a reasonable manner.

Consequential damages have always been allowed to be limited or excluded unless the limitation or exclusion is unconscionable. Limitations of consequential damages where a loss is commercial are ordinarily not considered unconscionable under New York law in accordance with the underlying policy that parties to an agreement are left free to shape their remedies to their particular requirements and reasonable agreements limiting or modifying remedies are to be given effect. In this particular case, the court held that trade practices including a standard limitation of liabilities clause would make it difficult for any party to show surprise. Absent express terms to the contrary, terms constituting usage of trade is a binding term of the agreement. Thus, if it constitutes usage of trade, a limited remedy for breach of warranty is enforceable, if it is not unconscionable and does not fail in its essential purpose.

It would appear from the above two cases that the acknowledgment forms or packing slips containing the exculpatory language or the disclaimer of liabilities are usually enforceable, especially where there are trade practices or where there has been a long course of dealing between the parties. The recommendation is to read the acknowledgment forms and the packing slips and understand the fact that you have to operate under their terms unless you actively dispute them and promptly communicate that you do not accept the terms.[9]

UNIFORM ELECTRONIC TRANSACTION ACT

The National Conference of Commissioners on Uniform State Laws (NCCUSL) has approved and recommended for enactment to all the states the Uniform Electronic Transaction Act (UETA) which applies to business and commercial transactions other than the execution of wills, codicils, or testamentary trusts. The Act also does not apply to the Uniform Commercial Code Section 1-107 (Waiver or Enunciation of Claim or Right after Breach), and Section 1-206 (Statute of Frauds) and Article 2 (sales) and Article 2a (lease). Thus, you cannot use electronic signatures for wills, waiver of rights, contracts controlled by Statute of Frauds, certain sales, and leases. The Act also does not apply to the Uniform Computer Infor-

---

[9]*Suzy Phillips Originals, Inc. v. Coville, Inc.*, 939 F. Supp. 1012 (E.D.N.Y. 1996).

mation Transaction Act and any other laws identified by a state. See Appendix I.

The UETA applies to all electronic records or an electronic signature created, generated, sent, communicated, received, or stored on or after the date that the state adopts the Act. The Act only applies to transactions between parties both of which have agreed to conduct transactions by electronic means. Whether they have agreed to conduct the transaction by electronic means is determined from the context and surrounding circumstances as well as the conduct of the parties. It is recommended to insert a clause in the contract consenting to the use of electronic signatures.

In essence, a record or signature may not be denied legal effect or enforceability solely because it is in electronic form. Furthermore, it follows that a contract that bears an electronic signature cannot be denied solely because it is in electronic form. The Act specifically provides that if a law other than the Act requires a record to be posted or displayed in a specific manner or to be sent, communicated, or transmitted by a specific method, or to contain information in a certain manner, the record must be posted or displayed, sent, or communicated by the method so specified by the other law. It allows other laws to supersede this law and where a specific method or specific terms are set forth that contradict or prohibit electronic transmission or electronic signatures or electronic contracts, the specific law other than the Act will prevail. Thus, statutory law cannot contractually be ignored.

The use of an electronic signature of a notary is permitted in the event that the notary is notarizing an electronic signature and provides that all the necessary information required to be included with the signature may be transmitted electronically.

A special section deals with the retention of records and allows the electronic record to be retained electronically and states that a paper record does not have to be maintained. In a judicial proceeding, evidence of a record of signature may not be excluded solely because it is in an electronic form. Before using UETA, consult with counsel.

CONSIGNMENT

The issue of whether a transfer of property is a consignment or a secured transaction presents itself many times before the courts. Usually, the courts rely on the intent of the parties, and where the question of intent is involved, the decision is subject to a review of the facts of each transaction.

In one case, the court stated that the intent is to be determined by an objective standard that considers the economic realities of the transactions rather than the actual intent of the parties. The court relied on four criteria that they felt would determine that the purpose of the transaction was to create a security interest and not a consignment:

1. The setting of the resale price by the consignee.
2. Billing the consignee upon shipment.
3. Commingling of proceeds or failure to keep proper accounts by the consignee.
4. Mixing consigned goods with goods owned by the consignee.

In contrast, certain factors indicate that the parties intend a true consignment:

1. Consignor retained control over the resale price of the consigned property.
2. Possession was delivered with authority to sell only upon the consent of the consignor.
3. The consignor may recall the goods.
4. The consignee was to receive a commission and not a profit on the sale.
5. The consigned property was segregated from other property of the consignee.
6. The consignor was entitled to inspect sales records and the physical inventory of the goods in the consignee's possession.
7. Consignee has no obligation to pay for the goods unless the goods are sold.

The criteria set by the courts seem to be sound, but unfortunately, many of the courts evaluate these transactions on a case-by-case basis and try to balance these factors to arrive at what they feel is a fair and equitable decision with each court selecting one or two criteria as critical and relegating the others as immaterial.[10]

---

[10]*In re Oriental Rug Warehouse Club, Inc.*, 205 B.R. 407 (Bankr. D. Minn. 1997); *Underwriters at Lloyds v. Shimer (In re Ide Jewelry Co., Inc.)*, 75 B.R. 969 (Bankr. S.D.N.Y. 1987).

CONSIGNMENT AND CREDITORS

A consignment of goods consists of the consignor delivering the goods to the consignee for the purpose of selling the goods. The consignor still owns the goods. The rights of creditors as to consigned goods is covered in UCC 2-326;

> Section 2-236: Sale on Approval and Sale or Return; Consignment Sales and Rights of Creditors.
>
> (1) Unless otherwise agreed, if delivered goods may be returned by the buyer even though they conform to the contract, the transaction is
>
>   (a) a "sale on approval" if the goods are delivered primarily for use, and
>
>   (b) a "sale or return" if the goods are delivered primarily for resale.
>
> (2) Except as provided in subsection (3), goods held on approval are not subject to the claims of the buyer's creditors until acceptance; goods held on sale or return are subject to such claims while in the buyer's possession.
>
> (3) Where goods are delivered to a person for sale and such person maintains a place of business at which he deals in goods of the kind involved, under a name other than the name of the person making delivery, then with respect to claims of creditors of the person conducting the business the goods are deemed to be on sale or return. The provisions of this subsection are applicable even though an agreement purports to reserve title to the person making delivery until payment or resale or uses such words as "on consignment" or "on memorandum." However, this subsection is not applicable if the person making delivery
>
>   (a) complies with an applicable law providing for a consignor's interest or the like to be evidenced by a sign, or
>
>   (b) establishes that the person conducting the business is generally known by his creditors to be substantially engaged in selling goods of others, or
>
>   (c) complies with the filing provisions of the Article on Secured Transactions (Article 9).
>
> (4) Any "or return" term of a contract for sale is to be treated as a separate contract for sale within the statute of frauds section of this Article (Section 2-201) and as contradicting the sale aspect of the contract within the provisions of this Article on parol or extrinsic evidence (Section 2-202).

Prior to the enactment of this section of the Uniform Commercial Code, creditors of the consignee (who receives the goods on consignment) could not rely on consigned goods in possession of the consignee because the title of the consignor (who delivers the goods on consignment) was superior to the claim of the creditor. The purpose of enacting the statute is to allow a creditor to attach a lien against property of a third person, which is in the consignee's possession on consignment, and to permit the creditor to treat such property as if it were owned by the consignee *under certain circumstances.*

Subdivision 3 spells out three separate and distinct exceptions and the purpose of the exceptions is to allow the consignor to protect himself by showing that the creditor had no right to assume that the goods were owned by the consignee. If the interest of the consignor is displayed by a sign or similar means identifying the consignor's interest in the property or if the filing provisions of the article on secured transactions that involves the filing of a financing statement is used, the consignor may protect its interest. An issue is where the person conducting the business is generally *not* known by his creditors to be substantially engaged in selling the goods of others, but the creditor had actual knowledge that the goods were subject to a consignment. In several states, the courts have held that the creditor's actual knowledge of the consignment before becoming a creditor is sufficient to meet the requirements of the exceptions set forth in Section 2-326; and the consignor will prevail.[11]

The minority view is that the creditor's knowledge of the debtor's possession of consigned property is totally irrelevant and the consignor's interest is junior to the creditor.[12]

As a general statement, where there is no evidence that the consignee's creditors are generally aware that the consignee is engaged in selling goods on consignment, the consignor (who delivers the goods to the consignee for the purposes of selling the goods on consignment) is bound to file a financing statement to prevent their property from becoming subject to the claims of the consignee's creditors.

> Credit and Collection Tip: *Where the creditors of the consignee are not totally aware of the fact that the consignee sells goods on consignment, and knowledge of this by the consignor may be difficult to ascertain and difficult to prove, the best course for the consignor is to file a financing statement. If it is common in the industry and it is known to most of the firms in the industry that this particular business does accept goods on consignment, the consignor would probably not be required to*

---

[11]*Belmont Int'l, Inc. v. American Int'l Shoe Co.*, 313 Ore. 112, 831 P. 2d 15 (1992) Supreme Court of Oregon; *GBS Meat Industry Pty., Ltd. v. Kress-Dobkin Co.*, 474 F. Supp. 1357 (W.D. Pa. 1979); *Eurpac Service Inc. v. Republic Acceptance Corp.*, 2000 WL 1228791 (Colo. App. Aug. 31, 2000).

[12]*In re State Street Auto Sales, Inc.*, 81 B.R. 215 (Bkrtcy. D. Mass. 1988)

file a financing statement. The best advice is when in doubt, file a financing statement.[13]

UNITED STATES WAREHOUSE ACT

The United States Warehouse Act clarified that electronic warehouse receipts are to be treated identically as paper receipts with respect to the perfection of a security interest under state law. Congress did not intend to give electronic receipts a super priority, but merely intended for electronic receipts to be on a parity with paper receipts and to be prioritized according to state law. See Chapter 10, Appendix I.

UNIFORM CUSTOM AND PRACTICES FOR DOCUMENTARY CREDITS—BACKGROUND

Originally the Uniform Customs and Practices for Documentary Credits (UCP) was not designed or intended to be law. It was prepared as standard terms to apply to letters of credit. Only those parties who chose to use these standard terms by a written agreement or by inserting a clause in the letter of credit that this letter of credit is subject to these standard terms, would actually use them. If parties chose to use a letter of credit without utilizing the standard terms of the UCP, than the Uniform Commercial Code would apply. Unfortunately, the Uniform Commercial Code does not set forth in detail all the obligations and procedures set forth in the UCP—and the reverse is also true.

What has happened is that the UCP has been almost universally adopted by the banks and is now a worldwide standard. An applicant wanting a letter of credit without utilizing the UCP would have difficulty locating a bank that would issue the letter of credit. The UCP has become the standard for issuing a letter of credit.

Imprinted on each letter of credit is usually a stamp or writing that the letter credit is subject to the UCP. As a result, the UCP could be identified as law, and operates as law since the courts apply the UCP as prevailing law. If the particular issue before the court is not covered by the UCP, the court will then apply the Uniform Commercial Code or the appropriate law of the particular country where the litigation is proceed-

---

[13]*In re Russell,* 254 B.R. 132 (Bkrtcy. D. Va. 2000).

ing. In today's environment, the UCP regulates and controls the issuance of both domestic and foreign letters of credit.

UNIFORM CUSTOMS AND PRACTICE FOR DOCUMENTARY CREDITS

The International Chamber of Commerce publishes a pamphlet known as the Uniform Customs and Practice for Documentary Credits, which is recognized as a set of rules governing the use of documentary credit in international commerce. The ICC states that banking associations and banks in more than 100 countries and territories have adopted the most recent revision. The 49 articles of the new Uniform Customs and Practice Act effective as of January 1, 1994 provided a working aid to bankers, lawyers, importers, exporters, and transport executives involved in international trade.

The pamphlet runs 60 pages and is divided into seven different categories as follows:

A. General Provisions and Definitions
B. Form and Notification of Credits
C. Liabilities and Responsibilities
D. Documents
E. Miscellaneous Provisions
F. Transferable Credit
G. Assignment of Proceeds

The rules cover the distinctions in extending credit that are considered separate transactions from sales or other contracts as well as instructions to issue the credits and the criteria and precise manner in which the credits must be issued. A section is devoted to the form and notification of the credits, including the revocation of a credit and the liability of the issuing and confirming bank. The rule states that the letter of credit or other document should indicate whether it is revocable or irrevocable. Obligations and liabilities of the banks, distinguishing between confirming banks and issuing banks are given considerable attention. The extent of examination of documents is set at reasonable care in ascertaining whether or not they appear on their face to be in compliance with the terms and conditions of the credit. Documents not stipulated in the credit will not be examined by the bank.

Almost 20 pages are devoted to identifying the various types of documents, from Letters of Credit to Marine/Ocean Bills of Lading to Air Transport Documents to Insurance.

In most international letters of credit, the letter of credit will be subject to the terms of the UCP so that the rules of the UCP will control the operation, procedures, and transfers of the funds pursuant to the letter of credit. Even domestic letters may also operate subject to the rules of the UCP. The document itself will bear terminology indicating the document is subject to the terms of the UCP. In those instances where the issue is not covered by the rules, the courts tend to apply the law of the particular country, such as in the United States, the appropriate section of the Uniform Commercial Code which covers letters of credit.

If the issuing bank determines that the documents appear on their face not to be in compliance with the terms and conditions of the credit, the bank may in its sole judgment approach the applicant for a waiver of the discrepancy. Nevertheless, documents that appear on their face to be inconsistent with one another will be considered as not appearing on their face to be in compliance with the terms and conditions of the credit.

Besides this pamphlet on the Uniform Customs and Practice for Documentary Credit, the ICC also publishes "The New ICC Guide to Documentary Credit Operations" which uses a combination of drafts, charts, and sample documents that illustrate the documentary credit process. The ICC also publishes "The New ICC Standard Documentary Credit Forms." These publications are all available from the International Chamber of Commerce, U.S. Counsel Inc., 1212 Avenue of the Americas, New York, NY 10036; (212) 354-4480.

UNIFORM CUSTOMS AND PRACTICES FOR DOCUMENTARY CREDITS—LETTERS OF CREDIT

A recent Circuit Court of Appeals decision in the 2nd Circuit reemphasized the effect of having the UCP (Uniform Customs and Practices for Documentary Credits) apply to a letter of credit. Section 14 (c & d) of UCP states as follows:

> (c)   if the Issuing Bank determines that the documents appear on their face not to be in compliance with the terms and conditions of the Credit, it may in its sole judgment approach the Applicant for a waiver of the discrepancy(ies). This does not, however, extend the period mentioned in sub-Article 13(b).

(d) If the Issuing Bank and/or Confirming Bank, if any, or a Nominated Bank acting on their behalf, decides to refuse the documents, it must give notice to that effect by telecommunication or, if that is not possible, by other expeditious means, without delay but no later than the close of the seventh banking day following the day of receipt of the documents. Such notice shall be given to the bank from which it received the documents, or to the Beneficiary, if it received the documents directly from him.

(ii) Such notice must state all discrepancies in respect of which the bank refuses the documents and must also state whether it is holding the documents at the disposal of, or is returning them to, the presenter.

(iii) The issuing Bank and/or Confirming Bank, if any, shall then be entitled to claim from the remitting bank refund with interest, of any reimbursement which has been made to that bank.

The court stated as follows:

Article 14 of the UCP allows an issuing bank to refuse to pay on a letter of credit if it determines that the documents appear on their face not to be in compliance with the terms and conditions of the credit (UCP Article 14(c)). However the issuing bank must give notice of its refusal by telecommunication or, if that is not possible by other expeditious means, without delay but no later than the close of the seventh banking day following the day of receipt of the documents and its notice must state all discrepancies in respective which the bank refuses the documents (UCP Article 14(d)(i)(ii)). Failure to comply with Article 14 notice provisions preclude the issuing bank from claiming that the documents are not in compliance with the terms and conditions of the credit (UCP Article 14(e)).

The bank failed to comply in that its first disclaimer was not sent by telecommunication and did not specify the grounds for the disclaimer. The bank was justifying its refusal based upon a fraud of the underlying transactions and that non-conforming documents were knowingly forwarded in violation of Article 13.

The discrepancies must be listed with specificity to substantiate the reason for the refusal to pay.[14]

---

[14]*Timothy W. v. Rochester, N.H., School Dist.*, 875 F. 2d 954 (1st Cir. 1989); *Hamilton Bank, N.A. v. Kookmin Bank*, 245 F. 3d 82 (2nd Cir. 2001).

CHAPTER 2
APPENDIX I

UNIFORM ELECTRONIC TRANSACTIONS ACT

Drafted by the National Conference of Commissioners on Uniform State Laws and by it approved and recommended for enactment in all the states at its Annual Conference Meeting in its one-hundred-and-eighth year in Denver, Colorado, July 23-30, 1999, without prefatory note and comments. Copyright © 1999 by the National Conference of Commissioners on Uniform State Laws (August 4, 1999). Copies of this Act may be obtained from: National Conference of Commissioners on Uniform State Laws, 211 E. Ontario Street, Suite 1300, Chicago, Illinois 60611, 312/915-0195.

UNIFORM ELECTRONIC TRANSACTIONS ACT

SECTION 1. SHORT TITLE. This [Act] may be cited as the Uniform Electronic Transactions Act.

SECTION 2. DEFINITIONS. In this [Act]:

(1) "Agreement" means the bargain of the parties in fact, as found in their language or inferred from other circumstances and from rules, regulations, and procedures given the effect of agreements under laws otherwise applicable to a particular transaction.

(2) "Automated transaction" means a transaction conducted or performed, in whole or in part, by electronic means or electronic records, in which the acts or records of one or both parties are not reviewed by an individual in the ordinary course in forming a contract, performing under an existing contract, or fulfilling an obligation required by the transaction.

(3) "Computer program" means a set of statements or instructions to be used directly or indirectly in an information processing system in order to bring about a certain result.

(4) "Contract" means the total legal obligation resulting from the parties' agreement as affected by this [Act] and other applicable law.

(5) "Electronic" means relating to technology having electrical, digital, magnetic, wireless, optical, electromagnetic, or similar capabilities.

(6) "Electronic agent" means a computer program or an electronic or other automated means used independently to initiate an action or respond to electronic records or performances in whole or in part, without review or action by an individual.

(7) "Electronic record" means a record created, generated, sent, communicated, received, or stored by electronic means.

(8) "Electronic signature" means an electronic sound, symbol, or process attached to or logically associated with a record and executed or adopted by a person with the intent to sign the record.

(9) "Governmental agency" means an executive, legislative, or judicial agency, department, board, commission, authority, institution, or instrumentality of the federal government or of a State or of a county, municipality, or other political subdivision of a State.

(10) "Information" means data, text, images, sounds, codes, computer programs, software, databases, or the like.

(11) "Information processing system" means an electronic system for creating, generating, sending, receiving, storing, displaying, or processing information.

(12) "Person" means an individual, corporation, business trust, estate, trust, partnership, limited liability company, association, joint venture, governmental agency, public corporation, or any other legal or commercial entity.

(13) "Record" means information that is inscribed on a tangible medium or that is stored in an electronic or other medium and is retrievable in perceivable form.

(14) "Security procedure" means a procedure employed for the purpose of verifying that an electronic signature, record, or performance is that of a specific person or for detecting changes or errors in the information in an electronic record. The term includes a procedure that requires the use of algorithms or other codes, identifying words or numbers, encryption, or callback or other acknowledgment procedures.

(15) "State" means a State of the United States, the District of Columbia, Puerto Rico, the United States Virgin Islands, or any territory or insular possession subject to the jurisdiction of the United States. The term includes an Indian tribe or band, or Alaskan native village, which is recognized by federal law or formally acknowledged by a State.

(16) "Transaction" means an action or set of actions occurring between two or more persons relating to the conduct of business, commercial, or governmental affairs.

SECTION 3. SCOPE.

(a) Except as otherwise provided in subsection (b), this [Act] applies to electronic records and electronic signatures relating to a transaction.

(b) This [Act] does not apply to a transaction to the extent it is governed by:

(1) a law governing the creation and execution of wills, codicils, or testamentary trusts;

(2) [The Uniform Commercial Code other than Sections 1-107 and 1-206, Article 2, and Article 2A];

(3) [Articles 3, 4, 4A, 5, 6, 7, 8, or 9 of the Uniform Commercial Code];

(4) [the Uniform Computer Information Transactions Act]; and

(5) [other laws, if any, identified by State].

(c) This [Act] applies to an electronic record or electronic signature otherwise excluded from the application of this [Act] under subsection (b) to the extent it is governed by a law other than those specified in subsection (b).

(d) A transaction subject to this [Act] is also subject to other applicable substantive law.

SECTION 4. PROSPECTIVE APPLICATION. This [Act] applies to any electronic record or electronic signature created, generated, sent, communicated, received, or stored on or after the effective date of this [Act].

SECTION 5. USE OF ELECTRONIC RECORDS AND ELECTRONIC SIGNATURES; VARIATION BY AGREEMENT.

(a) This [Act] does not require a record or signature to be created, generated, sent, communicated, received, stored, or otherwise processed or used by electronic means or in electronic form.

(b) This [Act] applies only to transactions between parties each of which has agreed to conduct transactions by electronic means. Whether the parties agree to conduct a transaction by electronic means is determined from the context and surrounding circumstances, including the parties' conduct.

(c) A party that agrees to conduct a transaction by electronic means may refuse to conduct other transactions by electronic means. The right granted by this subsection may not be waived by agreement.

(d) Except as otherwise provided in this [Act], the effect of any of its provisions may be varied by agreement. The presence in certain provisions of this [Act] of the words "unless otherwise agreed", or words of similar import, does not imply that the effect of other provisions may not be varied by agreement.

(e) Whether an electronic record or electronic signature has legal consequences is determined by this [Act] and other applicable law.

SECTION 6. CONSTRUCTION AND APPLICATION. This [Act] must be construed and applied:

(1) to facilitate electronic transactions consistent with other applicable law;

(2) to be consistent with reasonable practices concerning electronic transactions and with the continued expansion of those practices; and

(3) to effectuate its general purpose to make uniform the law with respect to the subject of this [Act] among States enacting it.

SECTION 7. LEGAL RECOGNITION OF ELECTRONIC RECORDS, ELECTRONIC SIGNATURES, AND ELECTRONIC CONTRACTS.

(a) A record or signature may not be denied legal effect or enforceability solely because it is in electronic form.

(b) A contract may not be denied legal effect or enforceability solely because an electronic record was used in its formation.

(c) If a law requires a record to be in writing, an electronic record satisfies the law.

(d) If a law requires a signature, an electronic signature satisfies the law.

SECTION 8. PROVISION OF INFORMATION IN WRITING; PRESENTATION OF RECORDS.

(a) If parties have agreed to conduct a transaction by electronic means and a law requires a person to provide, send, or deliver information in writing to another person, the requirement is satisfied if the information is provided, sent, or delivered, as the case may be, in an electronic record capable of retention by the recipient at the time of receipt. An electronic record is not capable of retention by the recipient if the sender or its information processing system inhibits the ability of the recipient to print or store the electronic record.

(b) If a law other than this [Act] requires a record (i) to be posted or displayed in a certain manner, (ii) to be sent, communicated, or transmitted by a specified method, or (iii) to contain information that is formatted in a certain manner, the following rules apply:

(1) The record must be posted or displayed in the manner specified in the other law.

(2) Except as otherwise provided in subsection (d)(2), the record must be sent, communicated, or transmitted by the method specified in the other law.

(3) The record must contain the information formatted in the manner specified in the other law.

(c) If a sender inhibits the ability of a recipient to store or print an electronic record, the electronic record is not enforceable against the recipient.

(d) The requirements of this section may not be varied by agreement, but:

(1) to the extent a law other than this [Act] requires information to be provided, sent, or delivered in writing but permits that requirement to be varied by agreement, the requirement under subsection (a) that the information be in the form of an electronic record capable of retention may also be varied by agreement; and

(2) a requirement under a law other than this [Act] to send, communicate, or transmit a record by [first-class mail, postage prepaid] [regular United States mail], may be varied by agreement to the extent permitted by the other law.

SECTION 9. ATTRIBUTION AND EFFECT OF ELECTRONIC RECORD AND ELECTRONIC SIGNATURE.

(a) An electronic record or electronic signature is attributable to a person if it was the act of the person. The act of the person may be shown in any manner, including a showing of the efficacy of any security procedure applied to determine the person to which the electronic record or electronic signature was attributable.

(b) The effect of an electronic record or electronic signature attributed to a person under subsection (a) is determined from the context and surrounding circumstances at the time of its creation, execution, or adoption, including the parties' agreement, if any, and otherwise as provided by law.

SECTION 10. EFFECT OF CHANGE OR ERROR. If a change or error in an electronic record occurs in a transmission between parties to a transaction, the following rules apply:

(1) If the parties have agreed to use a security procedure to detect changes or errors and one party has conformed to the procedure, but the other party has not, and the nonconforming party would have detected the change or error had that party also conformed, the conforming party may avoid the effect of the changed or erroneous electronic record.

(2) In an automated transaction involving an individual, the individual may avoid the effect of an electronic record that resulted from an error made by the

individual in dealing with the electronic agent of another person if the electronic agent did not provide an opportunity for the prevention or correction of the error and, at the time the individual learns of the error, the individual:

(A) promptly notifies the other person of the error and that the individual did not intend to be bound by the electronic record received by the other person;

(B) takes reasonable steps, including steps that conform to the other person's reasonable instructions, to return to the other person or, if instructed by the other person, to destroy the consideration received, if any, as a result of the erroneous electronic record; and

(C) has not used or received any benefit or value from the consideration, if any, received from the other person.

(3) If neither paragraph (1) nor paragraph (2) applies, the change or error has the effect provided by other law, including the law of mistake, and the parties' contract, if any.

(4) Paragraphs (2) and (3) may not be varied by agreement.

SECTION 11. NOTARIZATION AND ACKNOWLEDGMENT. If a law requires a signature or record to be notarized, acknowledged, verified, or made under oath, the requirement is satisfied if the electronic signature of the person authorized to perform those acts, together with all other information required to be included by other applicable law, is attached to or logically associated with the signature or record.

SECTION 12. RETENTION OF ELECTRONIC RECORDS; ORIGINALS.

(a) If a law requires that a record be retained, the requirement is satisfied by retaining an electronic record of the information in the record which:

(1) accurately reflects the information set forth in the record after it was first generated in its final form as an electronic record or otherwise; and

(2) remains accessible for later reference.

(b) A requirement to retain a record in accordance with subsection (a) does not apply to any information the sole purpose of which is to enable the record to be sent, communicated, or received.

(c) A person may satisfy subsection (a) by using the services of another person if the requirements of that subsection are satisfied.

(d) If a law requires a record to be presented or retained in its original form, or provides consequences if the record is not presented or retained in its original form, that law is satisfied by an electronic record retained in accordance with subsection (a).

(e) If a law requires retention of a check, that requirement is satisfied by retention of an electronic record of the information on the front and back of the check in accordance with subsection (a).

(f) A record retained as an electronic record in accordance with subsection (a) satisfies a law requiring a person to retain a record for evidentiary, audit, or like purposes, unless a law enacted after the effective date of this [Act] specifically prohibits the use of an electronic record for the specified purpose.

(g) This section does not preclude a governmental agency of this State from specifying additional requirements for the retention of a record subject to the agency's jurisdiction.

SECTION 13. ADMISSIBILITY IN EVIDENCE. In a proceeding, evidence of a record or signature may not be excluded solely because it is in electronic form.

SECTION 14. AUTOMATED TRANSACTION. In an automated transaction, the following rules apply:

(1) A contract may be formed by the interaction of electronic agents of the parties, even if no individual was aware of or reviewed the electronic agents' actions or the resulting terms and agreements.

(2) A contract may be formed by the interaction of an electronic agent and an individual, acting on the individual's own behalf or for another person, including by an interaction in which the individual performs actions that the individual is free to refuse to perform and which the individual knows or has reason to know will cause the electronic agent to complete the transaction or performance.

(3) The terms of the contract are determined by the substantive law applicable to it.

SECTION 15. TIME AND PLACE OF SENDING AND RECEIPT.

(a) Unless otherwise agreed between the sender and the recipient, an electronic record is sent when it:

(1) is addressed properly or otherwise directed properly to an information processing system that the recipient has designated or uses for the purpose of receiving electronic records or information of the type sent and from which the recipient is able to retrieve the electronic record;

(2) is in a form capable of being processed by that system; and

(3) enters an information processing system outside the control of the sender or of a person that sent the electronic record on behalf of the sender or enters a region of the information processing system designated or used by the recipient which is under the control of the recipient.

(b) Unless otherwise agreed between a sender and the recipient, an electronic record is received when:

(1) it enters an information processing system that the recipient has designated or uses for the purpose of receiving electronic records or information of the type sent and from which the recipient is able to retrieve the electronic record; and

(2) it is in a form capable of being processed by that system.

(c) Subsection (b) applies even if the place the information processing system is located is different from the place the electronic record is deemed to be received under subsection (d).

(d) Unless otherwise expressly provided in the electronic record or agreed between the sender and the recipient, an electronic record is deemed to be sent from the sender's place of business and to be received at the recipient's place of business. For purposes of this subsection, the following rules apply:

(1) If the sender or recipient has more than one place of business, the place of business of that person is the place having the closest relationship to the underlying transaction.

(2) If the sender or the recipient does not have a place of business, the place of business is the sender's or recipient's residence, as the case may be.

(e) An electronic record is received under subsection (b) even if no individual is aware of its receipt.

(f) Receipt of an electronic acknowledgment from an information processing system described in subsection (b) establishes that a record was received but, by itself, does not establish that the content sent corresponds to the content received.

(g) If a person is aware that an electronic record purportedly sent under subsection (a), or purportedly received under subsection (b), was not actually sent or received, the legal effect of the sending or receipt is determined by other applicable law. Except to the extent permitted by the other law, the requirements of this subsection may not be varied by agreement.

SECTION 16. TRANSFERABLE RECORDS.

(a) In this section, "transferable record" means an electronic record that:

(1) would be a note under [Article 3 of the Uniform Commercial Code] or a document under [Article 7 of the Uniform Commercial Code] if the electronic record were in writing; and

(2) the issuer of the electronic record expressly has agreed is a transferable record.

(b) A person has control of a transferable record if a system employed for evidencing the transfer of interests in the transferable record reliably establishes that person as the person to which the transferable record was issued or transferred.

(c) A system satisfies subsection (b), and a person is deemed to have control of a transferable record, if the transferable record is created, stored, and assigned in such a manner that:

(1) a single authoritative copy of the transferable record exists which is unique, identifiable, and, except as otherwise provided in paragraphs (4), (5), and (6), unalterable;

(2) the authoritative copy identifies the person asserting control as:

(A) the person to which the transferable record was issued; or

(B) if the authoritative copy indicates that the transferable record has been transferred, the person to which the transferable record was most recently transferred;

(3) the authoritative copy is communicated to and maintained by the person asserting control or its designated custodian;

(4) copies or revisions that add or change an identified assignee of the authoritative copy can be made only with the consent of the person asserting control;

(5) each copy of the authoritative copy and any copy of a copy is readily identifiable as a copy that is not the authoritative copy; and

(6) any revision of the authoritative copy is readily identifiable as authorized or unauthorized.

(d) Except as otherwise agreed, a person having control of a transferable record is the holder, as defined in [Section 1-201(20) of the Uniform Commercial Code], of the transferable record and has the same rights and defenses as a holder of an equivalent record or writing under [the Uniform Commercial Code], including, if the applicable statutory requirements under [Section 3-302(a), 7-501, or 9-308 of the Uniform Commercial Code] are satisfied, the rights and defenses of a holder in due course, a holder to which a negotiable document of title has been duly negotiated, or a purchaser, respectively. Delivery, possession, and indorsement are not required to obtain or exercise any of the rights under this subsection.

(e) Except as otherwise agreed, an obligor under a transferable record has the same rights and defenses as an equivalent obligor under equivalent records or writings under [the Uniform Commercial Code].

(f) If requested by a person against which enforcement is sought, the person seeking to enforce the transferable record shall provide reasonable proof that the person is in control of the transferable record. Proof may include access to the authoritative copy of the transferable record and related business records sufficient to review the terms of the transferable record and to establish the identity of the person having control of the transferable record.

[SECTION 17. CREATION AND RETENTION OF ELECTRONIC RECORDS AND CONVERSION OF WRITTEN RECORDS BY GOVERNMENTAL AGENCIES. [Each governmental agency] [The [designated state officer]] of this State shall determine whether, and the extent to which, [it] [a governmental agency] will create and retain electronic records and convert written records to electronic records.]

[SECTION 18. ACCEPTANCE AND DISTRIBUTION OF ELECTRONIC RECORDS BY GOVERNMENTAL AGENCIES.

(a) Except as otherwise provided in Section 12(f), [each governmental agency] [the [designated state officer]] of this State shall determine whether, and the extent to which, [it] [a governmental agency] will send and accept electronic records and electronic signatures to and from other persons and otherwise create, generate, communicate, store, process, use, and rely upon electronic records and electronic signatures.

(b) To the extent that a governmental agency uses electronic records and electronic signatures under subsection (a), the [governmental agency] [designated state officer], giving due consideration to security, may specify:

(c) the manner and format in which the electronic records must be created, generated, sent, communicated, received, and stored and the systems established for those purposes;

(2) if electronic records must be signed by electronic means, the type of electronic signature required, the manner and format in which the electronic signature must be affixed to the electronic record, and the identity of, or criteria that must be met by, any third party used by a person filing a document to facilitate the process;

(3) control processes and procedures as appropriate to ensure adequate preservation, disposition, integrity, security, confidentiality, and auditability of electronic records; and

(4) any other required attributes for electronic records which are specified for corresponding nonelectronic records or reasonably necessary under the circumstances.

(c) Except as otherwise provided in Section 12(f), this [Act] does not require a governmental agency of this State to use or permit the use of electronic records or electronic signatures.]

SECTION 19. INTEROPERABILITY. The [governmental agency] [designated officer] of this State which adopts standards pursuant to Section 18 may encourage and promote consistency and interoperability with similar requirements adopted by other governmental agencies of this and other States and the federal government and nongovernmental persons interacting with governmental agencies of this State. If appropriate, those standards may specify differing levels of standards from which governmental agencies of this State may choose in implementing the most appropriate standard for a particular application.]

SECTION 20. SEVERABILITY CLAUSE. If any provision of this [Act] or its application to any person or circumstance is held invalid, the invalidity does not affect other provisions or applications of this [Act] which can be given effect without the invalid provision or application, and to this end the provisions of this [Act] are severable.

SECTION 21. EFFECTIVE DATE. This [Act] takes effect ...

CHAPTER 2
APPENDIX II

UNIFORM COMMERCIAL CODE—
LETTERS OF CREDIT—ARTICLE 5

5-101. SHORT TITLE.

This Article shall be known and may be cited as Uniform Commercial Code—
Letters of Credit.

5-102. SCOPE.

(1) This Article applies

(a) to a credit issued by a bank if the credit requires a documentary draft or a
documentary demand for payment; and

(b) to a credit issued by a person other than a bank if the credit requires that the
draft or demand for payment be accompanied by a document of title; and

(c) to a credit issued by a bank or other person if the credit is not within sub-
paragraphs (a) or (b) but conspicuously states that it is a letter of credit or is
conspicuously so entitled.

(2) Unless the engagement meets the requirements of subsection (1), this Article does not apply to engagements to make advances or to honor drafts or
demands for payment, to authorities to pay or purchase, to guarantees or to
general agreements.

(3) This Article deals with some but not all of the rules and concepts of letters
of credit as such rules or concepts have developed prior to this act or may
hereafter develop. The fact that this Article states a rule does not by itself
require, imply, or negate application of the same or a converse rule to a situation not provided for or to a person not specified by this Article.

5-103. DEFINITIONS.

(1) In this Article unless the context otherwise requires

(a) "Credit" or "letter of credit" means an engagement by a bank or other person made at the request of a customer and of a kind within the scope of this Article (Section 5-102) that the issuer will honor drafts or other demands for payment upon compliance with the conditions specified in the credit. A credit may be either revocable or irrevocable. The engagement may be either an agreement to honor or a statement that the bank or other person is authorized to honor.

(b) A "documentary draft" or a "documentary demand for payment" is one honor of which is conditioned upon the presentation of a document or documents. "Document" means any paper including document of title, security, invoice, certificate, notice of default and the like.

(c) An "issuer" is a bank or other person issuing a credit.

(d) A "beneficiary" of a credit is a person who is entitled under its terms to draw or demand payment.

(e) An "advising bank" is a bank which gives notification of the issuance of a credit by another bank.

(f) A "confirming bank" is a bank which engages either that it will itself honor a credit already issued by another bank or that such a credit will be honored by the issuer or a third bank.

(g) A "customer" is a buyer or other person who causes an issuer to issue a credit. The term also includes a bank which procures issuance or confirmation on behalf of that bank's customer.

(2) Other definitions applying to this Article and the sections in which they appear are:

"Notation Credit".   Section 5-108.

"Presenter".   Section 5-112(3).

(3) Definitions in other Articles applying to this Article and the sections in which they appear are:

"Accept" or "Acceptance".   Section 3-410.

"Contract for sale".   Section 2-106.

"Draft".   Section 3-104.

"Holder in due course".   Section 3-302.

"Midnight deadline".   Section 4-104.

"Security".   Section 8-102.

(4) In addition, Article 1 contains general definitions and principles of construction and interpretation applicable throughout this Article.

5-104. Formal Requirements; Signing.

(1) Except as otherwise required in subsection (1)(c) of Section 5-102 on scope, no particular form of phrasing is required for a credit. A credit must be in writing and signed by the issuer and a confirmation must be in writing and signed by the confirming bank. A modification of the terms of a credit or confirmation must be signed by the issuer or confirming bank.

(2) A telegram may be a sufficient signed writing if it identifies its sender by an authorized authentication. The authentication may be in code and the authorized naming of the issuer in an advice of credit is a sufficient signing.

5-105. Consideration.

No consideration is necessary to establish a credit or to enlarge or otherwise modify its terms.

5-106. Time and Effect of Establishment of Credit.

(1) Unless otherwise agreed, a credit is established

(a) as regards the customer as soon as a letter of credit is sent to him or the letter of credit or an authorized written advice of its issuance is sent to the beneficiary; and

(b) as regards to beneficiary when he receives a letter of credit or an authorized written advice of its issuance.

(2) Unless otherwise agreed, once an irrevocable credit is established as regards the customer, it can be modified or revoked only with the consent of the customer, and once it is established as regards the beneficiary, it can be modified or revoked only with his consent.

(3) Unless otherwise agreed, after a revocable credit is established, it may be modified or revoked by the issuer without notice to or consent from the customer or beneficiary.

(4) Notwithstanding any modification or revocation of a revocable credit, any person authorized to honor or negotiate under the terms of the original credit is entitled to reimbursement for or honor of any draft or demand for payment duly honored or negotiated before receipt of notice of the modification or revocation, and the issuer in turn is entitled to reimbursement from its customer.

5-107. Advice of Credit; Confirmation; Error in Statement of Terms.

(1) Unless otherwise specified, an advising bank, by advising a credit issued by another bank, does not assume any obligation to honor drafts drawn or demands for payment made under the credit, but it does assume obligation for the accuracy of its own statement.

(2) A confirming bank, by confirming a credit, becomes directly obligated on the credit to the extent of its confirmation as though it were its issuer and acquires the rights of an issuer.

(3) Even though an advising bank incorrectly advises the terms of a credit it has been authorized to advise, the credit is established as against the issuer to the extent of its original terms.

(4) Unless otherwise specified, the customer bears as against the issuer all risks of transmission and reasonable translation or interpretation of any message relating to a credit.

5-108. "Notation Credit"; Exhaustion of Credit.

(1) A credit which specifies that any person purchasing or paying drafts drawn or demands for payment made under it must note the amount of the draft or demand on the letter or advice of credit is a "notation credit".

(2) Under a notation credit,

(a) a person paying the beneficiary or purchasing a draft or demand for payment from him acquires a right to honor only if the appropriate notation is made, and by transferring or forwarding for honor the documents under the credit, such a person warrants to the issuer that the notation has been made; and

(b) unless the credit or a signed statement that an appropriate notation has been made accompanies the draft or demand for payment, the issuer may delay honor until evidence of notation has been procured which is satisfactory to it but its obligation and that of its customer continue for a reasonable time not exceeding thirty days to obtain such evidence.

(3) If the credit is not a notation credit,

(a) the issuer may honor complying drafts or demands for payment presented to it in the order in which they are presented and is discharged pro tanto by honor of any such draft or demand;

(b) as between competing good faith purchasers of complying drafts or demands, the person first purchasing has priority over a subsequent purchaser even though the later purchased draft or demand has been first honored.

5-109. Issuer's Obligation to Its Customer.

(1) An issuer's obligation to its customer includes good faith and observance of any general banking usage but, unless otherwise agreed, does not include liability or responsibility

(a) for performance of the underlying contract for sale or other transaction between the customer and the beneficiary; or

(b) for any act or omission of any person other than itself or its own branch or for loss or destruction of a draft, demand, or document in transit or in the possession of others; or

(c) based on knowledge or lack of knowledge of any usage of any particular trade.

(2) An issuer must examine documents with care so as to ascertain that on their face they appear to comply with the terms of the credit but, unless otherwise agreed, assumes no liability or responsibility for the genuineness, falsification, or effect of any document which appears on such examination to be regular on its face.

(3) A non-bank issuer is not bound by any banking usage of which it has no knowledge.

5-110. Availability of Credit in Portions; Presenter's Reservation of Lien or Claim.

(1) Unless otherwise specified, a credit may be used in portions in the discretion of the beneficiary.

(2) Unless otherwise specified, a person by presenting a documentary draft or demand for payment under a credit relinquishes upon its honor all claims to the documents and a person by transferring such draft or demand or causing such presentment authorizes such relinquishment. An explicit reservation of claim makes the draft or demand non-complying.

5-111. Warranties on Transfer and Presentment.

(1) Unless otherwise agreed, the beneficiary by transferring or presenting a documentary draft or demand for payment warrants to all interested parties that the necessary conditions of the credit have been complied with. This is in addition to any warranties arising under Articles 3, 4, 7 and 8.

(2) Unless otherwise agreed, a negotiating, advising, confirming, collecting or issuing bank presenting or transferring a draft or demand for payment under a credit warrants only the matters warranted by a collecting bank under Article 4, and any such bank transferring a document warrants only the matters warranted by an intermediary under Articles 7 and 8.

5-112. Time Allowed for Honor or Rejection; Withholding Honor or Rejection by Consent; "Presenter".

(1) A bank to which a documentary draft or demand for payment is presented under a credit may without dishonor of the draft, demand or credit

(a) defer honor until the close of the third banking day following receipt of the documents; and

(b) further defer honor if the presenter has expressly or impliedly consented thereto.

Failure to honor within the time here specified constitutes dishonor of the draft or demand and of the credit [except as otherwise provided in subsection (4) of Section 5-114 on conditional payment].

Note: The bracketed language in the last sentence of subsection (1) should be included only if the optional provisions of Section 5-114(4) and (5) are included.

(2) Upon dishonor, the bank may unless otherwise instructed fulfill its duty to return the draft or demand and the documents by holding them at the disposal of the presenter and sending him an advice to that effect.

(3) "Presenter" means any person presenting a draft or demand for payment for honor under a credit even though that person is a confirming bank or other correspondent which is acting under an issuer's authorization.

5-113. INDEMNITIES.

(1) A bank seeking to obtain (whether for itself or another) honor, negotiation or reimbursement under a credit may give an indemnity to induce such honor, negotiation, or reimbursement.

(2) An indemnity agreement inducing honor, negotiation, or reimbursement

(a) unless otherwise explicitly agreed applies to defects in the documents but not in the goods; and

(b) unless a longer time is explicitly agreed expires at the end of ten business days following receipt of the documents by the ultimate customer unless notice of objection is sent before such expiration date. The ultimate customer may send notice of objection to the person from whom he received the documents and any bank receiving such notice is under a duty to send notice to its transferor before its midnight deadline.

5-114. ISSUER'S DUTY AND PRIVILEGE TO HONOR; RIGHT TO REIMBURSEMENT.

(1) An issuer must honor a draft or demand for payment which complies with the terms of the relevant credit regardless of whether the goods or documents conform to the underlying contract for sale or other contract between the customer and the beneficiary. The issuer is not excused from honor of such a draft or demand by reason of an additional general term that all documents must be satisfactory to the issuer, but an issuer may require that specified documents must be satisfactory to it.

(2) Unless otherwise agreed when documents appear on their fact to comply with the terms of a credit but a required document does not in fact conform to the warranties made on negotiation or transfer of a document of title (Sec-

tion 7-507) or of a certificated security (Section 8-306) or is forged or fraudulent or there is fraud in the transaction;

(a) the issuer must honor the draft or demand for payment if honor is demanded by a negotiating bank or other holder of the draft or demand which has taken the draft or demand under the credit and under circumstances which would make it a holder in due course (Section 3-302) and in an appropriate case would make it a person to whom a document of title has been duly negotiated (Section 7-502) or a bona fide purchaser of a certificated security (Section 8-302); and

(b) in all other cases as against its customer, an issuer acting in good faith may honor the draft or demand for payment despite notification from the customer of fraud, forgery, or other defect not apparent on the face of the documents but a court of appropriate jurisdiction may enjoin such honor.

(3) Unless otherwise agreed, an issuer which has duly honored a draft or demand for payment is entitled to immediate reimbursement of any payment made under the credit and to be put in effectively available funds not later than the day before maturity of any acceptance made under the credit.

(4) [When a credit provides for payment by the issuer on receipt of notice that the required documents are in the possession of a correspondent or other agent of the issuer. (a) any payment made on receipt of such notice is conditional; and

(b) the issuer may reject documents which do not comply with the credit if it does so within three banking days following its receipt of the documents; and

(c) in the event of such rejection, the issuer is entitled by charge back or otherwise to return of the payment made.]

(5) [In the case covered by subsection (4) failure to reject documents within the time specified in sub-paragraph (b) constitutes acceptance of the documents and makes the payment final in favor of the beneficiary.]

Note: Subsections (4) and (5) are bracketed as optional. If they are included, the bracketed language in the last sentence of Section 5-112(1) should also be included. As amended in 1977.

5-115. Remedy for Improper Dishonor or Anticipatory Repudiation.

(1) When an issuer wrongfully dishonors a draft or demand for payment presented under a credit, the person entitled to honor has, with respect to any documents, the rights of a person in the position of a seller (Section 2-707) and may recover from the issuer the face amount of the draft or demand together with incidental damages under Section 2-710 on seller's incidental damages and interest but less any amount realized by resale or other use or disposition of the subject matter of the transaction. In the event no resale or

other utilization is made, the documents, goods, or other subject matter involved in the transaction must be turned over to the issuer on payment of judgment.

(2) When an issuer wrongfully cancels or otherwise repudiates a credit before presentment of a draft or demand for payment drawn under it, the beneficiary has the rights of a seller after anticipatory repudiation by the buyer under Section 2-610 if he learns of the repudiation in time reasonably to avoid procurement of the required documents. Otherwise, the beneficiary has an immediate right of action for wrongful dishonor.

5-116. Transfer and Assignment.

(1) The right to draw under a credit can be transferred or assigned only when the credit is expressly designated as transferable or assignable.

(2) Even though the credit specifically states that it is nontransferable or nonassignable, the beneficiary may before performance of the conditions of the credit assign his right to proceeds. Such an assignment is an assignment of an account under Article 9 on Section Transactions and is governed by that Article except that

(a) the assignment is ineffective until the letter of credit or advice of credit is delivered to the assignee, which delivery constitutes perfection of the security interest under Article 9; and

(b) the issuer may honor drafts or demands for payment drawn under the credit until it receives a notification of the assignment signed by the beneficiary which reasonably identifies the credit involved in the assignment and contains a request to pay the assignee; and

(c) after what reasonably appears to be such a notification has been received, the issuer may without dishonor refuse to accept or pay even to a person otherwise entitled to honor until the letter of credit or advice of credit is exhibited to the issuer.

(3) Except where the beneficiary has effectively assigned his right to draw or his right to proceeds, nothing in this section limits his right to transfer or negotiate drafts or demands drawn under the credit.

As amended in 1972.

5-117. Insolvency of Bank Holding Funds for Documentary Credit.

(1) Where an issuer or an advising or confirming bank or a bank which has for a customer procured issuance of a credit by another bank becomes insolvent before final payment under the credit, and the credit is one to which this Article is made applicable by paragraphs (a) or (b) of Section 5-102(1) on

scope, the receipt or allocation of funds or collateral to secure or meet obligations under the credit shall have the following results:

(a) to the extent of any funds or collateral turned over after or before the insolvency as indemnity against or specifically for the purpose of payment of drafts or demands for payment drawn under the designated credit, the drafts or demands are entitled to payment in preference over depositors or other general creditors of the issuer or bank; and

(b) on expiration of the credit or surrender of the beneficiary's rights under it unused any person who has given such funds or collateral is similarly entitled to return thereof, and

(c) a charge to a general or current account with a bank if specifically consented to for the purpose of indemnity against or payment of drafts or demands for payment drawn under the designated credit falls under the same rules as if the funds had been drawn out in cash and then turned over with specific instructions.

(2) After honor or reimbursement under this section, the customer or other person for whose account the insolvent bank has acted, is entitled to receive the documents involved.

CHAPTER 3

Legal Remedies for Business Creditors

REVERSE PIERCING OF THE CORPORATE VEIL

The purpose of a corporation is primarily to shelter the shareholders, directors, and officers from personal liability. To take advantage of this umbrella, the officers, directors, and shareholders must operate the corporate entity as a separate corporate entity for the benefit of that corporate entity. In some instances, the same shareholder controls two different corporations and dominates both corporations to the extent that the corporations, their operations, and dealings are all within the control of the one shareholder. Sometimes, one corporation will liquidate or even file bankruptcy, leaving outstanding debts and judgments. Before ceasing business or filing a petition in bankruptcy, the corporation transfers its assets to the other corporation with or without consideration. Sometimes, circumstances present themselves to allow a creditor to pierce this corporate veil and hold that the corporations are alter egos of each other and that the solvent corporation should be liable for the debts of the insolvent or bankrupt corporation.

In recent years, suits based on piercing the corporate veil have increased and more and more creditors are recognizing that sophisticated debtors are using this corporate device to avoid payment of their debts. Piercing the corporate veil is a vague and illusory concept and applied by the courts in a discriminatory and subjective manner. It is not codified or statutory, but merely a common law creation to prevent a fraudulent use of the corporate umbrella.

When a corporate veil is pierced, the judges usually rely on various theories. The creation of the corporation is a privilege granted by the state and must not be abused. The arrangement among the corporation, the shareholders, and creditors is a contractual relationship and this contractual relationship should not be violated.

There are many criteria that the courts identify to justify piercing the corporate veil.

1. Common shareholders, stockholders, and directors.

2. Does the parent corporation own all or most of the stock of the other corporation or does the individual own the stock in both corporations?

3. Does the parent corporation finance a subsidiary or is the subsidiary allowed to use the line of credit of the parent?

4. Does one corporation have inadequate capital?

5. Does one corporation pay the salaries and the day-to-day expenses of the other corporation?

6. Does one corporation have no employees and no day-to-day expenses other than buying and selling merchandise at a profit?

7. Does one corporation have no assets and use its income to pay the expenses of the other corporation?

8. Does the individual treat the corporation as his own personal business, running personal expenses through the corporation?

9. Does the corporation maintain books?

10. Does one corporation fail to maintain corporate formality, such as directors' meetings, shareholders' meetings, minutes of these meetings, stock transfer books, etc.?

11. Is one corporation described by the other corporation as a department or division?

12. Do the directors and officers of one corporation take their direction from the other corporation? Did transfers of assets take place from one corporation to the other, rendering the corporation insolvent?

13. Was there extensive and pervasive control over the operation of the corporations by one individual?

14. Was there commingling of the properties or accounts of the corporation with the other corporation or with the individual?

15. Is there an absence of corporate records?

16. Is one corporation merely a facade for the personal operations of the dominant shareholder?

17. Do the financial statements of the two corporations clearly show overlapping and reliance on each other? Are the daily operations of one corporation being maintained by the other corporation?

The above listing identifies certain markers that recur regularly. Unfortunately, no standard has been established to tell you how many of these markers are necessary to induce a particular court to pierce the corporate veil nor is there any criteria to determine which markers receive heavy consideration. A review of the cases seems to indicate that each judge has his own criteria and each case seems to rest on its own set of facts.

Piercing the corporate veil requires a showing that the parent corporation dominates the subsidiary to such an extent that the latter is really an agent for or an instrumental part of the former, and the parent corporation used that control to commit fraud or some other wrong. A showing is usually required that the dominant party exercises complete control of the corporation with respect to the transactions, and such dominion was used to commit a fraud or wrong against the creditor which resulted in injury to the creditor. Complete domination is the key to piercing the corporate veil when the owners use the corporation as a mere device to further their personal agenda rather than the legitimate corporate interest. It makes no difference whether the corporation had been dominated by an individual or another corporation. If the separate entity concepts are so ignored that one corporation primarily transacts the business of the dominant corporation instead of its own, it may be called the other's alter ego, and corporate form may be disregarded to achieve an equitable result.

While the majority of the courts has determined that the reverse piercing of the corporate veil is a valid cause of action, a small majority has held that it is not a proper remedy.[1]

---

[1]*Scholes v. Lehman*, 56 F.3d 750 (7th Cir. 1995); *State v. Eastern*, 647 N.Y. Supp. 2d 904 (Sup. Ct. Albany Co. 1995); *American Fuel Corp. v. Utah Energy*, 122 F. 3d 130 (2nd Cir. 1997); *In re Richels*, 163 B.R. 760 (Bankr. Ed. Va. 1994).

FINANCING BY AFFILIATED COMPANY

The seller of a product or service often provides its own credit company which finances the transaction. The finance company is operated separately and distinctly from the equipment company and enters into the financing arrangement or lease arrangement, whichever is more appropriate, with the purchaser; the equipment company furnishes the equipment and is paid by the finance company. Most of these types of credit arrangements are several pages of fine print and it is incumbent upon the seller to be fully aware of the fine print. The disclaimers and liquidated damage clauses contained in the fine print are comprehensive and are designed primarily to protect the financing organization.

In the instance case, the court found that a particular agreement was not a consumer lease. Consumer leases are treated differently and consumers have additional protection when the product they purchase is being financed by an affiliated company. But courts are reluctant to change the terms of business agreements. This case happened in New Jersey and the court determined that the agreement was a finance lease, wherein the financial firm does not manufacture or supply the goods, but only acquires the goods or the right to possession in connection with the lease.

The portion of the disclaimer in the lease was common wherein it stated that the lessor, the credit company, shall not be deemed to have made any representation, warranty, or promise made by the seller of the product. Neither the seller nor the lessor shall act as or be deemed to be an agent of the other. The lessor shall not be bound by, or be liable for, any representation or promise made by the seller (even if the lessor is affiliated with the seller). The agreement also provided that the lessor shall have no liability to the lessee, the lessee's customers, or any third parties for any direct, indirect, special, or consequential damages arising out of the agreement. The lease provides that the agreement will not deprive the lessee of any rights it may have against any other person, i.e., the seller. Most of these financing agreements specifically state that the lessee shall look solely to the seller for any or all claims, representations, and warranties relating to the equipment. If a manufacturer's warranty is available, the lessee may rely on that agreement.

The court pointed out that the finance company performed no other function and its disclaimers were prominent in the lease and the lease provided that the purchaser had a right to pursue the seller for any warranties and representations. The fact that there was a close connection between the finance company and the seller is not of itself sufficient. Arguments might be made if the finance company was involved in the sale of the equipment or was involved in the delivery or maintenance of the equipment. But most finance companies are careful to be involved only in collecting payments, and totally remove themselves from any involvement in the sale or maintenance of the equipment.

The personal guarantee of the individual officer of the lessee was also deemed enforceable by the court. In this particular case, the telephone company was still in business and ultimately may answer for their breach of contract. The problem is that by the time the lessee takes the equipment company to court and obtains a judgment, the lessee itself may be out of business because the finance company will have repossessed all their equipment.

When entering into these types of transactions, the financial responsibility of the seller of the equipment is much more important than obtaining financing. If the seller of the equipment should file a petition in bankruptcy, the purchaser would have to seek out other firms to maintain and service the equipment. The charge for said services by third parties might be exorbitant compared to what the seller was charging. A careful reading of the finance agreement is important, but the most important ingredient is to know from whom you are purchasing the equipment and that they will stand behind the equipment.[2]

DUTY TO READ

A party who signs an instrument clearly infers to the other party that he has read the agreement and he may not later complain that he did not read the agreement and did not understand the agreement. If an individual has the capacity to read an agreement and to understand the agreement, he cannot complain that he did not read it and did not understand it. If this was not the case, it is fairly obvious that no one can rely on a signed document if the other party can merely avoid the agreement by stating that he did not read the agreement or did not understand the agreement. The same thing would apply to the acceptance of documents such as bills of lading, passenger tickets, insurance policies, bank books, and warehouse receipts, where these documents purport to be a contract between the parties. The party accepting these documents is assenting to the terms of the contract.

---

[2]*AT&T Credit Corp. v. Transglobal Telecom Alliance, Inc.*, 966 F. Supp 299 (D.N.J. 1997).

The courts over the years have carefully and systematically developed a number of exceptions to this rule. If the document is not legible or not easily read, a party is not bound by the fine print, or if it were in such small type and so long and so crowded that it was physically difficult to read the document, the court could readily believe that there was no assent. The courts are reluctant to enforce terms of contract not sufficiently called to the attention of one party, such as printed notices on letterheads, catalogs, or tags or printed notices inside of clothing. Some courts have been reluctant to enforce clauses that are printed on the reverse side of a document unless it is clearly and conspicuously referred to on the front side of the document. Purported contracts posted on desks, walls, or other public places may also be an exception unless the particular party to the contract actually observed the particular contractual terms or because the posting was so clearly conspicuous, the party should have observed the particular contractual terms. An example is an air traveler purchasing an insurance policy from a vending machine covering scheduled airline flights. Appearing next to the vending machine was a listing of the non-scheduled airline flights. The court held that it was a question of fact for a jury whether the passenger had been afforded sufficient notice of the limitation. Some statutes to be valid provide a set size and boldness of terms.

Another exception is where a party receives a document that the party has no reason to believe contains any contractual terms. This applies to the proverbial parking ticket or the ticket that is issued when a party checks his coat at the restaurant or the ticket that he receives when he delivers a package to a parcel checkroom. If a person without fault on his part assents to a document believing that it is something other than what it is, the instrument may be considered unenforceable. The question is whether consent to the terms of the contract is present and this determination is often decided on a case-by-case basis.

Whether the contractual provision is called sufficiently to the attention of a party to a contract depends upon whether a reasonable man acting in a reasonable manner and evaluating all the circumstances then and there prevailing would know that the terms were intended to be part of a proposed agreement between the two parties. A failure to read a document must be considered in view of all the circumstances then and there prevailing.

DUTY TO READ—FRAUD

Fraud and mistake are another exception to the rule of duty to read. This occurs where a particular party deliberately misrepresents what the contents of a writing or an agreement are and the other party relies on that oral representation and signs without having read the document. A minority of the courts will decide that the party had no right to rely on the oral representation because he was entering into a written contract, and a reasonable man should know that the written contract merges all the oral representations into the written contract. On the other hand, the majority of the courts feels a lack of mutual agreement is present between the parties and that the party who makes the misrepresentation is guilty of fraud and cannot enforce the contract.

A misrepresentation becomes more difficult where the contract specifically states that all oral representations made prior to the contract are merged into the contract. Even here a conflict exists among the courts with some courts stating that a failure to read the integration provision in the contract which merges the oral representation into the agreement precludes that party from offering the oral representation, even though it was a fraudulent one. Perhaps the better view is that a party is bound to know the contents of the paper that is signed.

Where one party procures another to sign a writing by fraudulently representing that it contains stipulations agreed upon, when in fact it does not, and relies on the faith of those representations and is induced to omit the reading of the contract, a false representation as to its contents may render it unenforceable and the party so defrauded is not precluded from contesting the validity of the contract.

DUTY TO READ—ADHESION CONTRACT

Contracts of adhesion are also exceptions to the rule. An adhesion contract is one in which an unconscionable bargain is entered into, due to a prodigious amount of bargaining power on behalf of the stronger party, which is used to the stronger party's advantage. In those cases, the contract is normally avoidable. An example would be the classic case where an individual purchased an automobile and the contract of purchase contained an express warranty that limited damages only to replacement of defective parts. In this instance, the individual suffered serious personal injuries. The court stated that the lawmakers did not authorize automobile manufacturers to use their grossly disproportionate bargaining power to relieve themselves from liability and to impose on the ordinary buyer, who in effect has no real freedom of choice, the grave danger of injury to himself and others that attends the sale of such a dangerous instrumentality as a defectively made automobile.

The issue of whether a consumer or a business is involved also is an important factor in these decisions. The courts tend to protect the consumer when the consumer is dealing with a business. The courts tend to leave the written contract stand in those situations between two businesses on the theory that the two businesses are sophisticated enough to understand that they have to read the written agreement.

In this area, it is difficult to set down black-and-white rules because for every decision that carves out an exception, the next court will say that the exception does not apply. The facts and circumstances of every case are always different and cases are rarely so similar that they are almost identical. Perhaps the best advice is to read the contract so that there will not be a need to avoid the terms of the written agreement. This applies even more so to bills of lading and documents of title and warehouse receipts because the courts apply a strict liability test to these instruments more so than to parking tickets and coat checkroom tickets.

STATUTE OF LIMITATIONS

The Statute of Limitations is designed to encourage a plaintiff to commence suit when the remedy becomes available so that potential and contingent suits are not indefinitely available to the creditor. The law encourages a plaintiff to commence suit as soon as practical after plaintiff discovers the availability of a remedy. A time frame is created within which a suit must be commenced. If the suit is not commenced within this time period, it is said to be barred by the Statute of Limitations. In general, it is more favorable to institute suits as soon as they accrue, since witnesses and evidence are readily available.

The important thing to remember is that each state has enacted its own specific Statute of Limitations. The statutes prescribe different time periods from state to state covering the same type of transactions; and the courts have different interpretations as to the application of the Statute of Limitations to these transactions. Most of the statutes, or at least the decision law in the states, allow the statute to be suspended if the defendant has left the state during the period covered by the Statute of Limitations.

In general, the Statute of Limitations in a contract case will run from when a breach of contract first occurred. In most situations dealing with demand notes, the time runs from when a demand is first made for payment. If the note is a time note, the demand must be made at the date of maturity of the note. With a contract of guarantee, the time frame begins to run from the time the obligation of the principal debtor first becomes due. This time frame would change radically if it was a guarantee of collection where the creditor must exhaust all remedies against the principal debtors before commencing suit against the guarantor. Notwithstanding these general statements, we must again emphasize that a review of state law is absolutely necessary.

RISKS OF LOSS

When commercial transactions were governed by the Uniform Sales Act, the question of which party had the risk of loss when the goods were in transit, such as on a train, plane, or a truck, depended upon which party had title at the time the accident happened. If the seller had title at the time the accident happened, the seller had to bear the loss and seek reimbursement from the insurance company. If title to the goods had already passed to the buyer, the buyer assumes the risk. There were no set rules. Each case presented a specific problem and often created additional questions. The end result was confusion and a significant amount of litigation.

The Uniform Commercial Code Sections 2-509 and 2-510 resolved many of the problems that existed under the Uniform Sales Act and Sections 2-319 and 2-320 have further resolved many of the problems by defining the term "F.O.B." Section 509 states that when a contract authorizes a seller to ship by carrier, if there is no requirement in the contract to deliver the goods at a particular specified location, the buyer assumes the risk of loss at the time the goods are delivered to the carrier. If the contract does require delivery at a specific designation and the goods are delivered there, the buyer assumes the risk of loss when the goods are tendered at the specific designation.

The term "F.O.B." (free on board) is defined as a delivery term. When the term "F.O.B. the place of shipment" is used, the seller must ship the goods and bear the expense of putting them into the possession of the carrier. Once in the possession of the carrier, the buyer assumes the risk of loss. When the term "F.O.B. place of destination" is used, the seller bears the expense and risk until delivery to the place of destination.

Most frequently, shipments are made "F.O.B. Seller's Place of Business," i.e., shipment contracts in which the seller agrees to make a contract for shipment and delivery of the goods into the possession of the carrier. The risk of loss passes to the buyer immediately upon delivery to the carrier. When the contract reads "F.O.B. Buyer's Place of Business," the risk of loss does not pass to the buyer until the carrier tenders the goods to the buyer at the buyer's place of business. It is assumed that the goods are delivered in a conforming condition and that the buyer has had reasonable notice to pick up the goods.

The actual address to which the seller is to deliver the goods as set forth in the contract has no bearing and will not affect the liability of either the seller or buyer—which is solely controlled by the "F.O.B." clause. If the term says "F.O.B. Seller's Place of Business" and then designates to what address the shipment is to be made, the seller's risk of loss ends when he delivers the merchandise to the carrier. The contract terms identify who is paying the expense of shipping, but this has no effect on the liability of the parties, which is controlled by the F.O.B. clause (nor would the fact that the seller is using his own trucks to ship the merchandise under a "F.O.B Place of Shipment" clause in the contract).

If there is no F.O.B designation in the contract, the risk of loss passes to the buyer immediately upon delivery to the carrier if no requirement is present to deliver at a particular designation. The parties may expressly provide in writing for any other terms and conditions that are contrary to the UCC and the written agreement would prevail.

SURETY—CONSTRUCTION CONTRACTS

Frequently, surety agreements are created in construction contracts where the owners of property obtain what is known as performance bonds from insurance companies. A case in New York clarified some of the issues and liabilities of the insurance company.

Contracts of surety are to be construed like other contracts so as to give effect to the intention of the parties. Once the liability and the meaning of the language in the surety contract has been determined, the responsibility of the surety is not to be extended or enlarged by construction or implication and is "strictissimi juris," which means the courts tend to interpret surety contracts strictly within the terms of the contract in the same manner as letters of credit are interpreted.

In general, third parties such as subcontractors or co-prime contractors have no right to recover from performance bonds for a contractor/principal's breach. Where a laborer sought to recover unpaid wages from a contractor's performance bond executed by the surety solely in favor of the owner, the judge concluded that such a bond was not intended to benefit anyone other than the named beneficiary (owner). Allowing a third party to assert a claim against a performance bond would frustrate the purpose of the bond since the purpose of the bond is to benefit the beneficiary and not third parties. To allow the third party to assert a claim against the performance bond, the amount of the performance bond would be reduced and the beneficiary would suffer. The court reasoned that if third parties were allowed to assert claims against the bond, sufficient monies would not be available to complete the performance, the purpose for which the bond was intended.

Another claim in the case was that the insurance company is itself liable for the delay, because they were stepping into the shoes of the contractor. Therefore, the third party could assert a claim against the insurance company since the contractor delayed the performance and the third party suffered damages. The court interpreted the contract strictly and stated that the insurance company had really become obligated to complete the work and did not step into the shoes of the prime contractor who defaulted in the performance, but stepped into the shoes of the beneficiary (the owner) and as the beneficiary under the contract, the insurance company was completing the work. In short, the obligations of the surety bond are solely for the benefit of the beneficiary, usually the owner of the property.

Sometimes, the contractor himself is the beneficiary and other times the subcontractors may be the beneficiaries under the surety agreement. A careful reading of the surety contract is essential. Sometimes, problems arise when the insurance company on the surety bond is competing with a bank that has a security interest in the accounts of the contractor. The surety is completing the job and should be entitled to the progress payments. On the other hand, the bank has a right to the progress payments to discharge their indebtedness. The bank filed a financing statement whereas the surety company had no opportunity to file a financing statement under its contract to complete the construction work (except as to the heavy equipment of the contractor). Consultation with counsel is recommended.[3]

NOTICE OF DEFECT

We continue to see cases where one party to a contract has failed to provide notice of the breach of the contract to the other party. In many instances it is an obvious defect and in some instances it is a defect that is not discovered until a later date.

Section 2-607 states as follows:

(2) acceptance of goods by the buyer precludes rejection of the goods accepted and if made with knowledge of a non-conformity cannot be

---

[3]*Anron Heating & Air Conditioning, Inc. v. City of New York,* Index No. 605981/97, 1998 N.Y. Misc. Lexis 520 (Sup. Ct., New York County, Nov. 4, 1998).

revoked because of it unless the acceptance was on the reasonable assumption that the non-conformity would be seasonably cured but acceptance does not of itself impair any other remedy provided by this article for non-conformity.

(3) where a tender has been accepted

    (a) the buyer must within a reasonable time after he discovers or should have discovered any breach, notify the seller of breach or be barred from any remedy...

The statute avers that within a reasonable time the party should notify the seller of the breach. The statute does not specify whether notice is oral, in writing, or whether you should use certified mail or overnight express. Many cases revolve around an oral notice that the other party denies receiving. Oral notice will meet the standards of this section if it is delivered within a reasonable time. The best of both worlds is to provide oral notice with a notation of whom you spoke to as well as the date and time, and to immediately mail to the seller written notice of the breach.

The written notice does not have to contain a detailed itemization of the nature of the breach nor in what respect the particular product was defective. The notice need not set forth any claim for damages, or of any threatened litigation, or of any other threat of a resort to a remedy. The notice only must inform the seller that the transaction involved a breach.

Whether the notice should be given by certified mail to establish the fact that the seller received notification of the breach or by use of an overnight express carrier where a record of delivery of the notice is available probably depends upon whether the purchaser of the product wishes to be cautious and upon the amount of the damages that the buyer will incur if the buyer is unable to prove notice to the seller.[4]

CREDITORS OF A BAILEE

In the western states, the branding of an animal creates evidence of ownership. However, a brand on livestock is only prima-facie evidence of ownership and is not per se ownership that may not be attacked by third parties. An agreement between the parties that one party retains ownership while the other party became a bailee and received possession of the

---

[4]*Aqualon Co. v. MAC Equipment,* 149 F. 3d 262 (4th Cir. 1998).

cattle is strong evidence that the ownership was retained in the name of the bailor.

In this particular case, the cattle were branded by the bailee and the creditor of the bailee of the cattle attempted to seize the cattle allegedly owned by someone other than the bailee. The mere fact that a bailee has possession of property does not mean that the creditor can attach this property if in fact it is a genuine bailment. The prevailing cases conclude that a security interest of a bailee's creditor does not attach to goods that are the subject of a bailment. The new brand was that of the bailee, but older brands were on the cattle. The last brand is not necessarily automatically dispositive of ownership.

Under the Wyoming statute, the brand, prima-facie ownership, was subject to rebuttal. Two brands were on the cattle and both of them could be treated as evidence of prima-facie ownership. A lien search under the bailee's name revealed no liens. The court ultimately held that the bailor maintained ownership of the cattle. The case also provided an analysis of the branding customs in the industry as well as the impact of separate agreements between the parties as to ownership and bailment.[5]

---

[5]*Estate of Harris v. Harris*, 218 F. 3d 1140 (10th Cir. 2000)

CHAPTER 4

Legal Issues of Consumers

ARBITRATION

The issue of whether a consumer is entitled to arbitration has been confronting the courts for the past several years and the decisions being rendered have not been consistent. The arbitration clauses are being used more frequently in today's environment for the purpose of avoiding class action suits and many corporations that sell to consumers are inserting in the agreement with the consumer that "any disputes must be resolved by arbitration." The courts favor arbitration since it means one more case that does not have to work its way through the overcrowded judicial system.

The creditors who lend the money to the consumers or the sellers who sell their merchandise to the consumers have passed the stage of using a simple "right to arbitrate," but are including in the arbitration clause certain terms and conditions that are forcing the courts to find that the arbitration clauses are unenforceable. An example is the arbitration clause that requires the debtor to arbitrate in a particular jurisdiction that may be thousands of miles from where the debtor resides or the debtor is required to absorb all of the costs and expenses of the arbitration or even half the expenses of the arbitration, where those expenses are extremely oppressive and unreasonable in relation to the amount in dispute.

One case recognized the general mandate in favor of arbitration which is prescribed by the Federal Arbitration Act, but at the same time rejected mandatory arbitration of non-written and implied warranty claims.[1]

Another case in the 11th Circuit also held that the arbitration agreement was unenforceable as to any claims asserted for breach of an express or written warranty, but for all other allegations, the court said the agreement required the parties to arbitrate their dispute.[2]

A case dealt with an arbitration clause that was contained in the software that was downloaded from one of the network providers. The software contained a click wrap agreement (an agreement appearing on the computer screen before the consumer uses the program) that required them to submit to arbitration in the State of Washington. In this instance, the court held that the agreement must be enforced despite some claims made by the plaintiff, but at the same time stated that the defendant could not require the proceedings to be held in the State of Washington.[3]

In another recent case, the court acknowledged the fact that the law favors contracts for arbitration between parties. No policy is in place compelling persons to accept arbitration of controversies in which they have not agreed to arbitrate. In the instant case, the Bank of America provided in their credit card agreement that they had the power of varying price or other performance in the contract. The court seemed to feel that the exercise of this power is subject to prescribed or implied limitations. The bank in this instance stated that it could change any term, condition, service, or feature of the credit account and the court held that this was ambiguous at least to the extent of whether the bank could unilaterally impose an alternative dispute resolution (ADR) clause. It was finally held that the customer did not consent to the unilateral imposition of an arbitration clause requiring that, upon the request of either party, any dispute must be resolved by arbitration, since nothing in the original agreement alerted customers that they might someday have to forfeit their right to a jury trial or a judicial forum. The courts favor arbitration, but at the same time are making an effort to prevent creditors from avoiding class actions by utilizing an arbitration clause in their contracts.

---

[1]*Boyd v. Homes of Legend, Inc.*, 981 F. Supp. 1423 (N.D. Ala. 1997).

[2]*Cunningham v. Fleetwood Homes of Georgia*, C.V. 99-PT-2605-E (N.D. Ala. March 30, 2000); *Rhode v. E & T Invs., Inc.*, 6 F. Supp.2d 1322 (M.D. Ala.), summary judgment granted in part, denied in part, 29 F. Supp.2d 1298 (M.D. Ala. 1998).

[3]*Lieschke v. RealNetworks, Inc.*, No. 99 C 7274, 99 C 7380, 2000 WL 198424 (N.D. Ill. Feb. 11, 2000).

ARBITRATION AGREEMENT— STRICT INTERPRETATION

The Federal Arbitration Act specifically states that an arbitration shall proceed "in the manner provided for in such agreement." Once the court has determined that it is satisfied as to the agreement for arbitration, the court shall make an order directing the parties to proceed to arbitration "in accordance with the terms of the agreement." Needless to say, arbitration agreements do not provide or allow for class actions.

The Circuit Court of Appeals in the 7th Circuit has held that the Federal Arbitration Act requires that the courts enforce the arbitration agreement according to its terms. The court acknowledged that the terms could conceivably allow a class action, but in the particular case a provision for a class action was not in the agreement and no express term in the agreement provided for class arbitration. Accordingly, *absent any express provision in the agreement providing for a class arbitration,* the courts do not have the authority to reform the agreement and order an arbitration panel to hear claims on a class basis pursuant to Rule 23.[4]

Considerable litigation on this point has taken place, but the large majority of the cases, with the exception of isolated cases under state law, prohibit arbitration of class claims even when they are brought under the Truth and Lending Act or the Fair Debt Collection Practices Act, both of which acts expressly allow class action proceedings. Where there is an agreement to submit to arbitration an existing dispute between the parties where the terms of the arbitration agreement clearly provide that the existing dispute shall be covered, the courts will generally enforce the agreement according to its terms.

That brings us to the issue of whether a bank can issue a "change in terms" notification to the consumer to include a mandatory arbitration clause in the credit card agreement. The great majority of the courts seem to have approved the bank's right to include a mandatory arbitration clause in the credit card agreement and will certainly give effect to the arbitration clause as to any future disputes.

One of the major problems is whether one party to an agreement has the right to alter the agreement without the consent of the other party. Whereas the federal courts are favorable to arbitration agreements under the Federal Arbitration Act, consumer attorneys have been attacking the arbitration agreements as oppressive and unconscionable on a wide vari-

---

[4]*Champ v. Siegel Trading Co.,* 55 F.3d 269 (7th Cir. 1995).

ety of grounds. Undoubtedly, the retroactivity of some of these "legal notices" will also be attacked.

A case in California held that the bank did not have an unequivocal right to deny the consumer a right to a jury trial and that the arbitration clause did not become part of the credit card agreement and could not be enforced against the cardholder. Because the bank did not deal with question of dispute resolution in the original cardholder agreement with the consumer, the court indicated that the bank did not have the right to change the terms of the cardholder agreement to now include a specific method of arbitration as the means to resolve a dispute between the parties.[5]

In other instances, the courts have found both technical and factual reasons not to enforce the change of terms notification, but in most cases the courts favor arbitration.

ARBITRATION—INSTALLMENT CONTRACT

An arbitration provision is installed in a retail installment contract in which both the buyer and the seller agree to submit to binding arbitration. The wife did not execute the arbitration contract. Even though the wife did not execute the retail installment contract, the wife was bound by the terms of the retail installment contract and the arbitration provisions. The court identified her as a third-party beneficiary who is not a party to the contract. Where the wife's claim is connected and intertwined with the husband's, since they both jointly owned the mobile home, she was bound by the arbitration contract almost as a matter of law.

The judicial system favors arbitration contracts as a general principle since anything that is capable of being arbitrated does not come within the jurisdiction of the courts. Any waiver of a right to arbitrate usually must be intentional and the party attempting to prove a waiver of an arbitration has a heavy burden.

ARBITRATION CLAUSE—CLICK WRAP

A New York case dealt with the issue of the purchase of a computer. In such transactions, no agreement or contract is entered upon the placement of an order or even upon the receipt of the goods. The contract is con-

---

[5]*Badie v. Bank of America*, 67 Cal. App. 4th 779, 79 Cal. Rptr. 2d 272 (1998) Court of Appeal of California, First Appellate District, Division Three.

summated only after the consumer has affirmatively retained the merchandise for thirty days within which the consumer has presumably examined the product, used the product, and read the agreement. In this particular case, the arbitration agreement clause was contained in the agreement that appeared on the computer screen.

Although the parties clearly did not possess equal bargaining power where a computer was bought from one of the major sellers, this factor alone does not create an adhesion contract. The consumer does have the ability to make the purchase elsewhere and also enjoys the express option to return the goods. The consumer is not in a "take-it-or-leave-it" position. If any of the terms of the agreement are unacceptable to the consumer, he or she can easily buy a competitor's product instead (either from a retailer or directly from a manufacturer) and reject the agreement by returning the merchandise.

While returning the goods to avoid the formation of a contract entails an affirmative action on the part of the consumer, and even some expense, this may be a tradeoff for the convenience and savings for which the consumer presumably opted when he or she chose to make a purchase by phone or mail as an alternative to on-site retail shopping. If the consumer does not read the agreement, or claims failure to understand or appreciate some term, the contract is not invalidated any more than such claim would undo a contract formed under other circumstances.

Under New York law, unconscionability requires a showing that a contract is both procedurally and substantially unconscionable when made. A showing of an absence of meaningful choice on the part of one of the parties together with contract terms unreasonably favorable to the other party is necessary. Ultimately, the court enforced arbitration with some modification.

This type of litigation will continue as the companies that do business with the consumers proceed to include arbitration clauses in contracts that they have with the consumer. The purpose of the arbitration clause is to avoid a class action suit that has become the stand-by of the cottage industry of consumer attorneys. If the seller can avoid a class action suit, the seller can deal with any damages that arise from arbitration agreements. The problem is that many of the sellers have drafted oppressive and burdensome arbitration agreements. In this scenario, the courts tend to look for some way to set aside the contract and permit the consumer to sue or be sued in his own community without incurring these expenses. These oppressive and burdensome arbitration agreements have led to conflicting decisions even with reasonable arbitration agreements. Nevertheless, where the arbitration agreement is reasonable and not oppressive to the consumer, the courts usually enforce the arbitration agreement since, in general, the entire judicial system is favorable to arbitration.

ARBITRATION—CLASS ACTIONS

The use of an arbitration clause has increased radically over the years in the area of credit cards and other transactions with consumers. One of the major reasons for the use of arbitration clauses is the ability of consumer attorneys to institute class actions. When an arbitration clause is used in a retail installment contract or in a lease or other credit agreement, the scope of the arbitration will be limited to the individual transaction with that individual consumer, and thus in the event of a violation of the FDCPA, FCRA, ECOA, or TILA, the violation would be limited to that individual consumer and no class action could be asserted by a consumer attorney. An arbitration is quicker and cheaper for both parties; and the disadvantage of not being able to appeal a bad decision by the arbitrator is overcome by the benefit to the creditor in that the creditor is not being faced with the threat of class action.[6]

DRAFTING ARBITRATION CLAUSES

The issue of drafting an arbitration clause has now become a significant problem, because creditors recognize that at some point in time, their mandatory arbitration clauses will be tested before a tribunal. The major issue to address is the extent and the content of the disclosure to the consumer. The costs to the consumer, the geographical considerations, the distance to be traveled by the consumer, the controlling law, and a variety of other criteria must be thoroughly evaluated. Some courts are favorable to arbitrations and most of these items present no problems. Other courts are favorable to the consumer and will apply the law on a strict liability basis, carefully examining each clause of the arbitration agreement. Some liberal judges find a technical violation that enables them to render the entire arbitration agreement invalid.

The notification to the consumer and the actual agreement of arbitration must be carefully drawn under the supervision of an attorney who is

---

[6]*Nationwide of Bryan, Inc., v. Dyer,* 969 S.W.2d 518 (Tex. App. Austin 1998) Consumer Identity Fraud.

fully experienced in this area. The pitfalls are numerous and the number of cases that have found unusual and unique reasons to deny arbitration are many. The broadest possible terms should be used to protect against the widest area of liability. Ambiguity in the arbitration agreement will certainly be decided against the creditor. Full disclosure of all the rights that the consumer has in a court proceeding should be clearly and conspicuously disclosed to the consumer and the consumer must be told that these rights will be forfeited in an arbitration.

Many lawyers suggest a wide variety of clauses to be included in arbitration clauses so that they will be upheld by the courts. Among the recommendations are the following:

- Be certain that the costs to be incurred by the consumer to conduct the arbitration are reasonable.
- Provide for more than minimal discovery during an arbitration.
- Require a written award.
- Allow the arbitrator the right to award injunctive or punitive relief.
- Do not make the consumer travel too far to attend the arbitration.
- Disclose all the rights the consumer is forfeiting—class action, jury trial, appeal.

In some instances suggestions are being made to specifically have the consumer waive a class action, although most of the cases have been fairly constant in stating that arbitration cannot include a class action.

As a general statement the Federal Arbitration Act has expanded to include the commerce clause so that it affects the state courts and supersedes inconsistent state laws and statutes. A lender would not have to necessarily comply with the state law, but may rely on the Federal Arbitration Act in the states where they do business. Most states encourage arbitration, but a few states (in particular Alabama) do not favor arbitration and many states set criteria to be met for the arbitration clause to be enforceable.

MANDATORY ARBITRATION—
SUPREME COURT DECISION

In view of the recent increase in the use of mandatory arbitration clauses to avoid exposure to class actions, a review of the decision of the Supreme Court of the United States on December 11, 2000 is in order. A consumer claimed that the mandatory arbitration clause in her contract to finance a mobile home violated the Truth and Lending Act. The agreement was silent as to the amount of costs that the consumer would have to pay to conduct the arbitration and did not protect her from substantial costs. Unfortunately, this decision has been reported in the newspapers as approving the enforcement of mandatory arbitration clauses, which is not exactly what the court held.

A careful reading reveals that nothing appeared in the record to indicate the amount of costs that the consumer would incur to arbitrate. The agreement was silent on the question of costs. Nothing in the deposition of the witnesses indicated the amount of costs the consumer might incur. Footnoting the decision, the court mentioned that the consumer assumed that there would be expenses of $500 for a claim under $10,000 (notwithstanding the fact that the American Arbitration Association limits consumer fees to $125 in arbitration cases valued under $10,000).

To invalidate the arbitration agreement in this instance would undermine the liberal federal policy favoring arbitration agreements. It also could conflict with the prior holdings that the party resisting arbitration must bear the burden of proving that the claims at issue are unsuitable for arbitration. The other interesting point to note about the decision is that there were four justices who dissented—a 5-4 decision.

The court stated the failure to specify costs was too speculative to justify the invalidation of an arbitration agreement and found the arbitration clause enforceable. Nevertheless, the court clearly indicated that if evidence was before the court that the costs incurred would be substantial and perhaps prohibitive, the decision might be different. The Supreme Court seems to be saying that arbitration clauses should not be oppressive, costly, or burdensome to the consumer and has not put a stamp of approval on arbitrations where the consumer will be unfairly treated.[7]

PAYDAY LENDING

Payday lenders across the country continue to make short-term loans to consumers at high interest rates. Many states do not have limitations on rates that lenders can make on small loans (New Hampshire, Wisconsin, Illinois, New Mexico, Idaho, Washington, and North Dakota).

---

[7]*Green Tree Financial Corp.—Alabama v. Randolph*, 531 U.S. 79, 121 S.Ct. 513, 148 L.E.2d 373(2000).

A number of states prohibit payday lending (most of the northeast from Maine down to South Carolina, Georgia, Alabama, Indiana, Michigan, South Dakota, Texas, Arizona, and Alaska). The remaining states, by and large, have laws that permit payday lending. In some of the states that prohibit payday lending, the lenders have formed relationships with the national banks and other financial institutions because these institutions have federal preemption authority to enable them to operate under federal laws and not the state laws that prohibit the practice.

Right now in Congress, several bills have been introduced to regulate the abuses of payday lending, including the usurious rates of interest, as well as prohibiting the relationships between the federally chartered financial institutions with payday lenders.

UNIFORM PROBATE CODE

Most claims against deceased parties survive the death of the deceased party and a suit normally may be instituted against the executor or the administrator of the estate. One of the primary functions of the executor/administrator is to pay any debts of the estate. If the assets are insufficient to pay the claim, the Uniform Probate Code, which has been adopted in many states with some variations, provides for priority setting forth the order in which the debts should be paid:

Funeral expenses

Debts and taxes deferred under federal law

Medical expenses of the deceased's last illness

Claims deferred under other state laws

Other claims

At one time, administrators or executors were empowered to prefer one creditor over another creditor within each class, but under the present Uniform Probate Code, each member of each class must receive an equal pro-rata share.

The Uniform Probate Code typically bars all claims unless presented within four months after the date of first publication of the notice to creditors. The Code provides that the administrator or executor must publish notice of debt in certain publications and notices of claims of debt owing to a creditor must be presented within a stated period of time. The particular period of time and the procedure for publishing a notice is governed by state law and a review of the particular statute is absolutely necessary. If a claim is not presented within the specified period of time in those states that have "non-claim" statutes, then the creditor is barred from asserting a claim against the estate. This presents problems because not every creditor is aware that the debtor is deceased and not every creditor sees the notice of publication of the deceased that does not appear on the front page of the newspaper (public figures excepted).

If the personal representative (executor or administrator) knows of the claim, it would appear reasonable that the personal representative should make some effort to notify the creditor. In many states, if the executor or administrator knows of the claim but complies with the terms of the statute and the creditor does not file within the required time, the claim may be barred. On the other hand, creditors have attacked successfully the unreasonableness of this statute and some courts adopt the attitude that notice by publication is sufficient only for creditors who are not reasonably ascertainable. Some creditors have successfully asserted claims against the executors and the distributees where an executor fails to notify ascertainable creditors.[8]

If a suit is pending at the time of death against the deceased, some conflict arises as to whether a presentation of a claim is or is not necessary. But the best advice is to file your claim. If the executor or administrator disallows a claim and notifies the creditor that the estate will not pay that claim, the creditor usually has a specified time within which to bring proceedings against the representative of the estate. Needless to say, the statutes from state to state vary considerably in time periods and requirements and consultation with counsel is recommended.

CHANGE IN TERM—FAILURE TO RECEIVE NOTICE

In the past few years many credit card companies have been issuing "change in terms" notices to credit card customers advising them that they will be subject to mandatory arbitration. In some cases, the credit card customers have raised the issue that they did not receive the notice of the change in terms. The credit card company must face the fact that when litigation is presented over this issue, they will have to offer evidence in the court that the customer did receive the "change in terms"

---

[8]*Tulsa Professional Collection Services, Inc. v. Pope*, 485 U.S. 478, 108 S.Ct. 1340 (1998).

notification. This may consist of detailed evidence of the procedures that were used in determining who would receive the "change in terms" notifications, the mailing procedures used by the credit card company, an offer of evidence of a check issued by the customer paying the bill in which the "change in terms" notification was enclosed, and perhaps any internal manuals or memos indicating the procedures that were used to be certain that the debtors received the "change in terms" notifications.[9]

CREDIT CARD USE—TELEPHONE CALLING CARD

A telephone credit card was stolen and the stolen card number was used for unauthorized charges for telephone calls overseas. The owner of the calling card defended on the grounds that under the Truth in Lending Act (TILA) Regulation Z, they were liable for no more than $50. Regulation Z covers identification cards that permit the consumer to defer payment on a purchase. The court agreed with the defendant that the calling cards were a type of credit card despite the fact that the plaintiff tried to override Regulation Z by arguing that the transaction was covered by a filed tariff with the Federal Communications Commission that states that the consumer would not be liable for any unauthorized use of calling cards before the consumer was notified of the loss. The court declined to allow the tariff to override the express provisions of Regulation Z.[10]

CREDIT CARD—SCHUMER BOX

Now that Charles Schumer is a Senator from New York, it appears that the Federal Reserve Board will finally issue new rules that will affect the solicitation of credit cards. Any solicitation under a law proposed by then-Representative Schumer must contain a box disclosing the interest rate and other conditions for using the card, known as the "Schumer box." A new proposed rule is being considered by the Federal Reserve that must contain the key long-term rate, also known as the annual percentage rate (APR) in 18-point type and other terms, including the method for calculating finance charges on the outstanding balance, minimum finance charges for each billing cycle, and fees, in 12-point type.

---

[9]*Kennedy v. Conseco Finance Corp.*, 2000 WL 1760943 (N.D. Ill, Nov. 30, 2000).

[10]*Telco Communications Group, Inc. v. Race Rock of Orlando, L.L.C.*, 57 F. Supp. 2d 340 (E.D. Va. 1999).

CREDIT CARD COMPANIES SETTLE

From the $160-million settlement that Sears paid due to their failure to file reaffirmation agreements plus the other settlements by some of the major department stores, the suits by the cottage industry of consumer attorneys continue. During the past year it was reported that Bank One settled a case for $40 million alleging improper charges to its credit card customers. Providian settled for $300 million following allegations of charges of deceptive sale tactics and followed up with another settlement of $105 million dealing with promotions to pay towing charges and other automobile expenses.

JOINT TENANTS

A tenancy in common is where each person owns his or her share of the property independent from other tenants and is free to sell an undivided interest. The one-half interest in the property could be disposed of by contract and deed as well as by a last will and testament. When a tenant in common conveys property or leaves it by will, the liens and mortgages and judgments still remain on the property.

Tenancy by the entirety is unique to married couples. Each tenant of the tenancy by the entirety owns all of the property and thus the surviving tenant by the entirety does not acquire the tenant's interest in real property because he/she already owned the entirety. The interest of the party who is deceased merely disappears from the record and with it all liens and claims against the interest of the deceased party.

A joint tenancy is somewhere in between a tenancy in common and tenancy by the entirety. A joint tenancy is composed of two persons not married. The joint tenant owns all of the property but at the same time may convey or sell the interest in the property or leave the property by last will. Title will vest in the surviving tenant at the moment of the decease of the other tenant, free of any liens or claims against the deceased tenant.

Joint tenancies and tenancies by the entirety can be attacked when a real property conveyance is made with no consideration by one of the joint tenants to the tenants by the entirety or the joint tenants. If the debtor has been rendered insolvent, in many of the states, a creditor can proceed to set aside the conveyance as fraudulent with respect to the creditors. The timing of the transfer by the debtor to the debtor and his wife is most important. The transfer must take place after the loan was granted and usually after the loan is in default. If a transfer is made while payments are current, the additional burden of proving that the debtor was insolvent at the time will have to be overcome. (See 2nd Edition, page 160.)[11]

ADDITIONAL CHARGES

The Uniform Consumer Credit Code provides that any agreement with respect to a consumer credit sale may not provide for any charges as a result of a default by the buyer other than authorized by the act. A provision in violation of this section is unenforceable. The Consumer Credit Code has been adopted in several western states.

INSTALLMENT PAYMENT HOLIDAY

A recent case dealt with the issue of payment holidays and the contention of the defendant that each deferral of payment was a new credit transaction and thus triggered a new disclosure requirement under the Truth in Lending Act. The court did not agree with the consumer citing the fact that both the lender and the consumer agreed to the payment holidays. Perhaps if the creditor had acted unilaterally, without agreement of the consumer, the result might have been different, although it is difficult to imagine the creditor offering a payment holiday unilaterally.[12]

HIPPA

The new regulations of the Health Insurance Patient Portability and Accountability Act require certain restrictions on the handling of health information in dealing with the consumer. The American Collectors Association is making the following recommendations to its members:

1. The medical provider should not be asked to send the verification information directly to the patient. The debt collector should send the information to the patient.

---

[11]*St. Theresa's Nursing Home v. Vuksanovich,* 268 A.D. 2d 421, 702 N.Y.S. 2d 92 (2000) Supreme Court of New York, Appellate Division, Second Department; *In re Granwell,* 20 N.Y. 2d 91, 228 N.E. 2d 779, 281 N.Y.S. 2d 783 (1967).

[12]*Begala v. PNC Bank, Ohio, Nat. Ass'n,* 163 F. 3d 948 (6th Cir. 1998).

2. The debtor should request the verification in writing and verification should include documentation that would clarify the amount of the debt owed and the creditor to whom the debt is owed. If the debtor requests the hospital's bill, the debt collector may furnish this upon the express written consent of the debtor before the bill is actually sent to the debtor. In many instances the hospital will require the debtor's written consent before it will release any medical information directly to the debt collector. If the request by the debtor for verification is sufficient to amount to consent to release the billing information, the medical provider should accept the debtor's request for verification. On the other hand, the medical provider may still insist on a direct letter of consent that the medical provider will probably furnish to the debt collector.

There is a two-year grace period before HIPPA becomes effective.

PRETEXTING

In April of 2001 the Federal Trade Commission reported that they had filed suit in three U.S. district courts to halt the operation of information brokers who use false pretenses, fraudulent statements, or impersonation to illegally obtain consumers' confidential financial information such as bank balances—and sell it. Obtaining consumers' private financial information, known as "pretexting," violates federal law and the courts have been asked to stop this illegal practice permanently. In each of the three cases the courts temporarily enjoined the defendants from continuing the illegal practices and imposed a partial freeze of assets pending a hearing.

The FTC screened over a thousand websites and reviewed five hundred print media advertisements and then identified about two hundred firms that offered to obtain and sell assets or bank account information to third parties. The fees range from $100 to $600. The obtaining of the information could injure consumers by invading their financial privacy or releasing the information to individuals who might use it to deplete a bank account or liquidate a stock portfolio or what is happening more frequently today—identity fraud.

Pretexting is a violation of Section 807(10) of the Fair Debt Collection Practices Act, which states that the use of any false representation or deceptive means to collect or attempt to collect any debt or to obtain information concerning the consumer is a violation of the Act. In most instances, the collection agency allows an outside vendor to obtain the information, but in the event the collection agency itself should engage in pretexting or a law firm should engage in pretexting, both the agency and the law firm would be in violation of the FDCPA. As of the writing of this *Supplement,* your author knows of no case where an agency or law firm was sued for engaging a "pretext" vendor on the grounds of agency or vicarious liability, but the exposure is present.

CHAPTER 4

APPENDIX I

These tables were prepared in 1996, and are furnished for guidelines and information. Significant and material changes may have been enacted since 1996.

STATE LAWS CONTROLLING ASSIGNMENT OF WAGES

State	When Permitted			On Wages	Limitations		Other
	Assignments Permitted for General Purposes	Assignments Permitted for Special Purposes Including Small Loans, Real Estate by Head of Family	Retail Installment Sales Assignments Prohibited		Notice to Employer Required	Written Assignment Required	
Alabama	All assignments of future wages unenforceable.						
Alaska		X		None			Employer cannot discharge employee because wages are subject to assignment for child support.
Arizona		X		10%		X	Spouse's consent required; 48 months' duration. Child support and spousal maintenance.
Arkansas		X		None	X^2	X	Assignment filed with county recorder. [7] Consent of wife required.
California	X^4	X^1	X^4	50%; amount sufficient to cover court ordered child report	X	X	Spouse's or parent's consent[11] (except for necessities). Must deny existence of other assignments.

Reprinted with permission of the National Association of Credit Management.

State					
Colorado	X[15,20]	Wages earned within 30 days from time of assignment. Limited to 50% of disposable earnings if assignor supporting spouse or child; otherwise 40%.	X[25] (Within 5 days)	X	Spouse must sign.[4] Child support. Wage assignment notice and certified copy of assignment must be served upon the employer by certified mail, or return receipt requested, or in any other manner prescribed in Rule 4 of the Colorado Rules of Civil Procedure.
Connecticut	Assignments void except for amounts due for support in public welfare cases or payments pursuant to a family support judgment.				
Delaware		None	X[2,25]	X	Assignments securing loans on "real estate or otherwise" need employer's written consent. Assignments given as security for loans prohibited under licensed lender law assignment for court imposed fines may be for total earnings consistent with federal law. Voluntary assignments authorized for support.
D.C.	All assignments of future wages unenforceable.[20]				
Florida	No wage assignment given to secure any loan is valid. Child support assignments are controlled by statute.				
Georgia	There are no statutory provisions pertaining to assignment of wages except for child support.				
Hawaii	X	None	X	X	Signed by spouse; limited to 20 months' duration if repayable in equal monthly installments or 12 months if repayable in any other manner. Assignments in employment agency contract must be in form approved by director of labor. Child support.[25]
Idaho	X[15]	None		X	Special provisions for court-ordered wage assignments for the support of minor children.
Illinois	X	15% of gross wages or weekly disposable wages equivalent to 40 times the federal minimum hourly wage, whichever is less.	X[25]	X	Special formal requirements for assignment and demand for wages. Child support or maintenance of spouse orders are exempt from general assignment provisions. Wages of states and local government and school district employees are not subject to assignment.
Indiana	X[15,19]	None[5]	X	X	Spouse's consent. Assignment to wage broker void unless interest on loan not more than 8% per year.
Iowa	X	None	X[2]	X	Child support: Voluntary and mandatory assignments for child support are subject to the federal garnishment restrictions. Spouse's consent required. Creditor may not take an assignment to secure a consumer credit debt. Employer bound to honor court-ordered assignment for child support.

State Laws Controlling Assignment of Wages

State	When Permitted		Retail Installment Sales Assignments Prohibited	On Wages	Limitations		Other
	Assignments Permitted for General Purposes	Assignments Permitted for Special Purposes Including Small Loans, Real Estate by Head of Family			Notice to Employer Required	Written Assignment Required	
Kansas	Assignment of earnings for debt arising out of consumer credit transaction unenforceable by the assignee and revocable by the consumer. Assignment is permitted for support and maintenance orders.						
Kentucky		X[8]	X[13]	10% Loans under $200 limited to 90 days from execution.	X[2]	X	Wage assignments to banks and trust companies as security for installment loans prohibited; and assignment for less than $200 must meet technical requirements of obtaining signed written statement of assignor and statement of name, address of each assignee. Not binding on employer unless he accepts same. Court must order either one or both parents to assign a portion of wages or salary for child support.
Louisiana	X[24]	X		The lesser of (1) 15% of the gross amount of wages, salary, commissions, bonuses and periodic payments pursuant to a retirement or pension plan for any work week, or (2) disposable earnings for a work week up to an amount equal to 30 times the federal minimum hourly wage. Void after 3 years.	X[2]		
Maine	X[20]	X[8]		None	X	X	
Maryland	X[18]	X	X	Six-month limitation.	X	X[3]	Must be signed and acknowledged by wage earner and recorded by clerk of district; spouse's consent and signature required; assignor must sign affidavit that interest limited to 6% per year.
Massachusetts	X[24]	X[24]	X	25% limited to two years on loans over $3,000; $10 per week for one year on loans under $3,000. Must comply with federal limitations.	X[2,25]	X	Signed by spouse.[3,9]

Reprinted with permission of the National Association of Credit Management.

State			Amount / Limitation				Remarks
Michigan	X[24]	X[18]	For householders with family assignment of 60% of wages permitted but not less than $15 a week less $2 per week for each legal dependent; for non-householders, 40% of wages permitted but not less than $10 per week.		X	X	Filed in district or municipal court. Child support provisions.
Minnesota	X[24]	X[20]	10% on assignment for small loan.	X[25]	X	X	Limited to 60 days except on excess of $1,500 per month. Signed by spouse.[3] Child support provisions
Mississippi		X[10]	None	X[2]		X	
Missouri	X[11,14]	X	Assignment permitted for that needed for periodic child support or maintenance.	X[2]		X	Court order for family support. [23]
Montana	X	X	10%*	X[25]		X	Signed and consented to by both spouses. Assignments of future wages to wage brokers invalid.[3] Court-ordered child support. Assignment filed with the county clerk's office.
Nebraska	X	X	Amount of weekly earnings subject to assignments shall not exceed the lesser of 25% of disposable weekly earnings or the amount by which disposable weekly earnings exceed 30 times federal minimum hourly wage, or 15% of disposable weekly earnings if wage earner is a head of a family.	Acknowledgment and consent of wage earner and spouse required.			Child support: Amount of disposal income withheld may not exceed maximum amount permitted under federal Consumer Credit Protection Act garnishment provisions.
Nevada	Assignment of wages is void if made at the time that an unsatisfied judgment exists against the maker. An assignment of wages is not valid if given as a security for a loan.						
New Hampshire	X[24]	X[12]	None	X[2]		X	See child support. [3,25]
New Jersey	Assignment of wages prohibited in most instances except by court order. [13,25]						
New Mexico	X	X	Up to 25% or 10% for small loan.	X		X	Signed by spouse.[3]

Reprinted with permission of the National Association of Credit Management.

STATE LAWS CONTROLLING ASSIGNMENT OF WAGES

State	When Permitted			Limitations			
	Assignments Permitted for General Purposes	Assignments Permitted for Special Purposes Including Small Loans, Real Estate by Head of Family	Retail Installment Sales Assignments Prohibited	On Wages	Notice to Employer Required	Written Assignment Required	Other
New York	X[19,24]	X	X	10% on indebtedness of under $1,000; no limit on excess amount provided wages exceed $85 per week.	X	X	Signature of spouse for small loan assignments; generally void if to secure loan of over 18% interest per year.[3,25]
North Carolina	X[24]	X[18]			X[2]		Action for assignment of future wages must be commenced within six months of execution.
North Dakota		X[14]	X	None			Assignment of future wages permitted only to satisfy judgment containing child support provisions. Court-ordered child support.
Ohio	Assignments invalid except for court-ordered support of spouse or minor child. Court Order Support: Employee may assign whatever portion of earning required to comply with the court order for support.						
Oklahoma	X[15]			Child support limited to 50% of disposable earnings for support of child or spouse; otherwise 40%.	X	X	
Oregon	X[14]	X		Amount withheld shall not be less than 25% of earnings plus employee fee or amount of support obligation plus $1, whichever is greater.			
Pennsylvania	X	X	X	None	X	X	Assignment of future wages to secure loan invalid unless accepted in writing by employer.
Puerto Rico	Except for payroll deductions permitted by statute, an employer may not deduct wages due to an employee in order to pay the same to any other person.						
Rhode Island	X[24]	X		One year from assignment; 10% for small loans. Limitation on assignments for court-ordered support payments. Court Order Child Sup-	X	X	Small loan assignment signed by spouse.[3]

Reprinted with permission of the National Association of Credit Management.

Voluntary assignment is to be in an amount sufficient to meet the support payments imposed by the court. Involuntary assignments are to be in an amount that satisfies the employee's responsibility in support payments, the employee's obligation to pay future support and any attorney's fees awarded.

State			Limitations			Remarks
South Carolina	X[20]		None	X[2]	X[1]	
South Dakota	X		Special limitations on assignments pursuant to small installment loan and consumer finance law.	X[3]	X	After default, employer has option of accepting and honoring assignment. Court-ordered child support.
Tennessee	X[24]		None	X[2]	X[25]	Court-ordered child support.
Texas	X	X[14]		X	X	
Utah	X[15]	X	50% of net earnings per court-ordered child support.			Court-ordered child support.
Vermont	X[1,24]	X[22]	10% for small loans; and trustee process law.	X	X[25]	Small loan assignment signed by spouse.[3] Wage assignment may not exceed the lesser of 25% of disposable earnings or 30 times the federal minimum hourly wage as prescribed by the Federal Consumer Protection Act.
Virginia	X		Small loan limited to 10%.	X[2]	X[25]	Small loan assignment signed by spouse.[3]
Washington	X[17]		50% of disposable income exempt for child support.	X[2]		Signed by spouse assignment and employer's acceptance filed with county auditor. Court-ordered child support. Assignment of future wages permitted only to secure loans up to $300.
West Virginia	X[16,24]		25% and limited to one year.	X[2]	X	Employee may revoke all assignments at will.
Wisconsin	X		Six-month limitation.	X[23]	X	Signed by spouse.[3]
Wyoming	Consumer transactions and loans under $200 except for bank loans. X[17]		None	X[2]	X	Signed by spouse. Child support. Special rules for loans under $200.

87

Reprinted with permission of the National Association of Credit Management.

[1] Necessities of life only.

[2] Assignment of future wages is not enforceable against the employer unless he has consented in writing.

[3] There are other technical limitations and requirements.

[4] Prohibited except for necessities of life.

[5] Assignments to wage brokers limited to part of wages to be earned within 30 days following date of assignment.

[6] Consumer loans only.

[7] Assignments of future wages given for less than $200 in money or goods and money.

[8] Prohibited in home repair contracts.

[9] Loans of over $3,000 limited to two years, assignments for loans under $3,000 limited to one year.

[10] To secure the purchases of goods.

[11] Assignment of future wages prohibited.

[12] Retail installment sales of motor vehicles only.

[13] Employer who withholds or assigns wages as well as assignee of wages who violates this Act deemed a disorderly person.

[14] Assignments for small loans prohibited.

[15] Assignments arising out of a consumer credit transaction are unenforceable by assignee and revocable by buyer, lessee, or debtor. These states have the UCCC in effect.

[16] No assignment of wages given to secure any loan is valid.

[17] Assignment of future wages given to secure loans of less than $300.

[18] Small loan licensee prohibited from taking an assignment of wages as payment or as security for a loan. Unenforceable by assignee and revocable by debtor.

[19] Employee must be given notice by certified mail 20 days before wage assignment is filed with employer.

[20] Consumer Protection Law forbids assignment of consumer's earnings by creditor as payment of security for payment of consumer credit sale or direct installment loan.

[21] Wage assignments may not be given to secure a loan under the Installment Loan and Finance Act.

[22] Consumers cannot agree to assign wages by contract.

[23] For court-ordered support only. Employers who discharge or discipline their employees because of court-ordered support assignments are liable for a maximum fine of $200 plus damages.

[24] Only future earnings may be assigned.

CHAPTER 5

Bankruptcy

AUTOMATIC STAY

Section 362 of the Bankruptcy Code states that a petition filed under the Bankruptcy Code operates to stay:

1. the commencement or continuation of all actions, the enforcement of any judgment.
2. any act to obtain possession of property of the debtor.
3. any act to create or enforce a lien.
4. any act to create or perfect a lien to the extent that such lien secures a claim that arose prior to the bankruptcy.
5. any act to recover a claim against the debtor that arose before the commencement.
6. setting off any debt against the debtor that arose before the filing of the petition.
7. continuation of any proceeding before the Tax Court concerning the debtor.

The first section deals with the fact that a creditor is prohibited from beginning any suit or continuing to prosecute a suit against the debtor that was commenced before the filing of the petition, or to recover a claim against the debtor that arose before the filing of a petition. This includes any type of proceeding whether judicial, administrative, or an arbitration proceeding. It applies only to the creditor's activity against the entity or individual that files the petition. If an action is pending against one of several defendants, the stay only prevents the continuation against the one defendant who filed the petition.

The second section deals with the enforcement of a judgment obtained before the petition was filed, either against the debtor personally or against property of the debtor's estate. The creditor cannot proceed with any levy, execution, or any other proceeding after judgment to collect or satisfy the pre-bankruptcy judgment.

The third section is one of the most important targets of the automatic stay in that it prohibits any effort to obtain possession or exercise control over any property of the debtor. The property of the debtor includes the debtor's legal and equitable interest in any property in which the debtor has an interest as of the date of the petition. The courts tend to look at this section with a broad brush and have applied this automatic stay to prevent the cancellation of licenses, commencement of a personal injury action against the debtor's insurer, the cancellation of insurance policies, the unilateral termination of contracts by non-debtor parties, and other similar types of actions by creditors designed to either protect the creditor's interest or in some manner coerce the debtor.

Property of the estate includes anything that the debtor controls or possesses whether the debtor may or may not have valid title to the property. The most comprehensive part of the automatic stay is that part which prohibits any attempt to collect or recover on any claim against the bankrupt that arose prior to the filing of the petition in bankruptcy. The creditor cannot coerce a debtor to pay an obligation, encourage the debtor to pay an obligation, or even tempt the debtor to pay an obligation after the petition was filed concerning a claim that arose prior to the petition.

A classic situation might be where the creditor refused to sell goods to the debtor in Chapter 11 on a cash basis when his sole purpose was to persuade the debtor to pay a debt that was incurred prior to the bankruptcy. A similar situation is where a college denied an individual a transcript of her grades, in the hope that it would persuade her to pay a debt that was incurred to the college prior to the bankruptcy.

The scenarios are endless and only limited by the creativity of the creditor, but the major thrust of the courts is to impress upon the creditor that no effort should be made to collect that debt whether by coercion, duress, offering a carrot or a stick, leading the debtor down the garden path, or committing some other action, the sole purpose of which is directly or indirectly to force the debtor into a position where he has to pay the debt that was incurred prior to bankruptcy.

The stay also prevents the filing of any lien on work that was done prior to the bankruptcy, such as a mechanics lien wherein the work was performed prior to the petition or a situation where the security agreement is being used to secure a claim that was incurred before the commencement of the bankruptcy case.

The creditor cannot set off a debt owed to the debtor against the debtor's liability to the creditor. In simple terms, if the creditor owes the debtor $500 and the debtor owes the creditor $500, he cannot offset mutual debts. The creditor still owes the debtor the full $500, whereas the debt from the bankrupt to the creditor of $500 will be paid according to the direction of the bankruptcy court depending upon the amount of money available for all the creditors. The courts in some instances have carved out certain exceptions to this rule.

There are various exceptions to the automatic stay and creditors should be aware of what these exceptions are. First, bankruptcy laws do not shield the bankrupt from being prosecuted criminally. Collection of alimony, maintenance, and support is not affected by the automatic stay unless it is coming from the property of estate. Normally, these claims are not discharged by the bankruptcy. The automatic stay does not affect certain governmental actions concerning the health and welfare of the population such as enforcing injunctions, judgments, or prosecuting actions for violations of various laws. There are certain exceptions to the automatic stay that deal with commodity transactions and with certain swap agreements that take place in the financial markets. Tax deficiencies may not be affected by the automatic stay and under certain conditions in non-residential real estate transactions, the automatic stay may be disregarded where there was an eviction in process of a business tenant. Other exceptions to the automatic stay are indigenous to certain industries and certain types of transactions.

Notwithstanding these certain specific exceptions to the automatic stay, the courts tend to treat the automatic stay liberally, and even these exceptions that are noted may be stayed if the proper application to court is made seeking such relief.

Violation of the stay may lead to sanctions by the bankruptcy court. A duty rests upon a creditor to comply with the automatic stay if the creditor has knowledge of the bankruptcy proceeding, even though written notice in the mail was not received. The estimate is that 1% of all first-class mail is not delivered, so a 1% chance exists that the bankruptcy notice was not received. Nevertheless, if word of mouth or other communication apprises the creditor of the fact of the bankruptcy, and the creditor proceeds notwithstanding this knowledge, violation of the provisions of the automatic stay may take place.

NOTICE OF SALE AFTER REMOVAL OF AUTOMATIC STAY

The creditor instructs their attorney to remove the automatic stay on a vehicle upon which they had a security interest. The attorney makes the necessary application to remove the stay. The attorney notifies the client creditor that the stay has been removed and the client may proceed with a public or private sale.

The creditor must recognize that the sale has to be conducted in accordance with the terms and conditions of the security agreement and the provisions of the statute of the state. Ergo, if there is a requirement that a notice of sale is to be delivered to the debtor or to any guarantors, the creditor must comply with that notice requirement. If the creditor should fail to deliver this notice, the creditor may forfeit any claim for deficiency, depending upon the provisions contained in the statute. The courts recognize that notice may be dispensed with if the collateral is perishable, or if its value threatens to decline speedily, or if it is customarily sold in a recognized market. This exception does not apply to machinery, vehicles, or other types of fixed assets.[1]

AUTOMATIC STAY—RECENT TRENDS

The clerk of the bankruptcy court usually provides to the creditor a notice of the various deadlines for filing a proof of claim. Notices are usually sent to the addresses listed by the debtor on his bankruptcy petition. If a creditor files a proof of claim with a different address, that will be the one used to mail the notices. For violations of the automatic stay, a notice by regular mail by the clerk is all that is necessary for the creditor to be apprised of the bankruptcy. If the creditor thereafter duns the debtor for a past due debt, the creditor violates the automatic stay.

The bankrupt will forward this dunning notice to an attorney. The attorney will then usually send a letter to the creditor advising of the bank-

---

[1]*Diamond Bank v. Carter (In re Carter)*, 203 B.R. 697 (Bankr. W.D. Mo. 1996).

ruptcy and the violation of the automatic stay if dunning continues. The bankrupt's attorney will sometimes telephone to contact the creditor, an offending law firm, or collection agency and advise them to stop dunning the debtor since the debtor has already filed a petition in bankruptcy.

What has happened recently are motions to punish the creditor, collection agency, or law firm for contempt for automatic stay violations. In some instances, the creditor, collection agency, or law firm, who is supposed to have received the letter from the bankrupt's attorney, claim they never received the letter. In fact, the letter from the attorney is not necessary if the clerk properly sent a notice of the bankruptcy to the creditor. Notice to the creditor in some jurisdictions is impugned to the collection agency and the attorney.

The bankruptcy judges are becoming annoyed that some of the major corporations are ignoring the bankruptcy notices and continuing to dun the debtor. Substantial fines ranging from $1,000 up to $10,000 for violations of the automatic stay are being awarded (and large fines for repeat violations), even though the violation may amount only to sending an additional letter. The moral of the story is that procedures should be installed so that bankruptcy notices reach the proper department and are properly noted on the debtor's account.

In one particular case, the party who violated the stay claims that they did not even receive the motion papers to punish the creditor, notwithstanding the attorney for the bankrupt signed an affidavit that the motion papers were mailed to the corporation. Since it was a contested motion, the motion papers had to be served through Section 7004 and the listing in the affidavit of service by the attorney should comply with Section 7004(3) where the creditor is a corporation:

> "upon a domestic or foreign corporation or upon a partnership or other unincorporated association, by mailing a copy of the summons and complaint to the attention of an officer, a manager or general agent, or to any other agent authorized by appointment or by law to receive service of process...."

FRAUD

The bankruptcy statute expressly prohibits the discharge of a debt that was obtained by false pretenses, false representation, or actual fraud (other than a statement respecting the debtor's financial condition). As to a misrepresentation of the debtor's or insider's financial condition, the debtor may be prohibited from obtaining a discharge as to the respective debt, but the debtor still may obtain a discharge for the entire bankruptcy.

In order to prevail, the creditor must prove that:

1. the debtor made a representation at the time that the debtor knew was false
2. the debtor made the representation deliberately and intentionally with the intention and purpose of deceiving the creditor
3. the creditor justifiably relied on such representation
4. the creditor sustained the loss and damage as the proximate result of the representation being made

Actual fraud by definition consists of any deceit, artifice, trick, or design involving direct and active operation of the mind used to circumvent and cheat another—something said, done, or admitted with the design of perpetrating a deceit or a deception. A silence regarding a material fact may constitute a false representation actionable under this section. The intent element does not require a finding of malice or personal ill will: all it requires is a showing of an intent to induce the creditor to rely and act on the misrepresentation in question.

Because direct proof of intent (the debtor's state of mind) is nearly impossible to obtain, the creditor may present evidence of the surrounding circumstances from which intent may be inferred. Intent to deceive will be inferred where a debtor makes false representation and the debtor knows or should know that the statement will induce another act. Justifiable reliance on the part of the plaintiff claiming to have been defrauded must be proved.

A person is justified in relying on a representation of fact even though he may have ascertained the falsity of the representation had he made an investigation. If a person sells land and states that it is free of encumbrances and the buyer relied on this statement, notwithstanding the buyer could have walked across the street to the office of the register of deeds and easily learned of an unsatisfied mortgage, justifiable reliance is present. Contributory negligence is no bar to a recovery because fraudulent representation is an intentional tort. On the other hand, a creditor cannot recover if he blindly relies upon a misrepresentation, the falsity of which would be obvious to him if he had utilized the opportunity to make a cursory examination or investigation.[2]

---

[2]*Leverett v. Oligschlaeger (In re Oligschlaeger)*, 239 B.R. 553 (Bankr. W.D. Mo. 1999).

CASH COLLATERAL

Section 363(c)(2) states as follows:

(A) The trustee may not use, sell or lease cash collateral under paragraph 1 of this subsection unless:

    (1) each entity that has an interest in such cash collateral consents

    (2) the court after notice and a hearing, authorizes such use, sale or lease in accordance with the provisions of this section.

The definition of "cash collateral" is that which is readily converted into cash, such as inventory and accounts receivable. Inventory is sold and the bankrupt has obtained cash or accounts receivable have been collected and converted into cash. The court takes the position that before the bankrupt can utilize this cash in a Chapter 11 proceeding to continue to operate the business, the bankrupt has two options: either obtain the consent of the secured creditor or obtain a hearing before the court on notice to the secured creditor. No other option exists. If the cash is utilized without obtaining consent and without a hearing, the bankrupt has violated Section 363(c)(2).

The bankrupt normally will contact the secured creditor or, in the alternative, will send out a notice for a hearing before the court. The creditor at that point can negotiate for adequate protection payments or some other adequate form of security so that the secured creditor will be protected. If the secured creditor and the debtor cannot reach an agreement, the court will design a solution usually not as favorable to the secured creditor as a negotiated agreement.

A secured creditor should take action where a creditor has a lien that can be converted into cash. The creditor should negotiate directly with the bankrupt to arrange for adequate security in the event the bankrupt intends to use the cash to operate the business. On the other hand, the secured creditor may take the position that Chapter 11 will not succeed and on proper grounds may oppose any use of the cash collateral.[3]

What occasionally happens is that the bankrupt utilizes the cash collateral without consent of the secured creditor or without serving a notice of a hearing. Several cases have addressed this issue and all of them seem to agree that a remedy should be afforded to the creditor. They do not agree on the type of remedy, since the statute is silent as to an available remedy where the bankrupt fails to comply with Section 363(c)(2).

---

[3]*Harvis Trien & Beck, P.C. v. Federal Home Loan Mortg. Corp.*, 153 F. 3d 61 (2nd Cir. 1998).

It appears that in the event the cash collateral is used without the consent of the secured creditor or without a hearing, the court will craft some type of remedy such as a replacement lien or a payment plan or hold an officer of the debtor, or perhaps the trustee, liable. One court did not agree with holding the trustee liable, but the court acknowledged that where the debtor misused the cash collateral, a fair and just remedy must be available to the creditor. The courts do not seem to accept, imply, or infer consent of the creditor—the consent must be in writing.

Nevertheless, at this point of the bankruptcy proceeding, whatever remedy is developed by the court will not be adequate to satisfy the secured party. Accordingly, it is recommended that the secured party act quickly when cash collateral is involved.[4, 5]

> **Credit & Collection Tip:** *If the secured party is of the opinion that the cash col-lateral will be used in the business, the secured party should take some affirmative action to bring this fact to the attention of the court and seek protection immediate-ly. Waiting for a bankrupt to act may result in serious harm. In addition, the secured party will be faced with Section 552(a) which denies a security interest in after-acquired inventory.*

PREFERENTIAL TRANSFERS

Under the Bankruptcy Code a trustee may recover certain transfers made by the debtor within 90 days before the bankruptcy petition was filed. A transfer by the debtor constitutes an avoidable preference if six elements are shown:

1. A transfer of an interest of the debtor in property
2. For the benefit of the creditor
3. On an account of an antecedent debt
4. Made while the debtor was insolvent
5. During 90 days before the date of filing
6. Enabling the creditor to receive more than such creditor would have received in a Chapter 7 liquidation of the estate

---

[4]*Freightliner Market Dev. Corp., v. Silver Wheel Freightlines, Inc.,* 823 F. 2d 362 (9th Cir. 1987).

[5]*Cargocaire Eng'g Corp., v. Dwyer (In re Gemel Int'l),* 190 B.R. 4 (Bkrtcy. D. Mass. 1995).

As a general rule, the courts tend to look at whether property transferred to a debtor within the 90-day period is a preference by applying the "diminution" of estate doctrine: where the transfer diminishes the fund to which creditors of the same class may be entitled for payment of the monies owed to such creditors to such an extent that other creditors will not obtain as great a percentage as the preferred creditor.

An exception to this rule is known as the "earmarking doctrine." The earmarking doctrine arose in cases in which a debtor owed money to a particular creditor under circumstances in which another party was the guarantor of the debtor's obligation. Where the guarantor paid to the old creditor the money owed by the debtor (bankrupt), the courts rejected the claim that such a payment was an avoidable preference. The rationale used to justify this was that no preferential transfer had occurred, because the transfer consisted of the new creditor's property (the guarantor), not the debtor's property, and no diminution to the debtor's estate resulted because the transaction merely substitutes one creditor for another.

In a recent case, the court extended this doctrine where the monies were paid to the debtor directly and the mere fact that the debtor may have had the power to divert the loan after it was deposited into the debtor's account does not amount to control of the funds by the debtor. The money was paid over to the debtor and the debtor thereafter paid the old creditor.[6]

RULE 911—BANKRUPTCY SANCTIONS

Rule 911 is the equivalent of Rule 11 of the Federal Rules of Civil Procedure that requires an attorney to sign all pleadings and all documents filed with the court to certify that the attorney has read the documents, that to the

> "best of the attorney's knowledge, information and belief formed after a reasonable inquiry, the pleading or document is well grounded in fact and is warranted by existing law or a good faith argument for the extension, modification or reversal of existing law and it is not interposed for any improper purpose such as to harass or cause unnecessary delay which may needlessly increase the cost of litigation or administration of the case."

---

[6]*Adams v. Anderson (In re Superior Stamp & Coin Co.)*, 223 F. 3d 1004 (9th Cir. 2000).

Rule 911 is presenting problems for attorneys signing affidavits attesting to the fact that the reaffirmation agreements signed by the bankrupt does not cause a hardship on the bankrupt. When a Chapter 7 case is started, the schedule filed by the debtor usually reveals that the debtor has few assets and insignificant income remaining after payment of monthly expenses to qualify for a Chapter 7 bankruptcy. At a later date, the attorney is executing an affidavit that a reaffirmation agreement is not a hardship upon the bankrupt debtor and that the debtor will be able to meet the payments. Where the payments are substantial, such as when a debtor wishes to continue the monthly payments on a car, and no major change in the debtor's position (such as acquiring a new job that pays more than his old job), the attorney who signs the petition and the affidavit (that has to accompany the reaffirmation agreement which thereafter is reviewed by the court) may fall into a catch-22 position.

Some of the courts now are beginning to look at Rule 911 and are inquiring as to whether the debtor will suffer a hardship in executing a reaffirmation or, in the alternative, whether the original schedules filed by the debtor were proper and correct. The end result is that attorneys should devote more attention to these affidavits than routinely signing them to enable the reaffirmation to be approved by the court, because several bankruptcy courts have taken the position that all reaffirmation agreements are to be reviewed by the court, not just those where the bankrupt debtor has not retained an attorney.[7]

WILLFUL AND MALICIOUS INJURY

An exception to discharge is Section 523(a)(6), which excepts from discharge a debt resulting from "willful and malicious injury by the debtor to another entity or to the property of another entity." This section of the Bankruptcy Code has caused considerable litigation and the courts are divided over the application of this section.

The section necessitates that the act must be willful, must be malicious, and must result in an injury. The malice does not have to be intentional, but may be shown by a total disregard for the safety of others knowing of the danger and even failing to use reasonable care to avoid injury.

---

[7]*In re Melendez*, 224 B.R. 252 (Bkrtcy. D. Mass. 1998); *In re Bruzzese*, 214 B.R. 444 (Bkrtcy E.D.N.Y. 1997).

The division of the courts seems to rest on the doctorate of "transfer intent" where the courts attempt to hold a party liable for injuries caused to other persons even though such injuries were not intended or foreseeable. If the act itself was wrongful and malicious, the theory is that the wrongdoer is liable for the consequences of the action even though an injury that was not intended may result.

The narrow approach to this standard is that the acts of the bankrupt must cause the injury intended. The Supreme Court, addressing this issue and evaluating intentional tort claims for a discharge in bankruptcy, followed the narrow criteria that required the victim to present evidence that the bankrupt intended the injury that was caused.

The Supreme Court decision arose in a medical malpractice case where the doctor was filing a bankruptcy petition after a judgment was obtained against him for which he did not carry insurance. The court took the position that he did not intend the patient (the creditor in this instance) to have suffered the harm as a result of his negligence in operating upon the creditor. The court distinguished between a deliberate and intentional injury and a deliberate intentional act that leads to an injury. In short, the court held that the doctor did not intend that the injury should happen.[8]

STRIPPING LIENS

Section 1322(b)(2) of the Bankruptcy Code states as follows:

> "the plan (debtor's plan of payment in Chapter 13) may modify the rights of holders of secured claims, other than a claim secured by a security interest in real property that is the debtors principle residence or of holders of unsecured claims or leave unaffected the rights of holders of any class of claims."

A "strip down" occurs when the balance on a mortgage ($71,000) is reduced to the market value of the security (home—$23,500).

Section 506 of the Bankruptcy Code provides as follows:

> "an allowed claim of a creditor secured by a lien on property in which the estate has an interest, or that is subject to set off under Section 563 of this title, is a secured claim to the extent of the value of such creditor's interest in the estate's interest in such property, or to the extent of the amount sub-

---

[8]*Kawaauhau v. Geiger*, 523 U.S. 57, 118 S. Ct. 974, 140 L. Ed. 2d 90 (1000).

ject to set off, as the case may be, and is an unsecured claim to the extent that the value of such creditor's interest or the amount so subject to set off is less than the amount of such allowed claim. Such value shall be determined in light of the purpose of the valuation and of the proposed disposition or use of such property, and in conjunction with any hearing on such disposition or use, or on a plan affecting such creditor's interest."

The Supreme Court considered the application by a debtor to "strip down" the homestead lenders' secured claim of $71,000 to the home's reduced value of $23,500. The Supreme Court prohibited this option under Section 506 by stating that Chapter 13 prohibits the debtor from reducing an unsecured homestead mortgage to the fair market value of the mortgage residence. The Supreme Court recognized that claims in bankruptcy could be broken down between secured and unsecured parts, but at the same time it concluded that Section 1322(b)(2) protected the unsecured components of a partially secured claim. Unfortunately, the Supreme Court did not decide whether its holding should be extended to wholly unsecured homestead mortgages.[9]

This issue has considerably divided the bankruptcy courts as well as the district courts. The majority view seems to follow the reasoning that the anti-modification provisions protect only the under-secured and not the wholly unsecured homestead lenders. Under this theory, if the mortgage was $50,000 and the security was worthless, the claim would automatically become an unsecured claim rather than a secured claim. The minority view takes the opposite position. The fact that a claim is under-secured does not mean that the mortgagee is limited by the valuation of its secured claim. The emphasis in this type of reasoning is on the homestead lender rather than on the value of the collateral that shields the claim from modification. Therefore, if it is a homestead lender, the secured mortgage is protected just as if the collateral was of some value. The Circuit Court of Appeals of 11th Circuit has provided an in-depth analysis of this issue and sided with the majority opinion.[10]

REAFFIRMATION

One creditor held both a secured and unsecured claim. The debtor wanted to reaffirm the secured claim, but the creditor stated that a reaffirma-

---

[9]*In Nobelman v. American Savings Bank*, 508 U.S. 324 (1993).

[10]*Tanner v. FirstPlus Fin., Inc. (In re Tanner)* 217 F. 3d 1357 (11th Cir. 2000).

tion of the secured claim would only be accepted if the bankrupt reaffirmed the unsecured claim. While it is perfectly acceptable for a secured creditor to enter into an agreement to reaffirm a secured claim, it is unacceptable for the creditor to predicate the entering of the reaffirmation on the secured claim as a condition to collect a separate unsecured claim. The court held that said action was a violation of the automatic stay.[11]

REAFFIRMATION CASES—PRIVATE ACTION

Several recent cases deal with the failure to file reaffirmation agreements and on balance it seems that the decisions were favorable. In the 1st Circuit in Massachusetts, where the Sears case was originally instituted, the court held that the failure to file a reaffirmation agreement may be enforced through the contempt powers of the bankruptcy courts by virtue of Section 105 (the proceeding is confined to the bankruptcy court). It did not address the issue of a private right of action.

Judge Posner in the 7th Circuit agreed with the 1st Circuit, but stated that no private right of action arises by virtue of failure to file the reaffirmation agreement and that the contempt powers of the bankruptcy court is the remedy for this type of a violation.

The 6th Circuit stated that Section 524 of the Bankruptcy Code does not provide a private right of action.[12]

INNOCENT PARTNERS

The nondischargeability of debts under Section 523(a)(2)(A) states that an individual debtor cannot obtain a discharge from any debt for money, property, or services to the extent it is obtained by false pretenses or a false representation or actual fraud. The statute states as follows:

(a) ˥ discharge...of this title does not discharge an individual debtor from any debtor

    (ii) for money, property, services or an extension, renewal or refinancing of credit to the extent obtained by

---

[11]*Jamo v. Katahdin Fed. Credit Union,* 253 B.R. 115 (Bankr. D. Maine 2000).

[12]*Bessette v. Avco Fin. Servs.,* 230 F. 2d 439 (1st Cir. 2000); *Cox v. Zale Delaware, Inc.,* 239 F 3d 910 (7th Cir. 2001); *Pertuso v. Ford Motor Credit Co.,* 233 F. 3d 417 (6th Cir. 2000).

(A) false pretenses, a false representation, or actual fraud other than statement respecting the debtors or an insiders financial condition.

The issue is the nature of the debt, not necessarily whether the debtor is culpable. In situations where partnerships are involved, the partners are vicariously liable for the debts of their co-partners. In this case, one of the partners used their authority to place another partner's money in a personal checking account and generated fictitious income statements to cover the fraud. The parties admitted their vicarious liability as imposed by law.

A petition in bankruptcy was filed by one of the partners and objections were filed due to fraud. The particular fraud was not committed in the ordinary course of business and no benefit accrued to the bankrupt partner by reason of the fraud. The court said that the receipt of benefit is not a requirement under Section 523(a)(2)(A). They stated "that the plain meaning of the statute is that debtors cannot discharge any debts that arise from fraud so long as they are liable to the creditor for fraud." The fact that the debtor is not the perpetrator of the fraud is not the issue. If the debtor is liable by reason of a fraud, even if the debtor received no benefit, under the Bankruptcy Code, the debtor is not entitled to a discharge.

Some bankruptcy courts require that the fraud be incurred in the ordinary course of business, although in this case in the 5th Circuit, the court did not delineate that as a criteria.[13]

BANKRUPTCY—PRIVACY

During 2000, the Toy Smart.com case was frequently in the media because the FTC filed an action against Toy Smart to prevent them from auctioning off their list of customers in a bankruptcy proceeding. Toy Smart was allegedly in violation of an offer made to their customers that the customer list would remain private and the names and addresses of their customers would not be shared, rented, or sold to any third party. The case was finally settled and Toy Smart agreed to abide by their agreement with the customers.

A study is being made by the Judicial Conference of the United States on the privacy implications of providing public access to court files and

---

[13]*In re M.M. Winkler & Associates*, 239 F. 3d 746 (5th Cir. 2001); *Strang v. Bradner*, 114 U.S. 555, 5 S. Ct. 1038, 29 L. Ed. 248 (1885).

more particularly with regard to bankruptcy files since a considerable amount of personal information is listed in the bankruptcy files. Certain bankruptcy information should be available to the courts and the interested parties to assure a fair and efficient administration of the bankruptcy estate. But on the other hand, certain information may be protected during the bankruptcy proceeding under the privacy laws of the Gramm-Leach-Bliley Act.

The study reportedly recommended that the policy should be balanced between efficiency and accountability and privacy, but the general public should have access to core information. Parties in interest should have access to the non-public highly sensitive data subject to reuse and redisclosure limitations. The bankruptcy system also should incorporate fair information principles of notice, consent, access, security, and accountability. The issue of privacy continues and will probably affect many other legal areas.

BANKRUPTCY REFORM ACT

Despite all the predictions and all the media attention to bankruptcy reform legislation and all the claims that the law will be passed imminently, as of the time this book is going to press, there is no new law and there are two different and distinct versions of the bill—one from the House and one from the Senate.

Some controversial amendments in the bill are causing the difficulty between the Democrats and the Republicans. The distinction is not between the House and Senate versions, it's between the Democrats and Republicans.

The primary controversy is over the homestead exemption where the Democrats want an absolute cap on this exemption and the Republicans are opposed to this since there is an unlimited cap in Texas, where President Bush was governor, and in Florida, where his brother Jeb Bush is governor.

The Senate bill was passed in March and the House bill was passed last year. The Senate bill made significant changes in the House bill. The bills would force more debtors to file under Chapter 13 which requires debtors to pay some of their debt if a "means test" indicates the ability to do so. A homestead exemption would set a cap on the equity a homeowner could protect. The proposed federal limit, $100,000 in the House bill and $125,000 in the Senate bill, supersedes state limits. The House cap would apply only to homes purchased within two years before filing.

Existing state laws would apply for homes purchased more than two years before a debtor filed a petition. Some states, such as Florida and Texas, have generous caps that would be eliminated.

In view of the horror of Sept. 11, 2001, the impact on the economy and the loss of jobs, the passage of the bankruptcy bill will probably not happen this year.

CHAPTER 6

Law Firms and Collection Agencies

MONITORING AND TAPING OF TELEPHONE CALLS

An area of concern for debt collectors as well as creditors is the ability and the desire to monitor, intercept, and tape telephone calls. Some readers may remember the prosecution of Linda Tripp when she taped a telephone call with Monica Lewinsky concerning her relationship with President Clinton. After the entire issue of Monica Lewinsky and President Clinton was finally resolved with the Senate's acquittal of the President following impeachment proceedings, the prosecution and media found a new issue in bringing charges against Linda Tripp for taping the telephone conversation with Monica without the consent of Monica (recently dismissed for lack of evidence). Certainly, at the time of the taping, Linda Tripp did not realize she was doing anything illegal. But before we consider the legal issues, let us understand the difference between intercepting, monitoring, and taping telephone calls.

INTERCEPTING TELEPHONE CALLS

The act of intercepting a telephone call consists of either taping or intercepting and listening to a telephone conversation carried on between two other parties. You are the third party listening to the conversation of two other parties. The example that comes first to mind may be from seeing movies where a person is seated in a van across the street with all types of electronic equipment, listening in on the telephone line while other people are talking. Often the telephone line being taped is that of an organized crime figure. This type of interception by third parties is expressly prohibited without first obtaining a court order. Before the governmental agency can obtain such an order, it is necessary for them to make a presentation before a judge to show that they have probable cause and sufficient evidence to warrant the interception of the telephone call. Under these circumstances, the court must be persuaded that a good reason is present for a governmental agency, such as the FBI or a district attorney, to eavesdrop on the conversation of two citizens.

MONITORING TELEPHONE CALLS

Federal laws govern telephone calls. The normal problem presented to the businessperson is the desire to intercept a call between a salesperson and the customer to be certain that the person is properly marketing the product of the employer. Telemarketing is the targeting of a select group of prospects on the telephone through the use of a sales force that utilizes a prepared script to market a designated product. Tele-promotion, a rather new development, is the persuasion of consumers through advertising to call a 900 number that provides some form of information for entertainment. These two methods of marketing have gained the attention of regulators because of their potential for abuse.

The employer is subject to federal law that allows employers to monitor its employees (sales force) by using a monitoring device installed by a local utility company (U.S. S.C. Section 2510 (5) (a) and Section 2511). Employers, on the other hand, must do the monitoring in the normal course of business and the monitoring must normally be limited in time and in scope and furthermore must not be used to intrude upon the privacy of an employee[1] (Appendix IV).

---

[1]*United States v. Harpel,* 493 F.2d 346 (10th Cir. 1974); *James v. Newspaper Agency Corp.,* 591 F.2d 579 (10th Cir. 1979); *Briggs v. American Air Filter Co.,* 630 F.2d 414 (5th Cir. 1980).

Most employers notify their employees that their conversations will be taped and that they will cease taping or monitoring at such time as the employee is not engaged in a call in the course of business. Employers have the employees execute written agreements wherein the employee is advised of the monitoring or taping program. A carefully drafted manual should be provided for the individuals conducting the monitoring or taping with express instructions as to the time and scope of the taping and procedures to use when encountering conversations on the telephone of a personal nature.

State Laws

Because states provide their own additional restrictions, a review of the state laws that deal with monitoring and taping a telephone conversation by an employer should be conducted. Informed consent of the employee is specified in many of the state laws and specifically is directed at notifying the employee and requiring the employer to obtain consent of the employee in writing. Many of the state laws are even more restrictively drawn, addressing the issues of the type of interception, the times when the interception will be done, when the interception will be terminated, and the manner of interception. Many employers will engage in a meeting with the employees so that the employees have the opportunity to ask questions concerning the monitoring or taping of the conversation. Sometimes, the monitoring and taping notification will be posted on a bulletin board in a clear and conspicuous language so that a new employee has easy access if an employee is hired without being notified of the taping program or is not required to execute a written agreement. Not all the states have major restrictions, but many of the state laws have nuances that should be reviewed.

State Laws as to Consent

Eleven states have laws requiring disclosure to employees when their phone calls are being monitored: California, Delaware, Florida, Georgia, Illinois, Massachusetts, Michigan, Montana, New Hampshire, Pennsylvania, and Washington. Many employers utilize a beep tone to identify the fact that employees are being monitored prior to the act of monitoring. This requirement is not present in all the state laws and is not present in the federal law. The statute in the State of Montana actually requires the consent of the customer to the monitoring and when the telephone beeps, the employee must notify the customer that the conversation is being monitored. The Massachusetts statute is similar to the Montana statute.

Taping Telephone Calls

To tape a telephone call from individual to individual requires a minimum amount of electronic equipment. In many of the new telephone systems that are sold with voice mail and electronic message receipt, you merely have to push a button on the system to record the conversation. The conversation is then recorded on your voice mail and you can record that voice mail conversation onto a tape recorder.[2]

With good reason, it probably would be permissible to monitor or tape an employee's telephone conversation, providing a reasonable purpose existed to tape the conversation even without the consent or notification or a written agreement with the employee. One set of circumstances was where a supervisor felt that the employee was collaborating with a competitor to divulge some trade secrets. The court did hold that this taping was an act in the normal course of business and was permissible.

Federal law allows the taping of a telephone conversation with the consent of either party. Accordingly, one of the parties may be the party who initiates the telephone call and the other party is the party who receives the telephone call. Under federal law, the party who makes the telephone call may tape the conversation without the consent of the individual who receives the call. President Nixon taped many telephone calls in his Oval Office both on the telephone and of those parties that were present in the office. The only one who consented to the taping was the President; none of the people who received the phone calls or who made the phone calls to the President or who were visitors to the Oval Office consented to the taping.

The great majority of the states allow taping of telephone calls with the consent of one party. Nevertheless, there is a group of states that does require the consent of both parties and they include California, Delaware, Florida, Georgia, Illinois, Maryland, Massachusetts, Michigan, Montana, New Hampshire, Pennsylvania, and Washington. A review of the state law is absolutely necessary before taping.

Federal Tariff

We attended a seminar where the presenter stated that before you tape a telephone call, a federal tariff requires the use of a beep tone and also requires the party using the beep tone to obtain the consent of the other party. This particular presentation included only half the story. A particu-

---

[2]*State v. Nova*, 361 So.2d 411 (Fla. 1978).

lar tariff does expressly state that you are required to use a beep tone and notify the other side that you are taping. But the only remedy available and the only penalty for a violation is that the telephone is removed and telephone service is terminated. The FCC at one time intended to abolish the rule, but failed to do so. I do not know of any of the Bell Companies or AT&T or any of the other telephone companies such as MCI, Sprint, or Cable & Wireless who have terminated telephone service because of the failure of the customer to use a beep tone or obtain consent of the other party.

Compliance with Laws of Other States

The question often asked when a call is made across state lines is whether the law of the state in which the telephone collector is located or where the recipient of the telephone call is located applies. For example, if the State of Maryland requires the consent of both parties and the State of New York requires only the consent of one party and your telephone collector is in New York and the ABC business is in Maryland, which state law applies? You should be complying with both the law in your state and the law of the state where the recipient of the telephone call resides. If the recipient's law requires consent of both parties, you should get the consent of both parties to a taping. Nevertheless, in practicality, you are subject to the laws in the state in which you reside. As a result, the party who initiates the call should be certain that they are complying with the laws of the state in which they reside.

Flagrant violations or continuing violations in a sister state might prompt the attorney general to seek the cooperation of the attorney general in your state to prevent you from violating the law of your sister state, but extradition to a sister state is rare except in serious cases.

Recorded Message

A recorded message that tells incoming callers that they may be monitored or recorded should provide sufficient notice to the customer that the telephone conversation is recorded. Whether this is express consent by the mere fact that the caller stays on the line is not really clear. Assuming that the customer does not protest and continues on the line and orders the merchandise, a sound basis may be made for the fact that the customer has consented. An additional precaution might be to use a beep tone and advise the customer the beep tone will signal the conversation is being recorded.

GRAMM-LEACH-BLILEY EXEMPTION

Under Gramm-Leach-Bliley, the Federal Trade Commission Commentary includes "collection agency, credit bureau" (16 CFR 65, page 33647). At the same time, the FTC states that a consumer has a customer relationship with a debt collector that purchases an account from the original creditor, but does not have this relationship with a debt collector that simply attempts to collect amounts owed to the creditor (16 CFR 65, page 11176).

An issue arises as to whether an attorney who is collecting debts is in fact a debt collector and whether the attorney would fall under the definition of a "collection agency" because he is a debt collector.

The American Bar Association has requested that the Federal Trade Commission clearly exempt attorneys from the application of the Gramm-Leach-Bliley Act on the grounds that the attorneys are subject to much more stringent and restrictive confidentiality than is provided for in GLB. Obviously, consumer attorneys will try to zero in on the fact that collection agencies are subject to Gramm-Leach-Bliley and will assert that agencies have an obligation to give a privacy notice to each debtor. GLB primarily provides for privacy notices to consumers who are "customers" of the financial institution, wherein the financial institution is providing some type of a service to the consumer. The collection agency or the law firm is not providing any service to the debtor. The collection agency or the law firm is representing the creditor and is an agent of the creditor. The obligation to comply with GLB is upon the creditor, not its agents who are merely acting in a representative capacity. The agents, of course, must provide the same degree of confidentiality that their clients provide, but it seems that there is no requirement that the agents must give a separate notice to the consumers.

This issue will probably be visited by the Federal Trade Commission again and probably by the courts before it is resolved.

APPENDIX I

WIRE AND ELECTRONIC COMMUNICATIONS INTERCEPTION AND INTERCEPTION OF ORAL COMMUNICATIONS

2510. DEFINITIONS AS USED IN THIS CHAPTER—

(1) "wire communication" means any aural transfer made in whole or in part through the use of facilities for the transmission of communications by the aid of wire, cable, or other like connection between the point of origin and the point of reception (including the use of such connection in a switching station) furnished or operated by any person engaged in providing or operating such facilities for the transmission of interstate or foreign communications or communications affecting interstate or foreign commerce and such term includes any electronic storage of such communication;

(2) "oral communication" means any oral communication uttered by a person exhibiting an expectation that such communication is not subject to interception under circumstances justifying such expectation, but such term does not include any electronic communication;

(3) "State" means any State of the United States, the District of Columbia, the Commonwealth of Puerto Rico, and any territory or possession of the United States;

(4) "intercept" means the aural or other acquisition of the contents of any wire, electronic, or oral communication through the use of any electronic, mechanical, or other device;

(5) "electronic, mechanical, or other device" means any device or apparatus which can be used to intercept a wire, oral, or electronic communication other than—

(a) any telephone or telegraph instrument, equipment or facility, or any component thereof, (i) furnished to the subscriber or user by a provider of wire or electronic communication service in the ordinary course of its business and being used by the subscriber or user in the ordinary course of its business or furnished by such subscriber or user for connection to the facilities of such service and used in the ordinary course of its business; or (ii) being used by a provider of wire or electronic communication service in the ordinary course of its business, or by an investigative or law enforcement officer in the ordinary course of his duties;

(b) a hearing aid or similar device being used to correct subnormal hearing to not better than normal;

(6) "person" means any employee, or agent of the United States or any State or political subdivision thereof, and any individual, partnership, association, joint stock company, trust, or corporation;

(7) "Investigative or law enforcement officer" means any officer of the United States or of a State or political subdivision thereof, who is empowered by law to conduct investigations of or to make arrests for offenses enumerated in this chapter, and any attorney authorized by law to prosecute or participate in the prosecution of such offenses;

(8) "contents", when used with respect to any wire, oral, or electronic communication, includes any information concerning the substance, purport, or meaning of that communication;

(9) "Judge of competent jurisdiction" means—

(a) a judge of a United States district court or a United States court of appeals; and

(b) a judge of any court of general criminal jurisdiction of a State who is authorized by a statute of that State to enter orders authorizing interceptions of wire, oral, or electronic communications;

(10) "communication common carrier" shall have the same meaning which is given the term "common carrier" by section 153(h) of title 47 of the United States Code;

(11) "aggrieved person" means a person who was a party to any intercepted wire, oral, or electronic communication or a person against whom the interception was directed;

(12) "electronic communication" means any transfer of signs, signals, writing, images, sounds, data or intelligence of any nature transmitted in whole or in part by a wire, radio, electromagnetic, photoelectronic or photooptical system that affects interstate or foreign commerce, but does not include—

(A) any wire or oral communication;

(B) any communication made through a tone-only paging device;

(C) any communication from a tracking device (as defined in section 3117 of this title); or

(D) electronic funds transfer information stored by a financial institution in a communications system used for the electronic storage and transfer of funds;

(13) "user" means any person or entity who—

(A) uses an electronic communication service; and

(B) is duly authorized by the provider of such service to engage in such use;

(14) "electronic communications system" means any wire, radio, electromagnetic, photooptical or photoelectronic facilities for the transmission of electronic communications, and any computer facilities or related electronic equipment for the electronic storage of such communications;

(15) "electronic communication service" means any service which provides to users thereof the ability to send or receive wire or electronic communications;

(16) "readily accessible to the general public" means, with respect to a radio communication, that such communication is not—

(A) scrambled or encrypted;

(B) transmitted using modulation techniques whose essential parameters have been withheld from the public with the intention of preserving the privacy of such communication;

(C) carried on a subcarrier or other signal subsidiary to a radio transmission;

(D) transmitted over a communication system provided by a common carrier, unless the communication is a tone-only paging system communication; or

(E) transmitted on frequencies allocated under part 25, subpart D, E, or F of part 74, or part 94 of the Rules of the Federal Communications Commission, unless, in the case of a communication transmitted on a frequency allocated under part 74 that is not exclusively allocated to broadcast auxiliary services, the communication is a two-way voice communication by radio;

[(F) Repealed. Pub. L. 104-132, Title VII, 731(2)(C), Apr. 24, 1996, 110 Stat. 1303]

(17) "electronic storage" means—

(A) any temporary, intermediate storage of a wire or electronic communication incidental to the electronic transmission thereof; and

(B) any storage of such communication by an electronic communication service for purposes of backup protection of such communication; and

(18) "aural transfer" means a transfer containing the human voice at any point between and including the point of origin and the point of reception.

CHAPTER 6
APPENDIX II

WIRE AND ELECTRONIC COMMUNICATIONS INTERCEPTION AND INTERCEPTION OF ORAL COMMUNICATIONS

2511. INTERCEPTION AND DISCLOSURE OF WIRE, ORAL, OR ELECTRONIC COMMUNICATIONS PROHIBITED

(1) Except as otherwise specifically provided in this chapter, any person who—

(a) intentionally intercepts, endeavors to intercept, or procures any other person to intercept or endeavor to intercept, any wire, oral, or electronic communication;

(b) intentionally uses, endeavors to use, or procures any other person to use or endeavor to use any electronic, mechanical, or other device to intercept any oral communication when—

(i) such device is affixed to, or otherwise transmits a signal through, a wire, cable, or other like connection used in wire communication; or

(ii) such device transmits communications by radio, or interferes with the transmission of such communication; or

(iii) such person knows, or has reason to know, that such device or any component thereof has been sent through the mail or transported in interstate or foreign commerce; or

(iv) such use or endeavor to use (A) takes place on the premises of any business or other commercial establishment the operations of which affect interstate or foreign commerce; or (B) obtains or is for the purpose of obtaining information relating to the operations of any business or other commercial establishment the operations of which affect interstate or foreign commerce; or

(v) such person acts in the District of Columbia, the Commonwealth of Puerto Rico, or any territory or possession of the United States;

(c) intentionally discloses, or endeavors to disclose, to any other person the contents of any wire, oral, or electronic communication, knowing or having reason to know that the information was obtained through the interception of a wire, oral, or electronic communication in violation of this subsection;

(d) intentionally uses, or endeavors to use, the contents of any wire, oral, or electronic communication, knowing or having reason to know that the information was obtained through the interception of a wire, oral, or electronic communication in violation of this subsection; or

(e) (i) intentionally discloses, or endeavors to disclose, to any other person the contents of any wire, oral, or electronic communication, intercepted by means authorized by sections 2511(2)(a)(ii), 2511(2)(b) to (c), 2511(2)(e), 2516, and 2518 of this chapter, (ii) knowing or having reason to know that the information was obtained through the interception of such communication in connection with a criminal investigation, (iii) having obtained or received the information in connection with a criminal investigation, and (iv) with intent to improperly obstruct, impede, or interfere with a duly authorized criminal investigation,

shall be punished as provided in subsection (4) or shall be subject to suit as provided in subsection (5).

(2)(a)(i) It shall not be unlawful under this chapter for an operator of a switchboard, or an officer, employee or agent of a provider of wire or electronic communication service, whose facilities are used in the transmission of a wire or electronic communication, to intercept, disclose, or use that communication in the normal course of his employment while engaged in any activity which is a necessary incident to the rendition of his service or to the protection of the rights or property of the provider of that service, except that a provider of wire communication service to the public shall not utilize service observing or random monitoring except for mechanical or service quality control checks.

(ii) Notwithstanding any other law, providers of wire or electronic communication service, their officers, employees, and agents, landlords, custodians, or other persons, are authorized to provide information, facilities, or technical assistance to persons authorized by law to intercept wire, oral, or electronic communications or to conduct electronic surveillance, as defined in section 101 of the Foreign Intelligence Surveillance Act of 1978, if such provider, its officers, employees, or agents, landlord, custodian, or other specified person, has been provided with—

(A) a court order directing such assistance signed by the authorizing judge, or

(B) a certification in writing by a person specified in section 2518(7) of this title or the Attorney General of the United States that no warrant or court order is required by law, that all statutory requirements have been met, and that the specified assistance is required,

setting forth the period of time during which the provision of the information, facilities, or technical assistance is authorized and specifying the information, facilities, or technical assistance required. No provider of wire or electronic communication service, officer, employee, or agent thereof, or landlord, custodian, or other specified person shall disclose the existence of any interception or surveillance or the device used to accomplish the interception or surveillance with respect to which the person has been furnished a court order or certification under this chapter, except as may otherwise be required by legal process and then only after prior notification to the Attorney General or to the principal prosecuting attorney of a State or any political subdivision of a State, as may be appropriate. Any such disclosure shall render such person liable for the civil damages provided for in section 2520. No cause of action shall lie in any court against any provider of wire or electronic communication service, its officers, employees, or agents, landlord, custodian, or other specified person for providing information, facilities, or assistance in accordance with the terms of a court order or certification under this chapter.

(b) It shall not be unlawful under this chapter for an officer, employee, or agent of the Federal Communications Commission, in the normal course of his employment and in discharge of the monitoring responsibilities exercised by the Commission in the enforcement of chapter 5 of title 47 of the United States Code, to intercept a wire or electronic communication, or oral communication transmitted by radio, or to disclose or use the information thereby obtained.

(c) It shall not be unlawful under this chapter for a person acting under color of law to intercept a wire, oral, or electronic communication, where such person is a party to the communication or one of the parties to the communication has given prior consent to such interception.

(d) It shall not be unlawful under this chapter for a person not acting under color of law to intercept a wire, oral, or electronic communication where such person is a party to the communication or where one of the parties to the communication has given prior consent to such interception unless such communication is intercepted for the purpose of committing any criminal or tortious act in violation of the Constitution or laws of the United States or of any State.

(e) Notwithstanding any other provision of this title or section 705 or 706 of the Communications Act of 1934, it shall not be unlawful for an officer, employee, or agent of the United States in the normal course of his official duty to conduct electronic surveillance, as defined in section 101 of the Foreign Intelligence Surveillance Act of 1978 as authorized by that Act.

(f)   Nothing contained in this chapter or chapter 121, or section 705 of the Communications Act of 1934, shall be deemed to affect the acquisition by the United States Government of foreign intelligence information from international or foreign communications, or foreign intelligence activities conducted in accordance with otherwise applicable Federal law involving a foreign electronic communications system, utilizing a means other than electronic surveillance as defined in section 101 of the Foreign Intelligence Surveillance Act of 1978, and procedures in this chapter and the Foreign Intelligence Surveillance Act of 1978 shall be the exclusive means by which electronic surveillance, as defined in section 101 of such Act, and the interception of domestic wire and oral communications may be conducted.

(g)   It shall not be unlawful under this chapter or chapter 121 of this title for any person—

(i)   to intercept or access an electronic communication made through an electronic communication system that is configured so that such electronic communication is readily accessible to the general public;

(ii) to intercept any radio communication which is transmitted—

(I)   by any station for the use of the general public, or that relates to ships, aircraft, vehicles, or persons in distress;

(II) by any governmental, law enforcement, civil defense, private land mobile, or public safety communications system, including police and fire, readily accessible to the general public;

(III) by a station operating on an authorized frequency within the bands allocated to the amateur, citizens band, or general mobile radio services; or

(IV) by any marine or aeronautical communications system;

(iii) to engage in any conduct which—

(I)   is prohibited by section 633 of the Communications Act of 1934; or

(II) is excepted from the application of section 705(a) of the Communications Act of 1934 by section 705(b) of that Act;

(iv) to intercept any wire or electronic communication the transmission of which is causing harmful interference to any lawfully operating station or consumer electronic equipment, to the extent necessary to identify the source of such interference; or

(v)   for other users of the same frequency to intercept any radio communication made through a system that utilizes frequencies monitored by individuals engaged in the provision or the use of such system, if such communication is not scrambled or encrypted.

(h)   It shall not be unlawful under this chapter—

(i)   to use a pen register or a trap and trace device (as those terms are defined for the purposes of chapter 206 (relating to pen registers and trap and trace devices) of this title); or

(ii) for a provider of electronic communication service to record the fact that a wire or electronic communication was initiated or completed in order to protect such provider, another provider furnishing service toward the completion of the wire or electronic communication, or a user of that service, from fraudulent, unlawful, or abusive use of such service.

(3)(a) Except as provided in paragraph (b) of this subsection, a person or entity providing an electronic communication service to the public shall not intentionally divulge the contents of any communication (other than one to such person or entity, or an agent thereof) while in transmission on that service to any person or entity other than an addressee or intended recipient of such communication or an agent of such addressee or intended recipient.

(b)   A person or entity providing electronic communication service to the public may divulge the contents of any such communication—

(i)   as otherwise authorized in section 2511(2)(a) or 2517 of this title;

(ii) with the lawful consent of the originator or any addressee or intended recipient of such communication;

(iii) to a person employed or authorized, or whose facilities are used, to forward such communication to its destination; or

(iv) which were inadvertently obtained by the service provider and which appear to pertain to the commission of a crime, if such divulgence is made to a law enforcement agency.

(4)(a) Except as provided in paragraph (b) of this subsection or in subsection (5), whoever violates subsection (1) of this section shall be fined under this title or imprisoned not more than five years, or both.

(b)   If the offense is a first offense under paragraph (a) of this subsection and is not for a tortious or illegal purpose or for purposes of direct or indirect commercial advantage or private commercial gain, and the wire or electronic communication with respect to which the offense under paragraph (a) is a radio communication that is not scrambled, encrypted, or transmitted using modulation techniques the essential parameters of which have been withheld from the public with the intention of preserving the privacy of such communication, then—

(i)   if the communication is not the radio portion of a cellular telephone communication, a cordless telephone communication that is transmitted between the cordless telephone handset and the base unit, a public land mobile radio service communication or a paging service communication, and the conduct is not that described in subsection (5), the offender shall be fined under this title or imprisoned not more than one year, or both, and

(ii) if the communication is the radio portion of a cellular telephone communication, a cordless telephone communication that is transmitted between the cordless telephone handset and the base unit, a public land mobile radio service communication or a paging service communication, the offender shall be fined under this title.

(c) Conduct otherwise an offense under this subsection that consists of or relates to the interception of a satellite transmission that is not encrypted or scrambled and that is transmitted—

(i) to a broadcasting station for purposes of retransmission to the general public; or

(ii) as an audio subcarrier intended for redistribution to facilities open to the public, but not including data transmissions or telephone calls,

is not an offense under this subsection unless the conduct is for the purposes of direct or indirect commercial advantage or private financial gain.

(5)(a)(i) If the communication is—

(A) a private satellite video communication that is not scrambled or encrypted and the conduct in violation of this chapter is the private viewing of that communication and is not for a tortious or illegal purpose or for purposes of direct or indirect commercial advantage or private commercial gain; or

(B) a radio communication that is transmitted on frequencies allocated under subpart D of part 74 of the rules of the Federal Communications Commission that is not scrambled or encrypted and the conduct in violation of this chapter is not for a tortious or illegal purpose or for purposes of direct or indirect commercial advantage or private commercial gain,

then the person who engages in such conduct shall be subject to suit by the Federal Government in a court of competent jurisdiction.

(ii) In an action under this subsection—

(A) if the violation of this chapter is a first offense for the person under paragraph (a) of subsection (4) and such person has not been found liable in a civil action under section 2520 of this title, the Federal Government shall be entitled to appropriate injunctive relief; and

(B) if the violation of this chapter is a second or subsequent offense under paragraph (a) of subsection (4) or such person has been found liable in any prior civil action under section 2520, the person shall be subject to a mandatory $500 civil fine.

(b) The court may use any means within its authority to enforce an injunction issued under paragraph (ii)(A), and shall impose a civil fine of not less than $500 for each violation of such an injunction.

CHAPTER 6
Appendix III

STORED WIRE AND ELECTRONIC COMMUNICATIONS AND TRANSACTIONAL RECORDS ACCESS

2701. UNLAWFUL ACCESS TO STORED COMMUNICATIONS

(a) Offense.—Except as provided in subsection (c) of this section whoever—

(1) intentionally accesses without authorization a facility through which an electronic communication service is provided; or

(2) intentionally exceeds an authorization to access that facility;

and thereby obtains, alters, or prevents authorized access to a wire or electronic communication while it is in electronic storage in such system shall be punished as provided in subsection (b) of this section.

(b) Punishment.—The punishment for an offense under subsection (a) of this section is—

(1) if the offense is committed for purposes of commercial advantage, malicious destruction or damage, or private commercial gain—

(A) a fine under this title or imprisonment for not more than one year, or both, in the case of a first offense under this subparagraph; and

(B) a fine under this title or imprisonment for not more than two years, or both, for any subsequent offense under this subparagraph; and

(2) a fine under this title or imprisonment for not more than six months, or both, in any other case.

(c) Exceptions.—Subsection (a) of this section does not apply with respect to conduct authorized—

(1) by the person or entity providing a wire or electronic communications service;

(2) by a user of that service with respect to a communication of or intended for that user; or

(3) in section 2703, 2404, or 2518 of this title.

CHAPTER 7

Checks, Notes, and Guarantees

LOST NOTES

All of us at one time or another have misplaced papers for an extended length of time and we do not wish to admit that the papers are lost. Under the UCC Section 3-309, a person is entitled to recover on a lost note. The section states as follows:

(a) a person not in possession of an instrument is entitled to enforce the instrument if (i) the person was in possession of the instrument and entitled to enforce it when loss of possession occurred, (ii) the loss of possession was not the result of a transfer by the person or a lawful seizure, (iii) the person cannot reasonably obtain possession of the instrument because the instrument was destroyed, its whereabouts cannot be determined, or it is in the wrongful possession of an unknown person or a person that cannot be found or is not amenable to service of process.

(b) a person seeking enforcement of an instrument under subsection (a) must prove the terms of the instrument and the person's right to enforce the instrument. If that proof is made, Section 3-308 applies to the case as if the person **seeking enforcement** had produced the instrument. The court may not **enter judgment** in favor of the person seeking enforcement unless it **finds that** the person required to pay the instrument is "adequately **protected**" against loss that might occur by reason of a claim by **another** person to enforce the instrument. Adequate protection may be provided by any reasonable means.

The section replaced an older section in the UCC wherein the owner of a lost instrument rather than the person in the possession of the instrument at the time of loss was entitled to enforce it.

The "adequate protection" wording is a flexible concept. A holder in due course may make demand for payment if the instrument was payable to bearer when it was lost or stolen. If the instrument was payable to the person who lost the instrument and that person did not endorse the instrument, no other person could be a valid holder in due course. Under a recent case, the FDIC sold a note after it was lost and issued an affidavit of a lost note to the plaintiff who sought to enforce the note. The defendants argued that plaintiff was not the party in possession at time of loss and could not utilize the revised UCC section. The court used the strict interpretation and stated "the plain language of the provision mandates that the plaintiff suing on the note must meet two tests, not just one: it must have been both in possession of the note when it was lost and entitled to enforce the note when it was lost." Under that theory, the plaintiff would not have been able to enforce the note.

Nevertheless in the instant case, the plaintiff was successful because there was a provision in the guarantee executed by the defendant that stated "any invalidity, irregularity, or enforceability of the obligation was hereby waived." This, or words of similar import, is a common clause in many guarantees. In the guarantees used by creditors that are only a few lines or are contained in credit applications or parts of other documents, where the president is guaranteeing the payment of the corporation's debt, this type of clause does not appear. Whether this reasoning would be successful in other jurisdictions is questionable since the initial note is not enforceable under the UCC and if such is the case, the court stretched when they created a new life and a new obligation by virtue of the guarantee (when the original obligation was unenforceable).[1]

---

[1]*Dennis Joslin Co. v. Robinson Broadcasting Corp.*, 977 F. Supp. 491 (D.D.C. 1997).

MUTUAL MISTAKE

Encoding errors by banks are common where a deposit by one customer is inadvertently credited to another customer's account because the wrong numbers are entered into the computer. The customer realizes the balance in the bank account unexpectedly has substantially increased by virtue of a mysterious deposit. The customer immediately withdraws the money from the bank account.

Shortly thereafter, the bank writes a letter to the customer to return the money and, of course, the customer has spent all the money by either repaying an indebtedness or making a handsome gift to a fiancee or, as happened in one case, the payee used the funds to operate a law practice, claiming reliance on the bank's mistake. The payee relied on a case where the customer used the money for the daily essentials of life and was not forced to repay the money to the bank. The courts in most of these cases hold that a mutual mistake occurred and the customer cannot be unjustly enriched.[2]

PAID-IN-FULL CHECKS—ACCORD AND SATISFACTION

Section 3-311 of the Uniform Commercial Code, designed to solve the problem of UCC 2-207 (which allows a recipient to deposit a check marked "paid in full," utilizing the magic words in the Uniform Commercial Code and suing for the balance), has now been passed in 47 of 50 states. Only New York, Rhode Island, and South Carolina have not passed the law. In fact, we are now beginning to see some litigation over the new section and a recent case in Connecticut pinpointed the efforts of a plaintiff's attorney, who altered a check by obliterating the language on the reverse side indicating that the check was to be treated as payment in full. The court properly held that under Section 3-311 in Connecticut the cashing of the check qualifies as an accord and satisfaction and the effort to obliterate the paid-in-full language and use the magic words of Section 3-311 was ineffective. A copy of Connecticut SGS Section 42A-3-311 appears in Appendix I.[3]

---

[2]*Bank One Trust Co. v. LaCour*, 721 N.E. 2d 491 (Ohio Ct. App., Franklin County 1999).

[3]Twin City Plumbing, Inc. v. William Hill, Inc., v. Homewood, 2000 Conn. Super. LEXIS 264 (Super. Ct. New Britain January 24, 2000).

FORGED ENDORSEMENT

Signatures on checks and notes are not often forged, but if you deal with enough checks and enough notes, somewhere along the line a signature does get forged. When an endorsement is forged on a check, a general rule applies shifting the risk of loss either upon the drawee bank for improper payment over a forged endorsement or to the drawer of the check when the fictitious payee exception applies. The official comment adopts the principle that the risk of loss for fraudulent endorsements by employees who are entrusted with responsibility for checks falls on the employer rather than the bank that takes the check or pays it, if the bank was not negligent in the transaction. The section is based on the belief that the employer is in a better position to avoid the loss by using care in choosing employees, in supervising them, and in adopting other measures to prevent forged endorsements on instruments payable to the employer or fraud in the issuance of instruments in the name of the employer. If the bank failed to exercise ordinary care, Subsection B allows the employer to shift loss to the bank to the extent of the bank's failure to exercise ordinary care.

In the official comment to the statute, several examples are afforded concerning forged checks. In one instance, a janitor finds a check and forges the employer's name on the check, cashes the check, and absconds with the money. In this case, the employer was not necessarily negligent unless the bank can show that the employer left the check negligently around for the janitor to find.

A second example is where the treasurer of a corporation, who is authorized to write the checks on behalf of the corporation, issues the check to himself and signs the check as an authorized officer of the corporation. The check is not forged although it was not authorized since no money was owed to the treasurer. Under these circumstances, the corporation is bound to pay the check.

A third example is a bookkeeper who steals a check payable to the employer and forges the employer's endorsement. The check is deposited to the employee's account and honored. The endorsement is effective as the employer's endorsement because the employee was a bookkeeper and she was entrusted with the check for bookkeeping purposes. The employer is liable.

A recent case in New York addressed this issue. An insurance company agent had an ongoing business understanding whereby the agent was responsible for processing requests for policy loans and dividend withdrawals. Under an established course of dealing, the agent had authority to verify the identity of the policyholder and the bona fide of the request for a loan or withdrawal, as well as the information necessary to process the request, to take receipt of the check, and to deliver it to the policyholder. The agency, on the undisputed facts, performed all of these steps necessary to process requests for policy loans or dividend withdrawals. The mutual agreement to proceed in this manner was surely intended to benefit both the insurance company and the agent.

The court found that the insurance company was responsible for the issuance of the checks because the insurance company was in a better position than the defendant to prevent the forgeries. The insurance company could have required authorization from the policyholders before issuing the checks, could have sent the checks directly to the payees, or could have delivered to them contemporary notice that an issued check was made out to them. The insurance company also might have prevented the forgeries through better supervision of the agent during the decade he was carrying out the fraudulent scheme.

In Appendix II, you will find Section 3-403, 404, 405, and 406 which deals with unauthorized signatures, fictitious payees, and employer's responsibility for fraudulent endorsements and forged signatures or alterations of instruments.[4]

ATTACHMENT OF BANK ACCOUNTS

One of the problems in attaching a bank account after a judgment is that the debtor will assert:

1. that the account is jointly held with another party;
2. that the monies do not belong to the depositor and that it is being held for someone else;
3. that the account is a direct deposit account that receives salary checks.

In reverse order, if it is a salary check, and the state law only permits a certain percentage of salary to be levied upon (such as in New York, where the limitation is 10%), then the creditor would be entitled to 10% of

---

[4]*Guardian Life Ins. Co. of America v. Chemical Bank*, 727 N.E. 2d 111 (N.Y. 2000)

that salary check and would not be entitled to levy on the entire amount in the account. An examination of the bank statement should be made to verify that only salary checks are deposited.

If it is money that the debtor claims belongs to someone else (such as his mother, sister, spouse, etc.), the attorney for the creditor should obtain sufficient documentation to establish that it is not the debtor's money. The burden of proof, of course, is upon the debtor, and if he cannot produce sufficient documentation, the creditor should make a motion in court to obtain the full amount.

If it is a joint account, the account should be labeled jointly between the husband and the wife. Under those circumstances, levy on half of the account and leave the other half of the account for the other party. If it is a joint account with right of survivorship, the debtor may argue successfully that you would have to wait to see who survives before executing on the monies in the account. If the wife survived, the creditor would not be entitled to any monies in the account and if the debtor survived, the creditor would be entitled to the full amount in the account. In most instances, in our practice, a settlement is made around 50% of the account.

The most dangerous aspect of attaching bank accounts is attaching a bank account with the wrong name, a typographical error in the account number, or some other clerical error that ends up attaching the wrong account. In these instances, the attorney for the creditor should act rapidly to remove the attachment because the creditor may be liable for damages that the account holder would sustain by reason of the account being attached inadvertently. Often, the error is with the bank and in these instances, the bank should also act quickly to remove the attachment. The problem is not so much if the attachment is only on the bank account for a day or two; but when the attachment remains for weeks or months, the damages could be significant.

AUTOMATED CHECK CLEARING HOUSE

The National Automated Check Clearing House Association was formed to provide for the electronic presentment of checks. Some merchants are utilizing this electronic presentment of checks to obtain a faster response after a check has been dishonored. The Automated Clearing House Network processes and delivers checks, but presentment and settlement is performed electronically among financial institutions. The trade association conducts the transactions under regulations of the U.S. Department of Treasury, which incorporates the operating rules of the Automatic Check

Clearing House and all members of ACH abide by these "NACHA Operating Rules."

Some checks are presented to the merchant and then electronically converted to debit items by using the Automatic Check Clearing House (ACH). If a paper check should become dishonored by the consumer's bank, the merchant is notified and then can present the check through the ACH Network only according to the rules of the network, which provide that the check may be presented a total of three times. Banks are only allowed to pay the face amount of these debit items. If merchants utilize the ACH, they must provide notice to the issuer of the check that the check will be sent through the ACH system. The rules do not provide how the notice must be sent, but a clear and conspicuous sign posted at the point of sale is appropriate, informing the issuer that the paper check will be presented electronically in the event it is returned for any reason.

No bad check fees may be charged to the person who signed the check unless a statement is signed by the consumer agreeing to allow the merchant to collect a fee for a return item. A copy must be furnished to the consumer of the writing. A stamp on the back of a check may also be appropriate.

A copy of the rules and regulations governing the ACH Network, the 2001 Edition, is currently available with rule changes and explains how to comply with these changes in the 2001 guide which implement the NACHA rule charges. The rules are available at www.NACHA.org. where you can buy the rules and regulations.

ORDINARY CARE—FACSIMILE SIGNATURES

Often a corporation wishes to use facsimile signatures on their checks. The normal procedure is to enter into an agreement with the bank, which provides that the bank has the authority to pay money against the facsimile signature. The language in these agreements varies, but in one case in Florida the agreement provided that the bank could pay any check when "bearing or purporting to bear" the facsimile signature. The plaintiff contended that the phrase was not a risk-shifting clause and served only to allow the bank to pay checks with facsimile signatures that have some technical defect in the ink such as smudges or a smear. The court disagreed and stated that the word "purport" covered the situation of a forgery which by its definition "purports to bear" a facsimile signature. On that ground alone the court held that the agreement was "risk shifting." The issuer of the check would bear the loss.

The agreement with the bank was not treated as an exculpatory clause since it was recognized that the bank did have a duty to exercise ordinary care. The bank does have a statutory duty of good faith and ordinary care and the plaintiff had a right to conduct depositions and other discovery to ascertain whether the bank acted with ordinary care.

Ordinary care in the banking environment does not necessarily mean that the bank should have examined the check for the forgery. Under many circumstances, the bank never looks at the signature line of a check and the failure to look at the signature line of the check or to examine the signature line would not necessarily be a lack of ordinary care, providing the bank was acting in a customary manner in the banking industry. If the banks actually reviewed (check by check) the signature line on each check, the entire banking system would probably come to a halt. The bank itself makes the decision which checks are examined, considering what the cost of reviewing the checks and the general damages they might incur by paying forged checks due to a failure to review the checks. The statutory definition of ordinary care would probably relieve the bank of any liability in most cases for losses from forgeries of the original signatures of the drawer.[5]

GUARANTEE—SEPARATE AGREEMENT

Often a guarantor will defend liability on the grounds that the debt against the principle debtor is void and therefore if the principal's debt is not valid, any claim against the guarantor should be invalid.

Unfortunately, the guarantee agreement executed by the guarantor usually contains some clause that provides that the guarantee is a continuing, absolute, and unconditional guarantee of payment regardless if the principal's debt is held to be invalid or unenforceable. In one case, the original obligation was found unenforceable because of certain omissions and irregularities in the agreements executed by the principal.

The court stressed that an agreement of guarantee is a separate agreement from the principal's obligation. As a separate agreement, the liability of the guarantor may be lesser or even greater than the liability of the principal. In another case, the principal's debt was released by the creditor, but the creditor still proceeded against the guarantor.

It has been pointed out elsewhere that agreements of guarantee used by institutions are comprehensive. Before execution, consultation with counsel is recommended and counsel should not be the same counsel

---

[5]*Arkwright Mutual Ins. Co. v. Nations Bank, NA.,* 212 F. 3d 1224 (11th Cir. 2000).

who is representing the principal. In plain simple terms, the guarantor should understand what the obligations are and exactly what the agreement provides.[6]

COMMERCIAL BAD FAITH

To hold a bank liable for fraud committed by a third party usually requires proof that the bank had full knowledge of the fraud, participated in the fraud, and benefited from the fraud. The fact that the bank knowingly or recklessly disregarded several "badges of fraud," including irregularities in the opening of the accounts and in the documents being submitted for the wire transfer, and knowing that the employee who handled the transaction lived on the same block as the party who committed the fraud and the rejection of wire transfers should have alerted the bank, are insufficient allegations to create an inference that the bank knew of or participated in the fraud.

A claim for commercial bad faith may arise if a plaintiff alleges facts that the principals of the bank were actual participants in the unlawful activity. Despite the fact several red flags were flying that should have alerted the bank to a fraud, or at least prompted the bank to investigate, and even though the bank acted negligently with regard to its conduct, allegations that a bank disregarded suspicious circumstances that may have induced the prudent banker to inquire do not suffice to state a claim for commercial bad faith. The bank's actions may be negligent and even grossly negligent, but this does not sufficiently allege the actual knowledge or the participation in the fraudulent action that supports a claim for commercial bad faith.

In this particular case, the plaintiff also alleged aiding and abetting in the fraud. To state a claim for aiding and abetting under New York law, a plaintiff must allege the existence of the fraud, knowledge of the fraud, and substantial assistance by the aider and abettor in achieving the fraud. The court pointed out that aiding and abetting also requires knowledge of the actual wrong. The test for aiding and abetting is similar to the test for commercial bad faith. Aside from knowledge, the bank would have had to provide substantial assistance, which means that the bank must affirmatively assist, help, conceal, or, by virtue of failing to act when required to do so, enable the fraud to proceed. The mere fact that participants in a

---

[6]*Manufacturers Hanover Trust Co. v. Green*, 95 A.D. 2d 507, 464 N.Y.S. 2d 474 (N.Y.A.D. 1st Dept. 1983); *Union Minot Ltd. v. Aon Fin. Prods.*, 2000 U.S. Dist. Lexis 10166 (S.D.N.Y. 2000) July 20, 2000.

fraudulent scheme use accounts at a bank to perpetrate the fraud does not rise to the level of substantial assistance necessary to state a claim for aiding and abetting.[7]

HOLDER IN DUE COURSE

A general principle is that a holder in due course must furnish value or consideration for a negotiable instrument. A promise not yet performed is not value. In one case, the court held that a law firm did not give value when it accepted a check as an advance retainer. The check was not issued by the client, for the client was the payee of the check and the client endorsed the check to the law firm. Thereafter, the drawer of the check stopped payment and asserted a defense against the client. The law firm sued the drawer on the grounds that the law firm was the holder in due course.

Because it was a check for an advance retainer and not payment for services already rendered, the court took an unusual view and held that until the firm billed against the retainer, no services were rendered and no value was given by the law firm. We believe the law firm was thoroughly surprised by the decision, and so were we!![8]

CHEX SYSTEMS

It was reported in the *Wall Street Journal* that Chex Systems, a database operated by E-Funds Corporation, a unit of the check printing company Deluxe Corporation, operates a database of checking account customers when a bank closes the account because a customer has not promptly repaid an overdraft. The account remains reported in the system for over five years even if the money owed to the bank is ultimately repaid. Almost 80% of the bank branches in the nation subscribe to this database.

The customers who are on the database often encounter difficulty opening a new account at another bank that is a member of the database, because many of the banks will not accept for a new account an applicant they find in the database.

---

[7]*Nigerian Nat'l Petroleum Corp. v. CitiBank, N.A.*, 1999 U.S. Dist. Lexis 11599 (S.D.N.Y. July 29, 1999); *Prudential-Bache Securities, Inc. v. Citibank, N.A.*, 73 N.Y. 2d 263, 536 N.E. 2d 1118, 539 N.Y.S. 2d 699 (1989).

[8]*Carter & Grimsley v. Omni Trading, Inc.* 306 Ill. App. 3d 1127, 716 N.E. 2d 320 (Ill. App. 3 Dist. 1999).

GUARANTEE FORMS

We are attaching in Appendix III four *simple* forms of guarantees which may be incorporated into credit applications or used separately. Nevertheless, in preparing any guarantee, we recommend consultation with experienced counsel to be certain that your documentation will survive litigation.

TRADE ACCEPTANCE

A trade acceptance is essentially a promissory note, but is drawn by the seller of goods on the purchaser and accepted by the purchaser. The purpose is to make the book account liquid and permit the holder to raise money before it is due under the terms of sale. Its principal function is to take the place of selling goods on an open account. When properly drawn, it is negotiable.

GUARANTEE PAYMENT OF MONEY

Where a guarantee consists of both monetary and non-monetary obligations, in that the defendant is guaranteeing performance or some other action that is not of a monetary nature, the creditor should divide the document into two separate guarantees rather than setting forth the obligations within the four corners of one guarantee. If one guarantee is being used, the terms of the guarantee should expressly state that the guarantee is an instrument for the payment of money *only* as to that portion of the guarantee that deals with money.

This eliminates some problems if the guarantee reached litigation and the dispute dealt with what performance was required of the guarantor.

GUARANTEES OF PAYMENT OR GUARANTEE OF COLLECTION

A guarantee of payment requires the guarantor to pay the indebtedness upon the happening of a default by the primary debtor. A guarantee of collection can only be enforced in the event the lender has made attempts to obtain payment from the debtor. In most instances, guarantees will not identify whether they are guarantees of payment or guarantees of collection. The court will review the terms of the guarantee to determine the intent of the parties.

Considerable litigation results from this distinction. Most guarantors will contend that the guarantee is one of collection, since lenders engage in diligent efforts to collect the debt from the primary borrower before commencing action against the guarantor.

Since most lenders want a guarantee of payment, it is important when drafting the guarantee that the proper wording is used.

> **Credit & Collection Tip:** *Consultation with an attorney is recommended with regard to the preparation and drafting of any guarantee, not only to be certain it is a guarantee of payment but also to include other appropriate terminology which will protect the lender.*

CASHIER'S CHECKS

Some courts will allow the bank to stop payment on a cashier's check if it was procured by fraud, since to honor the check would only assist in the fraudulent transaction. In this situation, the check should still be in the hands of the original payee. On the other hand, if the check was negotiated to a holder in due course, the bank could not refuse to pay the check. The issues of reliance by the payee when he received the check or whether the payee has really changed a position in reliance on the check seem to be factors that the courts consider in determining whether they are going to allow the bank to stop payment of the cashier's check.[9]

---

[9]*Associated Carriages, Inc. v. International Bank of Commerce*, 37 S.W. 3d 69 (Texas 4th District 2000).

CHAPTER 7
APPENDIX I

CGS §42A-3-311. ACCORD AND SATISFACTION BY USE OF INSTRUMENT

(a) If a person against whom a claim is asserted proves that (i) that person in good faith tendered an instrument to the claimant as full satisfaction of the claim, (ii) the amount of the claim was unliquidated or subject to a bona fide dispute, and (iii) the claimant obtained payment of the instrument, the following subsections apply.

(b) Unless subsection (c) applies, the claim is discharged if the person against whom the claim is asserted proves that the instrument or an accompanying written communication contained a conspicuous statement to the effect that the instrument was tendered as full satisfaction of the claim.

(c) Subject to subsection (d), a claim is not discharged under subsection (b) if either of the following applies: (i) The claimant, if an organization, proves that (i) within a reasonable time before the tender, the claimant sent a conspicuous statement to the person against whom the claim is asserted that communications concerning disputed debts, including an instrument tendered as full satisfaction of a debt, are to be sent to a designated person, office, or place, and (ii) the instrument or accompanying communication was not received by that designated person, office, or place.

(2) The claimant, whether or not an organization, proves that within ninety days after payment of the instrument, the claimant tendered repayment of the amount of the instrument to the person against whom the claim is asserted. This paragraph does not apply if the claimant is an organization that sent a statement complying with paragraph (1)(i).

(d) A claim is discharged if the person against whom the claim is asserted proves that within a reasonable time before collection of the instrument was initiated, the claimant, or an agent of the claimant having direct responsibility with respect to the disputed obligation, knew that the instrument was tendered in full satisfaction of the claim.

APPENDIX II

EXCERPTS FROM UNIFORM COMMERCIAL CODE: NEGOTIABLE INSTRUMENTS, ARTICLE 3, SEC. 403-407

3-403. UNAUTHORIZED SIGNATURE.

(a) Unless otherwise provided in this Article or Article 4, an unauthorized signature is ineffective except as the signature of the unauthorized signer in favor of a person who in good faith pays the instrument or takes it for value. An unauthorized signature may be ratified for all purposes of this Article.

(b) If the signature of more than one person is required to constitute the authorized signature of an organization, the signature of the organization is unauthorized if one of the required signatures is lacking.

(c) The civil or criminal liability of a person who makes an unauthorized signature is not affected by any provision of this Article which makes the unauthorized signature effective for the purposes of this Article.

3-404. IMPOSTERS; FICTITIOUS PAYEES.

(a) If an impostor, by use of the mails or otherwise, induces the issuer of an instrument to issue the instrument to the impostor, or to a person acting in concert with the impostor, by impersonating the payee of the instrument or a person authorized to act for the payee, an indorsement of the instrument by any person in the name of the payee is effective as the indorsement of the payee in favor of a person who, in good faith, pays the instrument or takes it for value or for collection.

(b) If (i) a person whose intent determines to whom an instrument is payable (Section 3-110(a) or (b)) does not intend the person identified as payee to have any interest in the instrument, or (ii) the person identified as payee of an instrument is a fictitious person, the following rules apply until the instrument is negotiated by special indorsement:

   (1) Any person in possession of the instrument is its holder.

   (2) An indorsement by any person in the name of the payee stated in the instrument is effective as the indorsement of the payee in favor of a person who, in good faith, pays the instrument or takes it for value or for collection.

(c) Under subsection (a) or (b), an indorsement is made in the name of a payee if (i) it is made in a name substantially similar to that of the payee or (ii) the instrument, whether or not indorsed, is deposited in a depositary bank to an account in a name substantially similar to that of the payee.

(d) With respect to an instrument to which subsection (a) or (b) applies, if a person paying the instrument or taking it for value or for collection fails to exercise ordinary care in paying or taking the instrument and that failure substantially contributes to loss resulting from payment of the instrument, the person bearing the loss may recover from the person failing to exercise ordinary care to the extent the failure to exercise ordinary care contributed to the loss.

3-405. EMPLOYER'S RESPONSIBILITY FOR FRAUDULENT INDORSEMENT BY EMPLOYEE.

(a) In this section:

(1) "Employee" includes an independent contractor and employee of an independent contractor retained by the employer.

(2) "Fraudulent indorsement" means (i) in the case of an instrument payable to the employer, a forged indorsement purporting to be that of the employer, or (ii) in the case of an instrument with respect to which the employer is the issuer, a forged indorsement purporting to be that of the person identified as payee.

(3) "Responsibility" with respect to instruments means authority (i) to sign or indorse instruments on behalf of the employer, (ii) to process instruments received by the employer for bookkeeping purposes, for deposit to an account, or for other disposition, (iii) to prepare or process instruments for issue in the name of the employer, (iv) to supply information determining the names or addresses of payees of instruments to be issued in the name of the employer, (v) to control the disposition of instruments to be issued in the name of the employer, or (vi) to act otherwise with respect to instruments in

a responsible capacity. "Responsibility" does not include authority that merely allows an employee to have access to instruments or blank or incomplete instrument forms that are being stored or transported or are part of incoming or outgoing mail, or similar access.

(b)   For the purpose of determining the rights and liabilities of a person who, in good faith, pays an instrument or takes it for value or for collection, if an employer entrusted an employee with responsibility with respect to the instrument and the employee or a person acting in concert with the employee makes a fraudulent indorsement of the instrument, the indorsement is effective as the indorsement of the person to whom the instrument is payable if it is made in the name of that person. If the person paying the instrument or taking it for value or for collection fails to exercise ordinary care in paying or taking the instrument and that failure substantially contributes to loss resulting from the fraud, the person bearing the loss may recover from the person failing to exercise ordinary care to the extent the failure to exercise ordinary care contributed to the loss.

(c)   Under subsection (b), an indorsement is made in the name of the person to whom an instrument is payable if (i) it is made in a name substantially similar to the name of that person or (ii) the instrument, whether or not indorsed, is deposited in a depositary bank to an account in a name substantially similar to the name of that person.

3-406. NEGLIGENCE CONTRIBUTING TO FORGED SIGNATURE OR ALTERATION OF INSTRUMENT.

(a)   A person whose failure to exercise ordinary care substantially contributes to an alteration of an instrument or to the making of a forged signature on an instrument is precluded from asserting the alteration or the forgery against a person who, in good faith, pays the instrument or takes it for value or for collection.

(b)   Under subsection (a), if the person asserting the preclusion fails to exercise ordinary care in paying or taking the instrument and that failure substantially contributes to loss, the loss is allocated between the person precluded and the person asserting the preclusion according to the extent to which the failure of each to exercise ordinary care contributed to the loss.

(c)   Under subsection (a), the burden of proving failure to exercise ordinary care is on the person asserting the preclusion. Under subsection (b), the burden of proving failure to exercise ordinary care is on the person precluded.

3-407. ALTERATION.

(a) "Alteration" means (i) an unauthorized change in an instrument that purports to modify in any respect the obligation of a party, or (ii) an unauthorized addition of words or numbers or other change to an incomplete instrument relating to the obligation of a party.

(b) Except as provided in subsection (c), an alteration fraudulently made discharges a party whose obligation is affected by the alteration unless that party assents or is precluded from asserting the alteration. No other alteration discharges a party, and the instrument may be enforced according to its original terms.

(c) A payor bank or drawee paying a fraudulently altered instrument or a person taking it for value, in good faith and without notice of the alteration, may enforce rights with respect to the instrument (i) according to its original terms, or (ii) in the case of an incomplete instrument altered by unauthorized completion, according to its terms as completed.

APPENDIX III

FOUR FORMS OF GUARANTY

Sample forms of guarantees are as follows:

FORM A

We (I) _____, the undersigned in consideration of you extending credit to _____ hereby guarantees the prompt payment of all debts from _____ to _____.

_____

FORM B

The undersigned hereby guarantees the prompt payment of all the obligations of _____ Corporation due and owing to _____ of which the undersigned guarantor is a stockholder. The undersigned hereby waives, presentment, demand, protest, notice of protest, notice of dishonor and any and all notices.

_____

FORM C

In order to induce _____ to extend credit to _____, the undersigned hereby guarantees the prompt payment of all obligations to _____ from _____.
The liability under this guaranty shall in no way be affected by the failure of _____ to give notice of any extension, compromise, adjustment or release or discharge of any party to the obligation or any party or guarantor liable on the obligation.

_____

FORM D

The obligation of the guarantor hereunder shall accrue immediately upon non-payment of the debt by _____ to _____ and _____ shall not be required to proceed against the primary obligor or any other secondary obligor. The undersigned hereby waives all rights to setoffs or counterclaims until the indebtedness from _____ to _____ is paid in full. The undersigned agrees to pay reasonable attorney's fees in the event the original obligation is turned over to an attorney for collection. This guaranty shall be enforced in accordance with the laws of the State of _____.

_____

CHAPTER 8

Repossesion of Property

CERTIFICATE OF TITLE—DUE PROCESS

Some state statutes do not require that any special notice be given to the debtor before the creditor obtains title to the vehicle after a repossession. Under the statute in Ohio the debtor was neither entitled to notice of the transfer of the repossession title nor was he entitled to a hearing.

In a recent case, the court held that allowing the secured party to obtain a repossession title without notice to the debtor and without a hearing violates the due process provisions of the U.S. Constitution. The case is presently up on appeal in the 6th Circuit and several banking associations have filed amici briefs.[1]

In another case involving a certificate of title state, a company financed the sales of vehicles from a dealer to several consumers, but the consumers were not able to obtain a certificate of title since the bank, which did "floor plan financing" for the dealer, held all the certificates of titles to all of the automobiles. The financer of the individual cars to the consumers had notice of the security interest of the bank, but argued that the consumers were buyers in the ordinary course of business, whose purchases extinguish the floor plan security interest of the bank. The court disagreed. No legal sales were made to the purported buyers and thus

---
[1]*Leslie v. Lacy*, 91 F. Supp. 2d 1182 (S.D. Ohio 2000).

they could not be considered buyers in the ordinary course of business. To have a legal sale, the buyer would have to receive title as required under the Certificate of Title Act of Texas.[2]

In the third case involving a certificate of title, Florida had specific legislation addressing ownership and title. A person acquiring a motor vehicle shall not acquire marketable title to the vehicle until he or she is issued a certificate of title to the motor vehicle. No court shall recognize the right, title, claim, or interest of any person in and to any motor vehicle sold, disposed of, mortgaged, or encumbered unless evidenced by a certificate title duly issued to that person in accordance with the provisions of the chapter. The court emphasized that title is not transferred to a creditor immediately on repossession. The creditor must present satisfactory proof in the form of an affidavit that the creditor is entitled to ownership and possession of the car. The creditor must pay a fee, must provide a lien holders 15 days' notice prior to requesting a certificate of title, and the former owner, such as the debtor in this case, has the ability to file a written protest to the issuance of a certificate of title. If a written protest is filed, a further 10-day period is required. Only after all of these conditions are met is a creditor with a repossessed vehicle able to obtain a new certificate of title and conclude a sale of the auto.[3]

PRE- AND POST-BANKRUPTCY REPOSSESSIONS

A repossession that occurs after the bankruptcy petition has been filed is considered a post-petition repossession. If the creditor has knowledge of the bankruptcy, the repossession would constitute a violation of the automatic stay contained in Section 362.

Not all post-petition repossessions result in damage awards. Where a creditor has received notice or has become aware of the pending bankruptcy proceeding, the creditor has a duty to make inquiry. If a repossession occurs after the petition is filed, but at a time prior to the creditor being informed of the filing (either by receipt of the notice from the court or notice by the debtor's counsel), the repossession would be void; but the creditor would not be liable for damages for the act of the repossession since there was no actual notice of the pendency of the bankruptcy case. It is not a willful violation and these instances have been described as technical or inadvertent. A creditor has an affirmative duty to undo any post-

---

[2]*Bank One Tex. N.A. v. Arcade Fin. Ltd.*, 219 F. 3d 494 (5th Cir. 2000).

[3]*In re Chiodo*, 250 B.R. 407 (Bkrtcy. D. Fla. 2000).

petition repossession immediately upon being notified of the pendency of the bankruptcy case even in the absence of any court order. Failure to do so will subject the creditor to damages.

Some repossessions occur pre-petition and the question is whether retention of collateral post-petition, which was lawfully repossessed pre-petition, constitutes a willful violation of the automatic stay. It is undisputed that property repossessed pre-petition, but not disposed of, remains the property of the estate of the bankrupt and cannot be disposed of post-petition without a court order.

The narrow focus of this is whether a creditor holding collateral repossessed pre-petition has an affirmative duty to turn its collateral over to the debtor and risk damages or whether the creditor has the right to hold the collateral pending a hearing. The issue is whether the creditor must make an immediate application for a hearing or whether the creditor can wait until the debtor makes an application for an adversary proceeding to recover the collateral from the creditor. Cases go both ways on this subject and it is difficult to determine the majority or the minority. The elements that seem to cause the conflict are contained in Section 542:

(a) Except as provided in subsection (c) or (d) of this section, an entity, other than a custodian, in possession, custody, or control, during the case, of property that the trustee may use, sell, or lease under section 363 of this title, or that the debtor may exempt under section 522 of this title, shall deliver to the trustee, and account for such property or the value of such property, unless such property is of inconsequential value or benefit to the estate.

(b) Except as provided in subsection (c) or (d) of this section, an entity that owes a debt that is property of the estate and that is matured, payable on demand, or payable on order, shall pay such debt to, or on the order of, the trustee, except to the extent that such debt may be offset under section 553 of this title against a claim against the debtor.

(c) Except as provided in section 362(a)(7) of this title, an entity that has neither actual notice nor actual knowledge of the commencement of the case concerning the debtor may transfer property of the estate, or pay a debt owing to the debtor, in good faith and other than in the manner specified in subsection (d) of this section, to an entity other than the trustee, with the same effect as to the entity making such transfer or payment as if the case under this title concerning the debtor had not been commenced.

The courts read the section as providing that an entity in possession of estate property shall deliver it to the trustee and this supports an automatic turnover duty with respect to any property repossessed pre-petition. On the other hand, the creditor is entitled to adequate protection of the creditor's interest as a pre-condition to the debtor's use of the property. The situation arises where the debtor may not even want the return of the property.

A recent case in Georgia has provided an excellent analysis of this situation and finally decided that no obligation rests on the creditor to make an application for the hearing, leaving the burden upon the debtor to make an application for a hearing to return the vehicle.[4]

POST-REPOSSESSION REQUIREMENTS

In Appendix I, we have put a table which is a state-by-state sample of post-repossession requirements for motor vehicles provided by Joseph D. Looney of Hudson Cook, LLP, Crofton, Maryland. The table sets forth: (1) the repo notice required, (2) within how many days it must be given, (3) the manner of mailing, (4) whether any right to reinstate must be given and any exceptions and the number of days, (5) what the amount includes in order to reinstate the loan, and (6) the notice of sale requirements that are necessary to place the vehicle at public or private sale.

CURE NOTICE

In Appendix II, we have provided a representative sample of pre-repossession requirements for motor vehicles (retail accounts). The table provides information on 31 states. These statutes are indigenous to each state and before any lender embarks upon using the cure notice, the lender should consult with experienced counsel in this area. The table details: (1) whether a cure notice is required, (2) the number of days to cure, (3) the manner of mailing the cure notice, (4) must a cure notice be given every time. If not, when. And (5) what the state requirements are for a cure notice. We hope the tables will be helpful to those parties engaged in the repossession of vehicles. Do not rely on the tables without reviewing the applicable state law, and consult with counsel since the tables were compiled in 1999 and the statutes may have been amended or modified.

---

[4]*Brown v. Joe Addison, Inc. (In re Brown)*, 210 B.R. 878 (Bankr. S. D. Ga. 1997).

One of the states not covered in the table is Maine. An analysis of the statute in Maine will hopefully illustrate the complexity of states' statutes and why it is necessary to embark on this procedure with care and thorough consideration.

Maine's Consumer Credit Codes regulate all consumer credit transactions (secured and unsecured). If a debtor defaults by failing to make payment within 10 days of the due date, M.R.S.A. Sections 5-510 and 5-511 require that a debtor be sent a written notice to cure prior to enforcing any contractual remedies, including accelerating the balance due or retaking possession of the secured property. A creditor must issue a 14-day written notice of default, which must describe the alleged default and allow the borrower the right to cure. The notice must include the name and telephone number of the creditor, the amount of payment to cure the default, and the last date payment must be made.

Notice may be sent by regular or certified mail. The 14-day time period does not begin until the consumer actually receives the notice. If the notice is sent by ordinary first-class mail, the date of receipt is determined by the date the consumer receives the mail. If a post office certificate is obtained, the date of receipt by the consumer will be judicially presumed to occur on the third calendar day after mailing.[5]

Using certified mail may not be the best way to proceed. If notice is sent by certified mail, return receipt requested, the date of receipt is determined by the date the consumer signs for the receipt, or the last date that delivery was attempted on unclaimed certified mail. The problem is that it may be difficult to determine the date of receipt unless the debtor completes the return receipt. Thus, a creditor may need to wait as long as four or five weeks to establish that the notice has been received so that the 14-day cure period may begin to run. If the debtor claims he did not receive the notice, the burden of proof is on the creditor to establish that notice was received. The recommended procedure is to mail by first-class mail and obtain a post office certificate of mailing. Without proof of compliance, a lawful act such as peaceful possession could be immediately transformed into a wrongful conversion and could expose the creditor to liability under state as well as federal laws.

The creditor is not required by statute to send an additional notice if the debtor should default again within one year. But it is important that proof of this notice be maintained with the same diligence that is accorded to the original agreement. If the original notice is lost or if no notice was sent, on the second default it is advisable to send another notice. A party

---

[5]*Griffin v. Chrysler Credit Corp.*, 553 A. 2d 653 (Me. 1989) Supreme Judicial Court of Maine.

who is purchasing paper in the State of Maine should obtain affidavits from the original creditor stating that the original creditor has complied with Maine statutory requirements for debtors residing in Maine. The affidavit should recite that the original creditor issued a proper statutory notice to cure, that the debtor failed to cure the default, and that the debt was accelerated prior to the sale. The notice to cure should also be provided.

The above furnishes a summary of some of the problems that will be faced in other states and why it is necessary that an in-depth review be made of each state's statute, and consultation with experienced counsel is recommended.

NOTIFICATION AND COMMERCIALLY REASONABLE SALES

The right to a deficiency is spelled out in the various state laws and most of them require specific procedures for a creditor to proceed against the debtor for a deficiency after the sale of a collateral. This right of deficiency exists only if the creditor strictly complies with the statutory requirements set forth. A co-debtor or guarantor is entitled to notice as a prerequisite to the collection of a deficiency from the co-debtor or guarantor. Although the various state laws may differ in many respects, almost all of them agree that co-debtors and guarantors must have notice of a sale of collateral.

The party seeking to proceed on a deficiency claim usually has the burden of proving compliance with the statutory requirements. In a case in Iowa, the court followed the ruling of their Court of Appeals, which held that mailing a notice to the address specified in the instrument itself does not necessarily satisfy the requirement of reasonable notification when the creditor learns prior to the sale that the debtor has not actually received the notice. In the instant case, the notice was mailed to a town that did not even exist in the State of Iowa and a ZIP Code that did not belong to the State of Iowa. The court reasoned that mailing a notice to an undeliverable address does not satisfy the reasonable notification requirement.

Merely sending the notification to the address specified on the security agreement or the financing statement would not be sufficient if the creditor was aware of a new address through their collection efforts. Before notification is sent, a review of the file should be made to be certain that the notification is sent to the most recent address. Perhaps, the best of both worlds would be to send to the address listed on the security agreement and financing statement and also to any other address that has come to the attention of the creditor.[6]

In many states, the failure to deliver notice will bar the creditor from proceeding against the debtor for a deficiency, but in some states, a creditor's failure to conduct the sale in a commercially reasonable manner or to deliver the required notice of the sale is not an absolute bar to obtaining a deficiency judgment. The failure to give notice or dispose of the collateral in a commercially reasonable manner results in a presumption that the collateral was worth at least the amount of the debt or that the amount that could have reasonably been obtained from a commercially reasonable sale of the collateral would be credited to the debt. The states that follow the latter premise credit the debtor with the true market value of the collateral and permit the creditor to proceed against the debtor for the deficiency.

The valuation of the collateral is left to the court to determine. The plaintiff presents the experts and the defendant presents the experts as to valuation and the end result is a battle of the experts. Many of the states utilize this formula and allow the creditor to obtain a deficiency even without notification or without a commercial reasonable sale, although a string of states totally bars a deficiency.[7]

TITLE LENDING

Sub-prime lending is a common term in the industry where auto finance companies extend credit to consumers who have poor credit ratings. Title lending practiced in many states is somewhat different. The consumer is seeking a small loan, usually less than $1,000. The title lender cuts a check for a one-month loan with interest ranging as high as 20% per month, which would run over 200% per year. The consumer then transfers title of the car to the lender and the lender usually insists upon a separate set of keys to the car so that they do not have to incur the expense of a tow job when time for repossession comes. As a rule, the lender will probably extend credit of no more than half the value of the car and in most instances, the car is probably valued at no more than $1,000 to $2,000.

While this is in the nature of a pawn operation, no federal regulation is in place to monitor this type of title lending. Regulation emanates from the states. Some of the states regulate or prohibit this type of lending, but

---

[6]*In re Huffman,* 204 B.R. 562 (Bankr. W.D. Mo. 1997).

[7]*Nationsbank of North Carolina v. American Doubloon Corp.,* 481 S.E. 2d 387 (N.C. Ct. App. 1997).

in many states, the lenders are successful in promoting favorable state legislation or the states themselves do not pay too much attention to enforcing their usury laws. In Florida, because the title lenders are classified as pawn shops, they do not have to return to the borrowers the excess if the sales price of the vehicle exceeds the unpaid loan balance. Some states such as Georgia and Tennessee have passed legislation favorable to title lenders. Regulation of title lending is through state laws and a careful examination of the state law is recommended. Nevertheless, the Uniform Commercial Code would still cover repossessions.

AFTER-ACQUIRED PROPERTY

Sometimes, a security agreement provides that the lien covers all inventory or all accounts receivable, but does not mention after-acquired property. Most courts adopt the theory that the Uniform Commercial Code contemplates that a security agreement should clearly spell out any claim to after-acquired collateral. Where the particular security is in the nature of revolving receivables, or revolving inventory, it would rarely, if ever, benefit a creditor to take a security interest in only the accounts receivable held by the debtor on the date of the security agreement or the inventory held by debtor on the date of the security agreement. These receivables and inventory would probably be liquidated in the normal course of the debtor's business and be replaced with new receivables throughout the business cycle. Therefore, it is incumbent upon the creditor to be certain that, in dealing with inventory or accounts receivable or any other type of revolving property, particular language is required to grant a security interest in inventory or accounts receivable to cover "after-acquired property."

The courts feel that it is neither onerous nor unreasonable to require a security agreement to set forth exactly what the collateral is. This position does not require the most exact and detailed description possible, but only a clear designation of any class of items intended to be collateral. It could be true that while many lenders, upon reading an agreement, would obtain an unambiguous explanation of its full meaning, some lenders might be misled and proceed without inquiry. The ease with which a secured party can eliminate the danger of misleading any reasonable subsequent lender suggests that specific language should be included.

Notwithstanding this sound reasoning, some courts treat inventory and accounts receivable to include after-acquired accounts receivable and after-acquired inventory on the theory that the parties did not intend that once the inventory or receivables are released, the lender would not have any security. Nevertheless, the reasoning of the majority of courts is sound and if you want protection, the specific words "after-acquired property" should be included in the security agreement.[8]

DEALERS-ONLY AUCTIONS

Is a dealers-only auction commercially unreasonable per se? The court said that such a holding would render dealers-only auctions (and possibly all wholesale auctions) unreasonable per se. The court did not hold that dealers-only auctions are commercially reasonable per se nor did they hold that they are commercially unreasonable per se. Plaintiff attempted to elicit testimony that Ford Credit would have been able to sell a car at retail at one of the Ford dealerships. A witness testified that the dealers would not repossess a car to put on their lot for sale. Dealers auctions are used because if the vehicle is sold privately, the commissions and cost deductions would have probably resulted in the same price. The fact that the vehicle could have bought a higher price at a different sale or on a different day is not sufficient to overcome the evidence of commercial reasonableness.[9]

[8]*Claytor v. Shenandoah Warehouse Co. (In re Shenandoah Warehouse Co.)*, 202 B.R. 871 (Bankr. W.D. Va. 1996).

[9]*Ford Motor Credit Co. v. Sagmiller (In re Estate of Sagmiller)*, 2000 ND 151, 615 N.W. 2d 567 (2000) Supreme Court of North Dakota.

CHAPTER 8

APPENDIX I

REPRESENTATIVE SAMPLE OF POST-REPOSSESSION REQUIREMENTS FOR MOTOR VEHICLES (RETAIL ACCOUNTS)—(COMPILED IN 1999)

	Post-Repo Notice Required?	Given Within No. of Days	Manner of Mailing?	Must Right to Reinstate Be Given? If Yes, Any Exceptions? No. of Days	Amounts to Reinstate	Notice of Sale Requirements
Alabama	No.	N/A	N/A	N/A	N/A	Reasonable notification of the time and place of any public sale, and reasonable notification of the time after which private sale or other intended disposition is to be made. Alabama Code § 7-9-504(3)
Arizona	No.	N/A	N/A	N/A	N/A	Reasonable notification of the time and place of public sale, and reasonable notification of the time after which private sale or other intended disposition is to be made. Arizona Rev. Stat. § 47-9504. The buyer is not liable for the deficiency if the original cash sale price of the vehicle was $1,000 or less. Arizona Rev. Stat. § 44-5501.B. Buyer liable if vehicle wrongfully damaged or if buyer refuses to give up vehicle. Id.

Reprinted with permission of Hudson Cook LLP.

State						
Colorado	No. Police must be notified at least one hour after, repossession occurs, name of owner, name of repossessor, name of mortgagee or assignee, and that repossessor must be licensed and bonded in Colorado. Colo. Rev. Stat. § 42-6-146; 4-9-503.5.	N/A	No.	N/A	N/A	Reasonable notice of sale. Colo. Rev. Stat. § 4-8-504. If the holder repossesses (with or without the aid of judicial process) or voluntarily accepts surrender of the vehicle, the buyer/co-buyer is not personally liable to the holder if the original cash sale price of the vehicle was $2,100 or less. Colo. Rev. Stat. § 5-5-103. Holder's remedies not limited to damages to vehicle because of conversion, destruction, or other wrongful conduct. Id.
Connecticut	If a notice of intent to repossess has not been provided to the buyer, holder must provide a written statement of the unaccelerated sum due under the contract and the actual and reasonable expenses of any retaking and storing (i.e., a reinstatement notice). Conn. Gen. Stat. § 36a-785(c). Notice must be given to local police dept. immediately after repossession if done without buyer's knowledge. Conn. Gen. Stat.§ 36a-785(a).	If a notice of intent to repossess has not been provided to the buyer, the statement must be mailed within 3 days of the retaking. Conn. Gen. Stat. §36a-785(c).	If a notice of intent to repossess has not been provided to the buyer, the statement must be mailed by registered or certified mail to the last known address of the buyer. Conn. Gen. Stat. § 36a-785(c).	If a notice of intent to repossess vehicle has not been provided, the vehicle must be retained in the state where it was repossessed for 15 days after repossession. Buyer has right to reinstate the contract and obtain possession of the vehicle within the 15-day period. If the voluntary notice of intent to repossess has been provided to the buyer, no right to reinstate need be given. Conn.Gen. Stat. § 36a-785(b).	Payment of past due payments under the contract at the time of repossession or upon performance or tender of performance of such other condition as may be named in the contract is precedent to the buyer's continued possession of vehicle, or upon performance or tender of performance of any other promise, and payment of the actual and reasonable expenses of any retaking and storage. Conn. Gen. Stat. § 36a-785(c). If the notice of intent to repossess or the reinstatement notice is not sent, the holder forfeits the right to claim payment for the actual and reasonable expenses of retaking and storage, and will also be liable for the actual damages suffered because of such failure. Id.	Not less than 10 days written notice of the time and place of any public sale, or the time after which any private sale or other intended disposition is to be made, either personally or by registered mail or by certified mail, return receipt requested, to the buyer at the last known place of business or residence. Sale must be not more than 180 days after repossession. Special sale procedure when vehicle taken by legal process. Conn. Gen. Stat. § 36a-785(d). Proceeds on resale shall be considered to be either the amount paid for the vehicle at the sale or the fair cash market value at the time of repossession, whichever is greater. Id. Fair cash market value is defined as 1/2 sum of average trade-in value plus average retail value as stated in NADA Guide Eastern Edition as of date of repossession. Conn Gen. Stat. § 36a-785(g). Buyer liable for deficiency balance if original cash sale price of vehicle more than $2,000. Id.
Delaware	No.	N/A	No.	N/A	N/A	Reasonable notification of the time and place of any public sale, and reasonable notification of the time after which any private sale or other intended disposition is to be made. Delaware Code Ann. § 9-504(3).

Reprinted with permission of Hudson Cook LLP.

	Post-Repo Notice Required?	Given Within No. of Days	Manner of Mailing?	Must Right to Reinstate Be Given? If Yes, Any Exceptions? No. of Days	Amounts to Reinstate	Notice of Sale Requirements
District of Columbia	Yes. Notice of repossession must be given to Metropolitan Police Dept. § 340.4 DCMR Notice of repossession must be given to buyer. § 341.4 DCMR No limits on scope of application.	Notice to police must be given within 1 hour of repossession. Notice to buyer must be given within 5 days of repossession. § 341.4 DCMR	Manner of giving notice to police not specified- presumably verbal. Notice to buyer must be given by personal service or by registered or certified mail, sent to the buyer's last known address, § 341.4 DCMR	Yes. Buyer has the right to cure and redeem vehicle within 15 days from the date holder's post-repossession notice delivered or mailed. Vehicle must be held in the District of Columbia or state or county in which consumer resides. §341.5 DCMR	Amount due under contract without acceleration and if notice of cure sent, costs of retaking and storing vehicle. Cure of any other defaults leading to repossession. §342.1 DCMR	10 days notice by personal service, registered or certified mail of the time and place of a public sale or auction or after which a private sale will take place; however, if less than 50% of sale price for the vehicle has been paid by buyer, buyer may demand public sale or auction within 15 days of receipt of post repo notice- demand must be accompanied by $15 fee. § 344.1 DCMR. If 50% or more of sale price has been paid, vehicle must be sold at public auction. § 344.2 DCMR.
Florida	No.	N/A	N/A	N/A	N/A	Reasonable notification of time and place of any public sale, and reasonable notification of the time after which any private sale or other intended disposition is to be made. Notice of sale must also be given to any guarantor. Fla. Stats. §679.504(3). Buyer is not liable for deficiency balance if balance at time of default is less than $2,000. Fla. Stats. §516.31.
Georgia	Yes. In order for holder to hold buyer liable for a deficiency: must give notice of buyer's right of redemption and right to demand public sale. § 10-1-36 O.C.G. No limits on scope of application.	Within 10 days after repossession. § 10-1-36 O.C.G.	Registered or certified mail to buyer at address shown on contract or last known address. §10-1-36 O.C.G.	Notice of holder's intention to pursue a deficiency claim shall include rights or redemption and right to demand public sale. § 10-1-36 O. C. G.	N/A	NOTE: If holder gives post repo notice, buyer may demand public sale of vehicle in writing sent to lender by certified/registered mail within 10 days of the posting of holder's post repo notice. § 10-1-36 O.C.G. If buyer elects public sale, sale must be held in state or county where original sale took place or state and county where the vehicle was repossessed. § 10-1-36 O.C.G.
Indiana	No.	N/A	N/A	N/A	N/A	Reasonable notification of the time and place of any public sale, or reasonable notification of the time after which any private sale or other intended disposition is to be made must be sent to the buyer. Indiana UCC § 9-504(3). If the holder repossesses or accepts a voluntary surrender of the vehicle and the original cash price was $3,000 or less, the buyer is not personally liable for the deficiency balance. Indiana UCCC § 5.103.

Reprinted with permission of Hudson Cook LLP.

State						
Iowa	No.	N/A	N/A	N/A	N/A	Reasonable notification of the time and place of any public sale or reasonable notification of the time after which any private sale or other intended disposition is to be made must be sent to the buyer. Iowa UCC § 9-504(3). Right to cure notice must be sent if vehicle voluntarily surrendered and buyer is to be liable for any deficiency balance. Iowa Credit Code § 537.5110.
Kansas	No.	N/A	N/A	N/A	N/A	Reasonable notification of the time and place of any public sale or reasonable notification of the time after which any private sale or other intended disposition is to be made must be sent to the buyer Kansas UCC § 9-504(3). Buyer not personally liable for deficiency balance if original sale price of vehicle less than $1,000. Kansas Stat. Ann. §16a-5-103.
Kentucky	No.	N/A	N/A	N/A	N/A	Reasonable notification of the time and place of any public sale or reasonable notification of the time after which any private sale or other intended disposition is to be made must be sent to the buyer. Kentucky UCC § 9-504(3). NOTE: The dealer's licensing section of the Kentucky Motor Vehicle Commission advises that consignment sales are not permitted in Kentucky.
Maryland	Subtitle 6: Yes. Md. Code Ann., Com. Law II § 12-624(d). "Goods" with a cash sale price $25,000 or less. Md. Code Ann., Com. Law II § 12-601. Subtitle 10: Yes. Md. Code Ann., Coml. Law II §12-1021(e). Vehicle purchased for personal, family, or household purposes. Md. Code Ann., Com. Law	Subtitle 6: Within 5 days of repossession. Md. Code Ann., Com. Law II §1-624(d). Subtitle 10: Within 5 days of repossession. Md. Code Ann., Com. Law II §12-1021(e).	Subtitle 6: Personal service or registered or certified mail to last known address Md. Code Ann., Com. Law II § 12-624(d). Subtitle 10: Personal service or registered or certified mail to last known address Md. Code Ann.,	Subtitle 6: Holder must retain vehicle in county where vehicle was sold to buyer or where repossessed for 15 days. Md. Code Ann., Com. Law II § 12-625(a). Both Subtitle 6 and Subtitle 10: For 15 days after the holder gives a required post-repossession notice, the buyer may redeem the vehicle. Md. Code Ann., Com. Law II §§ 12-625(a) and 12-1021(g). The notice must briefly state: (i) the right of the buyer to redeem the vehicle, and the amount payable for it; (ii) the rights of the	Subtitle 6: Past due payments, late charges, and if notice to cure given, actual and reasonable expenses of repossession and storage. Cure any other breach. Md. Code Ann., Com. Law II § 625(c). Subtitle 10: Amount due under agreement at time of redemption without giving effect of any provision which allows acceleration of any	Subtitle 6: If buyer has paid at least 50% of cash price of vehicle and requests in writing within 15-day period vehicle be sold at public auction, sent by registered or certified mail, vehicle must be so sold. Buyer must deposit lesser of 10% of time balance or $10 to cover costs of sale. If no deposit, holder may notify buyer in writing sent by registered or certified mail and if buyer fails to make deposit within 5 days after receives notice, right to have public sale forfeit. Public auction shall take place within 30 days from date buyer requested. sale. Holder shall give buyer at least 10 days notice of time and place of sale, sent

Reprinted with permission of Hudson Cook LLP.

	Post-Repo Notice Required?	Given Within No. of Days	Manner of Mailing?	Must Right to Reinstate Be Given? If Yes, Any Exceptions? No. of Days	Amounts to Reinstate	Notice of Sale Requirements
Maryland (Cont.)	II § 12-1001(d).		Com. Law II § 12-1021(e).	buyer with respect to resale, and his liability for a deficiency; and (iii) the exact location where the vehicle is stored and the address where any payment is to be made. Md. Code Ann., Com. Law II §§ 12-624(d) and 12-1021(g). If the default that lead to the current repossession occurred within 18 months of the last repossession, or if the buyer was guilty of fraudulent conduct or intentionally and wrongfully concealed, removed, damaged, or destroyed the vehicle or attempted to do so, and the vehicle was repossessed because of that conduct, the holder is not required to give the buyer notice of the right to redeem the vehicle. Md. Code Ann., Com. Law II §§ 12-624(e) and 12-1021(i)(l). Subtitle 6: Reinstatement rights need not be given if vehicle seized by police department and the vehicle was repossessed because of that seizure. Md. Code Ann. §12-625(d).	installment payable after that time. Md. Code Ann., Com. Law II, Com. Law II §12-1021(h)(1).	by registered or certified mail. Buyer liable for deficiency if original cash price of goods in excess of $2,000 and buyer has not paid at least 50% or has paid more than 50% but not requested a public auction. Written accounting must be sent to buyer containing specified information. Md. Code Ann., Com. Law II §12-626. Subtitle 10: At least 10 days before a public auction or private sale, the holder must notify the buyer in writing of the time and place of the sale, by certified mail, return receipt requested, sent to the buyer's last known address. Md. Code Ann., Com. Law II § 12-1021(j). In all cases of a private sale of a repossessed vehicle, a full written accounting containing specified information must be given to buyer and holder must retain a copy of the accounting for at least two years. *Id.*
Massachusetts	No. Within one hour after the vehicle is repossessed, the creditor must notify the local police dept. that the vehicle has been repossessed and identify the vehicle. M.G.L. c255B § 20C.	N/A	N/A	No.	N/A	Reasonable notification of the time and place of any public sale or reasonable notification of the time after which any private sale or any intended disposition is to be made must be sent to the buyer. Massachusetts UCC § 9-504.
Michigan	No.	N/A	N/A	N/A	N/A	Reasonable notification of the time and place of any public sale or reasonable notification of the time after which any private sale or other intended disposition is to be made must be sent to the buyer. Mich. Comp. Laws Ann. § 440.9504.

Reprinted with permission of Hudson Cook LLP.

Minnesota	No.	N/A	N/A	N/A		Reasonable notification of the time and place of any public sale or reasonable notification of the time after which any private sale or other intended disposition is to be made must be sent to the buyer. Minn. Stats. § 366.9-504. Buyer not liable for deficiency balance if original credit extended was more than $5,100. Minn. Stats. § 325G.22.
Missouri	No. A repossessor must give notice of repossession with the buyer's knowledge to a local law enforcement agency where the repossession occurred within 2 hours of repossession. Mo. Rev. Stat. § 304.155(12).	N/A	N/A	N/A		Reasonable notification of the time and place of any public sale or reasonable notification of the time after which any private sale or other intended disposition is to be made. Mo. Rev. Stat. § 400.9-504. NOTE: When a holder sells or otherwise disposes of collateral consisting of a motor vehicle with an original cash sale price of $7,500 or less, an action for a deficiency may not be commenced against the buyer until the holder has first given the buyer a detailed notice containing the name, address and telephone number of the holder to whom the payment of the deficiency is to be made, an identification of the vehicle sold, the date of the sale, the amount due the holder prior to the sale of the vehicle, the expenses deducted from the sale price, and the remaining deficiency. Mo. Rev. Stat. § 408.557.
Nevada	Yes, see note. NRS § 482.516. A repossession must be immediately reported to the police of sheriff's office where the repossession occurs. NRS § 482.518.	At least 10 days prior to sale. Within 60 days after repossession in order to collect a deficiency judgment. NRS § 482.516.	Not specified by statute.	No.	The buyer will be liable for any deficiency only if the notice is given within 60 days after repossession and includes an itemization of the balance and of any costs or fees for delinquency, collection or repossession. In addition, the notice must either set forth the computation or estimate of the amount of any credit for unearned finance charges or canceled insurance as of the	At least 10 days' written notice of intent to sell a repossessed vehicle must be given to all persons liable on the contract. The notice must be given in person or sent by mail to the buyer's address on the contract or the last known address, and: (i) set forth that there is a right to redeem the vehicle and the total amount required as of the date of the notice to redeem; (ii) inform such persons of their privilege of reinstatement of the security agreement, if the holder extends such a privilege; (iii) give notice of the holder's intent to resell

157

Reprinted with permission of Hudson Cook LLP.

	Post-Repo Notice Required?	Given Within No. of Days	Manner of Mailing?	Must Right to Reinstate Be Given? If Yes, Any Exceptions? No. of Days	Amounts to Reinstate	Notice of Sale Requirements
Nevada (Cont.)					date of the notice or state that such a credit may be available against the amount due. NRS § 482.516.	the vehicle at the expiration of 10 days from the date of giving or mailing the notice; (iv) disclose the place at which the vehicle will be returned to the buyer upon redemption or reinstatement; and (v) designate the name and address of the person to whom payment must be made. NRS § 482.516.
New Hampshire	No. Within 2 hours of repossession, any person who repossesses a vehicle must notify a police officer of the town or city, or if none, the county sheriff's dept., of the repossession, and give the name, address and telephone number of the owner and lienholder. N.H. Rev. Stat. Ann. § 262:3-a.	N/A	N/A	N/A	N/A	Reasonable notification of the time and place of any public sale, or reasonable notification of the time after which any private sale or other intended disposition is to be made. N.H. Rev. Stat. Ann. § 382-A:9-504(3).
New Jersey	No.	N/A	N/A	No.	N/A	Reasonable notification of the time and place of any public sale or reasonable notification of the time after which any private sale or other intended disposition is to be made. N.J. Rev. Stat. § 12A:9-504(3).
New York	Within 72 hours after taking possession, the secured party must mail or deliver a written notice to the buyer at the last known address. NY Pers. Prop. L. § 316. Installment sale of vehicle for personal, family, or household purposes. NY Pers. Prop. L. § 301(4).	The holder must mail or deliver a written notice to the buyer at the last known address within 72 hours of the repossession. NY Pers. Prop. L. § 316.	The holder must deliver a written notice to the buyer at the last known address within 72 hours of the repossession. NY Pers. Prop. L. § 316.	The notice must set forth: (i) the buyer's right to redeem the vehicle, (ii) the dollar amount necessary to redeem the vehicle; and (iii) the name, address and telephone number of the creditor the debtor may contact for additional information. NY Pers. Prop. L. § 316.	Past due payments, late charges, reasonable and actual costs of repossession and storing the vehicle, other performance required to cure default.	Reasonable notification of the time and place of any public sale or reasonable notification of the time after which any private sale or other intended disposition is to be made. NY Comm. Code § 9-504(3).

Reprinted with permission of Hudson Cook LLP.

State						
New York (Cont.)	The repossessor must immediately appear at a local police dept. to give notice of the repossession. Within 24 hours of the repossession, the holder must: (i) notify the DMV in person or by special delivery first class mail, and (ii) notify the vehicle's owner personally or by registered or certified mail. NY Veh. & Traf. L. § 425.					
North Carolina	No.	N/A	N/A	N/A	N/A	Reasonable notification of the time and place of any public sale, and reasonable notification of the time after which any private sale or other intended disposition is to be made. N.C. Stat. § 25-9-504(3). If surplus, it must be paid to buyer. Special proceedings to determine ownership of surplus if party to whom surplus should be paid is unknown. N.C. Stat. § 25-9-504.2.
Ohio	Yes, Ohio Rev. Code § 1317.12. "Goods" purchased primarily for personal, family, or household purposes. Ohio Rev. Code § 1317.01(d).	Within 5 days after taking possession. Ohio Rev. Code § 1317.12.	No specific requirement for mailing. If combined with notice of sale, must be sent certified mail, return receipt requested.	Buyer permitted to "cure" default by paying within 20 days or repossession or 15 days after notice sent, whichever is later. Right to cure default pursuant to these provisions may only be exercised once with respect to a single debt. Ohio Rev. Code § 1317.12.	Buyer must pay all past due installments, unpaid late charges, actual and reasonable expenses of repossession (provided that any portion over $25 need not be paid at the time of reinstatement but added to time balance) and a deposit by cash or bond in the amount of 2 installments to secure timely payment of future. Ohio Rev. Code § 1317.12. Holder may require buyer to pay transportation charges if vehicle returned to place of repossession at request of buyer. Id.	Disposition by public sale only 10 days' notice of time and place of sale and of minimum price for bid required. Notice must include statement that buyer will be liable for any deficiency. Notice must be sent by certified mail, return receipt requested, to buyer at last known address and to any other party known to have an interest in the vehicle. Notice of sale must be published at least 10 days prior to sale in a newspaper of general circulation in the county where the vehicle is to be held. Ohio Rev. Code § 1317.16.
Oregon	No.	N/A	N/A	N/A	N/A	Reasonable notification of the time and place of any public sale or reasonable notification of the time after which any private sale or other intended disposition is to be made. O.R.S. § 79.5040.

Reprinted with permission of Hudson Cook LLP.

	Post-Repo Notice Required?	Given Within No. of Days	Manner of Mailing?	Must Right to Reinstate Be Given? If Yes, Any Exceptions? No. of Days	Amounts to Reinstate	Notice of Sale Requirements
Pennsyl-vania	Yes. A written notice of repossession must be sent to a buyer of the motor vehicle. Also, within 24 hours after repossession, the repossessor must give notice to the local municipal police dept. or if no local police, to the PA State Police. 69 Pa. Stat. § 623.H.	No days specified, rather notice must be given "immediately" 69 Pa. Stat. § 623.D.	Personal delivery or registered or certified mail directed to the last known address of the buyer. 69 Pa. Stat. § 623.D.	Notice of repossession must: (i)set forth the buyer's right as to reinstatement of the contract if the holder extends the privilege of reinstatement and redemption of the motor vehicle, (ii) confirm an itemized statement of the total amount required to redeem the motor vehicle by reinstatement or repayment of the contract in full, (iii) give notice to the buyer of the holder's intent to resell the motor vehicle at the expiration of 15 days from the date of mailing such notice, (iv) disclose the place at which the motor vehicle is stored, and (v) must designate the name and address of the person to whom the buyer shall make payment, or upon whom he may serve notice. 69 Pa. Stat. § 623. D.	If reinstatement offered, past due payments, late charges, and if contract is in default more than 15 days at the time of repossession, actual and reasonable costs of repossession and storage, legal costs incurred in obtaining possession of the vehicle.	Reasonable notification of the time and place of any public sale or reasonable notification of the time after which any private sale or other intended disposition is to be made. 13 Pa. Stat. § 9504.
Rhode Island	No.	N/A	N/A	N/A	N/A	Reasonable notification of the time and place of any public sale or reasonable notification of the time after which any private sale or other intended disposition is to be made. R.I. Gen. Laws § 6A-9-504.
Tennessee	No.	N/A	N/A	N/A	N/A	Reasonable notification of the time and place of any public sale or reasonable notification of the time after which any private sale or other intended disposition is to be made. Tenn. Code Ann. § 47-9-504(3).
Texas	No.	N/A	N/A	N/A	N/A	Reasonable notification of the time and place of any public sale or reasonable notification of the time after which any private sale or other intended disposition is to be made. Tex. Rev. Civ. Statutes § 9.504(3).
Virginia	No.	N/A	N/A	N/A	N/A	Reasonable notification of the time and place of any public sale or reasonable notification of the time after which any private sale or other intended disposition is to be made. Code of Va. § 8.9.504(3).

Reprinted with permission of Hudson Cook LLP.

State					
Washington	No.	N/A	N/A	N/A	N/A	Reasonable notification of the time and place of any public sale or reasonable notification of the time after which any private sale or other intended disposition is to be made. Wash. Rev. Code Ann. § 62A 9-504. NOTE: A recent amendment to Washington's Article 9 of the UCC removed a non-uniform provision that prohibited the right to a deficiency under most consumer conditional sale contracts after repossession. Prior to this amendment, creditors holding consumer purchase money conditional sale contracts only had the following options on default: (i) repossess the collateral non-judicially and thereby lose the right to a deficiency, (ii) judicially foreclose but thereby retain the right to a deficiency. As a result of the amendment, which became effective July 27, 1997, a creditor no longer has to make the choice but may repossess and still have a right to a deficiency. Wash. Rev. Code Ann. § 62A 9-501.
Wisconsin	No. Wisconsin Consumer Act applies to consumer credit transactions of $25,000 or less. Wisc. Stats. § 421.202(6). NOTE: Self-help repossession not permitted. Replevin action to obtain possession of vehicle required. Wisc. Stats. § 425.205.	N/A	N/A	If the vehicle has been abandoned, the holder may take possession and send written notice to the buyer at the last known address. Buyer has right to recover vehicle in which case, costs incurred in returning the vehicle must be paid by holder. Wisc. Stats. § 425.207(2). The Wisconsin Consumer Act allows a consumer 15 days after non-judicial or commencement of judicial enforcement to cure the default and reinstate the contract. The creditor may not dispose of the vehicle until the period for redemption/reinstatement has passed.	All amounts in default plus reasonable and bona fide repossession costs, delinquency or deferral charges, court costs, filing and service fees. Wisc. Stats. § 425.208. The buyer must offer a performance deposit of 3 scheduled installments or minimum payments, or 1/3 of the total unpaid obligation, whichever is less.	Reasonable notification of the time and place of any public sale, or reasonable notification of the time after which any private sale or other intended disposition is to be made. Wisc. Stats. § 409.503(3). Buyer is not liable for vehicle repossessed or voluntarily surrendered if amount owing at the time of default was $1,000 or less. Wisc. Stats. § 425.209.

161

Reprinted with permission of Hudson Cook LLP.

	Post-Repo Notice Required?	Given Within No. of Days	Manner of Mailing?	Must Right to Reinstate Be Given? If Yes, Any Exceptions? No. of Days	Amounts to Reinstate	Notice of Sale Requirements
Puerto Rico	Repossession effected by filing with Secretary of Court affidavit of buyer's default. Laws of Puerto Rico, tit. 10, § 36. No limits on scope of application.	Secretary of Court cites parties into court to a hearing to be held within 10 days following the date of the citation. Laws of Puerto Rico, tit. 10, § 36.	Mailing by Secretary of Court not specified.	No. If buyer deemed to be in default, marshal ordered to seize the vehicle and deliver it to holder. Marshal files return with Court. Vehicle must be retained for 30 days following recovery. During 30-day period, buyer may reinstate account and recover possession of vehicle. Holder may choose between repossession of vehicle and action in court for the collection of money. If holder chooses repossession, it relinquishes right to collection action. Voluntary surrender of vehicle, with the consent of the holder, has same effect as repossession. Laws of Puerto Rico, tit. 10, § 36.	Amount of payments past due, late charges, actual and reasonable costs of repossession, storage.	If account is not reinstated and vehicle recovered by buyer within 30 days following repossession or surrender, vehicle may be disposed of by public auction sale. Vehicle must be sold within 30 days of expiration of first 30-day period. Laws of Puerto Rico, tit. 10, § 36.

APPENDIX II

REPRESENTATIVE SAMPLE OF PRE-REPOSSESSION REQUIREMENTS FOR MOTOR VEHICLES (RETAIL ACCOUNTS)

	Cure Notice Required?	No. of Days to Cure?	Manner of Mailing?	Must Cure Notice Be Given Every Time? If Not, When?	Requirements?
Alabama	No.	N/A	N/A	N/A	N/A
Arizona	No.	N/A	N/A	N/A	N/A
Colorado	Yes. After consumer has been in default for 10 days for failure to make a payment, send cure notice. Colo. Rev. Stat. § 5-5-111. Applies to consumer credit sales not to exceed $25,000. Colo. Rev. Stat. § 5-2-104(e).	Within 20 days after notice of right to cure is given. Colo. Rev. Stat. § 5-5-112.	Mail cure notice to buyer's last known address; certified or other special service is not required by law. Colo. Rev. Stat. § 5-5-111.	No. A notice of cure is required only when the default is for non-payment and only if no cure notice has been given to that buyer in the previous 12 months. Colo. Rev. Stat. § 5-5-112.	The notice must be in writing and state the holder's name, address, and telephone number. It must identify the transaction, state the buyer's right to cure, and the amount of the payment due (past due payments and late charges) and date by which the payment is due in order to cure the default. Colo. Rev. Stat. § 5-5-112. The buyer may voluntarily surrender the vehicle without receiving a notice of the right to cure the default.

Reprinted with permission of Hudson Cook LLP.

	Cure Notice Required?	No. of Days to Cure?	Manner of Mailing?	Must Cure Notice Be Given Every Time? If Not, When?	Requirements?
Connecticut	If vehicle held for outstanding balance on repossession, notice of intent to repossess must be given to buyer. Conn. Gen. Stat. § 36a-785. "Goods" includes motor vehicle used for personal, family, or household purposes having cash price of $50,000 or less. Conn. Gen. Stat. § 36a-770(c)(6). If notice of intent to repossess is not provided to buyer, a cure notice is required. Conn. Gen. Stat. § 36a-785.	No specific number of days to cure if notice of intent to repossess provided. Conn. Gen. Stat. § 36a-785. If no notice of intent to repossess is provided; must provide notice of right to cure within 3 days of repossession. In that event, the buyer has 15 days after repossession to cure. *Id.*	The notice of intent to repossess must be given to the buyer not less than 10 days prior to repossession by personal delivery or mailed, registered or certified mail. Conn. Gen. Stat. § 36a-785(b).	A cure notice is required only if notice of intent to repossess has not been given to the buyer. Conn. Gen. Stat. § 36a-785. Otherwise, if the buyer cures the default before the expiration of the cure period and the buyer later defaults again, it is recommended that another notice of intent to repossess the vehicle be provided to avoid the statutory right to cure.	The notice of intent to repossess must state the default and the period at the end of which the vehicle will be repossessed, and must briefly and clearly state buyer's rights under § 36a-785(b) of the Connecticut General Statutes in case the vehicle is repossessed. Conn. Gen. Stat. § 36a-785(b). Buyer may voluntarily surrender vehicle.
Delaware	No.	N/A	N/A	N/A	N/A
District of Columbia	Yes. A notice to cure must be given at least 10 days before any vehicle is repossessed. § 341.1 DCMR. See Note. No limits on scope of application.	At least 10 days prior to repossession. § 341.5 DCMR.	Personal service or registered or certified mail § 341.1 DCMR	Yes, unless buyer guilty of fraudulent conduct or intentionally and wrongfully concealed, removed, damaged or destroyed the vehicle or attempted to do so and vehicle is repossessed because of that conduct. § 343.2 DCMR NOTE: In order to (i) require the buyer to pay expenses of retaking and storing vehicle, and (ii) hold buyer liable for any deficiency, holder must give this notice. § 340.5, 341.1 & 342.1(c) DCMR.	Notice must explain: the default; action required to cure default; period after which vehicle will be repossessed; and the rights of the buyer if vehicle repossessed (i.e. right to cure, notice of sale, and right to demand public sale if 50% or more of vehicle sale price paid by buyer). §341.2 DCMR.
Florida	No. But, See Note.	N/A	N/A	N/A	NOTE: Where the lender has not insisted upon timely payments in the past, notice and demand for payment of past due payments would appear to be required before acceleration, based on case law. See *Commercial Credit Co. v. Willis*, 126 Fla. 444, 171 South 304, 1936 Fla. LEXIS 162B (1936); *Walker v. Ford Motor Credit Co.*, 484 So. 2d 61 (1986); *CJ Restaurant Enterprises, Inc. v. FMS Management Systems, Inc.*, 22 Fla. Law W.D. 1839, 1997 Fla. App. LEXIS 8642 (1997).

Reprinted with permission of Hudson Cook LLP.

State					
Georgia	No.	N/A	N/A	N/A	N/A
Indiana	No.	N/A	N/A	N/A	N/A
Iowa	Yes. Iowa Code § 537.5110(3). Vehicle for consumer purpose transactions of $25,000 or les[s] Iowa Code § 537.1301(12).	20 days from the date the notice is personally delivered to the buyer or from the date it is mailed to the buyer at the buyer's address. Iowa Code §§ 537.5110(4)(a) 537.5111(3).	Personally delivered or regular mail addressed to the buyer at the buyer's residence identified in the contract, or as subsequently identified by the buyer to the holder in writing. Iowa Code § 537.5111(3) and 537.1201(4).	A notice of right to cure must be delivered only *once* in any 365-day period. If the buyer defaults a second time within 365 days of a previous notice of right to cure, the notice need not be given again. Iowa Code § 537.5110(3).	The form of the notice is set forth in Iowa Code § 537.5111.
Kansas	Yes, the first time the buyer defaults and the holder wants to accelerate. Vehicles for consumer purpose with an amount financed of $25,000 or less. K.S.A. § 6a-1-301(10).	20 days after the notice is given. K.S.A. § 16a-5-111(2).	Personally delivered or mailed to the buyer's residence address identified in the contract or in a subsequent writing from the buyer. K.S.A. §§ 16a-5-110(1), 16a-1-201(6).	Cure notice must be given only once. The holder does not need to send a notice of right to cure again if the buyer cures the initial default and then defaults again. K.S.A. § 16a-5-111(3).	The form of the notice is set forth in K.S.A. § 16a-5-110(2).
Kentucky	No.	N/A	N/A	N/A	N/A
Maryland	Subtitle 6: Discretionary written notice of intention to repossess. Md. Code Ann. § 12-624. "Goods" cash sale price $25,000 or less. Md. Code Ann. § 12-601. Subtitle 10: Discretionary written notice of intent to repossess. Md. Code Ann. § 12-1021(c). Vehicle purchased for personal, family, or household purposes. Md. Code Ann. § 12-1001(d).	Subtitle 6: At least 10 days. Md. Code Ann. § 12-624(c). Subtitle 10: At least 10 days. Md. Code Ann. § 12-1021(c).	Subtitle 6: If notice of intent to repossess is given, must be sent by personal delivery or registered or certified mail to last known address. Md. Code Ann. § 12-624(c). Subtitle 10: If notice of intent to repossess is given, must be sent by personal delivery or registered or certified mail to last known address. Md. Code Ann. § 12-1021(d).	Subtitle 6: Notice is discretionary. If holder claims actual and reasonable expenses of retaking and storing the vehicle upon repossession, however, notice must be given. Md. Code Ann. § 12-625(d). Subtitle 10: Notice is discretionary. If holder claims actual and reasonable expenses of retaking and storing the vehicle upon repossession. However, notice must be given. Md. Code Ann. § 12-1021(h)(3).	Subtitle 6: The notice must state the default and any period at the end of which the vehicle will be repossessed and briefly state the rights of the buyer in case the vehicle is repossessed. Md. Code Ann. § 12-624(d). Subtitle 10: The notice must state the default and any period at the end of which the vehicle will be repossessed and briefly state the rights of the buyer in case the vehicle is repossessed. Md. Code Ann. § 12-1021(c).

Reprinted with permission of Hudson Cook LLP.

	Cure Notice Required?	No. of Days to Cure?	Manner of Mailing?	Must Cure Notice Be Given Every Time? If Not, When?	Requirements?
Massachusetts	Yes, if a consumer purpose transaction. M.G.L. c255B § 20A(b).	21 days after the notice is delivered. M.G.L. c255B § 20A(d).	Personal delivery or placed in U.S. Mail addressed to buyer at last known address. M.G.L. c255B § 20A(b).	The buyer gets 3 cures. If the buyer defaults a fourth time, no notice need be sent. M.G.L. c255B § 20A(b).	Buyer may cure default by paying past due payments and late charges, and curing any other default. M.G.L. c255B, § 2-A(e). Form provided.
Michigan	A creditor must send the co-signer a notice indicating that the primary obligor has become delinquent or defaulted on the obligation and that the co-signer is responsible for payment of the obligation. Mich. Comp. Laws Ann. § 445.272. A "co-signer" means a natural person who renders himself liable for the obligation of another person without compensation.** Mich. Comp. Laws Ann. § 445.271(c).	The co-signer must be given 30 days to respond to the notice by doing either of the following: (i) paying the amount then due under the obligation; (ii) making another arrangement satisfactory to the person to whom the obligation is owed. Mich. Comp. Laws Ann. § 445.272.	The co-signer notice must be sent by first class mail. Mich. Comp. Laws Ann. § 445.272. **A person who does not receive goods, services, or money in return for a credit obligation does not receive compensation within the meaning of this definition. Mich. Comp. Laws Ann. § 445.271(c)	Notice must be sent if holder intends to take any collection action against the co-signer. Mich. Comp. Laws Ann. § 445.272.	The co-signer notice must indicate that the primary obligation and that the co-signer is responsible for payment of the obligation. Mich. Comp. Laws Ann. § 445.272.
Minnesota	No, but See Note.	N/A	N/A	N/A	NOTE: Where the lessor or creditor has not insisted upon timely payments in the past, notice that the contract will be strictly interpreted in the future appears to be required before acceleration, based on case law. *Cobb v. Midwest Recovery*, 295 N.W.2d 232 (Minn. 1980).
Missouri	Yes, a cure notice is required to be given to a buyer and a co-signer for installment sale transactions where the cash sale price of the motor vehicle was $7,500 or less. See Mo. Rev. Stat. §§ 365.020(5); 365.145; 408.554.555.	20 days from the date the notice was given. Mo. Rev. Stat. §§ 408.554 and 408.555.	Personal delivery or by mailing the notice to last known address of the buyer and co-signer. Mo. Rev. Stat. § 408.554.	The buyer is entitled to the notice and right to cure only twice. Mo. Rev. Stat. § 408.555.3. However, on the second notice the holder must indicate that in the case of further default there is no right to cure. Mo. Rev. Stat. § 408.554.5	After a default consisting only of the buyer's failure to make a required payment for 10 days, the holder may neither accelerate nor take possession of vehicle until 20 days after a notice is given to the buyer and to all co-signers of the right to cure the default; and payment of the unpaid sums plus any unpaid delinquency charges will cure the default and restore the contract as though the default had not occurred. Mo. Rev. Stat. §§ 408.554 and 408.555.
Nevada	No, but See Note.	N/A	N/A	N/A	NOTE: Where the lessor or creditor has not insisted upon timely payments in the past, notice that the contract will be strictly interpreted in the future appears to be required before acceleration, based on case law. *Nevada Nat'l Bank v. Huff*, 94 Nev. 506, 582 P. 2d 364 (1978).

State				
New Hampshire	No.	N/A	N/A	N/A
New Jersey	No.	N/A	N/A	N/A
New York	No.	N/A	N/A	N/A
North Carolina	No.	N/A	N/A	N/A
Ohio	No.	N/A	N/A	N/A
Oregon	No.	N/A	N/A	N/A
Pennsylvania	No.	N/A	N/A	N/A
Rhode Island	No.	N/A	N/A	N/A
Tennessee	No.	N/A	N/A	N/A
Texas	Yes. See Note.	N/A	N/A	NOTE: Texas common law requires that debtors be provided with notice of intent to accelerate the debt and notice of acceleration. Notice of intent to accelerate a debt, in effect, provides the buyer with the opportunity to cure the default. The Texas Supreme Court has held that these common law rights may be waived by contract if the contract expressly provides for a waiver and expressly identifies the rights waived. *Shumway v. Horizon Credit Corp.*, 801 S.W.2d 890 (Tex. 1991). Forms Provided. *Also Note:* Where the lessor or creditor has not insisted upon timely payments in the past, notice that the contract will be strictly interpreted in the future appears to be required before acceleration, based on case law. *Ford Motor Credit v. Washington*, 573 S.W. 2d 616 (Tex. Civ. App. 1978).
Virginia	No.	N/A	N/A	N/A
Washington	No.	N/A	N/A	N/A

167

Reprinted with permission of Hudson Cook LLP.

	Cure Notice Required?	No. of Days to Cure?	Manner of Mailing?	Must Cure Notice Be Given Every Time? If Not, When?	Requirements?
Wisconsin	Yes. Wisc. Stats. § 425.104(1). Buyers in default on transactions of $25,000 or less (personal, family, or household purposes) must receive a cure notice.	15 days after notice is mailed. Wisc. Stats. § 425.105(1).	Not specified.	If the consumer has defaulted and cured twice in the preceding 12 months, there is no right to cure. Wisc. Stats. § 425.105(3).	Notice of default and right to cure must contain the name, address, and telephone number of the creditor (and other party to whom payment must be made) and a brief identification of the transaction. It must also state the nature of the default and the total payment, including an itemization of the delinquency charge, or performance necessary to cure the default, and the exact date by which the cure must occur. Wisc. Stats. § 425.104(2). NOTE: Self-help repossession is not permitted under the Wisconsin Consumer Act.
Puerto Rico	Yes. The holder must serve notice on the buyer if the buyer fails to pay any installment. The notice must be sent at the shortest possible time and before the next installment falls due. No limits on scope of application. Laws of Puerto Rico, tit. 10, § 760. Prior to repossession, the holder must file an affidavit with the Secretary of a Court showing the breach by the buyer. The Secretary will cite the parties to a hearing and order the marshall to seize the property if it appears the buyer has failed to comply with the contract. The marshall files a return with the Secretary. Laws of Puerto Rico, tit. 10, § 36. See Note.	No specific number of days specified. Laws of Puerto Rico, tit. 10, § 760.	No manner of mailing specified. Laws of Puerto Rico, tit. 10, § 760. Secretary of Court cites parties to a hearing to be held within 10 days of citation. Laws of Puerto Rico, tit. 10, § 36.	Yes.	Notice must specify failure to pay installment and corresponding late charge. Laws of Puerto Rico, tit. 10, § 760. NOTE: Holder may only accelerate if: (i) buyer in default for 3 consecutive payments; (ii) buyer in default one installment and if on 2 or more prior occasions buyer in default 2 or more consecutive installments; or (iii) buyer in default one or more consecutive installments and makes a partial payment and continues to pay, but continues to default for the remainder of the amount due for 3 consecutive installments following the date on which the partial payment was made. Laws of Puerto Rico, tit. 10, § 749.

168

Reprinted with permission of Hudson Cook LLP.

CHAPTER 9

Harassment, Intimidation, and Invasion of Privacy

GRAMM-LEACH-BLILEY ACT

On November 12, 1999, President Clinton signed into law the Gramm-Leach-Bliley, running about 400 or more pages, which will create some dramatic changes in the financial services industry. It constitutes an overhaul of various laws affecting the financial services industry that were enacted after the banking holiday in the early 1930's (when the banks were closed) and which were designed to avoid some of the provisions of the "Glass-Steagall Act" which separated the banking industry from other industries. The Act imposes an array of new requirements on financial institutions with respect to customer privacy. The FTC reported that compliance will be voluntary until July 1, 2001.

The new Act applies to any institution whose business engages in any activity that is financial in nature or incidental to a financial activity. Anyone actually engaged in this activity would be covered by the Act. The Act also covers activities that are now authorized for financial holding companies, which may cover such diverse activities as travel agencies. The broad definition in the Act might even extend to a one-time debtor-creditor relationship, even if the debtor-creditor relationship is minor or incidental to carrying on a business. The regulations may broaden or narrow terminology in the Act, but setting forth fine black-and-white limitations and restrictions will have to wait for the regulations to be issued.

The Act applies to non-public personal information that is obtained by the financial institution although no real definition of personal information is set forth. The financial institution must provide to the consumer clear and conspicuous disclosures concerning the privacy of the consumer, including its policies and practices on disclosing to affiliates, on protecting the information, and on disclosing information of customers who are no longer customers. The consumer certainly has an opportunity to opt out of sharing the financial information. The institution must make clear and conspicuous disclosure to the consumer of what information may be disclosed to third parties and how the consumer can make contact with the financial institution to opt out of said disclosure.

One cannot use false pretenses to obtain information maintained by or for a financial institution. The Act provides for criminal penalties. Under the new law, any person, including an attorney or a debt collector, could be fined substantial amounts or be imprisoned for contacting a financial institution to obtain financial information about a consumer under false pretenses.

The definition of a financial institution is broad and includes any loan or finance company, any credit card issuer, an operator of a credit card system, and any consumer reporting agency that compiles and maintains files on consumers on a nationwide basis (Section 603(p) of the Consumer Credit Protection Act). By including credit reporting agencies within the definition of the financial institution, persons who obtain credit reports must be careful that they do so only for permissible purposes.

Customers do not have any rights under the statute to bring lawsuits, but the Federal Trade Commission and the Federal Bank Regulatory Agency are designated as the agencies to enforce the Act.

A state law will prevail only to the extent that state authority is not inconsistent with the Act. If the state provides greater protection for the consumer, it is not deemed to be inconsistent. At least in this area, the banks were successful in not providing a private right of action to consumers and the cottage industry of consumer attorneys. In Appendix I, we have included a portion of the Gramm-Leach-Bliley Act, thirty-six pages dealing with the disclosure of non-public information and of fraudulent access to financial information.

By July 1, 2001 (the date the Act took effect), financial institutions must have provided notice to existing customers that they may opt out of sharing financial information. A consumer is anyone who obtains a financial product or a service, whereas a customer is someone who has a customer relationship with the financial institution. This means the customer is either depositing money with the bank or is investing or has already obtained some form of credit from the institution.

In the privacy area, the Act generally stated that financial institutions are required to give their customers the right to opt out of having information shared with third parties, but expressly allowing the banks to share with their affiliates. The financial institutions must establish clear policies as to the use of customer data, both at the time of establishing a customer relationship and yearly thereafter.

A privacy notice must be provided by the institution at the time of establishing any type of customer relationship prior to sharing any non-public information with non-affiliated third parties. This notice must be provided at least once during every 12-month period. The opt-out notice must contain a description of: (1) non-public information that is disclosed to affiliates and non-affiliated parties; (2) categories of parties to whom the information will be disclosed; and (3) policies regarding confidentiality and security of non-public personal information. These notices must be provided before any sharing of the information and this sharing will be performed unless the customer opts out. A reasonable means of opting out must be provided, such as reply form or toll-free number.

The consumer must be provided a 30-day window to opt out, but an opt-out received after the reasonable time will stop all future disclosures.

GRAMM-LEACH-BLILEY—
COLLECTION AGENCIES

The Act is somewhat hazy with regard to the application of the Act to collection agencies. Purchasers of debt are financial institutions under the Gramm-Leach-Bliley. As of the writing of this book, no case law has discussed to what extent collection agencies and/or law firms are subject to the Act. The Federal Trade Commission certainly has expressed the belief that debt collection agencies are financial institutions based on prior interpretations of the Bank Holding Company Act of 1956.[1]

GRAMM-LEACH-BLILEY—
SOCIAL SECURITY NUMBERS

Congress passed an act to include the social security number within the Gramm-Leach-Bliley Act. Specifically, the bill stated that notwithstanding any other provision of the Act, no financial institution may sell or purchase a social security number or a social security account number in a manner that violates the regulations. In essence, a social security number is financial information.

GRAMM-LEACH-BLILEY—
FINANCIAL INFORMATION

There is presently significant litigation concerning the issue of whether the name, address, and telephone number is financial information under the Financial Services Modernization Act (FSMA). The question is whether the term "nonpublic personal information," which is contained in the Financial Services Modernization Act, includes the name, address, and telephone number. The Federal Trade Commission in its final rules stated that the name, address, and telephone number was considered to be financial information.

These decisions will certainly affect the catalog owners and direct marketers as well as some of the websites with regard to the sharing of consumer information, both with affiliates and third parties, especially with regard to the right of the consumers to opt-out.

HIPPA

The Health Insurance Patient Portability and Accountability Act was passed in 1996 and on December 20, 2000 the privacy requirement rules were released by the U.S. Department of Health and Human Services. The

---

[1] *In re Wollin,* 249 B.R. 555 (Bkrtcy. D. Oregon 2000).

Act will have a significant impact upon "business associates" of health-care organizations, which include collection agencies and attorneys.

The new regulations provide consumers with new rights to control the release of their medical information, including advance consent for most disclosures of health information, the right to obtain documentation of disclosures, and the right to an explanation of the privacy rights and how this information is being used.

The final regulations deal directly with the procedures for releasing medical information. Patients are provided new rights to access their medical records and to know to whom the medical records were released. The disclosure of any medical records are restricted on a need-to-know basis and only for the purpose intended. New criminal and civil sanctions for violations of the rules now apply.

A valid business associate (collection agency or law firm) contract should include the use to which the medical information is intended and how the medical information will be protected from use other than its intended purpose. The healthcare provider should have the right to terminate the contract if there is a violation of the contract. The business associate should not disclose any medical information other than is permitted or required by the contract and use adequate protection to prevent the disclosure of the information to third parties. The business associate should be required to notify the healthcare provider if a violation of the contract occurs. The medical information released should always be available to the patient upon request by the healthcare organization.

The business associate also should organize its records so that the medical information is available to the Secretary of the Department of Health and Human Services, in the event it should be required to demonstrate that the healthcare provider has been complying with the HIPPA.

In the event the debtor requests verification information and disclosure of the medical services rendered, the debt collector should insist upon a request for verification information *in writing*. The documentation that should be furnished should clarify the amount of the debt and identify the proper creditor. If the debtor should request a copy of the billing statement, this request should be made in writing and should not be fulfilled merely upon an oral request over the telephone. The debt collector should request that the debtor specify the time period that is requested and the nature of the services rendered so that same may be readily identified by the healthcare provider. If the healthcare provider should request a written consent, which does occur, the debt collector should obtain the form of the consent from the healthcare provider and furnish it to the debtor to execute. The debtor should not be able to insist on the debt collector utilizing the request for verification as a substitute for the consent form provided by the medical provider. Nevertheless, this is an issue that should be taken up with the healthcare provider.

A written agreement should be entered into between the agency or law firm and the healthcare provider concerning their responsibilities under HIPPA. The contract should incorporate the requirements set forth in the final regulations which were promulgated.

The President had considered delaying the effectiveness of these rules but allowed the rules to take affect on April 14, 2001. The rules will probably be modified since this Administration seems to feel that some of the rules are unfair to the health industry. After April 14, 2003 a person who violates the rules will be subject to civil and criminal penalties, including a fine up to $250,000 and ten years in prison for the most egregious violations.

Since the law does not become effective until April 14, 2003, many of the trade associations will undoubtedly publish numerous articles on compliance with HIPPA. A careful reading of the law is necessary and consultation with counsel is in order. In the Appendix are appropriate excerpts from HIPPA.

INVASION OF PRIVACY

When the First Edition of this book was printed in 1996, the issue of privacy was just beginning to gain the attention of the state legislatures and Congress as well as becoming a growing concern of the American people. Four years later, the issue of privacy was raised in the presidential election in November of 2000 by both candidates, as it has become more and more a major concern of the population.

It should come as no surprise that the universe of credit and collection is also being impacted by the continuing obligation to respect the privacy of the consumer and to protect the security and the confidentiality of the personal information of the consumer.

In a case in Illinois, the husband was offered a home equity loan to pay off his credit card debts of over $100,000. The husband declined the offer of the home equity loan, but the loan officer was persistent and made several more solicitation calls at the husband's place of business. Notwithstanding that the husband declined all these offers, the loan officer again contacted the husband, telling him that he would like to talk to his spouse to advise her of the husband's debt situation and the advisability of a home equity loan. The husband declined again because he had taken extraordinary care to keep the amount of his debt concealed from his wife. Despite this declination, the loan officer did contact the wife and did disclose to her the amount of plaintiff's indebtedness to various credit card companies.

Plaintiff instituted a suit for invasion of privacy for disclosing private facts to his spouse about his credit card debt. The husband claimed that the disclosure caused a loss of reputation with his wife as well as marital disharmony and mental anguish.

The public disclosure of private facts does constitute an invasion of privacy providing the plaintiff can prove:

1. the defendant implemented publicity about the private life
2. the matter publicized was highly offensive to a reasonable person
3. the matter publicized was not of a legitimate public concern

As to the criterion number 1, this means that the matter must be made public by communicating it to the public at large or to so many persons that the matter must be regarded as substantially certain to become one of public knowledge. Nevertheless, an exception to this rule provides that the publicity element may be satisfied by disclosing the matter to a small number of persons who have a special relationship with the plaintiff such as fellow employees, club members, church, or family members.

Unfortunately, in this case the plaintiff was not able to persuade the court to use this theory. The court felt that the special relationship of small groups does not apply when the recipient of the information has a natural and proper interest in the information. The plaintiff's wife had a proper interest in knowing about the credit card debt because the amount of the credit card debt and the nature of the debt would have an ultimate effect upon her. She also had a legitimate concern in learning about the credit card debt because said debt decreases the value of her interest in the marital property and in plaintiff's estate, thereby potentially adversely affecting her future financial security in the event of divorce or plaintiff's death.

The defendant's disclosure of said information did not satisfy the publicity element for the public disclosure of private facts. The important aspect of the case is not so much that the court found in favor of the lender, but of the fact that the case probably would not have been brought five years ago. Today's climate presents a different temperature.[2]

---

[2]*John Doe v. TCF Bank Illinois*, 707 N.E. 2d 220 (App. Ct, Ill. 1999).

Truth is an absolute defense against a charge of defamation, but it is not a defense to an action for invasion of privacy. A real injury to the plaintiff arises from any disclosure of private facts to a small but intimately known circle. The public is not aware of the private facts before their disclosure and damage may result from the disclosure. In some situations, disclosure to a single person could qualify as a public disclosure if that particular person is the right person, although in most instances, the courts find that a single isolated disclosure is not sufficient to qualify as publicity.[3]

The details of a person's current and previous financial status are generally considered private facts, but if the information is in the public record or a trial record, it usually does not qualify as private.[4]

The more personal the information, the more offensive the disclosure. The issue is whether the circumstances would be more likely to lead to emotional distress or widespread and lasting damage. The intent of the party may also bear on the offensiveness of the invasion. Using private facts as a means of extorting payment or a settlement is more likely to offend a reasonable person.[5]

If the disclosure is made to the media, newsworthiness constitutes a legitimate public interest and newsworthiness has a low standard for legitimate public concern. To be newsworthy, information must only rise above the level of naked voyeurism. If it intrigues the general public and has some element of social relevance, it should be considered a legitimate public interest. In the credit and collection industry, the opportunities to disclose private information concerning businesses, whether they be corporations or partnerships or individuals, are always present. The use of this information must be considered before dissemination of this information to third parties. A legitimate purpose must exist in the dissemination, and a legitimate reason must be present to communicate the information obtained from the business on a credit application, financial statement, or any other means to induce you to do business with or extend credit to the party.

With privacy being splashed all over the media, the credit and collection manager must proceed cautiously.

---

[3]*Beaumont v. Brown*, 401 Mich. 80 (1977).

[4]*Biederman's of Springfield v. Wright*, 322 S.W. 2nd 892 (Mo. 1959); *Scottsdale Unified School District v. KPNX Broadcasting*, 188 Ari., 499 (1997).

[5]*American Credit Corporation v. U.S. Casualty*, 49 F.R.D. 314 (N.D. Ga. 1969).

PRIVACY AND CALLER ID

Caller ID is a recent technology that is now being offered in all fifty states. Most of the states have recognized the need to address the privacy concern of individuals affected by the service, by requiring the telephone companies to provide some form of call blocking. The Federal Communications Commission has also required telephone carriers to provide unblocking mechanisms. The problem with Caller ID legislation is that the governmental agencies have not addressed some of the problems, such as what happens when the use of Caller ID causes a violation of some other law, what happens when the laws from the various states differ substantially, and to what degree is the consumer able to use Caller ID to prevent telephone calls or prevent harassment.

The FDCPA states that a debt collector may not disclose the existence of a debt to anyone other than the consumer, his or her attorney, the spouse of the consumer, or a consumer reporting agency. A debt collector is at risk for revealing the fact that a debt is owed to anyone other than these parties. When a debt collector is attempting to locate a debtor, the debt collector is also restrained from disclosing that he/she is a debt collector unless specifically requested by the third party contacted.

Some states have additional restrictions that apply not only to agencies but also to creditors, such as Massachusetts, which restricts debt collection calls to two per week at home and one per month at work.

Caller ID technology also presents a serious problem to debt collectors who outsource collection of debts in the name of the creditor, but are using the telephone lines of the debt collector. When the debt collector calls, the Caller ID technology will reveal the telephone number of the debt collector/collection agency notwithstanding the fact that the debt collector is operating solely as an employee of the creditor and the message being delivered to the consumer is that the telephone call is from the creditor and not from a collection agency.

Some debt collectors have tried to make arrangements for only an alias or the initials of the company to be displayed on the Caller ID box. Unfortunately, an alias is still illegal in Connecticut, New Hampshire, North Dakota, and other states. Alaska, Connecticut, Illinois, Vermont, and Washington, require the full name of the debt collector. The most obvious solution, of course, is to use per-call blocking, except this presents a problem if the debt collector is utilizing a predictive dialer (automatic dialing of telephone numbers) and there is also the human factor of actually forgetting to dial the particular code. Human error in this area might expose the debt collector to liability notwithstanding the bona fide error defense. Other than per-call blocking, the debt collector can use per-line blocking, which probably is the best solution except that many calls will not be completed, since many of the receiving parties will not accept the call unless the sending party does disclose their name on the Caller ID screen. All states do not agree on per-line blocking and some only allow per-line blocking under certain conditions.

The other problem that a debt collector must be wary of is the fact that Caller ID will be able to identify the debt collector and count the number of telephone calls that are being made. In those states where a limit is placed on the telephone calls, the consumer now has an established record of how many calls were made.

Being aware of the regulations of Caller ID and operating within those regulations is essential to preventing exposure to violations of the FDCPA and other federal and state laws.

TELEGRAM—PRIVACY

The creditor sent a telegram to the debtor by using Western Union Telegraph Company and stating that the debtor "must have the March payment immediately or legal action" will be taken. The consumer alleged that there was an invasion of privacy and publishing of the libel was made to the employees of Western Union. The telegram was delivered to plaintiff's wife and thus the consumer was humiliated and embarrassed.

The court took a dim view of this particular suit. The right to sue for violation of the right of privacy is one of recent origin and has been restricted from the beginning. It is only applicable to the more flagrant breaches of decency and proprietary. To illustrate how restrictive the right is and how outrageous and indecent a violation must be to create a cause of action, the alleged violation must be dealt with as if it was true and published in good faith. The court held that no cause of action was set forth, because it is plain that a creditor has a perfect right to send a debtor a telegram in good faith and threaten legal action if the default continues. The court stated as follows:

> "There is still another reason (and there may be more) and that is that the protection afforded by the law to the right of privacy must be restricted to "ordinary sensibilities" and not to super sensitiveness or agoraphobia. There are some shocks, inconveniences and annoyances which members of society in their nature of things must absorb without the right of redress. It

would seem that one who was billed by mistake, would know of the mistake or could discover it, and that a publication to a few employees of a telegraph company who are not alleged to be acquainted with the alleged injured party would not offend the sensibilities of a person who has gone into debt and subjected himself to the standard communications of a civilized society."[6]

---

[6]*Davis v. General Finance & Thrift Corp.*, 80 Ga. App. 708, 57 S.E. 2d 225 (1950) Court of Appeals of Georgia.

CHAPTER 9
APPENDIX I

EXCERPT FROM GRAMM-LEACH-BLILEY ACT

TITLE V—PRIVACY
SUBTITLE A—DISCLOSURE OF NONPUBLIC PERSONAL INFORMATION

SEC. 501. PROTECTION OF NONPUBLIC PERSONAL INFORMATION.

(a) PRIVACY OBLIGATION POLICY.—It is the policy of the Congress that each financial institution has an affirmative and continuing obligation to respect the privacy of its customers and to protect the security and confidentiality of those customers' nonpublic personal information.

(b) FINANCIAL INSTITUTION'S SAFEGUARDS.—In furtherance of the policy in subsection (a), each agency or authority described in section 505(a) shall establish appropriate standards for the financial institutions subject to their jurisdiction relating to administrative, technical, and physical safeguards—

    (1)   to insure the security and confidentiality of customer records and information;

    (2)   to protect against any anticipated threats or hazards to the security or integrity of such records; and

    (3)   to protect against unauthorized access to or use of such records or information which could result in substantial harm or inconvenience to any customer.

SEC. 502. OBLIGATIONS WITH RESPECT TO DISCLOSURES OF PERSONAL INFORMATION.

(a) NOTICE REQUIREMENTS.—Except as otherwise provided in this subtitle, a financial institution may not, directly or through any affiliate, disclose to a nonaffiliated third party any nonpublic personal information unless such financial institution provides or has provided to the consumer a notice that complies with section 503.

(b) OPT OUT.—

    (1)   IN GENERAL.—A financial institution may not disclose nonpublic personal information to a nonaffiliated third party unless—

(A) such financial institution clearly and conspicuously discloses to the consumer, in writing or in electronic form or other form permitted by the regulations prescribed under section 504, that such information may be disclosed to such third party;

(B) the consumer is given the opportunity, before the time that such information is initially disclosed, to direct that such information not be disclosed to such third party; and

(C) the consumer is given an explanation of how the consumer can exercise that nondisclosure option.

    (2)   EXCEPTION.—This subsection shall not prevent a financial institution from providing nonpublic personal information to a nonaffiliated third party to perform services for or functions on behalf of the financial institution, including marketing of the financial institution's own products or services, or financial products or services offered pursuant to joint agreements between two or more financial institutions that comply with the requirements imposed by the regulations prescribed under section 504, if the financial institution fully discloses the providing of such information and enters into a contractual agreement with the third party that requires the third party to maintain the confidentiality of such information.

(c) LIMITS ON REUSE OF INFORMATION.—Except as otherwise provided in this subtitle, a nonaffiliated third party that receives from a financial institution nonpublic personal information under this section shall not, directly or through an affiliate of such receiving third party, disclose such information to any other person that is a nonaffiliated third party of both the financial institution and such receiving third party, unless such disclosure would be lawful if made directly to such other person by the financial institution.

(d) LIMITATIONS ON THE SHARING OF ACCOUNT NUMBER INFORMATION FOR MARKETING PURPOSES. A financial institution shall not disclose, other than to a consumer reporting agency, an account number or similar form of access number or access code for a credit card account, deposit account, or transaction account of a consumer to any nonaffiliated third party for use in telemarketing, direct mail marketing, or other marketing through electronic mail to the consumer.

(e) GENERAL EXCEPTIONS.—Subsections (a) and (b) shall not prohibit the disclosure of nonpublic personal information—

    (1)   as necessary to effect, administer, or enforce a transaction requested or authorized by the consumer, or in connection with—

(A) servicing or processing a financial product or service requested or authorized by the consumer;

(B) maintaining or servicing the consumer's account with the financial institution, or with another entity as part of a private label credit card program or other extension of credit on behalf of such entity; or

(C) a proposed or actual securitization, secondary market sale (including sales of servicing rights), or similar transaction related to a transaction of the consumer;

(2) with the consent or at the direction of the consumer;

(3) (A) to protect the confidentiality or security of the financial institution's records pertaining to the consumer, the service or product, or the transaction therein; (B) to protect against or prevent actual or potential fraud, unauthorized transactions, claims, or other liability; (C) for required institutional risk control, or for resolving customer disputes or inquiries; (D) to persons holding a legal or beneficial interest relating to the consumer; or (E) to persons acting in a fiduciary or representative capacity on behalf of the consumer;

(4) to provide information to insurance rate advisory organizations, guaranty funds or agencies, applicable rating agencies of the financial institution, persons assessing the institution's compliance with industry standards, and the institution's attorneys, accountants, and auditors;

(5) to the extent specifically permitted or required under other provisions of law and in accordance with the Right to Financial Privacy Act of 1978, to law enforcement agencies (including a Federal functional regulator, the Secretary of the Treasury with respect to subchapter II of chapter 53 of title 31, United States Code, and chapter 2 of title I of Public Law 91—508 (12 U.S.C. 1951–1959), a State insurance authority, or the Federal Trade Commission), self-regulatory organizations, or for an investigation on a matter related to public safety;

(6) (A) to a consumer reporting agency in accordance with the Fair Credit Reporting Act, or (B) from a consumer report by a consumer reporting agency;

(7) in connection with a proposed or actual sale, merger, transfer, or exchange of all or a portion of a business or operating unit if the disclosure of nonpublic personal information concerns solely consumers of such business or unit; or

(8) to comply with Federal, State, or local laws, rules, and other applicable legal requirements; to comply with a properly authorized civil, criminal, or regulatory investigation or subpoena or summons by Federal, State, or local authorities; or to respond to judicial process or government regulatory authorities having jurisdiction over the financial institution for examination, compliance, or other purposes as authorized by law.

SEC. 503. DISCLOSURE OF INSTITUTION PRIVACY POLICY.

(a) DISCLOSURE REQUIRED.—At the time of establishing a customer relationship with a consumer and not less than annually during the continuation of such relationship, a financial institution shall provide a clear and conspicuous disclosure to such consumer, in writing or in electronic form or other form permitted by the regulations prescribed under section 504, of such financial institution's policies and practices with respect to—

> (1) disclosing nonpublic personal information to affiliates and nonaffiliated third parties, consistent with section 502, including the categories of information that may be disclosed;
>
> (2) disclosing nonpublic personal information of persons who have ceased to be customers of the financial institution; and
>
> (3) protecting the nonpublic personal information of consumers.

Such disclosures shall be made in accordance with the regulations prescribed under section 504.

(b) INFORMATION TO BE INCLUDED.—The disclosure required by subsection (a) shall include—

> (1) the policies and practices of the institution with respect to disclosing nonpublic personal information to nonaffiliated third parties, other than agents of the institution, consistent with section 502 of this subtitle, and including—
>
> (A) the categories of persons to whom the information is on may be disclosed, other than the persons to whom the information may be provided pursuant to section 502(e); and
>
> (B) the policies and practices of the institution with respect to disclosing of nonpublic personal information of persons who have ceased to be customers of the financial institution;
>
> (2) the categories of nonpublic personal information that are collected by the financial institution;
>
> (3) the policies that the institution maintains to protect the confidentiality and security of nonpublic personal information in accordance with section 501; and
>
> (4) the disclosures required, if any, under section 603(d)(2)(A)(iii) of the Fair Credit Reporting Act

SEC. 504. RULEMAKING.

(a) REGULATORY AUTHORITY.—

> (1) RULEMAKING.—The Federal banking agencies, the National Credit Union Administration, the Secretary of the Treasury, the Securities and Exchange Commission, and the Federal Trade Commission shall each prescribe, after consultation as appropriate with representatives of state insurance authorities designated by the National Association of Insurance Commissioners, such regulations as may be necessary to

carry out the purposes of this subtitle with respect to the financial institutions subject to their jurisdiction under section 505.

(2)   COORDINATION, CONSISTENCY, AND COMPARABILITY.—Each of the agencies and authorities required under paragraph (1) to prescribe regulations shall consult and coordinate with the other such agencies and authorities for the purposes of assuring, to the extent possible, that the regulations prescribed by each such agency and authority are consistent and comparable with the regulations prescribed by the other such agencies and authorities.

(3)   PROCEDURES AND DEADLINE.—Such regulations shall be prescribed in accordance with applicable requirements of title 5, United States Code, and shall be issued in final form not later than 6 months after the date of the enactment of this Act.

(b) AUTHORITY TO GRANT EXCEPTIONS.—The regulations prescribed under subsection (a) may include such additional exceptions to subsections (a) through (d) of section 502 as are deemed consistent with the purposes of this subtitle.

SEC. 505. ENFORCEMENT.

(a) IN GENERAL.—This subtitle and the regulations prescribed thereunder shall be enforced by the Federal functional regulators, the state insurance authorities, and the Federal Trade Commission with respect to financial institutions and other persons subject to their jurisdiction under applicable law, as follows:

(1)   Under section 8 of the Federal Deposit Insurance Act, in the case of—
(A) national banks, Federal branches and Federal agencies of foreign banks, and any subsidiaries of such entities (except brokers, dealers, persons providing insurance, investment companies, and investment advisers), by the Office of the Comptroller of the Currency;
(B) member banks of the Federal Reserve System (other than national banks), branches and agencies of foreign banks (other than Federal branches, Federal agencies, and insured state branches of foreign banks), commercial lending companies owned or controlled by foreign banks, organizations operating under section 25 or 25A of the Federal Reserve Act, and bank holding companies and their nonbank subsidiaries or affiliates (except brokers, dealers, persons providing insurance, investment companies, and investment advisers), by the Board of Governors of the Federal Reserve System;
(C) banks insured by the Federal Deposit Insurance Corporation (other than members of the Federal Reserve System), insured State branches of foreign banks, and any subsidiaries of such entities (except brokers, dealers, persons providing insurance, investment companies, and investment advisers), by the Board of Directors of the Federal Deposit Insurance Corporation; and
(D) savings associations the deposits of which are insured by the Federal Deposit Insurance Corporation, and any subsidiaries of such savings associations (except brokers, dealers, persons providing insur-

ance, investment companies, and investment advisers), by the Director of the Office of Thrift Supervision.

(2) Under the Federal Credit Union Act, by the Board of the National Credit Union Administration with respect to any federally insured credit union, and any subsidiaries of such an entity.

(3) Under the Securities Exchange Act of 1934, by the Securities and Exchange Commission with respect to any broker or dealer.

(4) Under the Investment Company Act of 1940, by the Securities and Exchange Commission with respect to investment companies.

(5) Under the Investment Advisers Act of 1940, by the Securities and Exchange Commission with respect to investment advisers registered with the Commission under such Act.

(6) Under State insurance law, in the case of any person engaged in providing insurance, by the applicable state insurance authority of the state in which the person is domiciled, subject to section 104 of this Act.

(7) Under the Federal Trade Commission Act, by the Federal Trade Commission for any other financial institution or other person that is not subject to the jurisdiction of any agency or authority under paragraphs (1) through (6) of this subsection.

(b) ENFORCEMENT OF SECTION 501.—

(1) IN GENERAL.—Except as provided in paragraph (2), the agencies and authorities described in subsection (a) shall implement the standards prescribed under section 501(b) in the same manner, to the extent practicable, as standards prescribed pursuant to section 39(a) of the Federal Deposit Insurance Act are implemented pursuant to such section.

(2) EXCEPTION.—The agencies and authorities described in paragraphs (3), (4), (5), (6), and (7) of subsection (a) shall implement the standards prescribed under section 501(b) by rule with respect to the financial institutions and other persons subject to their respective jurisdictions under subsection (a).

(c) ABSENCE OF STATE ACTION.—If a state insurance authority fails to adopt regulations to carry out this subtitle, such state shall not be eligible to override, pursuant to section 45(g)(2)(B)(iii) of the Federal Deposit Insurance Act, the insurance customer protection regulations prescribed by a Federal banking agency under section 45(a) of such Act.

(d) DEFINITIONS.—The terms used in subsection (a) (1) that are not defined in this subtitle or otherwise defined in section 3(s) of the Federal Deposit Insurance Act shall have the same meaning as given in section 1(b) of the International Banking Act of 1978.

SEC. 506. PROTECTION OF FAIR CREDIT REPORTING ACT.

(a) AMENDMENT.—Section 621 of the Fair Credit Reporting Act (15 U.S.C. 1681s) is amended—

(1)   in subsection (d), by striking everything following the end of the second sentence; and

(2)   by striking subsection (c) and inserting the following:

(a) "REGULATORY AUTHORITY."—(1) The Federal banking agencies referred to in paragraphs (1) and (2) of subsection (b) shall jointly prescribe such regulations as necessary to carry out the purposes of this Act with respect to any persons identified under paragraphs (1) and (2) of subsection (b), and the Board of Governors of the Federal Reserve System shall have authority to prescribe regulations consistent with such joint regulations with respect to bank holding companies and affiliates (other than depository institutions and consumer reporting agencies) of such holding companies.

(2) "The Board of the National Credit Union Administration shall prescribe such regulations as necessary to carry out the purposes of this Act with respect to any persons identified under paragraph (3) of subsection (b)."

(b) CONFORMING AMENDMENT .—Section 621(a) of the Fair Credit Reporting Act (15 U.S.C. l681s(a)) is amended by striking paragraph (4).

(c) RELATION TO OTHER PROVISIONS.—Except for the amendments made by subsections (a) and (b), nothing in this title shall be construed to modify, limit, or supersede the operation of the Fair Credit Reporting Act, and no inference shall be drawn on the basis of the provisions of this title regarding whether information is transaction or experience information under section 603 of such Act.

Sec. 507. Relation to State Laws.

(a) IN GENERAL.—This subtitle and the amendments made by this subtitle shall not be construed as superseding, altering, or affecting any statute, regulation, order, or interpretation in effect in any state, except to the extent that such statute, regulation, order, or interpretation is inconsistent with the provisions of this subtitle, and then only to the extent of the inconsistency.

(b) GREATER PROTECTION UNDER STATE LAW.—For purposes of this section, a state statute, regulation, order, or interpretation is not inconsistent with the provisions of this subtitle if the protection such statute, regulation, order, or interpretation affords any person is greater than the protection provided under this subtitle and the amendments made by this subtitle, as determined by the Federal Trade Commission, after consultation with the agency or authority with jurisdiction under section 505(a) of either the person that initiated the complaint or that is the subject of the complaint, on its own motion or upon the petition of any interested party.

Sec. 508. Study of Information Sharing among Financial Affiliates.

(a) IN GENERAL.—The Secretary of the Treasury, in conjunction with the Federal functional regulators and the Federal Trade Commission, shall conduct a study of information sharing practices among financial institutions and their affiliates. Such study shall include—

(1) the purposes for the sharing of confidential customer information with affiliates or with nonaffiliated third parties;

(2) the extent and adequacy of security protection for such information;

(3) the potential risks for customer privacy of such sharing of information;

(4) the potential benefits for financial institutions and affiliates of such sharing of information;

(5) the potential benefits for customers of such sharing of information;

(6) the adequacy of existing laws to protect customer privacy;

(7) the adequacy of financial institution privacy policy and privacy rights disclosure under existing law;

(8) the feasibility of different approaches, including opt-out and opt-in, to permit customers to direct that confidential information not be shared with affiliates and nonaffiliated third parties; and

(9) the feasibility of restricting sharing of information for specific uses or of permitting customers to direct the uses for which information may be shared.

(b) CONSULTATION.—The Secretary shall consult with representatives of state insurance authorities designated by the National Association of Insurance Commissioners, and also with financial services industry, consumer organizations and privacy groups, and other representatives of the general public, in formulating and conducting the study required by subsection (a).

(c) REPORT.—On or before January 1, 2002, the Secretary shall submit a report to the Congress containing the findings and conclusions of the study required under subsection (a), together with such recommendations for legislative or administrative action as may be appropriate.

SEC. 509. DEFINITIONS.

As used in this subtitle:

(1) FEDERAL BANKING AGENCY.—The term "Federal banking agency" has the same meaning as given in section 3 of the Federal Deposit Insurance Act.

(2) FEDERAL FUNCTIONAL REGULATOR.—The term "Federal functional regulator" means—

(A) the Board of Governors of the Federal Reserve System;

(B) the Office of the Comptroller of the Currency;

(C) the Board of Directors of the Federal Deposit Insurance Corporation;

(D) the Director of the Office of Thrift Supervision;

(E) the National Credit Union Administration Board; and

(F) the Securities and Exchange Commission.

(3) FINANCIAL INSTITUTION.—

(A) IN GENERAL.—The term "financial institution" means any institution the business of which is engaging in financial activities as described in section 4(k) of the Bank Holding Company Act of 1956.

(B) PERSONS SUBJECT TO CFTC REGULATION.—Notwithstanding subparagraph (A), the term "financial institution" does not include any person or entity with respect to any financial activity that is subject to the jurisdiction of the Commodity Futures Trading Commission under the Commodity Exchange Act.

(C) FARM CREDIT INSTITUTIONS.—Notwithstanding subparagraph (A), the term "financial institution" does not include the Federal Agricultural Mortgage Corporation or any entity chartered and operating under the Farm Credit Act of 1971.

(D) OTHER SECONDARY MARKET INSTITUTIONS.—Notwithstanding subparagraph (A), the term "financial institution" does not include institutions chartered by Congress specifically to engage in transactions described in section 502(e)(1)(C), as long as such institutions do not sell or transfer nonpublic personal information to a nonaffiliated third party.

(4) NONPUBLIC PERSONAL INFORMATION.—

(A) The term "nonpublic personal information" means personally identifiable financial information—

(i) provided by a consumer to a financial institution;

(ii) resulting from any transaction with the consumer or any service performed for the consumer; or

(iii) otherwise obtained by the financial institution.

(B) Such term does not include publicly available information, as such term is defined by the regulations prescribed under section 504.

(C) Notwithstanding subparagraph (B), such term—

(i) shall include any list, description, or other grouping of consumers (and publicly available information pertaining to them) that is derived using any nonpublic personal information other than publicly available information; but

(ii) shall not include any list, description, or other grouping of consumers (and publicly available information pertaining to them) that is derived without using any nonpublic personal information.

(5) NONAFFILIATED THIRD PARTY.—The term "nonaffiliated third party" means any entity that is not an affiliate of, or related by common ownership, or affiliated by corporate control with the financial institution, but does not include a joint employee of such institution.

(6) AFFILIATE.—The term "affiliate" means any company that controls, is controlled by, or is under common control with another company.

(7) NECESSARY TO EFFECT, ADMINISTER, OR ENFORCE.—The term "as necessary to effect, administer, or enforce the transaction" means—

(A) the disclosure is required, or is a usual, appropriate, or acceptable method to carry out the transaction or the product or service business of which the transaction is a part, and record or service or maintain the consumer's account in the ordinary course of providing the financial service or financial product, or to administer or service benefits or claims relating to the transaction or the product or service business of which it is a part, and includes—

(i) providing the consumer or the consumer's agent or broker with a confirmation, statement, or other record of the transaction, or information on the status or value of the financial service or financial product; and

(ii) the accrual or recognition of incentives or bonuses associated with the transaction that are provided by the financial institution or any other party;

(B) the disclosure is required, or is one of the lawful or appropriate methods, to enforce the rights of the financial institution or of other persons engaged in carrying out the financial transaction, or providing the product or service;

(C) the disclosure is required, or is a usual, appropriate, or acceptable method for insurance underwriting at the consumer's request or for reinsurance purposes, or for any of the following purposes as they relate to a consumer's insurance: account administration, reporting, investigating, or preventing fraud or material misrepresentation, processing premium payments, processing claims, administering insurance benefits (including utilization review activities), participating in research projects, or as otherwise required or specifically permitted by Federal or State law; or

(D) the disclosure is required, or is a usual, appropriate, or acceptable method in connection with—

(i) the authorization, settlement, billing, processing, clearing, transferring, reconciling, or collection of amounts charged, debited, or otherwise paid using a debit, credit, or other payment card, check, or account number, or by other payment means;

(ii) the transfer of receivables, accounts, or interests therein; or

(iii) the audit of debit, credit, or other payment information.

(8) STATE INSURANCE AUTHORITY.—The term "State insurance authority" means, in the case of any person engaged in providing insurance, the State insurance authority of the state in which the person is domiciled.

(9) CONSUMER.—The term "consumer" means an individual who obtains, from a financial institution, financial products or services which are to be used primarily for personal, family, or household purposes, and also means the legal representative of such an individual

(10) JOINT AGREEMENT.—The term "joint agreement" means a formal written contract pursuant to which two or more financial institutions jointly offer, endorse, or sponsor a financial product or service, and as may be further defined in the regulations prescribed under section 504.

(11) CUSTOMER RELATIONSHIP.—The term "time of establishing a customer relationship" shall be defined by the regulations prescribed under section 504, and shall, in the case of a financial institution engaged in extending credit directly to consumers to finance purchases of goods or services, mean the time of establishing the credit relationship with the consumer.

SEC. 510. EFFECTIVE DATE.

This subtitle shall take effect 6 months after the date on which rules are required to be prescribed under section 504(a)(3), except—

(1) to the extent that a later date is specified in the rules prescribed under section 504; and

(2) that sections 504 and 506 shall be effective upon enactment.

SUBTITLE B—FRAUDULENT ACCESS TO FINANCIAL INFORMATION

SEC. 521. PRIVACY PROTECTION FOR CUSTOMER INFORMATION OF FINANCIAL INSTITUTIONS.

(a) PROHIBITION ON OBTAINING CUSTOMER INFORMATION BY FALSE PRETENSES.—It shall be a violation of this subtitle for any person to obtain or attempt to obtain, or cause to be disclosed or attempt to cause to be disclosed to any person, customer information of a financial institution relating to another person—

(1) by making a false, fictitious, or fraudulent statement or representation to an officer, employee, or agent of a financial institution;

(2) by making a false, fictitious, or fraudulent statement or representation to a customer of a financial institution; or

(3) by providing any document to an officer, employee, or agent of a financial institution, knowing that the document is forged, counterfeit, lost, or stolen, was fraudulently obtained, or contains a false, fictitious, or fraudulent statement or representation.

(b) PROHIBITION ON SOLICITATION OF A PERSON TO OBTAIN CUSTOMER INFORMATION FROM FINANCIAL INSTITUTION UNDER FALSE PRETENSES.—It shall be a violation of this subtitle to request a person to obtain customer information of a financial institution, knowing that the person will obtain, or attempt to obtain, the information from the institution in any manner described in subsection (a).

(c) NONAPPLICABILITY TO LAW ENFORCEMENT AGENCIES.—No provision of this section shall be construed so as to prevent any action by a law enforcement agency, or any officer, employee, or agent of such agency, to obtain customer information of a financial institution in connection with the performance of the official duties of the agency.

(d) NONAPPLICABILITY TO FINANCIAL INSTITUTIONS IN CERTAIN CASES.—No provision of this section shall be construed so as to prevent any financial institution, or any officer, employee, or agent of a financial institution, from obtaining customer information of such financial institution in the course of—

    (1)   testing the security procedures or systems of such institution for maintaining the confidentiality of customer information;

    (2)   investigating allegations of misconduct or negligence on the part of any officer, employee, or agent of the financial institution; or

    (3)   recovering customer information of the financial institution which was obtained or received by another person in any manner described in subsection (a) or (b).

(e) NONAPPLICABILITY TO INSURANCE INSTITUTIONS FOR INVESTIGATION OF INSURANCE FRAUD.—No provision of this section shall be construed so as to prevent any insurance institution, or any officer, employee, or agency of an insurance institution, from obtaining information as part of an insurance investigation into criminal activity, fraud, material misrepresentation, or material nondisclosure that is authorized for such institution under state law, regulation, interpretation, or order.

(f) NONAPPLICABILITY TO CERTAIN TYPES OF CUSTOMER INFORMATION OF FINANCIAL INSTITUTIONS.—No provision of this section shall be construed so as to prevent any person from obtaining customer information of a financial institution that otherwise is available as a public record filed pursuant to the securities laws (as defined in section 3(a)(47) of the Securities Exchange Act of 1934).

(g) NONAPPLICABILITY TO COLLECTION OF CHILD SUPPORT JUDGMENTS.—No provision of this section shall be construed to prevent any state-licensed private investigator, or any officer, employee, or agent of such private investigator from obtaining customer information of a financial institution, to the extent reasonably necessary to collect child support from a person adjudged to have been delinquent in his or her obligations by a Federal or State court, and to the extent that such action by a state-licensed private investigator is not unlawful under any other Federal or State law or regulation, and has been authorized by an order or judgment of a court of competent jurisdiction.

SEC. 522. ADMINISTRATIVE ENFORCEMENT.

(a) ENFORCEMENT BY FEDERAL TRADE COMMISSION.—Except as provided in subsection (b), compliance with this subtitle shall be enforced by the Federal Trade Commission in the same manner and with the same power and authority as the Commission has under the Fair Debt Collection Practices Act to enforce compliance with such Act.

(b) ENFORCEMENT BY OTHER AGENCIES IN CERTAIN CASES.—

    (1)   IN GENERAL.—Compliance with this subtitle shall be enforced under—

        (A) section 8 of the Federal Deposit Insurance Act, in the case of—

            (i) national banks, and Federal branches and Federal agencies of foreign banks by the Office of the Comptroller of the Currency;

            (ii) member banks of the Federal Reserve System (other than national banks), branches and agencies of foreign banks (other than Federal branches, Federal agencies, and insured State branches of foreign banks), commercial lending companies owned or controlled by foreign banks, and organizations operating under section 25 or 25A of the Federal Reserve Act, by the Board;

            (iii) banks insured by the Federal Deposit Insurance Corporation (other than members of the Federal Reserve System and national nonmember banks) and insured State branches of foreign banks by the Board of Directors of the Federal Deposit Insurance Corporation; and

            (iv) savings associations the deposits of which are insured by the Federal Deposit Insurance Corporation by the Director of the Office of Thrift Supervision; and

        (B) the Federal Credit Union Act, by the Administrator of the National Credit Union Administration with respect to any Federal credit union.

    (2)   VIOLATIONS OF THIS SUBTITLE TREATED AS VIOLATIONS OF OTHER LAWS.—For the purpose of the exercise by any agency referred to in paragraph (1) of its powers under any Act referred to in that paragraph, a violation of this subtitle shall be deemed to be a violation of a requirement imposed under that Act. In addition to its powers under any provision of law specifically referred to in paragraph (1), each of the agencies referred to in that paragraph may exercise, for the purpose of enforcing compliance with this subtitle, any other authority conferred on such agency by law.

SEC. 523. CRIMINAL PENALTY.

(a) IN GENERAL.—Whoever knowingly and intentionally violates, or knowingly and intentionally attempts to violate, section 521 shall be fined in accordance with title 18, United States Code, or imprisoned for not more than 5 years, or both.

(b) ENHANCED PENALTY FOR AGGRAVATED CASES.—Whoever violates, or attempts to violate, section 521 while violating another law of the United States or as part of a pattern of any illegal activity involving more than $100,000 in a 12-month period shall be fined twice the amount provided in subsection (b)(3) or (c)(3) (as the case may be) of section 3571 of title 18, United States Code, imprisoned for not more than 10 years, or both.

Sec. 524. Relation to State Laws.

(a) IN GENERAL.—This subtitle shall not be construed as superseding, altering, or affecting the statutes, regulations, orders, or interpretations in effect in any state, except to the extent that such statutes, regulations, orders, or interpretations are inconsistent with the provisions of this subtitle, and then only to the extent of the inconsistency.

(b) GREATER PROTECTION UNDER STATE LAW.— For purposes of this section, a State statute, regulation, order, or interpretation is not inconsistent with the provisions of this subtitle if the protection such statute, regulation, order, or interpretation affords any person is greater than the protection provided under this subtitle as determined by the Federal Trade Commission, after consultation with the agency or authority with jurisdiction under section 522 of either the person that initiated the complaint or that is the subject of the complaint, on its own motion or upon the petition of any interested party.

Sec. 525. Agency Guidance.

In furtherance of the objectives of this subtitle, each Federal banking agency (as defined in section 3(z) of the Federal Deposit Insurance Act), the National Credit Union Administration, and the Securities and Exchange Commission or self-regulatory organizations, as appropriate, shall review regulations and guidelines applicable to financial institutions under their respective jurisdictions and shall prescribe such revisions to such regulations and guidelines as may be necessary to ensure that such financial institutions have policies, procedures, and controls in place to prevent the unauthorized disclosure of customer financial information and to deter and detect activities proscribed under section 521.

Sec. 526. Reports.

(a) REPORT TO THE CONGRESS.—Before the end of the 18-month period beginning on the date of the enactment of this Act, the Comptroller General, in consultation with the Federal Trade Commission, Federal banking agencies, the National Credit Union Administration, the Securities and Exchange Commission, appropriate Federal law enforcement agencies, and appropriate State insurance regulators, shall submit to the Congress a report on the following:

(1) The efficacy and adequacy of the remedies provided in this subtitle in addressing attempts to obtain financial information by fraudulent means or by false pretenses.

(2) Any recommendations for additional legislative or regulatory action to address threats to the privacy of financial information created by attempts to obtain information by fraudulent means or false pretenses.

(b) ANNUAL REPORT BY ADMINISTERING AGENCIES.—The Federal Trade Commission and the Attorney General shall submit to Congress an annual report on number and disposition of all enforcement actions taken pursuant to this subtitle.

SEC. 527. DEFINITIONS.

For purposes of this subtitle, the following definitions shall apply:

(1)   CUSTOMER.—The term "customer" means, with respect to a financial institution, any person (or authorized representative of a person) to whom the financial institution provides a product or service, including that of acting as a fiduciary.

(2)   CUSTOMER INFORMATION OF A FINANCIAL INSTITUTION.— The term "customer information of a financial institution" means any information maintained by or for a financial institution which is derived from the relationship between the financial institution and a customer of the financial institution and is identified with the customer.

(3)   DOCUMENT.—The term "document" means any information in any form.

(4)   FINANCIAL INSTITUTION.—

(A) IN GENERAL.—The term "financial institution" means any institution engaged in the business of providing financial services to customers who maintain a credit, deposit, trust, or other financial account or relationship with the institution.

(B) CERTAIN FINANCIAL INSTITUTIONS SPECIFICALLY INCLUDED.—The term "financial institution" includes any depository institution (as defined in section 19(b)(1)(A) of the Federal Reserve Act), any broker or dealer, any investment adviser or investment company, any insurance company, any loan or finance company, any credit card issuer or operator of a credit card system, and any consumer reporting agency that compiles and maintains files on consumers on a nationwide basis (as defined in section 603(p) of the Consumer Credit Protection Act).

(C) SECURITIES INSTITUTIONS.—For purposes of subparagraph (B)—

(i) the terms "broker" and "dealer" have the same meanings as given in section 3 of the Securities Exchange Act of 1934 (15 U.S.C. 78c);

(ii) the term "investment adviser" has the same meaning as given in section 202(a) (11) of the Investment Advisers Act of 1940 (15 U.S.C. 80b-2(a)); and

(iii) the term "investment company" has the same meaning as given in section 3 of the Investment Company Act of 1940 (15 U.S.C. 80a-3).

(D) CERTAIN PERSONS AND ENTITIES SPECIFICALLY EXCLUD-ED.—The term "financial institution" does not include any person or entity with respect to any financial activity that is subject to the jurisdiction of the Commodity Futures Trading Commission under the Commodity Exchange Act and does not include the Federal Agricultural Mortgage Corporation or any entity chartered and operating under the Farm Credit Act of 1971.

(E) FURTHER DEFINITION BY REGULATION.—The Federal Trade Commission, after consultation with Federal banking agencies and the Securities and Exchange Commission, may prescribe regulations clarifying or describing the types of institutions which shall be treated as financial institutions for purposes of this subtitle.

APPENDIX II

GRAMM-LEACH-BLILEY— FDIC PRIVACY OF CONSUMER FINANCIAL INFORMATION

FIL-3-2001
January 22, 2001,

TO: CHIEF EXECUTIVE OFFICER AND COMPLIANCE OFFICER

SUBJECT: *FDIC Creates Privacy Rule Handbook to Assist Banks With Compliance*

The attached *Privacy Rule Handbook* was produced by the Federal Deposit Insurance Corporation (FDIC) to help financial institutions comply with the final rule governing the privacy of consumer financial information and implement effective consumer privacy policies.

The Gramm-Leach-Bliley Act of 1999 (GLBA) established new requirements for financial institutions to provide new privacy protections to consumers. Specifically, Title V of GLBA requires a financial institution to issue privacy notices and provide consumers with an opportunity to opt out of certain types of information sharing. The FDIC developed and adopted a final regulation with other financial institution regulators to implement the GLBA privacy provisions. The FDIC's rule, 12 C.F.R. Part 332, was distributed to FDIC-supervised banks with Financial Institution Letter (FIL) 34-2000, dated June 5, 2000.

Although the privacy rule's effective date is November 13, 2000, compliance is not mandatory until July 1, 2001. Mandatory compliance was extended in the final rule to provide banks with sufficient time to develop the necessary notices and procedures to implement the rule. **It is imperative that banks use this interim period to develop a privacy compliance strategy to achieve full compliance by July 1, 2001.**

This *Handbook* is designed to help banks prepare for the July 1, 2001, deadline. First, the *Handbook* explains the basic requirements of the privacy rule. Second, the *Handbook* provides suggestions for implementing the requirements of the privacy rule to meet the July 1 deadline. Third, the *Handbook* suggests activities to monitor and maintain compliance over time. Finally, the *Handbook* describes in greater detail key terminology in the rule and provides other helpful resources.

The *Privacy Rule Handbook* does not impose any new requirements on banks. Rather, it provides a summary of the rule's requirements and suggestions to help banks develop and implement effective consumer privacy policies and procedures. The *Handbook* uses the term "bank" to mean those financial institutions that must comply with Part 332.

For more information about the privacy rule, please contact the FDIC regional office responsible for supervising your bank, or call Ken Baebel, Assistant Director in the Division of Compliance and Consumer Affairs, on (202) 942-3086.

Stephen M. Cross

Director

Attachment: *Privacy Rule Handbook* (see attached pages)

Distribution: FDIC-Supervised Banks (Commercial and Savings)

NOTE: Paper copies of FDIC financial institution letters may be obtained through the FDIC's Public Information Center, 801 17th Street, NW, Room 100, Washington, DC 20434 (800-276-6003 or 202-416-6940).

Section One:
Overview of privacy rule requirements

The privacy rule governs when and how banks may share nonpublic personal information about consumers with nonaffiliated third parties.

The rule embodies two principles—notice and opt out. In summary:

- **All** banks must develop **initial** and **annual** privacy **notices.** The notices must describe in general terms the bank's information sharing practices.
- Banks that share non public personal information about consumers with nonaffiliated third parties (outside of opt out exceptions delineated in the privacy rule) must also provide consumers with:
  - an opt out notice
  - a reasonable period of time for the consumer to opt out

A few **key terms** *used throughout the privacy rule are critical to application. Refer to* **Section Four** *of this guide for an explanation of:*

- *nonpublic personal information*
- *the distinction between consumers and customers*
- *nonaffiliated third party*

Exceptions to opt out: A consumer cannot opt out of all information sharing. First, the privacy rule does not govern information sharing among affiliated parties. Second, the rule contains exceptions to allow transfers of nonpublic personal information to unaffiliated parties to process and service a consumer's transaction, and to facilitate other normal business transactions. For example, consumers cannot opt out when nonpublic personal information is shared with a nonaffiliated third party to:

- market the bank's own financial products or services
- market financial products or services offered by the bank and another financial institution (joint marketing)
- process and service transactions the consumer requests or authorizes
- protect against potential fraud or unauthorized transactions
- respond to judicial process
- comply with federal, state, or local legal requirements

*Applying exceptions: A bank may have to satisfy disclosure and other requirements to make the rule's opt out exceptions applicable. For example, the **joint marketing exception** requires a **contractual agreement** between two nonaffiliated financial institutions to:*

a) jointly offer, endorse, or sponsor the financial product or service, and

b) limit further use or disclosure of the consumer information transferred

In addition, the bank must include a separate statement in the privacy notice disclosing the joint marketing agreement.

Prohibition on sharing account numbers: The privacy rule prohibits a bank from disclosing an account number or access code for credit card, deposit, or transaction accounts to any nonaffiliated third party for use in marketing. The rule contains two narrow exceptions to this general prohibition. A bank may share account numbers in conjunction with marketing its **own products** as long as the service provider is not authorized to directly initiate charges to the accounts. A bank may also disclose account numbers to a participant in a private label or affinity credit card program when the participants are identified to the customer. **An account number does not include a number or code in encrypted form as long as the bank does not also provide a means to decode the number.**

Limits on reuse and redisclosure: The privacy rule limits reuse and redisclosure of nonpublic personal information received from a nonaffiliated financial institution or disclosed to a nonaffiliated third party. The specific limitations depend on whether the information was received pursuant to or outside of the notice and opt out exceptions.

State Law: A provision under a State law that provides greater consumer protection than provided under the GLBA privacy provisions will supercede the Federal privacy rule. The bank will be obligated to comply with the provisions of that

State law to the extent those provisions provide greater consumer protection than the Federal privacy rule. The Federal Trade Commission determines whether a particular State law provides greater protection.

Privacy Notices

Every bank must develop initial and annual privacy notices—*even if the bank does not share information with nonaffiliated third parties.*

Content of notices: The initial, annual, and revised notices include, as applicable:

- **categories of information a bank collects** (all banks)
- **categories of information a bank may disclose** (all banks, except a bank that does not intend to make any disclosures or only makes disclosures under the exceptions may simply state that)
- **categories of affiliates and nonaffiliates to whom a bank discloses nonpublic personal information** (all banks sharing nonpublic personal information with an affiliate or with a nonaffiliated third party)
- **information sharing practices about former customers** (all banks)
- **categories of information disclosed under the service provider/joint marketing exception** (only those banks relying on this exception)
- **consumer's right to opt out** (only those banks that disclose outside of exceptions)
- **disclosures made under the Fair Credit Reporting Act** (only those banks providing the FCRA opt out notice)
- **disclosures about confidentiality and security of information** (all banks)

A revised notice may be required when a bank changes its information sharing practices.

The following table reflects the rule's requirements for delivering initial, annual, and revised notices to consumers and customers.

Type of Notice	Who gets it	Delivery
Initial privacy notice (all banks)	• all existing bank customers • all new bank customers after July 1, 2001 • consumers who are not customers	• **no later than July 1, 2001** • when the customer relationship is established 　only if the bank intends to share nonpublic personal information about the consumer with a nonaffiliated third party
Annual privacy notice (all banks)	• customers	• at least once in any period of 12 consecutive months while the customer relationship continues
Revised privacy notice (as applicable)	• customers and consumers who are not customers	• **before** the bank shares nonpublic personal information in a manner not described in the most recent notice delivered to the customer or consumer

Opt Out Notice

The final rule provides that an **opt out notice** is adequate if it:

- identifies all the categories of nonpublic personal information the bank intends to disclose to nonaffiliated third parties
- states the consumer can opt out of the disclosure
- provides a reasonable method for the consumer to opt out, such as a toll-free telephone number

The table below summarizes the rule's requirements for delivering an opt out notice.

Type of Notice	Who gets it	Delivery
Opt out notice (only banks that share outside of exceptions)	• customers and consumers who are not customers	• **before** the bank shares nonpublic personal information about the customer or consumer and the information sharing is not permissible under the privacy rule opt out exceptions

The opt out right: If a bank intends to share nonpublic personal information outside the exceptions, it must also:

- provide consumers with a **reasonable opportunity to opt out.** Examples in the privacy rule give consumers **30 days** to respond to the opt out notice when the bank delivers the notice by mail or electronically
- **comply** with a consumer's opt out direction **as soon as reasonably practicable** when the direction is received after the initial opt out period elapses
- **comply** with the opt out direction until revoked in writing by the consumer

Delivering notices: The initial, annual, revised, and opt out notices may be delivered in writing or, if the consumer agrees, electronically. An oral description of the notice is not sufficient.

Section Two
Get Ready for July 1, 2001

A bank's strategy for achieving full compliance by July 1, 2001, will vary depending on the complexity of the bank and the progress it has already made in complying with the requirements of the rule. The level of effort a bank will expend depends in large part on:

- the bank's previous efforts to assess or disclose information sharing practices
- the bank's decisions about sharing nonpublic personal information after July 1, 2001
- the volume, if any, of consumers and customers who must receive an opportunity to opt out before information sharing with nonaffiliated third parties can take place.

Nearly all banks, however, can take the following four steps to create a comprehensive and effective privacy compliance strategy:

- establish a timeline for compliance
- develop privacy policies and notices
- deliver notices
- prepare to respond to consumers

1. Establish a timeline for compliance

A timeline designating important checkpoints prior to July 1, 2001, is a good place to start and can be instrumental to ensuring timely compliance.

A bank may want to establish timeframes to:

Assess current information sharing practices	Obtain input and approval from management	Prepare to respond to public inquiries
Draft privacy policies and consumer notices	1. Deliver initial notices to customers 2. Deliver opt out notices to consumers and costomers as applicable	Process opt out directions from consumers and customers

A specific process for certifying completion of the various steps identified in the bank's privacy compliance strategy will help managers keep track of progress. When establishing due dates for specific activities, build in time to receive input and feedback from senior management and other stakeholders. Every bank should consider:

- **Involving the Board of Directors:** A board-approved privacy policy is not required by the rule, but it can be an effective way to involve the board of directors in developing a privacy compliance strategy. A board-sanctioned privacy policy can be useful in communicating the bank's overall privacy commitment and strategy to the entire organization.
- **Involving representatives from each bank department** Most likely a senior bank officer will oversee development and implementation of the privacy compliance strategy. Nevertheless, participation from each department in the bank will help ensure nothing is overlooked. This approach will also help policy makers identify information sharing practices or consumer privacy issues unique to a specific department or to a financial product or service.

2. Develop privacy policies and notices

Use this opportunity to evaluate and establish institutional privacy objectives, and communicate to potential customers and consumers the bank's customer service philosophy.

- Create a comprehensive inventory of information collection and information sharing practices at the bank. The inventory will help ensure practices are properly disclosed in the bank's privacy notices. For every department, review:

- all applications and forms used to collect information about consumers

- marketing practices

- vendor contracts

- electronic banking and Internet activities

- fee income accounts

- record retention policies

Affiliates: **If a bank has any affiliates, the inventory should include information-sharing practices with affiliates. Although the privacy rule does not place any restrictions on information sharing with affiliates, it does require disclosure of these practices in the and annual notices. Furthermore, the privacy rule requires the initial and annual notices include applicable Fair Credit Reporting Act affiliate information sharing opt out notices.**

- *Assess current information collection and information sharing practices* in light of the privacy rule obligations and the bank's objectives. Determine which practices should continue after July 1, 2001. This may be a good time to involve the bank's Board of Directors. Consider:

  - whether any current practices would be prohibited under the rule

  - which practices must be disclosed in the privacy notices and whether opt out rights apply

  - whether account numbers are shared only as permitted by the rule

  - whether information received from other financial institutions is shared only as permitted by the rule's reuse and redisclosure limitations

  - whether to adopt voluntary privacy standards developed by relevant trade associations. Those standards could be good indicators of industry norms and consumer expectations

- *Draft privacy notice(s).* Create a list of information collection and information sharing practices that must be disclosed to consumers. This list can help you categorize practices per the rule requirements and decide how to structure notices. The privacy rule provides a variety of disclosure options. For example, banks may develop:

  - one initial privacy notice that covers all the information sharing practices of the bank

  - an assortment of initial notices for different customer relationships or different types of financial products or services

  - one initial notice that covers the practices of the bank along with one or more of its affiliates Likewise, the opt out notice may be structured in a variety of ways.

When drafting privacy notices, consider:

- **Sample clauses** provided in Appendix A in the rule. Banks may use the sample clauses to the extent they accurately reflect the bank's practices.

Most likely, the initial and annual privacy notices will be identical. If required, the opt out notice may be combined with the initial and annual notices.

- **Fair Credit Reporting Act requirements and information security standards.** The federal banking agencies have issued two proposed rules that may affect the compliance strategy and the content of privacy notices.

The *Proposed Security Standards for Customer Information* describe the agencies' expectations for implementing technical and physical safeguards to protect customer information. *The Proposed Fair Credit Reporting Regulations* cover the opt out provisions of the Fair Credit Reporting Act.

Both proposals will be finalized in the near future. When issued, the final rules will be available on the FDIC's Web site: www.fdic.gov. In the meantime, the proposals are posted on the Web site.

3. Deliver notices

- Identify consumers and customers who must receive the initial and opt out notices. It is important to identify all groups of existing customers, consumers, and former customers who must get the initial privacy notice and opt out notification. Some banks may need to coordinate several databases and a variety of departments to identify everyone who must receive a notice.

Opt out notices for joint account holders: The privacy rule allows banks to provide a single privacy and opt out notice when two or more consume(jointly obtain a financial product or service. However, any of the joint consumers may exercise the right to opt out. The opt out notice provided to joint account holders must explain how the bank will treat an opt out direction by a joint consumer and give one joint consumer the ability to opt out on behalf of all of the joint consumers.

- *Establish timeframes for mailing or otherwise delivering notices.* Remember:
  - **All existing bank customers must receive an initial privacy notice no later than July 1, 2001.**
  - **Existing bank customers, consumers who are not customers, and former bank customers** have the right to opt out if the bank is sharing nonpublic personal information about them with nonaffiliated third parties outside the exceptions.
  - Information sharing subject to opt out cannot continue after July 1, 2001, until the initial and opt out notices are delivered and a reasonable opt out period has elapsed. Therefore, banks that intend to share nonpublic personal information outside the exceptions after July 1, 2001 should deliver notices well before July 1.

4. Prepare to respond to consumers

- *Develop opt out procedures.* All banks sharing nonpublic personal information outside of the exceptions will need to develop procedures for consumers to exercise an opt out, as well as procedures for processing and complying with opt out directions. The opt out procedures should include:
  - tracking the initial opt out opportunity (e.g., the first 30 days after the initial notice is delivered)
  - recording opt outs received from consumers
  - maintaining the opt out mechanism(s), such as a toll-free telephone number, electronic mail, or an opt out form with boxes to check
  - complying with opt out directions received after the initial opt out opportunity elapses
- *Respond to public inquiries.* Customer service representatives and other bank employees should be prepared to answer questions from consumers about the new privacy notices. Depending on the number of employees answering consumer phone calls, it may be a good idea to provide scripts to help employees respond to questions from the public. In addition, it may be helpful to have extra copies of the privacy notice readily available for mailing or handing out to consumers.

Section Three:
Maintaining Compliance Beyond July 1, 2001

The following activities can help a bank achieve and maintain compliance with the privacy rule.

- Develop controls to monitor ongoing compliance. Consider mechanisms for monitoring:
  - delivery of initial and annual notices to customers
  - delivery of initial notice to consumers who are not customers, if applicable
  - compliance with opt out directions, if applicable
  - accuracy of privacy notices, including prior approval for:
    - new marketing arrangements
    - new or renewed vendor contracts
    - disclosure of account numbers
    - affiliate-referral programs
    - reuse of consumer information received from another financial institution
- Train employees. All employees should understand the bank's policies and procedures for complying with the privacy rule. Some employees will need

to be able to explain the bank's privacy policies to customers and to businesses providing services to the bank.

- Audit for compliance. Periodic audits will help management assess risk and verify the effectiveness of the compliance program. The Federal Financial Institutions Examination Council (FFIEC) will release interagency privacy examination procedures before July 1, 2001. The exam procedures will be a useful tool in developing a privacy audit program.

The interagency exam procedures will be mailed directly to insured depository institutions as soon as they are finalized. The procedures will also be available on the FDIC's Web site at www.fdic.qov when complete.

Section Four:
Learn the Lingo

Learning the lingo will help you understand and comply with the privacy rule. This section provides an explanation of key terminology.

Who must comply with the FDIC's privacy rule?

The FDIC's privacy rule refers to financial institutions that must comply with the rule as "you." For example, when the rule states that "you must provide a notice" it means all entities subject to this rule must provide a notice. The following definition of "you" explains the types of entities subject to the rule:

You: The banks that must comply with the FDIC's rule are—

(1) FDIC-supervised banks

(2) insured state branches of foreign banks

(3) subsidiaries of FDIC-supervised banks and insured state branches of foreign banks, with certain exceptions, such as insurance and securities or brokerage subsidiaries

Although the FDIC's rule only applies to certain banks and some of their subsidiaries, all financial institutions must comply with similar privacy rules adopted by their supervisory agencies. For example, although securities subsidiaries of FDIC-supervised banks do not have to comply with the FDIC's privacy rule, they do have to comply with a similar privacy rule adopted by the Securities and Exchange Commission.

Who is protected by the privacy rule?

The privacy rule protects "consumers." **All consumers receive the same privacy protections.**

However, a subset of consumers defined as **customers** must receive certain disclosures, such as an annual privacy notice, that need not be provided to consumers who are not customers.

Thus, it is important to know the distinction between consumers and customers to understand the different disclosure requirements under the privacy rule.

Consumer: Any individual who is seeking to obtain or has obtained a financial product or service from a bank for personal, family, or household purposes is a consumer of that bank. The definition of consumer includes individuals who:

- **apply for** a financial product or service (e.g., a loan or a deposit account) for personal, family, or household purposes
- **actually obtain** a financial product or service (e.g., a loan or a deposit account) for personal, family, or household purposes

Customer: As the following diagram reflects, customers are a subset of consumers. A customer is a consumer with whom a bank has a **continuing relationship**. Although the rule does not define "continuing relationship," it provides examples of transactions that are and are not considered continuing relationships. Consumers who have a deposit account, obtain a loan, or obtain an investment advisory service are considered customers. See Section 332.3(i).

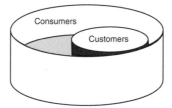

Additional guidance regarding the customer relationship can be found in the Supplemental Information (the preamble) of the rule, which notes that a continuing relationship is established "where a consumer typically would receive some measure of continued service following, or in connection with, a transaction." See page 35168, Federal Register, Vol. 65, No.106.

The next diagram depicts the relationship between all individuals who do business with a bank and those who meet the regulatory definitions for **consumers** and **customers**. As the diagram shows, only a portion of the individuals who conduct business with a bank are consumers under the privacy rule. For example, individuals are not considered consumers under this rule if they are commercial clients, grantors or beneficiaries of trusts for which the bank is trustee, or participants in an employee benefit plan that the banks sponsors.

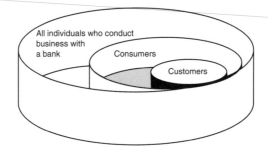

What type of information is protected by the privacy rule? The rule identifies three primary categories of information:

- publicly available information
- personally identifiable financial information
- nonpublic personal information

Nonpublic personal information **is the category of information protected by the privacy rule.** The definitions for publicly available information and personally identifiable financial information work together to describe and define nonpublic personal information.

- *Publicly available information* is any information a bank reasonably believes is lawfully publicly available. The **nature** of the information, **not the source** of the information, determines whether it is publicly available information for purposes of the privacy rule. For example, even if a bank obtains customers' telephone numbers or the assessed value of their residences directly from the consumers, this information will be considered publicly available if the bank has a reasonable basis to believe the information could have been lawfully obtained from a public source. A reasonable belief exists if a bank has determined that (a) the information is of the type that is generally available to the public and (b) the individual has not blocked such information from public disclosure. This means, for example, that a bank can consider a customer's phone number to be publicly available, but only if the bank takes steps to determine the phone number is not unlisted.

- *Personally identifiable financial information* is any information a bank collects about a consumer in conjunction with providing a financial product or service. This includes:

  - information provided by the consumer during the application process (e.g., name, phone number, address, income)

  - information resulting from the financial product or service transaction (e.g., payment history, loan or deposit balances, credit card purchases)

  - information from other sources about the consumer obtained in connection with providing the financial product or service (e.g., information from a consumer credit report or from court records)

Personally identifiable financial information also includes any information that "is disclosed in a manner that indicates that the individual is or has been your consumer." See Section 332.3(o)(2)(i)(D). **Thus, the very fact that an individual is a consumer of a bank is personally identifiable financial information.**

- *Nonpublic personal information*, the category of information protected by the privacy rule, consists of:

  1. Personally identifiable financial information that is not publicly available information; and

2. Lists, descriptions, or other groupings of consumers that were either

    a. **created using** personally identifiable financial information that is not publicly available information, or

    b. **contain** personally identifiable financial information that is not publicly available information.

A list is considered nonpublic personal information if it is **generated** based on customer relationships, loan balances, or other personally identifiable financial information that is not publicly available. A list is also considered nonpublic personal information if it **contains** any nonpublic personal information.

For example, in jurisdictions where mortgage documents are public records, the names and address of all individuals for whom a bank held a mortgage would not be nonpublic personal information since it was generated using publicly available information and contained only publicly available information. The list would become nonpublic personal information, however, if it contained current loan balances or if it was generated using only those customers with current mortgage loan balances in excess of a certain amount.

The two categories of non public personal information are depicted in the following diagram.

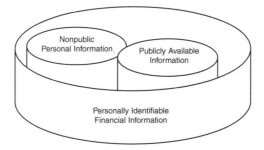

Who are nonaffiliated third parties?

The privacy rule restricts information sharing with nonaffiliated third parties. The rule defines nonaffiliated third parties as persons or entities except affiliates and persons jointly employed by a bank and a nonaffiliated third party. Affiliates generally include a bank's subsidiaries, its holding company, and any other subsidiaries of the holding company. See Section 332.3(a), Section 332.3(d), and Section 332.3(g).

The privacy rule does not impose limitations on information sharing with affiliates. It does, however, require disclosure of such information sharing policies and practices. (Note: The rules governing the sharing of information between a bank and its affiliates are set forth in the Fair Credit Reporting Act.)

Although the privacy rule most commonly uses the term "nonaffiliated third parties," there are some instances in which a distinction is made between nonaffiliated financial institutions and all other nonaffiliated third parties. Readers should pay particular attention to these distinctions. See Section 332.13.

Other Resources

A variety of resources are available to help banks understand the privacy rule and related issues. Some of the most significant are listed below. All FDIC material can be found at www.fdic.gov.

FDIC Financial Institution Letter titled *Final Rule on the Privacy of Consumers' Financial Information*, (FIL-34-2000 dated June 5, 2000).

FDIC Financial Institution Letter titled *Proposed Regulations Implementing the Fair Credit Reporting Act*. (FIL-71-2000 dated October 26, 2000).

FDIC Financial Institution Letter titled *Proposed Security Standards for Customer Information*, (FIL-43-2000 dated July 6, 2000).

FDIC Financial Institution Letter titled *Internet Web Site Privacy Survey Report*, (FIL-113-99 dated December 27, 1999).

FDIC Financial Institution Letter titled *Online Privacy of Consumer Financial Information*, (FIL-86-98 dated August 17, 1998).

Transcript of *"Is It Any of Your Business? Consumer Information, Privacy, and the Financial Services Industry,"* an interagency public forum hosted by the FDIC, March 23, 2000.

Office of the Comptroller of the Currency's Bulletin titled Privacy Laws and Regulations, (September 8, 2000) available at www.occ.treas.gov.

Office of Thrift Supervision's Memorandum to Chief Executive Officers titled *Privacy Preparedness Check-up*, (September 29, 2000) available at www.ots.treas.gov.

APPENDIX III

GRAMM-LEACH-BLILEY— FINANCIAL PRIVACY REGULATIONS

The federal agencies (the FTC, FDIC, Federal Reserve Board, OCC, OTS, and NCUA) have promulgated regulations to implement the financial privacy provisions of the Gramm-Leach-Bliley Act ("GLB Act"). These new rules will require financial institutions to (I) disclose their privacy policies and practices regarding sharing consumers' nonpublic personal information with affiliated and non-affiliated third-parties and (2) give consumers the right to opt-out of having this information shared with the non-affiliated third parties.

• WHEN DO THE RULES TAKE EFFECT?

Although the rules are effective as of November 13, 2000, the "full compliance date" is July 1, 2001. Full compliance means that all initial privacy notices and opt-out provisions must be delivered to customers before July 1, 2001, and if consumers' nonpublic personal information is to be disclosed without interruption to a non-affiliated third party of a financial institution, the consumers must have been given a reasonable opportunity to opt-out prior to that date.

• WHICH ENTITIES MUST COMPLY WITH THE REGULATIONS?

The rules will affect all "financial institutions" (as very broadly defined) and those entities to which financial institutions disclose "nonpublic personal information" about consumers. "Financial institutions" are any entities that are "significantly engaged" in any financial activity listed in section 4(k) of the Bank Holding Company Act. Financial activities include: (1) lending, (2) credit reporting, (3) debt collecting, (4) exchanging or transferring money, (5) investing for others, (6) insuring or indemnifying against loss or (7) dealing in securities.

Reprinted with the permission of Marcus Heyder, Anne Fortney, and Lovells.

Under this definition, "financial institution" includes not only creditors and lessors but also loan servicers, mortgage brokers, auto dealers, consumer reporting agencies and debt collectors.

"Significantly engaged" is undefined, but the regulations offer some guidance in the form of examples of entities not significantly engaged in financial activities, such as a merchant who allows an individual to "run a tab." The regulations do not specifically address whether or not a retailer that arranges for a non-affiliated financial institution to offer the retailer's customers a private label credit card is a financial institution. They also do not specifically exempt all special-purpose securitization entities from the definition of financial institution.

- **WHAT INFORMATION IS COVERED BY THE REGULATIONS?**

The regulations cover "nonpublic personal information." Both the GLB Act and the regulations define the term as: (i) personally identifiable financial information, or (ii) a consumer list (and publicly available information pertaining to the customers on that list) that has been derived using personally identifiable financial information that is not publicly available.

The regulations, however, define "personally identifiable financial information" so broadly as to include information that is not intrinsically financial in nature. "Personally identifiable financial information" is (i) any information that a consumer provides to a financial institution in order to obtain a financial product or service, (ii) any information resulting from a transaction between the consumer and the financial institution, or (iii) any information about a consumer that a financial institution otherwise obtains in connection with providing a financial product or service to the consumer. Thus, any information that a financial institution obtains from a consumer or an applicant and *any* information resulting from the consumer's transaction is personally identifiable financial information and is included within the definition unless it is "publicly available information." For example, if a consumer provides information to a financial institution when applying for a loan or credit card, that information and the fact that the consumer has become the financial institution's customer is "nonpublic personal information" unless it is publicly available information. Similarly, information collected by the financial institution through an Internet "cookie" (an information collecting device from a web server) placed on that customer's computer when he accesses his account is nonpublic personal information unless it is publicly available.

- **WHAT KIND OF INFORMATION IS "PUBLICLY AVAILABLE INFORMATION"**
  AND THUS EXCLUDED FROM THE DEFINITION OF "NONPUBLIC PERSONAL
  INFORMATION"?

Financial institutions may freely disclose any information that is "publicly available" as defined by the regulations. Information is publicly available if a financial institution has a "reasonable basis to believe" it is lawfully made available to the general public from (i) government records, (ii) widely distributed media, or (iii) disclosures to the public required to be made by the government. A financial institution has a reasonable basis to believe information is lawfully made available if the institution takes steps to determine (i) that the information is of the type that is available to the general public; and (ii) that a consumer who may exercise control over the distribution of that type of information has, in fact, not directed that the information be unavailable to the public. For example, the regulations provide that a financial institution has a reasonable basis to believe a telephone number is publicly available if the number is in the telephone book, or a consumer informs the institution that the number is not unlisted. (The regulations do not address how a financial institution is to make this determination in the case of existing customers who have not been asked whether their telephone number is unlisted.)

The regulations also provide that financial institutions might have a reasonable basis to believe that mortgage loan information is publicly available as long as the financial institution, has determined that the mortgage information is included on the public record in the relevant jurisdiction. Regarding other types of information, the FTC cautions in its Supplemental Information that, even if information is of a type generally available, a financial institution should not automatically assume that an individual's information is publicly available, especially if an individual has some measure of control over the information's availability.

• TO WHOM MUST FINANCIAL INSTITUTIONS GIVE DISCLOSURE NOTICES ABOUT PRIVACY POLICIES AND OPT-OUT PROVISIONS?

The regulations establish two categories of people who must receive notices: "customers" and "consumers." A "consumer" means an individual who obtains (or has obtained) a financial service or product from a financial institution when that financial product or service is to be used for personal, family or household purposes. (The term also includes a consumer's legal representative.) The term includes an applicant for such a financial product or service, regardless of whether the application is accepted. "Consumers" also includes an individual who provides nonpublic personal information to a financial institution to determine whether he or she may qualify for a financial product or service regardless of whether the product or service is ever provided.

A consumer differs from a customer in that a customer has a continuing customer relationship with a financial institution. The distinction is not always obvious. A one-time transaction may be sufficient to establish a customer relationship, depending on the nature of the transaction. However, a consumer will not become a customer simply by repeatedly engaging in isolated transactions that would by themselves be insufficient to establish a customer relationship, such as withdrawing funds from an ATM.

- ## What type of notices must financial institutions provide to customers and consumers?

Essentially, a financial institution must provide "initial privacy notice," an "annual privacy notice" and "opt-out notices." The regulations also provide for "revised privacy notices" when disclosure policies and practices change. Customers and consumers are accorded different privacy protections under the regulations. A consumer (including an applicant or a pre-application inquirer) receives a financial institution's privacy policy (or "short-form" thereof) and opt-out notice *only* if a financial institution intends to disclose nonpublic information about the consumer to non-affiliated third parties. A customer, on the other hand, gets notices of the institution's privacy policy regardless of whether the financial institution discloses the customer's nonpublic personal information.

When there are joint account holders, a financial institution may provide one privacy notice (it may provide more at its discretion), but must honor requests from one or more account holders for separate notices.

- ## Are there model forms for the privacy and notices?

In response to industry requests, the regulations include model forms to facilitate compliance. The model forms may be used if they accurately state the financial institution's policies, and they must include illustrative examples, as applicable.

- ## What information must a financial institution include in a privacy notice?

Generally, a privacy notice must disclose the "categories" of "nonpublic personal information" a financial institution collects and shares with affiliates and non-affiliated third parties. It also must disclose the "categories" of such affiliates and non-affiliated third parties who receive nonpublic personal information. The categories should include the level of detail that is in the following phrases: "information from the consumer," "information from a consumer reporting agency" and "non-profit organizations." These categories should be followed by "a few examples." The privacy notice must disclose the financial institution's policies on sharing information about former customers. The notice must inform a customer or consumer of the right to opt-out of nonpublic personal information sharing. A financial institution may state generally that it makes disclosures to non-affiliated third parties "as permitted by law" to describe disclosures made pursuant to one of the exceptions in the regulations. Under certain circumstances involving consumers, financial institutions may provide a "short-form" initial notice along with an opt-out notice, stating where and how the more complete privacy disclosure may be obtained. A financial institution may provide "simplified notices" to customers if the financial institution will not disclose that customer's nonpublic personal information to an affiliate or a non-affiliated third party.

- **WHAT INFORMATION MUST A FINANCIAL INSTITUTION INCLUDE IN AN OPT-OUT NOTICE?**

An opt-out notice must accurately explain that a customer or consumer has the right to opt-out of allowing a financial institution disclose nonpublic personal information to a non-affiliated third party and provide the customer or consumer a reasonable means to opt-out. The notice must state the categories of nonpublic personal information that the financial institution discloses, as well as the categories of non-affiliated third parties to whom such disclosures are made.

- **WHEN MUST A FINANCIAL INSTITUTION SEND PRIVACY AND OPT-OUT NOTICES?**

A financial institution must provide a privacy policy notice (or "short-form" thereof) and an opt-out notice to a consumer who is not a customer (such as an applicant) before it discloses any nonpublic personal information to a third party. A financial institution must provide an initial privacy policy notice not later than the time of establishing a customer relationship. This initial privacy policy notice must include an explanation of the opt-out right if the financial institution intends to disclose nonpublic personal information. The institution must also provide existing customers with notice of its privacy policy once every twelve months. In all cases, opt-out notice must be provided prior to disclosing any nonpublic personal information. The institution must also give a consumer or customer sufficient time to exercise the opt-out right before disclosing this information.

The regulations provide examples of when a customer relationship is established, but do not provide a general rule explaining the actual event that marks the establishment of a customer relationship. For example, a customer relationship is established when a consumer opens a credit card account with a financial institution or executes a lease for personal property with the institution. However, the regulations do not address whether the date a credit card application is approved or the date when the customer first uses a credit card should be the date of establishing the relationship. A financial institution establishes a customer relationship with a consumer when it originates a loan to the consumer. When a financial institution transfers the servicing rights to that loan to another financial institution, the customer relationship transfers as well, but the customer remains a consumer of the original institution.

In two instances, a financial institution may provide the initial notice *after* the customer relationship is established, though it must provide the notice within a reasonable amount of time. First, later notice is permissible if the customer relationship is not established at the customer's election. For example, if a financial institution acquires the servicing rights to a customer's loan and the customer does not have a choice about the acquisition, the acquiring financial institution would have to provide an initial notice within a "reasonable time" upon transfer of the relationship. Second, a later notice may be provided if the consumer's transaction would be substantially delayed by requiring the notice to be given by the time the customer relationship is established and the consumer agrees to receive the notice at a later time. An example is when a transaction is conducted over the telephone. The regulations do not define "reasonable time" for giving later notices to the customer.

A financial institution need not send a new initial privacy notice each time a customer obtains a new financial service or product from that institution. A new notice must be sent only if the institution's notice is not accurate with respect to the new product or service.

A financial institution must provide an annual notice at least once in any consecutive twelve month period. The institution may define the period, but must apply it to the customer on a consistent basis. A financial institution need not provide an annual notice to a former customer. The regulations provide examples, but no firm defining moment, as to when a customer becomes a "former customer." For example, in the case of a closed-end loan, when the customer has paid the loan in full and the financial institution has charged off the loan, the customer becomes a "former customer."

- ## HOW MAY A FINANCIAL INSTITUTION DELIVER A PRIVACY OR OPT-OUT NOTICE TO A CONSUMER OR CUSTOMER?

Delivery of privacy and opt-out notices may be accomplished by hand delivery, mail, or, in connection with electronic transactions, on an electronic site. The regulations do not permit oral delivery of the notices alone, either in person or by telephone.

In the case of initial notices on a website, a consumer or customer must acknowledge receipt of the notice on the site as a step in the process of obtaining a financial product or service. For ATM transactions, the opt-out notice may be displayed on the ATM machine screen, and the consumer must be required to acknowledge receipt before proceeding with the transaction. For other isolated transactions, a financial institution must provide the privacy and opt-out notices at the time of the transaction, and require the consumer to make the opt-out decision prior to completing the transaction. A financial institution is not required to send annual notices to customers who have indicated that they want no communications about their customer relationship from the financial institution.

- ## HOW MAY A CUSTOMER OR CONSUMER EXERCISE THE OPT-OUT RIGHT?

A financial institution provides a reasonable means for a consumer or customer to exercise the opt-out right if it designates check-off boxes in a prominent position on the relevant forms with the opt-out notice; includes a reply form that includes the address to which the form should be mailed; provides an electronic means to opt-out, such as a form that can be sent via electronic mail or a process at the financial institution's web site (provided that the consumer has agreed to electronic delivery of information); or provides a toll-free number that consumers or customers may call to opt-out. However, if a consumer or customer must write his own letter to exercise the opt-out right, the means are unreasonable. The FTC's Supplementary Information states that a financial institution may require each consumer or customer to opt-out through a specific means, as long as that means is reasonable for the consumer or customer and is one of the means enumerated above (or is comparable).

• HOW ARE OPT-OUT RIGHTS APPLIED TO JOINT ACCOUNT HOLDERS?

In the case of joint accounts, financial institutions may provide opt-out notices to only one account holder, unless one or more of the account holders requests a separate notice.

Any of joint account holders may exercise the right to opt-out. The financial institution has the option of (1) treating the opt-out by any joint account holder as applying to all of the account holders or (2) permitting each joint consumer to opt-out separately. However, the financial institution may *not* require all joint account holders to opt-out.

• WHAT ARE THE EXCEPTIONS TO THE NOTICE AND OPT-OUT REQUIREMENTS?

An exception for the *opt-out only* applies for service providers and joint marketing, but the financial institution must contract with the service provider or marketer to protect against inappropriate disclosure or use of nonpublic personal information.

The following other exceptions apply to the disclosure, as well as, requirements:

- A *"processing and servicing"* exception permits a financial institution to disclose nonpublic personal information "as necessary to effect, administer or enforce a transaction" that a consumer requests or authorizes. This exception includes servicing or processing, private label card functions, securitizations and secondary market sales.

- The consumer may *consent* to disclosure of nonpublic personal information, as long as the consent has not been revoked. The FTC expressly declined to clarify whether consent must be specific and express or whether it can be implied, such as in the case where the financial institution shares information under a co-brand arrangement, private label product or three-party sales financing transaction and the nature of the product *requires* the information sharing. However, the Supplemental Information to the FTC Rule states that financial institutions should "take steps to ensure that the limits of the consent are well understood by both the financial institution and the consumer."

- The notice and requirements also do not apply to disclosures:
    - To protect the confidentiality or security of the financial institution's records on its consumers,
    - To protect against or prevent fraud, unauthorized transactions, claims or other liability,

- To facilitate institutional risk control or to resolve consumer disputes or inquiries,

- To the consumer's legal representative, fiduciary or similar representative,

- To provide information to insurance rate advisory organizations, guaranty funds or agencies, rating agencies, standards assessors, attorneys, accountants and auditors,

- To the extent specifically permitted or required under other laws, to law enforcement agencies, state insurance agencies, self-regulatory organizations or a public safety examination,

- To a consumer reporting agency or from a consumer report,

- In connection with a proposed or actual sale, merger, or similar business transfer (if the disclosure concerns solely consumers of such business or unit),

- To comply with applicable laws or legal requirements, government investigations or judicial process.

- ## UNDER WHAT CIRCUMSTANCES MAY A FINANCIAL INSTITUTION DISCLOSE ACCOUNT NUMBERS TO NON-AFFILIATED THIRD PARTIES?

Account numbers and account access devices only may be disclosed to affiliates of the financial institution, to a consumer reporting agency or to a financial institution's agent or service provider that performs marketing for the financial institution. They may be disclosed to a participant in a private label credit card program where the participants in the program are identified when the customer enters into the program. Account numbers may be disclosed in encrypted form to other non-affiliated third parties as long as the financial institution does not provide the recipient with a means to decode the number.

- ## WHAT ARE THE LIMITS ON REDISCLOSURE AND REUSE OF INFORMATION?

The regulations' restrictions on redisclosure and reuse of nonpublic personal information by a non affiliated third party apply whether or not the third party is a financial institution. Generally, nonpublic personal information may be redisclosed and reused consistent with the consumer's or customer's opt-out decision. Thus, an entity may redisclose information that was not received pursuant to one of the exceptions, only (1) to affiliates of the financial institution that disclosed the information; (2) to the entity's own affiliates; or (3) to other parties if the original financial institution could have disclosed the information to such parties in light of its own disclosure policies and the consumer's or customer's opt-out decision. The information also may be redisclosed and reused under some, but not all, of the exceptions. Nonpublic personal information that is received by an entity pursuant to an exception (other than the service providers and joint marketing exception) may be redisclosed only (1) to the affiliates of the initial financial institution that disclosed the information (2) to the entity's own affiliates, and the information may be used and disclosed by the entity only for the purposes of the exception under which it received the information.

Because entities that receive nonpublic personal information from financial institutions are restricted in how they can reuse and redisclose such information by the initial financial institution's privacy policies and the consumers' opt-out decisions, the FTC's Supplementary Information observes that the receiving entities must have procedures in place so they can continually monitor the status of such decisions.

CHAPTER 10

Secured Lending: Mortgages, Security Interests, and Uniform Commercial Code 9

REVISED UCC 9—TRADE NAMES

Section 9-402 (7) states as follows:

> "A financing statement sufficiently shows the name of the debtor if it gives the individual partnership or corporate name of the debtor, whether or not it adds other trade names or names of partners."

Recite the proper corporate name, the proper partnership name, and the proper individual name. The use of the trade name is superfluous, and *without the proper corporate name* will result in an unperfected filing. The state of Texas in adopting the revised UCC 9 provides in Section 9-503 that "a financing statement that provides only the debtors trade name does not sufficiently provide the name of the debtor." Even if the trade name was substantially similar to the corporate name, it would not be sufficient. The Texas statute also states that a financing statement that provides the name of the debtor is not rendered ineffective by the absence of a trade name or other name of the debtor.

As the states adopt Revised Article 9, they may modify or attempt to clarify Revised UCC 9, but essentially the basic statute states that the filing must be in the individual, partnership, or corporation name.[1]

NOTICE OF SALE

Despite the many cases involving the issue as well as the checklists used by financial institutions and the many articles written on the subject, creditors still fail to give notice to the debtors of a sale.

We have another case where the debtor abandoned the property and the creditor did not give notice of the sale. Section 9-504 of the Uniform Commercial Code sets forth as follows:

> "Unless collateral is perishable or threatens to decline speedily in value or is of a type customarily sold on recognized market, reasonable notification of the time and place of any public sale or reasonable notification of the time after which any private sale or other intended disposition is to be made shall be sent by the secured party to the debtor, if he has not signed after default a statement renouncing or modifying his right to notification of sale. A reminder that notice should also be sent to guarantors, co-signers, co-makers, etc."[2]

DRAGNET CLAUSE—RELATEDNESS RULE

A "dragnet clause" provides that the collateral described in a security agreement secures any new advances, extension, renewals, or refinancing. It may secure any other amounts that the debtor may owe to their lender now or in the future.

---

[1]*Stanton v. Texas Drug Co., (In re Stanton)* 254 B.R. 357 (Bkrtcy. E.D. Tx. 2000).

[2]*Brockbank v. Best Capital Corp.,* 341 S.C. 372, 534 S.E. 2d 688 (2000) (Supreme Court of South Carolina).

The "relatedness rule" serves to limit the application of a future advance clause to those advances that are of the same class as the primary transaction. The relatedness rule developed prior to the enactment of the Uniform Commercial Code and was a reflection of the disfavor with which the courts viewed dragnet clauses in security agreements, notwithstanding the fact they were common. This device is abused when a lender, relying on a broadly drafted clause, seeks to bring within the shelter of his security arrangements claims against the debtor that are unrelated to the financing that was contemplated by the parties. The courts have regularly curbed such abuses no matter how well the clause is drafted, for the future advances to be covered must be of the same class as the primary obligation or so related to it that the consent of the debtor to its inclusion may be inferred.

One particular court has set down four tests to be applied in the application of the relatedness rule.

1. Whether the indebtedness allegedly covered by the mortgage containing said dragnet clause is specifically intentional.
2. Whether the other indebtedness allegedly covered is of the same class as the debt referenced in the mortgage.
3. Whether the indebtedness was intended to be separately secured.
4. Whether the mortgagee relied on the dragnet clause in making further loans.

Under these tests, it would seem that any future advance must be used for the same purpose as the original advance. The debtor should have some knowledge of the presence of the dragnet clauses, although some courts feel this is cured by the mere execution of the security agreement. As to the question of the lender relying on the dragnet clause, this particular test is not an essential ingredient in most decisions.

The "same class" test is also applied rather differently by various courts. Some courts will treat loans of a business nature as the same class. Loans to satisfy an overdraft business checking account were not related to a prior loan. While courts do not generally approve of dragnet clauses, whether or not the court will uphold the terms in the security agreement or the mortgage agreement appears to be decided more on a case-by-case basis than by any fixed precedent. While the reasons for enforcing or for not enforcing the dragnet clause vary from state to state and from court to court, most of the courts pay lip service to the "relatedness rule" in holding some relationship must exist between the original indebtedness and the future advance and some inferred consent by the debtor. Both issues are subjective, and no black-and-white line is drawn.[3]

CONTINUATION STATEMENT

The Uniform Commercial Code provides in Section 9-403 the following:

> "A filed financing statement is effective for a period of five years from the date of filing. The effectiveness of a filed financing statement lapses on the expiration of the five-year period unless a continuation of statement is filed prior to the lapse....A continuation statement may be filed by the secured party within 6 months prior to the expiration of the five-year period."

The number of filings that occur on the last day of the five-year period lead to significant litigation over the measurement of the five-year period. Despite a six-month window within which to file a continuation statement, the tendency of a certain portion of the population to do things at the last minute apparently applies equally to the filing of financing statements.

Unfortunately, the measurement of the five-year period is not bright line and that's what causes the litigation. Many states have time computation statutes that refer to a particular act that must be done within a specific period of time. The time computation statute identifies the first day of the act as well as the last day of the act and usually explicit exclusions of certain days and inclusions of certain days are contained in the statute. If you are one of the many who decide to file on what you believe is the last day of the five-year period, review the time computation statute in the particular state. Your author cannot provide assurance that a time computation statute exists in every state and in those states where a statute does not exist, you must review the case law of the state to find the correct last day. The lesson: File at least a week prior to the five-year period—or even a month before.[4]

YIELD SPREAD PREMIUMS

Real Estate Settlement Procedures Act of 1974 (RESPA) prohibits the payment to a mortgage broker of kickbacks for referral of prospects to lenders seeking a federally backed mortgage.

---

[3]*In re Wollin*, 249 B.R. 555 (D. Or. 2000).

[4]*Bank of Holden v. Bank of Warrensburg*, 15 S.W. 3d 758 (2000) Court of Appeals of Missouri, Western District.

Section 8 of RESPA prohibits:

"any person from giving and any person from accepting any fee, kickback, or other thing of value pursuant to any agreement or understanding that business shall be referred to any person."

In plain and simple language, kickbacks or referral fees are not allowed. On the other hand, the law does provide for an exemption if the payments are compensation for goods or facilities actually furnished or for services actually performed. The test set by HUD (Department of Housing and Urban Development) in March 1, 1999 basically consists of a two-pronged criteria:

"Were the goods or facilities actually furnished or services actually performed for the total compensation and if they were actually performed, were they reasonably related to the value of the goods and services or facilities furnished."

About two years prior to the issuance of the March 1, 1999 policy statement, the leading case on the subject set forth a slightly different criteria to determine a violation. In the Culpepper case, if the fee is tied to the goods, facilities, or services purchased and only after it passes this test, you determine if the amount is reasonable.

The Culpepper decision was a situation where the broker was paid for an above par loan and it was held that the yield spread premium did not constitute a reasonable payment for goods or for services and did not fall within any of the exceptions. The court felt that the broker spent the same amount of time and the same quality and quantity of services whether it originated an above par loan, a par loan, or below par loan, and was only paid the additional fee when they generated an above par loan. On a motion for a re-hearing before the 11th Circuit, the Circuit Court of Appeals left open the fact that a lender might prove as a defense that a yield spread premium may be a legitimate payment for brokerage services. They flatly rejected that a yield spread premium is illegal per se.

This test was set forth in the lower court and then the 11th Circuit vacated the lower courts' denial of the class action claims and the motion for class certification and also decided to apply the HUD test. The case was remanded back to the district court. Several other cases in Alabama, Minnesota, and New York have also dealt with this particular problem.

Prior to the issuance of the HUD Policy Statement in March of 1999, the minority of the courts applied the test used in Culpepper with the majority of courts, leaning toward the test which ultimately became the policy statement of HUD. The core of the policy statement is as follows:

A. Goods or facilities must actually be furnished or services actually performed for the total compensation paid.

B. The total compensation must be reasonably related to the value of the goods or facilities that were actually furnished or services that were actually performed.

So long as the total compensation is justified, it is irrelevant whether all or part of the compensation is calculated with reference to the interest rate and it is irrelevant whether the components are paid entirely by the borrower, entirely by the lender, or partially by the lender and partially by the borrower. The HUD policy statement adopts the Independent Banker's Association of America letter in restating the list of 14 services that must be performed by a mortgage broker in connection with the origination of the loan. Sufficient origination work must be performed and at least 5 additional services identified. The reasonableness of the compensation uses a market value test in the policy statement. Payments to the broker must be no greater than the amount normally charged for similar services, goods, or facilities.

The violation causing the most litigation is the situation where a mortgage broker refers a prospect and earns a fee of a rate of interest higher than the lender required (yield spread premium). This additional fee is paid because the rate of interest that the borrower is paying is higher than the rate of interest that the lender advised the broker would be the minimum required. Whether the fee falls within the Culpepper test or the HUD test is still an open question, depending upon the facts and circumstances of each particular case. At the time of this writing, it still has not been resolved. Up to this point, the courts have interpreted the statute with a narrow approach. Whether added fees are illegal kickbacks or whether they are connected to the volume or the value of the business referred is still an open issue. In Culpepper, the court looked for any excess payment to the broker, but found that the fee was a fair market price paid to the broker for the loan and was not a referral fee. Even though the fee may be categorized as a referral fee, if it turns out that it is payment for goods, then it is not a referral fee. Furthermore, if a fee is paid by the borrower to a mortgage broker, this certainly would not constitute a violation of the statute.[5,6]

---

[5]*Culpepper v. Inland Mortgage Co.*, 132 F. 3d 692 (11th Cir. 1998); *Dujanovic v. MortgageAmerica, Inc.*, 185 F.R.D 660 (N.D. Ala. 1999); *McCrillis v. WMC Mortg. Corp.*, 133 F. Supp. 2d 470 (S.D. Miss. 2000).

[6]*Golon v. Ohio Sav. Bank*, 1999 WL 965593 (N.D., Ill. 1999); *Schmitz v. Aegis Mortgage Corp.*, 48 F. Supp. 2d 877 (D. Minn. 1999); *Brancheau v. Residential Mortg.*, 187 F.R.D 591 (D. Minn. 1999).

ACCOUNTS RECEIVABLE— FINANCING—FACTORING

One form of accounts receivable financing is known as "factoring arrangements" which are common in the textile industry and other industries. The factor (finance company) purchases the account receivable from the debtor corporation and assumes all the credit risk. The factor buys the account under an agreement that does not provide for any recourse or charge back against the debtor corporation if the account proves uncollectible. The factor will purchase the account for a percentage less than the face amount of the account receivable and in essence becomes the owner of the account. This fee represents the compensation for the factor assuming all the risks of collection. Under such an arrangement, neither the debtor corporation nor any of its creditors have any legitimate concern with any disposition that the factor may make of the accounts receivable. The factor is under no obligation to furnish the debtor corporation with a notice of sale or disposition of the said accounts receivable, because the factor is the owner.

Under another form of accounts receivable financing, the finance company (as distinguished from a factor) does not assume the credit risk, but still receives an assignment of the accounts receivable and advances money to debtor corporation (usually 2/3 to 4/5 of the face amount of the invoice). The finance corporation retains a right of full or limited recourse or charge back to the debtor corporation (or any guarantors) for any accounts that are uncollectible. Any disposition of the accounts receivable by the finance company under the terms of their agreement requires the finance company to provide notice to the debtor corporation or the guarantor, for such disposition may increase a deficiency claim or reduce a possible surplus to which the debtor corporation may be liable or entitled.[7]

JUDICIAL FORECLOSURE

Judicial foreclosure is a procedure available in all states wherein the mortgagor commences a suit to foreclose a real estate mortgage. The foreclosure procedure is heavily regulated by each state. In most states, a choice is available of judicial foreclosure, as distinguished from non-judicial foreclosure.

---

[7] *Al Gailani v. Riyad Bank Houston Agency*, 22 S.W.3d 560 (Tex. App. 2000).

In judicial foreclosure, a suit has to be commenced against the debtor in the same manner as any suit is instituted. The procedure varies from state to state; but, in general, before a judgment can be entered, procedures in many states have to be undertaken by the court to determine that no hardship will be inflicted upon the debtor and, in some instances, a person appointed by the court reviews the entire foreclosure proceeding to determine that it was properly performed and to determine that the amount claimed to be due is accurate. If a judgment of foreclosure is obtained, the creditor may hold a public sale after publication in the newspaper and, after the sale and application to the court, proceed against the debtor for the deficiency, if there is a deficiency. The procedures are enumerated in the statutes in the various states and require meticulous compliance. In a few states, this procedure can be accomplished within sixty or ninety days. In most states, the uncontested procedure takes at least six to eight months and, in some states, the procedure can run from a year to a year and a half to even two years or more before the creditor can obtain title to the property and obtain a deficiency judgment. If the foreclosure is contested, no estimate of the length of time to complete should be made.

NON-JUDICIAL FORECLOSURE

The non-judicial foreclosure is available in approximately thirty-five states and is heavily regulated, with the procedure carefully enumerated in the statutes of the respective states. The procedure requires sending out notices of a proposed sale by personally serving this information upon any person who has an interest in the property and publishing the sale over a period of weeks prior to the sale that a public sale may be held. A deficiency can be obtained against the debtor if the property does not bring sufficient monies. The advantages of a non-judicial sale is that usually it can be accomplished in a speedier time frame than the judicial foreclosure, from sixty to a hundred twenty days on average, although some states may still take as long as a year.

DEED IN LIEU OF FORECLOSURE

In order to avoid a judicial foreclosure and a non-judicial foreclosure, sometimes a creditor will accept a deed offered by the debtor in lieu of proceeding with the foreclosure. The debtor executes a deed in the same manner as an owner would to a purchaser and the lender becomes the owner of the property. The debtor may feel the property is worth more than the mortgage and may offer to sell the property to the mortgagee in consideration of a certain amount above the mortgage. The normal situation is where the value of the property is somewhat less than the balance due on the mortgage and the creditor accepts the deed and waives any further proceeding against the debtor. One of the strong motivating forces of a deed in lieu of foreclosure is the desire of the borrower to avoid the stigma of a foreclosure proceeding.

The lender must understand that the offering of a deed in lieu of foreclosure is not a defense to the lender's foreclosure action. If the lender believes the property is worth substantially less than the mortgage, the lender would be advised to institute a foreclosure action and obtain a deficiency judgment against the debtor—assuming the debtor possesses assets in addition to the property in question.

The courts do not look kindly on deeds in lieu of foreclosure since they feel that somehow the lender has coerced the debtor into transferring the property for an amount less than the value of the property. The lender and the borrower are not in equal bargaining positions and, if this is the case, the borrower at a later date might pursue a suit to set aside the transfer.

Another problem is where the debtor files a petition in bankruptcy shortly after the transfer is made. Any transfer made within ninety days of the petition, or within one year of the filing if the transfer is made to an insider, may be set aside. If the transfer is for an inadequate consideration, it also may be set aside. The lender must exercise caution.

Obtaining a title insurance policy is absolutely essential because the lender must treat this deed in lieu of foreclosure in the same way that any buyer would treat the purchase of any property and review all the potential liens or potential claims against the property.

Fraudulent Transfer

Another problem with the deed in lieu of foreclosure is that the courts sometimes frown upon this transaction because they feel the lender is somehow persuading the debtor into executing the deed. The conveyance may be a fraudulent transfer or a transfer without adequate consideration because the lender enjoyed an unconscionable advantage over the borrower.

If a transfer is made without adequate consideration, the borrower at a later date may move to set aside the transfer. If the debtor files a bankruptcy petition, the lender is faced with some additional problems when accepting a deed in lieu of foreclosure, for any transfer made by the bankrupt within ninety days prior to the filing of a bankruptcy petition or within one year of the filing if the transfer is made to an insider (relative or owner) may be set aside. A transfer made for an inadequate consideration may be considered a fraudulent transfer and is subject to being set aside by the trustee in bankruptcy. Fraudulent transfers may be set aside if they are made within a year prior to the filing of a bankruptcy petition and in some states, the statute of limitations for a fraudulent transfer exceeds the one-year period set forth in the bankruptcy court.

Appraisal

The lender can exercise caution to overcome some of these risks of a deed in lieu of foreclosure. The first and probably the most important is to obtain an independent appraisal of the property to establish that the fair market value of the property is equal to or less than the amount of the mortgage debt. Most problems arise because an appraisal has not been made and the debtor claims that the value of the property was greater than the amount of the mortgage and the debtor was coerced or unduly influenced into executing the deed. The independent appraisal can be used if the debtor files a bankruptcy and the trustee asserts a fraudulent transfer or a transfer made without adequate consideration. The risk of a trustee asserting a preference with regard to the transfer will remain in any deed in lieu of the foreclosure, where the debtor is threatening to file a bankruptcy petition or the financial condition of the debtor indicates that a bankruptcy petition is imminent.

As a normal course of doing business, a title company usually will not issue a title policy unless the independent appraisal shows that the value of the property is somewhat below the amount of the debt. The title policy issued to the lender is a policy that was issued to protect a mortgagee. When the lender accepts a deed in lieu of foreclosure, the lender should obtain an owner's policy, as opposed to a lender's policy. The title insurance company may want to approve the independent appraisal or may want to conduct the appraisal themselves before issuing a policy.

No Interest in Property

The lender should not permit the borrower to have any further interest in the property, such as any option to purchase, a right of first refusal when the lender sells, or any type of a lease. The risk is that the court might interpret such relationships between the lender and the borrower as creating a mortgage in lieu of a transfer of property. If the courts determine that it is a mortgage, the lender would be in the same place he was before and would be faced with a judicial or non-judicial foreclosure, rather than a deed in lieu of foreclosure. The lender also must treat this deed in lieu of foreclosure in the same way that one would treat the purchase of any property, and review all other liens or potential claims against the property.

Merger of Title

Where the same person owns a mortgage and the property, the mortgage merges into the title and disappears. This concept is disadvantageous to the lender, for if the transfer to the lender should ever be set aside, the lender wants to maintain the mortgage. Accordingly, the lender will usually set forth in their agreements with the debtor that the mortgage shall remain alive and the mortgage will maintain its priority over any other liens that were filed after the date of the original mortgage. Nevertheless, to keep the mortgage alive, the debt must be kept alive in the same manner and the settlement agreement between the parties must establish that the debt is to remain alive to support the fact that the mortgage will remain alive. This is usually solved by the lender agreeing not to sue the debtor on the debt, in exchange for the deed in lieu of foreclosure providing that the transfer is never set aside, and providing that the debtor does not file a petition in bankruptcy.

This section touches only the highlights of a deed in lieu of foreclosure. Considering a deed in lieu of foreclosure requires the balancing of various choices to be made, and consultation with an experienced attorney is recommended.

COOPERATIVE APARTMENTS

The owner of the condominium is the fee owner of the apartment and a portion of the common areas. The legal status is in the nature of ownership of real estate, and a condominium is treated as real property. A deed or mortgage is used to transfer ownership in the same manner as real estate is transferred or mortgaged.

A cooperative apartment involves two types of relationships, both of them not in the nature of ownership in real estate. The first relationship is that of a stockholder in a corporation and the second relationship is that of a lessee who enjoys a lease relationship with the parent corporation (the cooperative). Cooperative ownership is treated as personal property. When a lease terminates, the tenant would normally owe to the landlord the rent up until the time the lease was terminated, the use and occupancy after the lease was terminated during the time that the tenant still remained in the apartment and, finally, there would probably be a clause in the lease that would require the tenant to pay to the landlord the balance of the rent required under the lease after subtracting any rent that the landlord collected from renting the premises during the term of the lease. The normal cooperative relationship involves the long-term lease together with stock ownership in the corporation. The party who is the lessee and the owner of the stock must be one and the same party.

It is common in cooperatives that the stock cannot be sold or transferred without the consent of the cooperative board and, at the same time, that the lessee cannot sub-lease the premises without the consent of the cooperative board. If a cooperative board is to terminate a lease and evict a tenant for non-payment, usually the agreement with the cooperative board permits the cooperative board to cancel the stock certificates and issue a new stock certificate to whomsoever the cooperative board decides to lease the premises to, and to issue a new certificate to this party as well as a new lease.

Some courts have rejected this particular posture and do not allow the cooperative board to cancel the stock and issue a new stock certificate when the lease is terminated. The reverse situation also can come into play where the owner of the stock certificate dies and leaves the stock to an heir who is not suitable to the board. Some leases provide that the lease would terminate and automatically come to an end. This also presents problems to the cooperative board.[8]

A sale of a cooperative apartment is, in reality, a sale of the stock of the cooperative apartment and has nothing to do with the leasehold interest. The rights of a cooperative tenant flow from stock ownership and not from the proprietary lease which merely creates a landlord-and-tenant relationship between the cooperative corporation and the stockholder.[9]

COOPERATIVE APARTMENTS— SECURITY INTERESTS

Article 9 of the Uniform Commercial Code covers the obtaining of security interests in cooperatives. The use of financing statements and security agreements is the appropriate filing method under the Uniform Commercial Code. The tenant grants to the cooperative a security interest in the right, title, and interest to the shares of stock in the co-op, and the agreement includes pledging the leasehold interest as security. Some states

---

[8]*United States v. 110-118 Riverside Tenants Corp.*, 886 F. 2d 514 (2nd Cir. 1998).

[9]*State Tax Comm'n v. Shor*, 378 N.Y.S. 2d 222 (Sup. Ct. New York County 1975), aff'd 385 N.Y.S. 2d 290 (App. Div. 1st Dep't 1976), aff'd 371 N.E. 2d 523 (1977).

require the filing of a financing statement at the place where the mortgage and deed are filed for the real estate. A review of the UCC of the particular state is recommended.

As to foreclosure of a co-op, several options are available under the Uniform Commercial Code. First, a co-op may be sold under Section 9-504, which provides that the sale shall take place in a commercially reasonable manner, and the proceeds shall be applied in the same way as any sale under a security interest. Second, a tenant may proceed under 9-505, in which the board accepts the shares in full discharge of the obligation of the debtor, which rarely happens except where the debtor wishes to avoid a deficiency, and the collateral is clearly worth the debt. Third, judgment may be obtained and the creditor in some states may execute on the stock ownership or may make application under state law for a turnover of the stock or lease. Of course, in all of these situations, selling the cooperative is still subject to the approval of the board pursuant to the agreements with the board.

Judgment liens attach to a debtor's real property, but do not attach to personal property. Since most states treat co-op ownership as personal property, a recorded judgment lien would not attach to the shares or the leasehold interest. Whether a recorded mechanics lien can attach to the leasehold would probably depend upon the laws of the particular state. If the leasehold is considered real estate, the answer would be in the affirmative. On the other hand, if the leasehold is considered personal and not real estate, a recorded mechanics lien would not create a lien on the leasehold interest.

LIABILITY OF LEASING COMPANY

An issue that receives a fair share of litigation is whether a leasing company that is closely affiliated with an automobile manufacturer, a distributor, and a dealer, but still is a separate entity is subject to a customer's defense of breach of warranty. Can the leasing company enforce a vehicle lease over a defense that the vehicle suffers from manufacturing defects due to a breach of the new car warranty? This issue comes up frequently before the court and somehow each case is a little bit different from every other case, and the facts of each case are relevant to the decisions.

In the case at hand, the dealer made the debtor acknowledge that there were no express warranties regarding the vehicle as to its condition, merchantability, or fitness for use and that the contract disclaimed any implied warranties. The contract provided that the manufacturer's dispute-resolution system must be utilized before taking any action if there was a dispute regarding the manufacturer's warranty. A creditor selected a luxury car offered by the "Ray Caten Motorcar Corp." and leased the vehicle. He used a form of lease provided by the Mercedes-Benz Credit Corporation (MBCC) and executed a lease for a new Mercedes-Benz at a monthly rate of $1419.00. The total payments were $68,100. The lease provided for an assignment by Caten to MBCC pursuant to the terms of the dealer automobile purchase and lease agreement between the debtor and the MBCC, and the certificate of title was issued by MBCC.

When a transferee knew, controlled, or participated in the underlying transaction, the holder-in-due-course status is neither necessary nor desirable. Underlying the decision was the inequality and bargaining power between the typical consumer and lender. The lender not only enjoyed more economic and bargaining power, but greater expertise, along with the ability to write an adhesion contract that unduly favored the lender. The court denied holder-in-due-course status to finance companies whose involvement with the seller's businesses and whose knowledge of the terms of the underlying sale agreement was pervasive.

The court held that a consumer lessee may raise a breach of warranty claim against the lessor when a significantly close relationship exists between the seller, manufacturer, and the lessor and any attempt to disclaim such obligations by contract is unenforceable. The court relied upon Article 2A of the UCC which says that the courts will determine case by case whether the finance lessors are affiliates of the supplier of goods. The court apparently felt that Mercedes-Benz met all the criteria and that it was a question of which component in the chain of distributions of products will bear the loss due to a manufacturing defect, the manufacturer, its finance company, or its franchisee. If a truly independent lender finances a consumer's acquisition of a car, it is ordinarily expected that the lender will not be responsible if the car is a lemon. This was a New Jersey case. In most instances, the courts will lean towards the lender.[10]

---

[10]*Mercedes-Benz Credit Corp. v. Lotito*, 703 A. 2d 288 (N.J. Super. Ct. App. Div. 1997).

CHAPTER 10
APPENDIX I

UNITED STATES CODE ANNOTATED TITLE 7. AGRICULTURE CHAPTER 10—WAREHOUSES

259. SECURITY INTERESTS

(a) Receipts for products stored

Except as provided in subsection (b) of this section, for all agricultural products stored for interstate or foreign commerce, or in any place under the exclusive jurisdiction of the United States, in a warehouse licensed under this chapter *original receipts shall be issued by the warehouseman conducting the same,* but no receipts shall be issued except for agricultural products actually stored in the warehouse at the *time of the* issuance thereof.

(b) Transfer of agricultural products stored in warehouses

(1) Notwithstanding any other provision of this chapter, if a warehouseman, because of a temporary shortage, lacks sufficient space to store the agricultural products of all depositors in a licensed warehouse, the warehouseman may, in accordance with regulations issued by the Secretary of Agriculture and subject to such terms and conditions as the Secretary may prescribe, transfer stored agricultural products for which receipts have been issued out of such warehouse to another licensed warehouse for continued storage

(2) The warehouseman of a licensed warehouse from which agricultural products have been transferred under paragraph (1) shall deliver to the rightful owner of such products, on request, at the licensed warehouse where first deposited, such products in the amount, and of the kind, quality, and grade called for by the receipts or other evidence of storage of such owner.

(c) Central filing system records in lieu of receipts for cotton stored; delivery of cotton; electronic transmission facilities between warehouses and systems; system records equivalent to receipts and ownership interests; recordation and enforcement of liens in central filing system; warehousemen's liens unaffected; conditions for delivery on demand of cotton stored

(1)(A) Notwithstanding any other provision of Federal or State law, the Secretary of Agriculture, or the designated representative of the Secretary, may provide that in lieu of issuing a receipt for cotton stored in a warehouse licensed under this chapter or in any other warehouse the information required to be included in a receipt (i) under section 260 of this title in the case of a warehouse licensed under this chapter or (ii) under any applicable State law in the case of a warehouse not licensed under this chapter shall be recorded instead in a central filing system or systems maintained in one or more locations in accordance with regulations issued by the Secretary.

(B)   Any such record shall state that the cotton shall be delivered to a specified person or to the order of the person.

(C)   This subsection and subsection (d) of this section shall not apply to a warehouse that does not have facilities to electronically transmit and receive information to and from the central filing system. Nothing in this subsection shall be construed as to require a warehouseman to obtain the facilities.

(2) Notwithstanding any other provision of Federal or State law:

(A)   The record of the possessory interests of persons in cotton included in any such central filing system shall be deemed to be a receipt for the purposes of this chapter or State law and shall establish the possessory interest of persons in the cotton.

(B)   Any person designated as a holder of an electronic warehouse receipt authorized under this subsection and subsection (d) of this section shall, for the purpose of perfecting the security interest of the person under Federal or State law with respect to the cotton covered by the warehouse receipt, be considered to be in possession of the warehouse receipt. If more than one security interest exists in the cotton reflected on the electronic warehouse receipt, the priority of the security interests shall be determined by the applicable Federal or State law. This subsection is applicable to electronic cotton warehouse receipts and any other security interests covering cotton stored in a cotton warehouse regardless of whether the warehouse is licensed under this chapter.

(3)   A warehouseman conducting a warehouse covered under this subsection, in the absence of a lawful excuse, shall, without unnecessary delay, deliver the cotton stored in the warehouse on demand made by the person named in

the record in the central filing system as the holder of the receipt representing the cotton, if demand is accompanied by—

(A) an offer to satisfy a valid warehouseman's lien, as determined by the Secretary; and

(B) an offer to provide an acknowledgment in the central filing system, if requested by the warehouseman, that the cotton has been delivered.

(d) Administration of central filing system or systems; imposition and collection of fees; fund as depository for fees, late payment penalties, and investments; fund monies available for expenses

(1) The Secretary shall (under such regulations as the Secretary may prescribe) charge and provide for the collection of reasonable fees to cover the estimated costs to the Department of Agriculture incident to the functioning and the maintenance of any central filing system or systems referred to in subsection (c) of this section that is administered by the Department of Agriculture.

(2) The Secretary may provide for the fees to be collected by persons operating the central filing system administered by the Department from those persons recording information in the central filing system at such time and in such manners as may be prescribed in regulations issued by the Secretary.

(3) The fees shall be deposited into a fund which shall be available without fiscal year limitation for the expenses of the Secretary incurred in carrying out subsection (c) of this section and this subsection. Any sums collected or received by the Secretary under this chapter and deposited to the fund and any late payment penalties collected by the Secretary and credited to the fund may be invested by the Secretary in insured or fully collateralized, interest-bearing accounts or, at the discretion of the Secretary, by the Secretary of the Treasury in United States Government debt instruments. The interest earned on the sums and any late payment penalties collected by the Secretary shall be credited to the fund and shall be available without fiscal year limitations for the expenses of the Service incurred in carrying out subsection (c) of this section and this subsection.

CHAPTER 10
APPENDIX II

INTERNET LENDING AND COMPLIANCE WITH SECTION 8 OF RESPA[1]

Grant E. Mitchell, ESQ.[2]
Reed Smith LLP

INTRODUCTION

I was in charge of RESPA interpretations for many years. But that ended on April 1, 1999, so anything that I say about HUD's view must be viewed with a caveat—I do not speak for current or future Administrations, even though matters involving RESPA interpretations evolve slowly. And, of course, I would recommend that you hire your own counsel if you intend to create any sort of online mortgage lending arrangement.

RESPA is the Real Estate Settlement Procedures Act, a far-reaching federal law which Congress enacted in December, 1974, and which applies to almost all residential mortgage loan transactions, whether they are undertaken by pen, typewriter, computer, or the Internet. RESPA requires disclosures in covered transactions, it provides criminal and civil penalties for those who fail to follow

[1]Portions of these materials were published in the March 2000 issue of the MBA's *Mortgage Banking* magazine at page 84 under the title *A Twentysomething Does Online Lending.*

[2]Grant E. Mitchell is an attorney with the DC office of Reed Smith Shaw & McClay LLP. Prior to April 1999 he was the Senior Attorney for RESPA at the Department of Housing and Urban Development (HUD). Mr. Mitchell acknowledges the substantial contributions of Robert M. Jaworski in the preparation of these materials. Robert M. Jaworski is a partner in Reed Smith's Princeton, New Jersey office and a former Deputy Commissioner of the New Jersey Department of Banking. Both are members of the Reed Smith Consumer Financial Services Group.

Reprinted with the permission of Grant E. Mitchell.

A version of these materials was published in the *Quarterly Report* of the Consumer Finance Law Conference, Oklahoma City University of Law, and use of them here is gratefully acknowledged.

the rules; it also frequently referees who wins and loses in the online mortgage loan business.[3]

A. RESPA REFERRAL FEE PROHIBITION

The statute is deceptively simple. RESPA §8 and Regulation X prohibit a person from paying or receiving a "thing of value" pursuant to any "agreement or under-standing" that business incident to a "settlement service" involving a "federally-related mortgage loan" shall be referred, and this includes loan origination, defined as taking of loan applications, loan processing and the underwriting and funding of such loans. 12 U.S.C. §2607(a); 24 C.F.R. §3500.14(b). With limited exceptions, Regulation X provides that "any referral of a settlement service is not a compensable service," *Id.* On the other hand, RESPA §8 never prohibits a pay-ment by a lender to its duly appointed agent or contractor for services actually performed in the origination, processing, or funding of a loan, or a payment to any person of a "bona fide" salary or compensation or other payment for "goods or facilities actually furnished or for services actually performed." 24 C.F.R. §3500.14(g)(I)(iii) and (iv).

The dilemma in the e-commerce world (and frequently the paper-commerce world) is that the prohibitions run contrary to the business generation instincts of the "marketing people." "If I can get enough eyes to my site who eventually translate into customers for a lender, why shouldn't I be well-rewarded for my success?" Similar questions have been raised since the dawn of RESPA. Califor-nia case law involving commercial real estate transactions allows finder's fees to be paid[4]; many believed they should be permissible in residential real estate transactions as well. HUD said no.[5] Later, HUD also disallowed payments by a lender to real estate brokers, even though a state regulatory board allowed them.[6]

Economists occasionally suggest that a paid referral is economically cheaper than requiring a business to sift through a sea of uninterested persons to find the few who care for its product. Nonetheless, this view has not prevailed in the resi-dential real estate regulation context, and this may be because the precept that "a man's home is his castle" has been transmuted into the official policy of the Fed-eral government, and perhaps, the state governments as well—witness the special tax treatment accorded home purchase costs, the ongoing subsidy in the IRS tax

---

[3] Attachment A sets forth some commonly used terms described in RESPA and online mortgage lending

[4] See *Tyrone v. Kelley*, 9 Cal. 3d1, March 9, 1973; also *Grant v. Marinell*, 112 Cal. App. 3d 6172 (Novem-ber 1980); *Preach v. Rainbow*, Cal. App. 4th 1941 (January 1993).

[5] Letter from Robert Hollister dated February 25, 1978, collected in Barron's *Federal Regulation of Real Estate and Mortgage Lending*, Fourth Edition, Opinion 30.

[6] Letter from Grant Mitchell dated February 8, 1994, collected in Barron's *Federal Regulation of Real Estate and Mortgage Lending*, Fourth Edition, New Opinion 1.

code for interest paid during the life of the loan, the elimination of capital gains on residential property for all but the most expensive homes, and the nurturing of a well-established and well-funded secondary market to provide liquidity for home loans. Seen in this light, it is not surprising that a potential homebuyer and home-owner, who, at least twenty-six years ago when RESPA was first passed, was an infrequent venturer into home finance, would be accorded special consumer protections by the Congress. And despite wishful thinking that cyberworld is so clear, so simple, and so representative of the working of a perfect market that fraud and calumny will disappear, this is not yet proven and the laws of the paper world, including RESPA, are likely to remain.

In addition to the RESPA rules that were substantially revised in 1992[7], there have been three important issuances from HUD that bear on online mortgage lending. They are: the Retsinas, or IBAA, letter (IBAA letter, February 14, 1995), which itemizes a number of common origination services and sets forth a minimum number of services that a person would have to perform to justify compensation in a mortgage lending transaction (IBAA Test); the Computer Loan Origination Policy Statement of 1996 (CLO Statement, 61 Fed Reg. 29255, June 7, 1996), which sets forth broad policies showing how HUD views computer loan originations; and the HUD Policy Statement 1999-1 Regarding Mortgage Broker Fees (Broker Fee Statement, 64 Fed Reg. 10080, March 1, 1999), which sets forth important principles regarding compensable goods and services and cross-references the IBAA letter as providing useful information regarding compensable services.

I will now examine some common questions concerning the legality under RESPA §8 of certain practices connected with the marketing of mortgage loans in the e-commerce world. Using the HUD pronouncements mentioned above as a guide, I will attempt to provide answers to these questions, or at least give some thoughts on how HUD might be expected to address them.

B. SOME QUESTIONS AND ANSWERS REGARDING INTERNET LENDING

Question 1. Suppose a lender enters into an agreement with a Website Operator whereby the Website Operator creates a "hyperlink" on its website by which visitors can "click through" to the lender's website and be offered a special program of rates and terms? May the lender pay the Website Operator a fee based on the number of people who visit the Website Operator's website, or on the number of people who "click through" to the lender's website? How much of a fee can be paid by the lender to the Website Operator?

Answer: Payment based on the number of people who visit the Website Operator's website would appear analogous to payment advertisement being

---

[7]57 Fed. Reg. 49600, November 2, 1992.

based on the publication's circulation numbers. HUD has never questioned such payments, which, it seems, can rather convincingly be characterized as payment for a "good" (advertising space) or for "services" (the service of disseminating information to the public about the lender's products).

In addition, HUD has in the past approved payments for a list of potential customers.[8] It seems that a payment to the Internet Website Operator based on the number of "click throughs" can be perceived as payment for a stream of prospects, at least insofar as there is no obvious "endorsement" of the lender and/or its products by the Website Operator.[9] However, these payments would undoubtedly have to be minimal, say, a maximum of several dollars per item, and payments for comparable prospects list or advertising rates in the industry would likely be used for comparison. To be logically entitled to achieve greater payments, it would appear that the Website Operator would have to be in a position to undertake or contract to perform, and actually perform, settlement type services.

Question 2. If only minimal fees can be paid, how can the Website Operator legally earn greater fees? Must the Website Operator perform a variety of loan services as specified in the IBAA letter to receive more substantial compensation, including (say) a flat fee or a percentage fee per loan? Would such an arrangement meet the safe harbor provisions of 24 C.F.R. 3500.14(g)(1)(iii) and (iv)?

(a) *Under the IBAA Test.* It appears arguable that payments to the Website Operator of a flat fee for, or a percentage of the amount of, each loan originated through the Website Operator's website could only be characterized under the IBAA Test as a permissible payment by the wholesale lender if the Website Operator is performing or arranging for performance of origination-type services. The test for compensability would be whether the services provided by the operator satisfied the threshold level of origination services set forth in the IBAA Letter (Listed Services).

Some relatively ministerial duties that the Website Operator can undertake would include taking the borrower's application, initiating/ordering verifications of employment and deposits, initiating/ordering requests for mortgage and other loan verifications, initiating/ordering appraisals, and ordering flood certifications. In addition, the Website Operator could also be seen as performing "counseling services" for the borrowers through the display on its website of detailed information concerning the loan rates and terms available from the wholesale lender, and through its display and maintenance of a toll-free telephone number through which a consumer can obtain additional information and/or answers to questions concerning, possibly, the home buying and financ-

---

[8]See letter dated March 24, 1994 from Grant E. Mitchell, Senior Attorney for RESPA, collected in Barron's *Federal Regulation of Real Estate and Mortgage Lending*, Fourth Edition. "Payment for a 'prospects' list does not violate RESPA."

[9]The March 24, 1994 letter indicates that there is no violation "so long as the payment . . . is not further conditioned upon . . . an endorsement of the product being offered by the seller of the list."

ing process, how closing costs and monthly payments would vary under each product, helping the borrowers to understand and clear credit problems, etc. Since these activities arguably include the taking of a loan application and at least five additional Listed Services, one could conclude that the services provided by the Website Operator to the wholesale lender would meet the first part of the IBAA Test and would therefore be compensable.

As to whether the fee paid to the Website Operator would satisfy the second part of the IBAA Test, i.e., whether the fee can be seen as reasonably related to the services actually provided, would depend on whether comparable fees are paid under similar marketing arrangements. To support the reasonableness of the fee paid to the Website Operator, market data showing that the fee is in fact competitive in the marketplace for similar services in the geographical regions in which it is offered would be needed.

In the Broker Fee Statement, HUD cautioned that the IBAA Letter is not dispositive in analyzing more costly mortgage broker transactions where more comprehensive services are provided. As noted, the particular program reviewed by HUD in the IBAA Letter involved the performance of six Listed Services in return for a flat fee of about $200. 64 Fed Reg. 10085, fn. 6. To achieve a higher fee, the Website Operator should arguably perform more than six and, to be safe, as many of the Listed Services as possible.

(b) *Under the CLO Test.* The Website Operator's website could be viewed as constituting a CLO as defined in the CLO Statement, i.e., a computer system used by a consumer to facilitate choice among alternative lenders and/or loan products offered in connection with a particular RESPA-covered real estate transaction. The website provides to consumers who visit them almost all of the information and services identified by HUD in the CLO Statement as being representative of the information and services provided through a CLO.

Although the website may apparently be characterized as a CLO if Listed Services are being performed via the website, it may be more appropriate to analyze the services under the Broker Fee Statement and the IBAA Test rather than under the CLO Statement. This is because the circumstance where the borrower and lender are brought together and an application is taken through the website, the website can be said to meet the definition of a "mortgage broker" in regulation. As previously indicated, the CLO Statement states that if a CLO elects to operate as a mortgage broker, the mortgage broker compensation rules apply.

On the other hand, if the website were to be used only for general marketing purposes, rather than for brokerage or origination-type services similar to those set forth in the IBAA letter, resort to the CLO Statement to determine whether or not fees paid for such marketing services are compensable under RESPA would appear appropriate. The CLO Statement says simply that payments made to a CLO Operator do not violate RESPA §8 so long as services are provided to the customer by virtue of the CLO and the payment is reasonable in relation to those services. Under the CLO Statement, no specific form of payment is prescribed or prohibited and, in particular, payments based on closed loans are permitted, so long as the payments are reasonable in the marketplace for the services provided. However, in 1996 at least, HUD frowned on the concept of a single-lender CLO, indicating in the CLO Statement that "if a CLO lists only one settlement service provider and only presents basic information to the consumer on the provider's products, then there would appear to be no or nominal compensable services provided by the CLO to either the settlement service provider or the consumer, only a referral."[10]

Question 3. Does it matter if settlement services are automated?

Answer. There is no indication in RESPA, Regulation X or any official HUD interpretation of RESPA or Regulation X that mortgage processing or underwriting services performed by a person are to be treated differently if performed in an automated manner. To the contrary, what little has been said by HUD on the subject appears to indicate that the performance of mortgage processing and underwriting services will be treated essentially the same under RESPA whether performed manually or in an automated manner.

For example, in the Broker Fee Statement, HUD acknowledges that the "advent of computer technology has, in some cases, changed how a broker's settlement services are performed," and indicates that "[f]or ... services [other than the Listed Services] to be acknowledged as compensable under RESPA, they should be identifiable and meaningful services *akin to* those identified in the IBAA [L]etter including, for example, the operation of a ...[CLO] or an automated underwriting system (AUS)]." 64 Fed. Reg. at 10085 (emphasis added).

In addition, HUD specifically addressed in the CLO Policy Statement the provision of settlement services through the use of a CLO (which by its very nature is automated), and indicated that it would essentially employ the traditional RESPA §8 analysis to determine whether or not payment for such services is permissible under RESPA §8.

Not examined here is the more complicated question as to whether a Website Operator could outsource some or all of its mortgage processing or underwriting services to an entity jointly owned by the Website Operator and a lender. However, there is no obvious reason why the same rules that apply to affiliated business arrangements generally would not also apply to online structured arrangements such as this.

Question 4. Is providing access to the Website Operator's website a facility or goods for which the Website Operator can be compensated in addition to the compensation for services that the Website Operator performs?

Answer. Arguably, payments for providing access to a website can be characterized as payments for "goods" (analogous perhaps to payments for print advertisements) or for a "facility" (the "rental" of space on the website that customers can "visit") and where they can "meet" with the functional equivalent of

---

[10] 61 Fed. Reg. 29255 (June 7, 1996).

a loan officer and obtain information about the lender's products and submit a loan application. Under this argument, such payments would be permissible so long as reasonably related to the value of the website access furnished.

Furthermore, HUD has indicated in the Broker Fee Statement that mortgage brokers may furnish compensable goods and facilities in addition to performing compensable services, and has provided examples.

> [A]ppraisals, credit reports, and other documents required for a complete loan file may be regarded as goods, and a reasonable portion of the broker's retail or "store-front" operation may generally be regarded as facilities for which a lender may compensate a broker. 64 Fed Reg. 10085.

Again, accepting the argument that providing access to the website constitutes "goods" or a "facility," it would appear that the Website Operator may be reasonably compensated for providing such access in addition to receiving compensation for origination services.

Question 5. If marketing a lender's products through a Website constitutes "goods" or a "service" for which the Website Operator can be compensated, are some methods of determining compensation more defensible than others?

Answer. If the compensation to be paid to the Website Operator is to be determined by the number of closed loans that came to the lender through the Website Operator's website, it seems possible that the compensation could be deemed an impermissible payment for a referral. The argument, borrowed from some recent judicial decisions analyzing the legality under RESPA §8 of the payment of yield spread premiums to brokers[11] would be that if the wholesaler pays a fee to the Website Operator for marketing services based on closed loans, never pays a fee for marketing services for loans that do not close or for which no application is made, and there is no significant difference in the marketing services provided with respect to all visitors to the Website Operator's website, it is possible for a court or HUD to conclude that the payment is not for the marketing services, but rather is a prohibited finder's fee.

However, HUD has never specifically disapproved payments to mortgage brokers based on closed loans, and, in fact, has indicated in an informal letter that percentage compensation based on closed loans does not necessarily violate RESPA §8.[12] Rather, HUD stated that it would first look to see whether the payment is for services actually performed and in doing so would consider whether,

---

[11]*Culpepper v. Inland Mortgage*, 953 F., Supp. 367 (N.D. Ala) (reversed in part, vacated in part, 132 F.39 692 (1988).

[12]Letter from Grant E. Mitchell dated October 9, 1992 collected in *Pannabecker, The RESPA Manual: A Complete Guide to the Real Estate Settlement Procedure Act*, A.S. Pratt and Sons, Arlington, Virginia, at A8-147.

in an arm's length transaction, a purchaser would buy the services at or near the amount charged. HUD also stated that, "[t]he fact that others pay comparable prices for similar services may be relevant to this inquiry." *Id.* Additionally, as indicated above, HUD has clearly indicated that CLOs may charge settlement service providers a fee for each closed transaction arising from the use of the CLO. 61 Fed. Reg. 29257 (June 7, 1996).

Less problematic, clearly, is compensation paid by a lender for the marketing services of a Website Operator as a flat fee, assuming it is paid regardless whether or not a loan closes. The only apparent issue in such a scenario would be whether the flat fee was reasonable in relation to the marketing services provided. Somewhat less clear than a flat fee would be a fee based on the number of "hits" on the lender's website that came through the hyperlink from the Website Operator's website, or a fee based on the total number of "hits" on the Website Operator's website, with the former being more susceptible than the latter to the argument that because of the manner in which the fee is determined it should not be considered to be *for* services.

Question 6. Co-branding arrangements between one entity with access to potential customers and another entity with a product to sell are quite common on the Internet. Do co-branding arrangements involving residential mortgage lenders present special problems or limitations with respect to RESPA §8?

Co-branding presents the same type of RESPA problems as do finder's fees. It would appear that the co-brander, which is typically not in the settlement service business, is being paid a fee in exchange for steering its associated customers to the preferred lender or other settlement service provider. While a fee on the order of a reasonable fee paid for a selected prospects list as set forth in Question 1 above may be allowable, additional compensation without additional services such as the Listed Services would appear suspect under Section 8.

There have been several attempts to amend RESPA to allow co-branding arrangements, covertly during last-minute discussions regarding the 1996 Budget Act as well as in two other bills.[13] However, no such proposal has ever been enacted. Treasury and HUD and other opponents of this amendment have argued, so far successfully, that allowing payments to one group that performs no services, including groups yet unformed and for purposes unclear, would essentially eviscerate the "anti-referral fee" concept which is the essence of Section 0(a) of RESPA.

Thus, co-branding in circumstances where the non-settlement services party performs no services, including Internet co-branding arrangements, will likely continue to be viewed by HUD as a violation of Section 8.

---

[13]Financial Regulatory Relief and Economic Efficiency Act, FRREEA of 1997 (S. 1407, 105th Congress), and FRREEA of 1999 (S. 576, 106th Congress).

C. LENDER PAYMENTS TO REAL ESTATE AGENTS OR BROKERS

How can real estate agents or brokers get paid by lenders, in view of RESPA's prohibition of compensated referrals? This is a subject that has had considerable airing and generated considerable misinformation for several years. I will discuss here what RESPA and HUD have actually said on the subject. I am not talking about loans insured under any FHA program (which is administered by HUD). FHA has had a strict "one fee per transaction" rule for most of its history; as a generalization, if a fee is paid to a person acting as agent, that person cannot get another fee in that transaction.

Payments to Bona Fide Employees

RESPA Section 8 also permits payments by an employer to its employee (but not an independent contractor) for referral activities. 24 C.F.R. § 3500.l4(g)(vii) (the "Employee Exemption"). However, where the employee is making the referral to a company that is not his/her employer, that company may not pay the employee or the employee's company for the referral. 24 C.F.R. §3500.14(b).

(a) WARNING: Bona Fide employees only! HUD has stated:

Individuals may not be hired on a part-time basis to make referrals because of their access to consumers as settlement service providers. Sham employment arrangements, such as a title company paying a one hour "salary" to a real estate agent who provides a referral, and issuing a W-2 for "services" rendered to justify compensating a referral are, and will continue to be, violations of RESPA. 61 Fed. Reg. 29238,29243 (June 7, 1996).

See also, Industry Frequently Asked Questions ("FAQs") about RESPA, posted on the RESPA Homepage at www.hud.gov:

May real estate agents who are independent contractors be considered employees under the "employer-employee" exemption, for purposes of being allowed to be paid referral fees from employers?

No. Exemption applies only to bona-fide employees.

(b) Definition of *"Bona Fide Employees"*

Except for its statement that an independent contractor is not an employee and its warning about sham employment arrangements, there is no specific guidance in Regulation X or from HUD as to who qualifies as a *"bona fide* employee" for purposes of the Employee Exemption. Because HUD has not provided a definition of a *"bona fide employee"* one is forced to look elsewhere for guidance.

The general test relied on by the Internal Revenue Service ("IRS") to determine if a person is an employee has been applied for many purposes outside of federal tax law, e.g., worker's compensation and state income tax withholding. Under this test, the relationship of employer and employee exists when the employer has the right to control and direct the individual who performs the services, not only as to the result to be accomplished by the work, but also as to the details and means by which the result is accomplished. In other words, an employee is subject to the will and control of the employer, not only as to what is to be done but how it is to be done. In this connection, it is not necessary that the employer actually direct or control the manner in which the services are performed; it is sufficient that it has the right to do so.

To help determine whether a worker is an employee or an independent contractor under the common law, the IRS has established a twenty-factor test based upon common law principles (the "twenty-factor test"). The twenty factors indicate what degree of control by the business over a worker is sufficient to establish an employer-employee relationship. The degree of importance of each factor varies depending on the occupation and the factual context in which the services are performed. The twenty factors are designed only as guides for determining whether an individual is an employee; special scrutiny is required in applying the twenty factors to assure that form is not elevated over substance.

Under the twenty-factor test, the following factors indicate the existence of an employer-employee relationship:

1. *Instructions to Worker.* The business requires compliance with its instructions, either oral or written, concerning when, where and how the worker is to perform his or her required duties.

2. *Training.* The business trains the worker to perform in a particular manner. Such training may include requiring an experienced employee to work with the worker, corresponding with the worker, or requiring the worker to attend meetings.

3. *Integration into Business Operations.* The business integrates the worker's services into its operations to such a degree that the success or continuation of the business depends upon the worker's performance.

4. *Requirement that Services Be Rendered Personally.* The business requires that services be rendered by the worker personally. This demonstrates that the business is interested in the methods used to accomplish the work as well as in the results. However, if the business allows the worker to delegate the responsibility for the performance of his or her duties, this would be a factor indicating that the worker is an independent contractor.

5. *Hiring, Supervising and Paying Assistants.* The business hires, supervises or pays any assistants to the worker. However, if the worker hires, supervises or pays his or her own assistants pursuant to an oral or written contract under which the worker is responsible only for the attainment of a result, this would be a factor indicating that the worker is an independent contractor.

6. *Continuity of the Relationship.* The business has a continuing relationship with the worker. A continuing relationship may exist where work is performed at frequently recurring, although irregular, intervals.

7. *Setting the Hours of Work.* The business sets the hours of work for the worker.

8. *Requirement of Full-Time Work.* The business requires the worker to work full-time. If the worker is free to work when and for whom he or she chooses, this would be a factor indicating that the worker is an independent contractor.

9. *Working on Employer Premises.* The business requires that work be performed on the business's premises. Work done off the business's premises, such as at the worker's office, indicates some freedom from control. The importance of this factor depends on the nature of the services involved and the extent to which an employer generally would require employees to perform similar services on the employer's premises.

10. *Setting the Order or Sequence of Work.* The worker is not free to follow his or her own pattern of work, but must follow the established routines and schedules of the business. Often, however, because of the nature of an occupation, a business does not set such routines or schedules. Nevertheless, it should be sufficient to indicate an employer-employee relationship if the business makes it clear to the worker that the business can, if it so desires, set such routines or schedules.

11. *Requiring Oral or Written Reports.* The business requires that the worker submit regular oral or written reports.

12. *Payment by Hour, Week, Month.* The worker's payment of salary is determined by the hour, week, or month, provided that this method of payment is not just a convenient way of paying a lump sum agreed upon as the cost of a job. Payment made by the job or on a straight commission basis generally indicates that the worker is an independent contractor.

13. *Payment of Workers' Business or Traveling Expenses.* The business retains the right to regulate and monitor the worker's business activities such as by paying a worker's business and/or traveling expenses.

14. *Furnishing Worker's Tools and Materials.* The business furnishes tools, materials and other equipment to the worker necessary for the performance of the worker's services.

15. *Working for More than One Business at a Time.* The worker performs services for one business only or for several businesses that are part of the same service arrangement. Conversely, if the worker performs services for a number of unrelated businesses at the same time, this would be a factor indicating that the worker is an independent contractor.

16. *Right to Discharge Worker.* The business retains the right to discharge the worker. Conversely, an independent contractor cannot be fired so long as the independent contractor produces a result that meets contractual specifications.

17. *Right to Terminate.* The worker retains the right to terminate his or her relationship with the business at any time without incurring liability. On the other hand, the following factors indicate the existence of an independent contractor relationship:

18. *Significant Investment by Worker.* The worker makes a significant investment in facilities used by the worker, such as the maintenance of an outside office rented at fair value from an unrelated party. Conversely, the worker's lack of such investment indicates dependence on the business's facilities and, therefore, is a factor indicating an employer-employee relationship.

19. *Realization of Profit or Loss by Worker.* The worker can realize a profit or suffer a loss as a result of his or her services, i.e., the worker has entrepreneurial risk. As such, the worker is deemed to have an "investment" in the project. This factor works in conjunction with factors 5, 13, and 14 above. Ordinarily, an employee cannot lose money in his or her occupation whereas an independent contractor who hires his own assistants, buys his own equipment, and pays his own expenses bears such a risk.

20. *Availability of Worker's Services to the General Public.* The worker makes his or her services available to the general public on a regular or consistent basis.

D. DISCUSSION

Because the IBAA Letter is quoted with approval in an "official interpretation" of HUD (the March 1, 1999 Policy Statement), the IBAA Letter arguably represents an official interpretation of HUD upon which reliance may be placed. Assuming that to be the case, if a person actually performs at least the threshold services in the IBAA letter for every loan application for which the person receives payment and it can be demonstrated that the payment received is reasonably related to the market value of the services actually performed, one can argue that the payments do not violate Section 8 because they are fair market compensation for actual services provided.

On the other hand, because HUD has not provided a definition of "bona fide employee," no definitive assurance can be given that under any circumstance real estate agents will be able to satisfy the Employee Exemption, unless and until HUD provides further guidance, and, given the extensive criminal and civil penalties under RESPA, reliance on this exception alone appears to be highly problematic.

E. CONCLUSION

Some say twenty-five years of RESPA is enough—the Internet will so commoditize mortgage loans that referral fees and kickbacks will be squeezed out. Others are not so sure. There is a strongly held view that a referee, or perhaps a sheriff, is still needed to bring order to the cyber-frontier. The residential mortgage market has long been made national by Fannie Mae and Freddie Mac. In such an environment, clear national rules governing compensation arrangements in Internet mortgage loan transactions are needed, and particularly in view of the fact that technology that facilitates online mortgage lending also facilitates enforcement efforts against RESPA violators. Thus, any website is now available for a compliance audit at the click of a mouse on a PC on every desk of every federal regulator.

I believe HUD can, and should, in conjunction with other federal efforts on encryption and digital signatures complete its efforts to establish Internet online mortgage transactions rules.

ATTACHMENT A

E-COMMERCE AND RESPA
Commonly used terms in online mortgage lending

"Single lender site"—a site that displays only the owner/lender's information and application materials for access to potential borrowers.

"Multi-lender sites"—a site that provides information regarding more than one lender and allows potential borrower to select a lender for further processing.

"Content site"—a website that contains information, commercial advertising, and, possibly loan content information, which a potential borrower may select.

"Click-through"—an icon on a website that a potential borrower can click to be sent to another website.

"Framing"—a seamless process where the computer view goes from one site to a linked site without any obvious indication that the user has left the original site.

"Link"—a connection with icon on a website that a Website Operator puts on its site, usually for some charge, so that a potential borrower can be sent to another website (see click-through).

"Hyperlink"—a link that, when clicked, automatically dials up the linked website.

"Impression"—a method of counting each time a website is visited.

"Section 8 of RESPA"—a criminal and civil federal statute administered by the Department of Housing and Urban Development. Section 8(a) prohibits compensated referrals of settlement service business, and penalizes both the giver and the receiver; Section 8(b) prohibits kickbacks, fee splitting and unearned fees.

"Affiliated business arrangement"—an exception to Section 8 of RESPA, which allows one company in the settlement services business to have profit-making interest in another company in the settlement services business, so long as the provisions of a safe harbor are followed—to use of the related provider (with limited exceptions), disclosure of ownership must be made, and the exchange of fees between the companies is limited. However, an employer may pay its own employees for referrals to an affiliated business company. An affiliated business (AfBA) disclosure informs the borrower of some of the important details of such an arrangements.

"Settlement service"—any service provided in connection with a prospective or actual residential mortgage settlement covered by RESPA (almost every residential real estate transaction where lender takes a lien on the property).

SUMMARIZING THE UCC ARTICLE 9 REVISIONS

Dan L. Nicewander
Gardere Wynne Sewell LLP

I. INTRODUCTION AND NEW VOCABULARY

This article will highlight a few selected changes in revised Uniform Commercial Code (UCC) Article 9.[1] Revised Article 9 was intended to be effective July 1, 2001 in those states that adopt it. However, some states, such as Alabama, Florida and Mississippi, have adopted it with a later effective date of January 1, 2002. Also, it is now clear that some important states will not have adopted it by July 1, 2001.

Revised Article 9 is medium neutral and parties may communicate with the filing office by means of records communicated and stored in media other than paper. The term "writing" has been replaced by "record" and "signed" has been replaced by "authenticated." "Communicate" and "send" include the act of transmitting both tangible and intangible records.

The definition of "consumer goods" is substantially the same as the definition in old Section 9.109. However, the definitions of "consumer debtor," "consumer obligor," "consumer-goods transactions" and "consumer transaction" have been added in connection with various new (and old) consumer-related provisions and to designate certain provisions that are inapplicable in consumer transactions.

II. STYLE OF DRAFTING

Revised Article 9 may initially seem more like the Internal Revenue Code than old Article 9 with numerous cross-references to other sections, though once the read-

---

[1]Portions of this outline are based upon materials originally prepared by Professor John Krahmer of Texas Tech School of Law and portions are based upon materials originally prepared by Stan Pieringer of Locke Liddell & Sapp LLP.

Reproduced with the permission of Daniel L. Nicewander and Gardere Wynne Sewell LLP.

er becomes a little familiar with this law, it becomes more user-friendly. That's why a CD-ROM sold by Professor John Krahmer of Texas Tech Law School is invaluable. You can click forward and then back click without using all your fingers and pieces of paper to make all the cross-references. If you are using a book, be prepared to flip pages.

III. NEW TYPES OF COLLATERAL

Revised Article 9 applies to several new types of collateral. For some of the new types of collateral, filing a financing statement is not the proper, or the only way, to perfect a security interest.

Type of Collateral	Method(s) of Perfection	
Commercial deposit accounts	Control	(if the account is with the secured party, the secured party automatically has control; otherwise, a Deposit Account Control Agreement is required)
Letter-of-credit rights	Control	(issuer of or nominated person under letter of credit must consent to the assignment in writing)
Electronic chattel paper (chattel paper that is not on "paper," but was originally created in electronic form and has been "signed" electronically)	Control	(requires special technology)
Commercial tort claims	Filing	(but description must be specific to perfect)
Health care insurance receivables (a new type of Account)	Filing	
Credit card receivables (a new type of Account)	Filing	
Software	Filing	(unless state has enacted special law for software)
Manufactured homes	Filing	(unless state certificate of title statute applies)
As-extracted collateral (oil, gas or other minerals in which the security interest is created before extraction and attaches upon extraction)	Filing *locally*	(mortgage recording office)
Accounts arising from the sale or lease of intangible personal property	Filing	
"Payment Intangibles" (general intangibles where the obligor's principal obligation is to pay money)	Filing	
Supporting obligations (letter-of-credit right, guaranty or other secondary obligation that supports the payment or performance of an account, chattel paper, a document, a general intangible, an instrument, or investment property)	Automatic if security interest in the supported collateral is perfected	

Goods held by a bailee	• If bailee has issued a negotiation document for the goods, (i) possession of the document or (ii) filing • If bailee has issued a non-negotiable document for the goods, (i) issuance of a document by the bailee in the secured party's name, (ii) notification to bailee, or (iii) filing • If bailee has issued no document at all, the bailee must authenticate a record acknowledging that it holds the goods on behalf of the secured party

IV. UNIFORM FORMS NOW CONTAINED IN STATUTE

Uniform forms for financing statements, continuation statements, termination statements, certain post-default notices and the like are contained in Revised Article 9.[2] Filings can be made electronically.[3] In the 1999 Legislative Session, the Texas Legislature also adopted provisions regarding electronic filing that became effective immediately to make it clear that such filings were available under the old Chapter 9.[4] Revised Article 9 will not change existing Texas law in this regard.

V. CENTRALIZED FILING NOW THE NORM

Except for fixture filings and filings covering timber or minerals (designed "as-extracted collateral" in Revised §9-l02(a)(6)), UCC filings are centralized in the Office of the Secretary of State in the Revised Article 9.[5] This represents only a modest change from the non-uniform version of old §9-40l that was previously in effect in Texas. The non-uniform Texas amendment dealing with the rights of persons as interest owners in oil and gas production at old §9-319 has been continued by the revision as Revised §9-343.

VI. RULES FOR IDENTIFYING THE DEBTOR CLARIFIED AND TEST OF IDENTIFICATION STANDARDIZED

The standards for specifying the name of the debtor used in a financing statement are clarified and a statutory test based upon the search logic used by the filing office is stated for determining whether the name is seriously misleading.[6] There is no longer as much discretion for the court to find that the wrong name is "close enough."[7]

---

[2]*See* Revised UCC Article 9 §9-521.

[3]*See* Revised UCC Article 9 §9-516.

[4]*See* SB478 and SB479.

[5]*See* Revised Article 9 §9-501(a).

[6]*See* Revised Article 9 §9-502(a)(1), 9-503, and 9-506(c).

[7]*See also ITT Commercial Finance Corp. v. Bank of the West,* 166 F.3d 295 (5th Cir. 1999), where the court used this test as part of the basis for its decision under old Article 9.

VII. GENERIC FINANCING STATEMENT DESCRIPTIONS ALLOWED

The description of collateral in a financing statement can be extremely broad. For example, a description of "all assets" or "all personal property" is acceptable.[8] Note, however, that this allowance of super-generic descriptions does not extend to descriptions in the security agreement.[9] Fixture filings and timber or mineral filings continue to require real estate descriptions and a local filing.[10]

VIII. CHANGES TO THE FINANCING STATEMENT

New National UCC-1 Form. Revised Article 9 contains a uniform national form of financing statement. However, some states may vary this form, and not all states have enacted Revised Article 9 yet, *so the secured party still needs to be sure it is using the right UCC-1 form for the state where you are filing.*

Debtor's Signature No Longer Required. Under Revised Article 9, the debtor does not have to sign the financing statement. The secured party must have authorization to file the financing statement, but a signed security agreement counts as authorization.[11]

Filing Before Closing. If you intend to file financing statements prior to the security agreement being executed at closing, each debtor should provide a specific authorization in a separate document signed before closing.

Get the Debtor's Name Right. Revised Article 9 places a great deal of importance on having the debtor's legal name appear correctly on the financing statement. The debtor's organizational documents and certificate of existence will enable you to confirm the debtor's correct legal name. *Do not use the debtor's trade name or d/b/a on the financing statement. Use only the correct legal name, and take extra care to avoid spelling or typographical errors.*

Get the Debtor's Address Right. The address of the debtor must be accurate for filing under Revised Article 9. If the debtor is an organization that has more than one place of business, you must use the address of its chief executive office (where the president/CEO are located) on the financing statement. If the debtor is an organization that has only one place of business, the debtor's place of business is its chief executive office. If the debtor is an individual, the individual's primary residence address must be used.

---

[8]*See* Revised §9-504(2).

[9]*See* Revised §9-108(c).

[10]*See* Revised §9-502(b).

[11]*See* Revised §§9-502 and 9 509.

Include the Debtor's Tax ID/Social Security Number. Under Revised Article 9, tax identification numbers for organizations and social security numbers for individual debtors must be included on the financing statement.

Filing Offices Must Accept Filings. Under Revised Article 9, filing offices are required to accept financing statements as they are presented as long as the correct filing fee is included. Therefore, never assume that the filing office will screen the filing for omitted information, typographical errors, etc. *The financing statement must be right when it leaves your control.*

IX. RISK OF REFUSED FILING SHIFTED TO FILER; REASONS FOR REFUSAL LIMITED

The first filer will lose to a subsequent purchaser who relies on the absence of a financing statement if the filing office wrongfully failed to accept the filing, but will prevail against a subsequent party if the filing was accepted but was incorrectly indexed.[12] The limited number of reasons why a filing may be rejected is specifically stated.[13]

X. ELECTRONIC AGREEMENTS ALLOWED

While a security agreement under Revised Article 9 can still take the form of a written document signed by the debtor, revised Article 9 also contemplates the use of security agreements that take the form of a "record" stored in an electronic or other medium that are retrievable in a perceivable form (e.g., printouts from a computer disk). To be an effective security agreement, such a record must be "authenticated," and this could be done by means such as an encryption that identifies the authenticating party.[14]

XI. DEFINITION OF PROCEEDS EXPANDED AND TRACING APPROVED

The definition of proceeds has been expanded under the Revised Article 9 to make it clear that the term includes whatever the debtor receives upon sale, lease, license, exchange, collection, distribution, loss or other disposition of collateral.[15]

---

[12]*Compare* Revised §9-516(b) *with* Revised §9-517.

[13]*See* Revised §§9-516(b) and 8-520(a). *See also* safe harbor form at §9-521.

[14]*See* Revised §§9-102(a)(7), 9-102(a)(70), and 9-203.

[15]*See* Revised §§9-102(a)(65) and 9-203(e)(I).

Tracing is specifically approved as a means of tracking proceeds.[16] However, proceeds traced into a bank account may be subject to a higher priority claim by the bank.[17]

XII. DEFINITION OF PURCHASE MONEY SECURITY INTEREST EXPANDED AND CLARIFIED; DUAL-STATUS RULE ADOPTED

The definition of "purchase money security interest" has been expanded and clarified and, in addition, Revised Article 9 statutorily adopts the "dual-status" rule in non-consumer transactions to protect renewal or refinancing of purchase money transactions.[18] This should help avoid the "transformation rule" that has been a problem in the refinancing of purchase money interests under the old Article 9.[19] The limitation to transactions other than consumer goods transactions leaves to the court the determination of the proper rules in consumer goods transactions. The court is instructed not to draw any inference from this limitation.

XIII. RULES FOR PERFECTING SUBSTANTIALLY CHANGED

Revised Article 9 changes the choice-of-law rule governing filing for most tangible collateral from the jurisdiction in which the collateral is located to the jurisdiction where the *debtor* is "located."[20] Where is the debtor "located"?[21] Same rules as before, with three big changes:

- "Registered organizations," such as corporations or limited liability companies, are located in the state under whose law the debtor is organized. This has caused Revised Article 9 to be called the Delaware Relief Act![22]

- Individual debtors are located at their principal residence.[23]

---

[16]*See* Revised §9-315(b)(2).

[17]*See* Revised §§9-104, 9-327.

[18]*See* Revised §9-103(f).

[19]*See* the discussion of the "dual-status" rule and the "transformation" rule in John Krahmer, *Annual Survey of Texas Law: Commercial Transactions*, 51 S.M.U. L.Rev. 799-800 (1998).

[20]Revised Article 9 §9-301.

[21]Revised Article 9 §9-307.

[22]Revised Article 9 §9-307(e).

[23]Revised Article 9 §9-307(b)(1).

- Special rules exist for determining the location of the United States and registered organizations under the laws of the United States. The U.S. is located in District of Columbia.[24]

If a debtor is located in a jurisdiction whose law does not require public notice as a condition of perfection, the entity is deemed located in the District of Columbia.[25] The underlying policy is that the result should depend upon the availability of public information.

But consider: Where is the forum? A filing in the District of Columbia on a company located in Brussels perhaps will not impress the court very much if the bankruptcy filing is in Belgium. But Canadian provinces are generally the only places outside the U.S. that meet the criteria for public notice as a condition of perfection.

Special rules apply to certificates of title,[26] deposit accounts,[27] investment property[28] and letter-of-credit rights.[29] The law of the depositary bank's jurisdiction governs the perfection and priority of a security interest in a deposit account. The bank's jurisdiction is defined by a series of rules, and the first is the agreement between the bank and its depositor. For letter-of-credit rights: If the issuer is located in a state, the law of that state controls; if the issuer is not located in a state, the law of the debtor's location controls.

There are also new choice-of-law rules governing priority: Except where otherwise provided, priority is determined by the law of the jurisdiction in which the debtor is located. However, for goods, instruments, money, negotiable documents, and chattel paper, priority is determined by the law of the jurisdiction in which the *collateral* is located. The "last event" test has been dropped. Special rules apply for goods covered by a certificate of title, for deposit accounts, for letter-of-credit rights, for investment property, and agricultural liens.[30]

XIV. CHANGES IN PRIORITY RULES

Sections 9-317 and 9-342 of Revised Article 9 include several new priority rules. Revised Article 9 changes the rule that security interests that are perfected by control rank equally. Under Revised Article 9, the security interest first perfected by

---

[24]Revised Article 9 §9-307(f).

[25]Revised Article 9 §9-307(c).

[26]Revised §9-303.

[27]Revised §9-304.

[28]Revised §9-305.

[29]Revised §9-306.

[30]*See* Revised §§9-337, 9-327, 9-329, 9-328, 9-322.

control will have priority over security interests later perfected by control. First in time will be first in right.

Purchase money security interests (PMSIs) will be allowed in intangible collateral. It is not clear under old Article 9. New §9-103 makes it clear that a security interest in collateral may be both a PMSI as well as a non-PMSI. Consignments are treated as PMSIs in inventory. Section 9-324(f) contains new rules for PMSIs in software embedded in goods. This follows the priority accorded the goods in which the software is embedded. Old §9-319, a non-uniform Texas provision providing for the perfection without filing of liens to secure the obligations of first purchasers of oil or gas production, lives on in Texas at Revised §9-343.

XV. TRANSITION RULES

Article 3 of S.B. 1058, enacting Texas Revised Article 9 in 1999, contains the transition provisions. These provisions are not part of the Revised Article 9 in Texas. In the uniform text of the UCC the transition rules are largely in Revised Article 9 Part 7. Texas did not adopt Part 7 of the Revised Article 9. Nonetheless, the Texas transition rules are essentially those of the uniform test and this oversight was corrected by S.B. 433 passed in May 2001. One of the reasons for having a nationally uniform effective date was to minimize the impact of the transition, which will be particularly difficult in view of Revised Article 9's expanded scope, new definitions, the changes it works in choice-of-law rules for perfection and priority, and its expansion of the methods of perfection. A good chart of the transition rules has been prepared by Steve Weise.[31]

The Official Comment to Revised §9-701 describes the "horrendous complications" that are likely after July 1, 2001 if old Article 9 is in effect in some jurisdictions and not in others. This is almost certain to be the case. For example, the proper place to file to perfect (and therefore the status of a particular security interest as perfected or un-perfected) will depend upon whether matter is litigated in a state with old Article 9 or a state with Revised Article 9.

In those states that have enacted it, Revised Article 9 will apply to all transactions, even those entered into prior to 2001. The transition rules are a Swiss cheese of rules, exceptions to rules and exceptions to exceptions to rules, and special, wild card rules. The simple news is that a security interest that is enforceable and perfected under old Article 9, and which would be perfected under Revised Article 9, continues perfected under Revised Article 9. No surprise here.[32] A security interest that is enforceable and perfected under old Article 9, but for which the applicable requirements for enforceability and perfection under Revised Article 9 have not been satisfied, will remain perfected under Revised Article 9,

---

[31]*See The New Article 9* (Second Edition) published by the America Bar Association.

[32]Revised §9-703 (a).

though not necessarily for the period it would have remained perfected under old Article 9. This grace period is one year for perfection by means other than filing, unless the security interest meets Revised Article 9 requirements for enforceability and perfection before that year expires.[33]

Revised §9-705(c) provides that a financing statement filed in the proper jurisdiction under old Article 9 remains effective for all purposes, despite the fact that Revised Article 9 would require the filing of a financing statement in a different jurisdiction, until the earlier of (1) the time the filing would have lapsed under the law of the old jurisdiction, or (2) June 30, 2006. So interested parties will have to search both jurisdictions until July 1, 2006.

As noted above, if a security interest was perfected (by means other than filing) under old Article 9 or common law, perfection is preserved for one year after July 1, 2001, unless during that year the security interest is perfected in the manner prescribed by Revised Article 9. So, there may be some additional bankruptcy filings in July 2002 as debtors seek to take advantage of inadvertently lapsed perfection. This lapse rule would apply, for example, in the case of a security interest perfected by the filing of a financing statement other than in the jurisdiction where the debtor is "located" as defined in Revised Article 9. If the secured party satisfies the requirements of Revised Article 9 within that period, it remains perfected. If not, it becomes un-perfected.

Filing a continuation statement under Revised Article 9 does not necessarily continue the effectiveness of a financing statement filed under old Article 9.[34] However, a continuation statement filed after Revised Article 9 becomes effective and in compliance with Revised Article 9 will continue the perfection of a financing statement filed in the same office in that jurisdiction.

All other continuations must be made by filing a new "initial financing statement."[35] If a new initial financing statement is filed before Revised Article 9 becomes effective, it will live, until it would run out under the old law. If it is filed after the Revised Article 9 becomes effective, it will live for the period as provided in Revised Article 9.

Revised §9-308 states that Revised Article 9 will determine the priority of conflicting claims to collateral; however, if the relative priorities of the claims were "established" before Revised Article 9 came into effect, old Article 9 will determine priority. So, if two secured parties have a fixed priority with respect to a known item of collateral under existing law, that priority will be preserved, even if Revised Article 9 would compel a different or even opposite result. One example is as follows:

Under old Article 9, in 1999 a financing statement is filed that attempts to perfect a security interest in license fees as an account. The security interest is not

---

[33]Revised §9-703(b).

[34]Old Texas §9-305(d).

[35]Old Texas §9-306.

perfected under old Article 9 because license fees are not accounts under old Article 9.

- In 2000, a second secured party files a financing statement covering general intangibles and so becomes perfected as to the license fees.

- Revised Article 9 would make the "bad" 1999 filing "good" (because Revised Article 9 defines license fees as accounts), but because the relative priorities were established before Revised Article 9 became effective, the second secured party will nevertheless retain priority.

XVI. DEBTOR REQUESTS AND NOTICES

Revised Article 9 places several obligations on secured parties that arise upon receipt of notice from the debtor, including notices about the release of deposit accounts, electronic chattel paper, investment property, and letter-of-credit rights, notifications to account debtors that have been notified of the assignment of the accounts to the secured party, requests for an accounting of the debt and the collateral, requests for release of collateral, requests for an explanation of calculation of surplus or deficiency, and requests for termination statements.[36] The secured party has to respond to these requests within ten (10) to fourteen (14) days, depending on the type of request. Failure to do so can create a great deal of liability.

XVII. FORECLOSURE

Revised Article 9 makes major changes in the repossession and sale of consumer goods.[37] These changes go into effect for all loans on the effective date of Revised Article 9.

XVIII. WHAT SHOULD A SECURED PARTY DO

Under Revised Article 9, if a debtor is a business entity such as a corporation, limited partnership, limited liability partnership, or limited liability company, the financing statement should be filed *in the state where the debtor is organized*. This is a change from the old "principal place of business" rule. This new rule, combined with Revised Article 9's new emphasis on getting the debtor's name right on the financing statement, means that it is now more important than ever that the secured party get for each debtor:

---

[36]*See* Revised §§9-208, 9-209, 9-513, and 9-616.

[37]*See* Revised §§9-601 through 9-624.

- Copies of the debtor's organizational documents, including
  - for a general partnership, limited partnership, or limited liability partnership the partnership agreement;
  - for a corporation, the articles of incorporation;
  - for a limited liability company, the articles of organization.
- Certificates of existence and good standing (if applicable) from state officials in the state where the borrower is organized.

These documents will confirm where the secured party needs to file against the borrower and will confirm the debtor's legal name. If the debtor is an individual, a sole proprietorship, an unincorporated association, general partnership or other entity that is not registered or organized with any state's office, then the place of filing continues to be governed by the old "principal place of business" rule.

Revised Article 9's transition rules for the place-of-filing change provide that place-of-business filings under old Article 9 will continue to be effective until their lapse date, even if Revised Article 9 requires filing in a different state (the state of organization). *This transition rule means that, until five (5) years after the effective date of Revised Article 9 (July 1, 2006, for debtors with principal places of business in Texas, Arizona, New Mexico or Nebraska; January 1, 2007, for debtors with principal places of business in Alabama or Florida), the secured party must order UCC searches in both the old Article 9 place-of-business state and the Revised Article 9 state of organization.* Otherwise, the secured party may miss a prior perfected security interest.

Also, because Revised Article 9 has not been adopted in every state and will not go into effect in some states where it has been adopted until January 1, 2002, *after July 1, 2002, the secured party must determine on every loan the secured party closes whether or not either (i) any collateral, or (ii) the borrower/pledgor's principal place of business, is located in a state in which Revised Article 9 has not been adopted or is not effective.* If the answer to either the collateral or the place of business analysis is "yes," then the secured party must file in both the state where the collateral/place of business is located and the state where the borrower/pledgor is located under Revised Article 9. The secured party may check on the Internet for Revised Article 9's status in a particular state by browsing to http://www.krahmer.net/maps/map1.htm.

CHAPTER 11

Fair Debt Collection Practices Act

MEANINGFUL INVOLVEMENT OF DEBT-COLLECTOR

Two cases in the 7th Circuit dealt with collection agencies and one comforting decision came from the Circuit Court of Appeals in the 7th Circuit.

Two of the cases dealt with Evanston Northwestern Healthcare Corporation and were decided a few months apart. The first case set forth in detail what participation by a collection agency is necessary so that a creditor shall not be deemed to be the actual debt collector and, therefore, subject to liability. The court specified the following situations as evidence the agency is not meaningfully involved:

1. The collection agency is a mere mailing service or performs only ministerial functions.
2. The letter states that if the debtor does not pay, the debt will be referred for collection.
3. The collection agency is paid merely for sending letters rather than a percentage of debts collected.

4. The collection agency does not receive any payments or forwards all payments to the creditor.

5. If the debtor fails to respond to the letters, the collection agency has no further contact with the debtor, or the creditor decides whether to pursue collection.

6. The collection agency does not receive the files of the debtor.

7. The collection agency never discusses with the creditor the collection process or what steps should be taken with certain debtors.

8. The collection agency cannot initiate phone calls to the debtor.

9. Correspondence received by the collection agency is forwarded to the creditor.

10. The collection agency has no authority to negotiate collection of the debts.

11. The letters do not state the collection agency's address or phone number.

12. The letter directs questions or payments to the creditor.

13. The creditor has substantial control over the content of the letters.

On the other hand, the court laid out the evidence that indicates a creditor is not acting as a debt collector:

1. The collection agency provides traditional debt collection services for the creditor, such as direct contact with debtors, locating debtors' assets, and referrals to collection attorneys.

2. Accounts remain with the collection agency if the debtor does not pay after the receipt of a letter.

3. The collection agency has authority to decide to pursue debts that remain unpaid after letters are sent.

4. The collection agency provides follow-up services.

5. The creditor pays only for successful collection efforts.

6. The creditor exercises only limited control over the collection agency.

7. The collection agency retains information about the debtors.

8. The letter states the collection agency's telephone number and address.

9. The collection agency drafts the letters.

10. The collection agency collects debts for others.

11. The collection agency answers debtors' inquiries.
12. The collection agency recommends how to pursue debtors.

The court, after examining what the creditor did in the particular case, held that the creditor is solely a creditor and not subject to the liability of the Fair Debt Collection Practices Act. It is interesting that the courts laid out thirteen items that show that the creditor is participating in the collection of the debt and twelve items that show that the creditor is not participating in the collection of the debt. Unfortunately, the court has not set forth any black-and-white numerical formula for determining whether or not a creditor is liable under the FDCPA. When a court sets forth formula criteria to make a determination, other judges latch onto these simple formulas but often apply them in different ways. What is important about this case is that the judge then considered eight different activities of the collection agency and made a decision, based on these eight activities, that the creditor was not liable.

In the second case involving the same hospital, the court found that the hospital was not a debt collector and liable under the Fair Debt Collection Practices Act. This case was decided only three months after the prior case in 1999. The judge in this case cited the criteria that was used in the prior case and stated candidly that he was persuaded by the prior judge's reasoning and, for the same reason, he decided that the hospital creditor was not liable. Now we have two cases that have utilized this criteria set forth by Judge Norgel and we have a feeling that these criteria will receive attention in other cases. We therefore recommend to creditors in the 7th Circuit that they read these criteria carefully.[1]

From the 7th Circuit, a comforting decision was rendered by Chief Judge Posner of the Circuit Court of Appeals. This decision by Judge Posner and the wording of the decision is probably the most comforting decision that your author has read in the past ten years, especially out of the 7th Circuit. One must remember that the 7th Circuit has always been the most liberal circuit. More decisions come out of the western district and the northern district of the 7th Circuit than any other districts in the country on Fair Debt Collection Practices Act, and the great majority of them have been favorable to the consumers.

In this case, the Chief Judge dealt with a collection agency and a question of whether the creditor is participating in the collection of the

---

[1]*Larson v. Evanston Northwestern Healthcare Corp.,* No. 98 C 0005, 1999 WL 518901 (N.D. Ill. July 19, 1999); *Morency v. Evanston Northwestern Healthcare Corp.,* No. 98 C 8436, 1999 WL 754713 (N.D. Ill. Sept. 14, 1999).

debt. The facts presented stated that the Book-of-the-Month Club had an arrangement with their agency wherein they sent the name and address of the customer to the agency, which writes the customer demanding payment of the amount due and stating that further collection efforts may ensue, if the demand is ignored. Before mailing the letter, the agency runs a computer check to eliminate debtors whom it would be futile to dun, such as debtors in bankruptcy, since the debts to the Book-of-the-Month Club were so small it would not warrant filing a claim in bankruptcy. The dunning letters are a collaborative product of both the agency and the creditor, and the letters direct the customer to pay the Book-of-the-Month Club directly.

The letter lists the phone number for the agency, but it is a number for messages only and the messages are forwarded to the creditor rather than being handled by the agency. If the letter fails to elicit payment, the creditor will notify the agency, which may send another letter and if it does, the sequence may be repeated until the agency is convinced that the debtor is not going to pay in response merely to the demand. A flat fee is paid for each letter. If the letters fail to produce payment of the debt, the creditor retransmits the name and the address to the agency; it is then up to the agency to decide what to do. Because the debts are small, the agency usually does nothing further, and if it does do anything further, it keeps 35% of the money obtained from the debtor.

As to the suit started against a shareholder of the agency, the court attacked the attorney for the consumer and stated that the plaintiffs are represented by an experienced practitioner in consumer-finance litigation, who should be sanctioned for what amounts to a malicious prosecution. The FDCPA is not aimed at the shareholders or debt collectors operating in a corporate form unless some basis is shown for piercing the corporate veil, which was not attempted in the instance case. These were strong words emanating from the Chief Judge on the Circuit Court of Appeals of the 7th Circuit, but things improved as the decision went on. The court added that the joinder of these defendants (stockholders) illustrates the all-too-common abuse of the class action as a device for forcing the settlement of meritless claims and, thus, is a mirror image of the abusive tactics of debt collectors, at which the statute is aimed.

While the agency did accept the flat rate for each letter, since the balances are small, we may assume that the agency is limited to sending a series of dunning letters. The court stated, "If the debtors are smart, they probably know that if they tough it out, eventually the letters will cease coming and that will be the last they will hear of the matter until they discover they have earned a lousy credit rating. They are, nevertheless, in the clutches of a bona fide collection agency which, if the letters fail to collect the debt, may sue." That not being enough, the Chief Judge added the following comment, "It is ironic that the named plaintiffs of the class action directed against the debt collectors should be accusing the debt collector of being insufficiently aggressive in its effort to collect debts owed by the members of the class."

A second claim was made concerning the rights of Colorado residents (see last section of this chapter). The argument made was that referring to the rights of the Colorado residents implies that non-residents of Colorado do not have similar rights, whereas the Fair Debt Collection Practices Act confers similar rights on debtors. Again, the comfort level increases when the Circuit Court stated "in other words, the reader of the paragraph is assumed to react by saying to himself, 'since I am not a resident of Colorado, I guess I have no right to limit further communications from this pesky debtor collector' ... this is a fantastic conjecture ... to say the least, that recipients of such letters, unless they happen to be class action lawyers specializing in consumer-finance litigation, have any idea of what specific federal or state rights they might have." Notwithstanding the tone of the decision, the last paragraph is worth reading:

> "Any document can be misread. The Act is not violated by a dunning debt letter that is susceptible of an ingenious misreading, for then every dunning letter would violate it. The Act protects the unsophisticated debtor but not the irrational one."

Nevertheless, one aspect of the decision is troublesome. The agency accepted phone calls on tape, and transmitted the tape to the creditor. Is this different from the agency sending mail unopened to the creditor, and leaving the burden of response on the creditor? Isn't this one of the main practices prohibited by the FDCPA to prevent agencies from selling their names on letters? We seriously doubt this will pass muster in the other circuits, even if the agency is otherwise involved.[2]

MEANINGFUL INVOLVEMENT—ATTORNEY

Two cases dealt with the issue of attorneys conducting mass mailings. Both cases were in the 2nd Circuit and both were decided favorably to the attorney. Unfortunately, one of them was an unpublished opinion.

---

[2]*White v. Goodman*, No. 98-4180, 98-4328, 98-4329 CA., 7th Cir. (January 11, 2000).

In the first case, defendant law firm mailed collection letters to the plaintiff to collect debts. Each letter was printed and mailed from defendant's office by its employees. Each letter was a form letter, drafted and approved by the attorneys at the defendant's law firm. Approximately 67,000 letters were mailed. The second letter stated that if payment is not made, "legal action may become necessary." The letters did not bear any signature and only contained the firm name of the defendant and his or her address, and they were described as the attorneys for the creditor. An individual attorney participated in and/or directly supervised the review of every single file before any letter was sent to verify the data, and then an attorney directed each pre-approved form letter be sent after individual consideration. The court also stated that the attorney "supervised each and every step of the process."

The court held that the attorney did not violate Section 1692e(3) of the FDCPA since the attorney, or a group of attorneys, both literally and actually supervised and controlled the production and sending of the letters. This alone distinguished the case totally from *Clomon v. Jackson*. In *Clomon*, the attorney was only hired part-time and the agency issued a million collection letters a year. The attorney in that case did not actually review each debtor's file and he played no day-to-day role in the debt collection process. The court emphasized that the defendant is a law firm that sends the letters on its own letterhead rather than lending its letterhead to a collection agency, and that the attorneys controlled and supervised the production and mailing of the letters, and stated that the case was more like *Goldberg v. Winston & Morrone, P.C.*, #95 Civ. 9282, 1997 U.S. Dist. Lexis 352i, *3@15 (S.D.N.Y. March 25, 1997), where the letters were sent by defendant attorneys, as they were here, but were sent by the creditor under the supervision of the defendant attorneys, rather than by a debt collection agency as in *Clomon*.

The court stated that in the *Goldberg* decision, Judge Kaplan denied summary judgment because if an attorney exercises a sufficient degree of control or supervision over the sending of the collection letters and management of individual cases, his signature or facsimile thereof is not misleading under *Clomon*. The court also referred to *Avila v. Rubin*, 84 F. 3d 222 (7th Cir. 1996), affirming a finding of an FDCPA violation where the defendant attorney was a majority owner of the agency, but did not personally prepare, sign, or review any of the letters.

What made this case significant was that they reviewed the statement in *Clomon v. Jackson* that "there will be few, if any, cases in which a mass-produced collection letter bearing facsimile of an attorney signature will comply with" the FDCPA. The court concluded that the interpretation by the courts in this and other circuits has made it clear that *Clomon* does not flatly ban the mass mailing letters using a facsimile signature. The court stated that a mass mailing of debt collection letters from an attorney will not violate the FDCPA under certain circumstances.

> "*Clomon* establishes that an attorney sending dunning letters must be directly and personally involved in the mailing of the letters in order to comply with the scriptures of FDCPA. This may include reviewing the file of individual debtors to determine if and when a letter should be sent or approving the sending of letters based on the recommendation of others."

The court in the instant case summarized it as follows:

> "In short, the process through which collection letters are sent must be directly controlled or supervised by an attorney for the mass mailing to be permissable."

The words in *Clomon*, "based on the recommendation of others," clearly define that an attorney need not review each file providing, in substitution thereof, he directly controls or supervises the entire operation.

The plaintiff in the case presented the argument that it was physically impossible for the attorney to review up to 60,000 collection letters annually, and that mathematically, each attorney would have to handle 21,000 letters or roughly 400 per week or 80 per day. Judge Korman addressed this by stating that "this number is not so high that the lawyers could not provide their requisite review." Since the clients were two regulated public utilities and the City University of New York, such a review could be done in a matter of minutes. The court addressed this issue because the plaintiff stated that defendant's affidavit was false because it was physically impossible. But this does not detract from the fact that the court held for the defendant on the grounds that they supervised and controlled the operation and that they did not necessarily have to see and review personally each file.[3]

The next decision was also handed down by Judge Korman and, needless to say, the result was somewhat the same. In this case, the individual defendant spent 90% of her time on collection duties and scanned the initial referral from the hospital on the computer before the first letter was sent to the debtor. The defendant conducted the scan in about two to four hours to check the information in each referred account to see whether anything unusual appeared in the data, such as abnormal names, amounts, addresses, services, or any other data that would be at a variance with the normal. If there is a variance, the attorney deleted the

---

[3]*Kapeluschnik v. Leschack Grodensky P.C.*, 96-CB-2399 (E.D. N.Y. August 25, 1999).

account before a letter was sent. After the attorney's initial scan, the defendant would apportion a number of the files to several supervisors for an in-depth review, reviewing about one-third to one-half of the files personally. The in-depth review included a review of the address, the services rendered, payments made, whether a payment is made by an insurance company, workmen's compensation, disability, other information, and a review of the collection activity. The defendant law firm received about 400 referrals a week or 1,800 a month. While the defendant attorney scanned each account, she did not conduct an in-depth review on all the accounts. The attorney was directly involved with the debtors who write, call, or come to the office, supervised the staff, set the procedures, and created a manual the staff follows. The attorney reviewed each file before suit was brought and attended court when cases were prosecuted. The attorney dealt directly with the client.

The problem in this particular case was that the defendant law firm occupied space on the same floor as the collection agency that referred the accounts to them. The collection agency received a referral from the hospital and thereafter referred the accounts to the law firm. The agency and the law firm shared a computer system, although once the accounts were referred to the law firm, the agency had no further involvement and the law firm instructed the system's operator to refer them to a fulfillment house to print the letters.

The court looked at the fact that the law firm occupied space on the same floor as the agency, shared a computer system and a system's operator with the agency, and also shared a receptionist with the agency. The court rejected the argument that this was sufficient to establish that the agency controlled the law firm. The law firm operated totally independently, hired their own personnel, paid their own bills, and the partner supervised and controlled the whole operation to the total exclusion of any employees or staff of the agency.

We have devoted space to the exact circumstances of each case so that other attorneys will understand in detail exactly what duties they have to perform to conduct a mass mailing. In this particular decision, the court also distinguished the facts in *Clomon* from the facts of the instant case. The attorney for the plaintiff raised the issue that the defendant attorney had an obligation to make further inquiry than merely to scan the accounts, but the court felt that the attorney is entitled to rely on the objectively reasonable representation of the client, citing several cases. The court again cited *Goldberg v. Winston & Morrone P.C.* and noted the absence "of any authority that it is misleading for a non attorney law firm employee to do the work of the firm." *Danielson v. Hicks*, No. Civ. 3-94-1053, 1995

W.L. 767290 (D. Minn. 1995) was cited, wherein it was stated that it was not false or misleading when dunning letters came from a paralegal rather than an attorney.

Clomon and *Avila* set forth that if the attorney supervised and controlled the operation, there was no violation of the FDCPA. The plaintiff attorneys in their suits zeroed in on a review of the letter itself, but *Clomon* and *Avila* are devoid of any inference that the attorney must review the letter. Both *Clomon* and *Avila* allege that an attorney should review the file, but this review is equivalent to being directly and personally involved. In *Clomon*, this personal involvement "may include reviewing the file ... or approving the sending of letters based on the recommendation of others." No reference is made to personally reviewing the actual letter.

Many attorneys who are sending a large number of letters are taking the time and effort to sign each and every letter, and certainly this should be a strong firewall to preventing a lawsuit by a consumer attorney. On the other hand, the case law seems to be clear that supervision and control is the key to compliance with the Fair Debt Collection Practices Act and the use of a facsimile signature, as stated in the *Kartivich* decision, is immaterial. However, do not state in your letter that "you personally reviewed the account."

It is hoped that the above two cases, in addition to *Dalton v. FMA Enter. Inc.*, No. 95-396-CIV-FTM-17, 1997 WL 48871 (M.D. Fla., February 3, 1997), *Kartavich v. Winston & Morrone P.C.*, 96-C-08930S USDC W.D. Wisc. (February 19, 1997), and *Anthes v. TransWorld Systems Inc.*, 765 F. Supp. 162 (D. Del. 1991), put to rest many of these suits that are based solely on the fact that the attorney is mailing a large number of letters over a facsimile signature. The problem that created all these suits is that *Clomon v. Jackson* and *Avila v. Rubin* seemed to indicate that the attorney had to personally review each file as well as each letter, although no reference was made to a letter in either case. Thus, when a consumer attorney saw a facsimile signature, the attorney concluded that there was a violation of the FDCPA. Fortunately, that is not the case, for a trail of cases clearly sets forth that control and supervision on a day-to-day basis is meaningful involvement.

A major case dealing with mass mailing was sympathetic to the defendant. With regard to plaintiff's claim that Wexler sent them a form letter bearing only a firm signature that is not manually signed by an attorney, the court responded by saying that "the issue, however, is not who signed the letter, or how it was produced, but rather whether it falsely represents or implies that it came from an attorney when in fact it did not." In response to the allegation that the attorneys did not spend as much time on each file as they should, the court said "the quality of Wexler's law practice is not an issue." The case is on appeal.[4]

Credit & Collection Tip: *In some cases, the attorney relies on the fact that each file has been individually reviewed by an attorney. While this certainly is a defense, it is recommended to include the additional defense that the attorney supervises and controls the operation of his office, and is meaningfully involved on a day-to-day basis.*

COLLECTION ACTIVITY IN THIRTY-DAY PERIOD

In the First Edition of *Complete Guide to Credit and Collection Law,* we stated that many collection agencies and law firms are conservatively writing a simple non-threatening initial letter and taking no additional action during the thirty-day period. In effect, the debtor is receiving a thirty-day grace period to dispute the debt.

In the Second Edition of our book, we still maintained that the courts seem to say that little or no action should be taken during the thirty-day period and that the courts stretched to allow the debtor that thirty-day free grace period.

Nevertheless, it is not a violation to institute suit during the thirty-day period, even though the act of advising the consumer that suit will be started within the thirty-day period may be a violation. Technically, the act does not prohibit dunning a debtor during the thirty-day period if it can be done without overshadowing the right to dispute the debt, i.e., cannot demand payment in any way to contradict the right to dispute.

The 6th Circuit was the first circuit that seemed to allow a reminder letter during the thirty-day period. The reminder letter contained a specific clause that stated, "if we are not notified that your debt has been paid before April 4, 1996, and if this debt is not disputed, we shall advise you of our final position regarding the status of your account." This phrase in the second collection letter apparently persuaded the 6th Circuit to allow the sending of this letter during the thirty-day period.[5]

On March 31, 2000, the Federal Trade Commission issued an opinion letter to the American Collectors Association in response to a request for two advisory opinions concerning the FDCPA. The first question was whether the FDCPA permits a collection agency to either demand pay-

---

[4]*Boyd v. Wexler,* 2000 WL 1727781 (N.D. Ill. Nov. 21, 2000).

[5]*Smith v. Computer Credit, Inc.,* 167 F.3d 1052 (6th Cir. 1999).

ment or take legal action during the pendency of the thirty-day period for disputing a debt in situations where a debtor has not notified the collection agency that the debt is disputed. The FTC stated that Congress did not specify that collectors must cease collection efforts during the dispute period if consumers send nothing in writing. The Commission pointed out that they have voiced this opinion many times to Congress. They cited two recent decisions. One in the 7th Circuit stated that the debt collector is perfectly free to sue within the thirty days, but the debt collector must cease his efforts at collection during the interval between being asked for verification of the debt and mailing the verification to the debtor.[6]

This decision was handed down by Judge Posner, Chief Judge of the 7th Circuit Court of Appeals, who once tried to write what he believed was a "safe letter" (which letter was not accepted in another circuit). Judge Posner appears to be somewhat frustrated and annoyed at the consumer attorneys for bringing suits for technical violations.

The Federal Trade Commission also cited *Smith v. Computer Credit Inc.*, which was referred to in the Second Edition of our book, as evidence of the fact that a debt collector does not have to stop its collection efforts during the thirty-day period, but must ensure that its efforts do not threaten the consumer's right to dispute the validity of the debt. The Commission believes that the thirty-day time frame is a dispute period in which the consumer may insist that the collector verify the debt, and not a grace period within which all collection efforts are prohibited.

Unfortunately, the opinion letters of the Federal Trade Commission are not binding on the courts. Notwithstanding the opinions of the Federal Trade Commission, the courts frequently do not follow the policy of the Commission. It is necessary to examine the law in the particular circuit on this subject and counsel must make a judgment call as to whether they can sustain these arguments before they embark on a collection effort within that thirty-day period. Until recently, one might say that the liberal 7th Circuit would not permit either suit or a determined collection effort within the thirty-day period. On the other hand, Judge Posner changed that perspective during 1998 and 1999. The 6th Circuit has now addressed the problem. Nevertheless, the remaining circuits have not produced any decisions on this point and, while two circuits may be persuasive on the other circuits, there is no guarantee that neither the 9th Circuit in California on the West Coast nor the 2nd Circuit in New York would necessarily

---

[6]*Bartlett v. Heibl*, 128 F.3d 497, 501 (7th Cir 1997)

follow the other circuits. Until such time as the other circuits handle this issue, we recommend that the debt collector consult with counsel.

TIME BARRED DEBTS

In a 1987 case, *Kimber v. Federal Financial Corp.*, 668 F. Supp. 1480 (M.D., Ala. 1987), the district court found that a debt collector who had instituted a suit on a time barred debt violated the FDCPA because there was a threat to sue the debtor. A recent case in Texas found no violation where no threat of any legal action was contained in the writing sent to the debtor. The letter only stated the creditor would make further attempts to collect the debt.[7]

A case in the 8th Circuit states that in the absence of a threat of litigation or act of litigation, a violation of the FDCPA does not take place merely when a debt collector attempts to collect a valid debt that is barred by the statute of limitations in the state where the debtor resides.[8]

BUSINESS DEBTS

In the Second Edition, we referred to the case of *Moore v. Principle Credit Corporation*, W.L. 378 387 (N.D. Mass. 1998), where contacting the individual at his home converted the debt from a business debt to a consumer debt, because the call was made to the home residence. In that particular case, flagrant violations were at issue and we opined that the court was stretching to find some way to hold the collection agency liable.

In a later case, the plaintiff cited *Moore v. Principle Credit* to support a violation where the debtor's credit card was used to purchase commercial equipment and the collection agency sent letters to the debtor's home. Nevertheless, the court was unpersuaded by the *Moore* case and stated that it was unclear whether the obligation for computer programs in the *Moore* case was incurred for personal or business use. However, the *Moore* case concluded that even if the debt had been business related, collection calls to a home converted the debt, placing it within the FDCPA breach.

An 8th Circuit court rejected this conclusion and stated that if a communication to the debtor's home converted a commercial debt into an

---

[7]*Johnson v. Capital One Bank*, 2000 WL 1279661 (W.D. Tex., May 19, 2000).

[8]*Freyermuth v. Credit Euro Services*, No. 00-2661, 2001 U.S. App. Lexis 7662 (8th Cir., 4/27/01).

obligation under the FDCPA, it would be tantamount to an amendment of the clear intent of Congress. The court further held that commercial obligations are beyond the FDCPA's reach and that the 8th Circuit Court of Appeals recognizes that the FDCPA applies to obligations that arise from "consumer transactions."[9]

OPTION TO PAY DEBT BY CREDIT CARD

We have a case in Ohio (albeit an unreported decision) that stated setting forth a credit card option of payment in a dunning letter to the consumer is not a violation of the FDCPA since there was nothing in the letter to compel the debtor to use the option, and the option was not unconscionable or deceptive.[10]

The case relied on an unreported decision in 1997. Despite this new decision, significant problems are present with using the credit card as an option, and it is the opinion of the author that before we can feel comfortable in using this device, we really should be able to rely on a reported decision from another circuit. (See page 512, *Complete Guide to Credit and Collection Law*, Second Edition.)

PORTFOLIO PURCHASES

The question of whether the purchase of portfolios is subject to the Fair Debt Collection Practices Act not only involves the issue of whether the buyer is purchasing delinquent accounts for the purpose of the collection, but also depends upon the particular statutes in certain states.

A review of the collection agency statute in the particular state is pertinent when a decision is made for the first time to purchase the portfolio of accounts. Some of the statutes not only will cause the purchase to become subject to the FDCPA, but, at the same time, may require the purchaser to obtain a collection agency license in the state. A review of the state law is in order.

In addition, under certain state laws, sales, finance and lender's licenses may also be required, depending upon the laws of the respective state. These types of laws provide certain restrictions on the types of loans

---

[9]*Duffy v. Landberg*, 133 F.3d 1120 (C.C.A. 8th Cir. 1998); *Holman v. West Valley Collection Servs., Inc.*, 60 F. Supp. 2d 935 (D. Minn. 1999).

[10]*Miller v. Credit Collection Servs.*, C-3-98-490 (S.D. Ohio, Sept. 13, 2000).

that may be granted, and it may be incumbent upon the purchaser to comply with said law. Before such step is taken, a review of the state laws is absolutely necessary.

COLORADO FDCPA

The Colorado Revised Statutes Section 12-14-105(3) states:

> (a) If a consumer notifies a debt collector or collection agency in writing that:
> ...
> (II) The consumer refuses to pay a debt or the consumer wishes the collection agency to cease further communication with the consumer, then the debt collector or collection agency shall not communicate further with the consumer with respect to such debt except:
>
> (A) To advise the consumer that the collection agency's further efforts are being terminated;
>
> (B) To notify the consumer that the collection agency or creditor may invoke specified remedies which are ordinarily invoked by such collection agency or creditor; or
>
> (C) Where applicable, to notify the consumer that the collection agency or creditor intends to invoke a specified remedy permitted by law.
>
> (b) If such notice from the consumer is made by mail, notification shall be complete upon receipt.
>
> (c) In its initial written communication to the consumer, the collection agency shall include notification of the consumer's rights under this subsection (3). If such notification is placed on the back of the written communication, there shall be a statement on the front notifying the consumer of such fact.

The problem with the statute is that many agencies incorporate this notice requirement in their letter, but mail the letter to debtors in states other than Colorado. Several suits were started on the grounds that the Colorado statute misleads unsophisticated consumers from other states into believing that the right to end debt collection communications belongs exclusively to Colorado residents. Unaware of their parallel Section 1692C(c) rights, these consumers will likely continue to receive unwanted contacts.

Thereafter, a case in Illinois decided that the debtor failed to meet the mandate in the letters because the unsophisticated consumer could read the notice on the back of the letters and be misled to believe that only Colorado residents had the right to have a debt collector cease communication. The court held that the information about the debtor's right to cease collector contact was presented in a misleading manner. The court did suggest in a footnote that the letters include the safe harbor language used in another case, which was as follows:

> "We are required under state law to notify consumers of the following rights. This list does not contain a complete list of the rights consumers have under state and federal law."[11]

The circuit court in Illinois decided in favor of the debt collector on substantially similar circumstances.[12]

The best advice is to consult with counsel, review these cases carefully, and to use infinite wisdom in drafting the wording.

In addition, on May 25, 2000, the governor signed a law that changed the Colorado's Fair Debt Collection Practices Act and will require third-party debt collectors to notify consumers of their right to request that collectors cease contact at the debtor's home or work and request that collectors cease all contact with the debtor. Accordingly, when preparing the magic wording under the Colorado Statute, the debt collector should consider the new law in Colorado.

JURY AWARD—$15 MILLION

The State of Texas is large and it is even larger when it comes to awarding damages in consumer trials. It is reported that the court awarded $15 million for knowingly and intentionally causing injury to an elderly person. Five million dollars was awarded for actual damages and ten million for punitive damages. It seems that the plaintiff made phone calls, including threats of throwing the debtor in jail, even though the debtor claimed she did not sign the papers and furnished the plaintiff samples of her signatures and signed an affidavit of forgery at the plaintiff's request.[13]

---

[11]*Jenkins v. Union Corp.*, 999 F. Supp. 1120 (N.D. Ill. 1998); *Brown v. ACB Business Servs. Inc.*, 1996 WL 469588 (S.D.N.Y. August 16, 1996).

[12]*White v. Goodman*, 1998 WL 850814 (N.D. Ill.).

[13]*Perez v. Greenpoint Credit Corp.*, 99-357 (DuVou County District Court, October 9, 2000).

TELEPHONE COLLECTION

Many states have more restrictive requirements when making telephone calls to debtors. Some examples of those requirements are as follows:

a. New York—New York City has passed a mirror image of the Fair Debt Collection Practices Act and has included in the Act business debts as well as consumer debts. New York City law requires the debt collector to include in all communications with the debtor that the communications are being used to collect a debt or to obtain information that will be used for that purpose. New York City also provides that communicating with the consumer more than twice during a seven-day period is excessively frequent.

b. Connecticut—A debtor may not contact a consumer at his place of employment if he has reason to know that the employer prohibits such communication. With regard to all communications, a debt collector must disclose that the communication is an attempt to collect a debt and that any information obtained will be used for that purpose.

c. Massachusetts—When making a telephone call, a debt collector must disclose the name of the agency and the personal name of the individual making the communication as well as the agency's telephone number and office hours.

d. Minnesota—A collection agency shall not imply or suggest in any communication with the debtor that healthcare services will be withheld in any emergency situation.

The American Collectors Association has compiled a book entitled *ACA's Guide to State Collection Laws and Practices* (2000 Edition). For information concerning other states that have such laws, you may obtain this book from the American Collectors Association at the following address: 4040 W. 70th Street, Minneapolis, MN 55435 (952-928-8000).

DUPLICATION OF EFFORTS

A judge finally recognized the fact that some of the billed legal work by a consumer attorney was duplicate work undertaken in a similar case by the same attorney. The attorneys litigated similar issues before the judge in another case concerning similar problems. The judge denied a portion of the attorneys fees.[14]

---

[14]*Riter v. Moss & Bloomberg, Ltd.*, 2000 WL 1433867 (N.D. Ill., Sept. 26, 2000).

MINI-MIRANDA WARNING

The mini-Miranda warning is still required in all oral or written communications to debtors living in Connecticut, North Carolina, New York City, Texas, and Wyoming and must be included in all written communications in Hawaii, Vermont, and the District of Columbia.

RECEIPT—VALIDATION NOTICE

As a general rule, a debt collector does not need to establish that a validation notice was actually received by the debtor and a mere denial by the debtor that they did not receive the letter is insufficient as a matter of law to rebut the overall presumption of receipt.

A suggestion might be that any letters that contain the validation notice and are returned as undeliverable should be retained in the file. In the event litigation develops, the letter marked undeliverable may be used.[15]

IMPUTED KNOWLEDGE

Consumer attorneys attempt to create the situation wherein they notify the creditor that the consumer attorney is representing the debtor. The debtor does not pay the debt and thereafter the creditor forwards the case either to a collection agency or to an attorney. The attorney of the collection agency thereafter prepares a letter and mails it to the consumer directly, since the creditor failed to notify the collection agency or law firm that the creditor received an appearance by an attorney on behalf of the consumer.

Two cases considering the situation offer a direct conflict. Both cases are in New York. The first case took the position that the creditor's knowledge that the consumer has an attorney is not automatically imputed to the debt collector. The consumer must come forward with proof that the firm had actual knowledge of the communications. In that case, the law firm specifically denied that it had any knowledge that the consumer had retained an attorney.

In a second case the creditor did have actual notice of plaintiff's legal representation but failed to disclose that fact to its debt collector. The court felt that permitting creditors to engage in such a limited disclosure would eviscerate the protections afforded debtors by the FDCPA. The statute

---

[15]*Mahon v. Credit Bureau, Inc.* F. 3d 1197 (9th Cir. 1999); *Simmons v. Miller*, 970 F. Supp. 661 (S.D. Ind. 1997).

does not require that the debt collector have actual knowledge of the legal representation. Knowledge can be imputed to the debt collector when the creditor has such knowledge and fails to convey it to its debt collector at the time its seeks collection.

Furthermore, the court felt that when the collection agency or law firm accepted the file, the attorney's name and address could be readily ascertained from the creditor. The court cited the statute (15 USC 1692 C (a)(2) itself which states:

> "If the debt collector knows the consumer is represented by an attorney with respect to such debt and has knowledge of, or can readily ascertain, such attorneys name and address...a debt collector may not communicate with a consumer in connection with the collection of any debt."

A creditor has a duty when turning over a file to his debt collector to convey all the material facts regarding the claim. The court moved the burden of liability to the creditor for failure to notify the debt collector. The court's reasoning, perhaps, is that if the debt collector is sued, the debt collector will then implead the client for indemnification for failure to advise the debt collector that the debtor had retained legal counsel with respect to the debt.

Unfortunately, the landscape isn't as level as the court feels. If the client advises the debt collector that they orally communicated this to the debt collector, it is highly unlikely that the debt collector will seek reimbursement from the client or will join the client as a third party in the suit seeking indemnification for any liability because of the client's failure to provide the debt collector notice.

Probably the only moral of the story is that the debt collector and the law firm should notify the client in writing that the law does require the creditor to notify the debt collector. Perhaps this will cause the creditor to be careful when referring claims to the debt collector, and advise the debt collector when an attorney has contacted the creditor on behalf of the debtor with respect to the debt.[16]

CONFUSION—OVERSHADOWING

A case before the 7th Circuit addressed the issue of whether a letter allegedly confused an unsophisticated debtor. The letter provided for

---

[16]*Powers v. Professional Credit Servs.*, 107 F. Supp. 2d 166 (N.D.N.Y., 2000); *Jones v. Weiss*, 95 F. Supp. 2d 105 (N.D.N.Y., 2000); *Micare v. Foster & Garbus*, 2001 WL 197821 (N.D., Feb. 21, 2001).

prompt payment during the 30-day period and to call the office immediately. Both of the consolidated cases were before the court after the district court granted the defendant's motion to dismiss. The 7th Circuit decided that the test to be used is not whether those statements in the letter contradict or overshadow the validation notice, but whether the unsophisticated debtor was confused. If this 7th Circuit decision is followed, it would appear that a motion to dismiss a complaint because language in the letter contradicts or overshadows the validation notice would never be successful merely by alleging confusion.[17]

IMMEDIATE PAYMENT

A recent case in the 3rd Circuit offers further evidence that rather than finding technical violations, the courts are now looking for technical explanations to hold that the debt collector did not violate the FDCPA. In this particular case, the letter stated:

> "We shall afford you the opportunity to pay this bill immediately and avoid further action against you."

The court treated this as an "option" and not as an "overshadowing." The court offered that the debtor has the option to either pay the debt immediately and avoid further action or exercise his rights under the 30-day validation notice to dispute the validity of the debt.

Frankly, the author believes that if this case was decided five to eight years ago, it would have gone the other way and the court would have certainly agreed with the earlier leading case in the 3rd Circuit (*Graziano v. Harrison*, 950 F. 2d 107 (3rd Cir., 1991). But in today's environment, the courts are becoming more evenhanded in their effort to protect the consumer and are recognizing that the debt collectors are doing their best to comply with the law. As a result, the courts are sometimes reluctant to reward consumer attorneys for technical violations.

CLASS ACTION—OFFER OF JUDGMENT

A new strategy in class actions seems to be developing in the court in the wake of two recent cases. In the first case, the defendant made an offer of

---

[17] *Johnson v. Revenue Management Corp.*, 169 F. 3d 1057 (7th Cir., 1999).

judgment for $1,000 plus the costs of the action and reasonable attorneys fees incurred up to the date of the offer. When plaintiff rejected the offer, defendant moved to compel plaintiff to accept the offer pursuant to Rule 68 and moved to dismiss the complaint pursuant to Rule 12(b)(1). The judge in that case found that the offer of judgment rendered the claim moot. The claim became moot when the parties lacked a legally cognizable interest in the outcome. The plaintiff must have a personal stake in the litigation. Without such a personal stake, the court lacks subject matter jurisdiction and the case must be dismissed.

The court in this case dismissed the complaint for lack of subject matter jurisdiction and entered judgment against the debtor in accordance with Rule 68 offer of judgment, and retained jurisdiction to determine the amount of reasonable attorney's fees and costs. The plaintiff responded that the debtor had not offered to compensate the class and the judge stated that while this argument may have some validity after class certification, it did not apply because no class had been certified and no motion had been made for certification.

In the second case, the plaintiff neither accepted nor rejected the Rule 68 offer of judgment. However, the court reasoned that the plaintiff must do one or the other and whichever he chooses, the prize is the same. If he accepts the offer, the case is moot. If he declines, the case would be indistinguishable from the prior case and the court reasoned that he would compel them to accept the offer.

A second distinction from the prior case was that the defendant had not moved to dismiss the action, but the court pointed out that it is well established that even if the parties do not address the issue, a court may dismiss an action when it appears that jurisdiction may be lacking. In the prior case there was no class certification before the court, while in the current case the plaintiff did bring such a motion for class certification well before the offer of judgment. If the claim of the named plaintiff becomes moot before class certification, the entire case is to be dismissed for lack of subject matter jurisdiction because a class action cannot be maintained unless there is a named plaintiff with a live controversy, both at the time the complaint is filed and at the time the class is certified. Because the issues of mootness and class certification in many cases are inextricably interwoven, there are exceptions to the rule.

The court considered the motion for class certification and denied said motion, awarded the plaintiff $1,000 of the $3,000 lump sum offer, which was the statutory damages and took under consideration the issue of attorney's fees. Both of these cases were in the 2nd Circuit and the second case certainly gave strong support to the reasoning in the first case.

Hopefully this theory will expand to other courts in the 2nd Circuit and even beyond.

Notwithstanding the above, a recent case in California held that a Rule 68 offer of judgment did not moot the debtor's individual claims because a mere offer of settlement without acceptance does not moot an action. In this instance, the plaintiffs rejected the offer and since they did not obtain relief, the court determined they still had a cognizable interest in the outcome of the action.[18]

CLIENTS AND CLIENT'S INFORMATION

A case in the Circuit Court of Appeals of the 4th Circuit reemphasized the court's statement in *Jenkins v. Heintz* that debt collectors are not liable for attempting to collect valid certified amounts owed to their client. In *Jenkins v. Heintz* the court did not say that the debt collector's status as an attorney should add a requirement of independent legal analysis for each aspect of the creditor's claim. To interpret the FDCPA as treating lawyers and debt collectors unequally would contort the statute's meaning and ignore Congress's drafting and the Supreme Court's interpretation.

The court in this instance refused to combine Rule 11 (which obligates an attorney to conduct a reasonable investigation into a claim) with the FDCPA to create a heightened duty of investigation for lawyer-debt collectors engaged in ordinary debt collection.[19]

CONSUMER CREDIT TRANSACTION— WISCONSIN

Although the case was not brought under the Fair Debt Collection Practices Act, the court held that a hospital that provided uninsured medical service to an injured minor patient in which the financial obligation was payable in installments, was not a consumer credit transaction subject to the Wisconsin Credit Act. No agreement existed at the time that the services provided could be paid in installments and the hospital's customary

---

[18]*Ambalu v. Rosenblatt, et. al.*, 194 F.R.D. 451 (E.D.N.Y. 2000); *Wilner v. OSI Collection Services, Inc.*, 198 F.R.D. 393 (S.D.N.Y. 2001); *Littledove v. JBC & Associates, Inc.*, 2000 WL 33141223 (E.D., Cal. Dec. 22, 2000).

[19]*Jenkins v. Heintz*, 124 F. 3d 824 (7th Cir. 1997); *Amond v. Brincefield, Hartnett & Associates, P.C.*, 175 F. 3d 1013 (4th Cir. 1999).

practice was not to allow patients the option of installment plans at the time of rendering services, but only after attempts to collect the debt were unsuccessful. The court properly held that any installment payment transaction that would qualify for the Consumer Credit Transaction Act must be made before services were rendered. After the debt was in default, an agreement permitting the debtor to pay over time would not constitute such an agreement to permit the transaction to become a consumer credit transaction.[20]

[20]*Dean Med. Ctr., S.C. v. Conners,* 2000 WI App. 202, 618 NW 2d 194 (2000) Court of Appeals of Wisconsin.

APPENDIX I

SPECIAL STATE TEXT REQUIREMENTS FOR DUNNING NOTICES

Prepared by American Collector's Association, Inc.
Compliance Department, Last Updated
July 18, 2000

What follows is a listing of state statutes for those states which have special text requirements for dunning notices. Those states not listed either do not have statutes or rules addressing special text requirements or their statutes or rules have requirements which are similar to those under the Fair Debt Collection Practices Act. Please note that this document does not contain information on any statutory requirements regarding the collection of checks. This information is based upon research completed by ACA's Compliance Department, and, while care has been taken to research the laws as carefully as possible, the Association will not be responsible for omissions. This information is not intended as legal advice and should not be used as such. Before acting on the advice contained within this document, please discuss the issues raised with your own legal counsel.

ARKANSAS

Special Text or Address Requirements

(a) ☛A collection agency shall use only the Agency name or tradestyle exactly as it appears on the Agency's license issued by the SBCA [Arkansas State Board of Collection Agencies] in all communication, (e.g., ABC Collection Agency cannot use a name such as ABC Acceptance Company) except for skiptracing and envelopes.

(b)   **When an Agency communicates with a debtor, the Agency must disclose, in a written or telephone communication, the specific reason for the communication, the name of the creditor, the registered name of the Agency, the date of communication in written communication, and in oral communication, the identity of the collector making the contact.** Arkansas State Board of Collection Agencies Rules and Regs., § XIV (Rule current as of end of 1999, last revised October 16, 1997). (emphasis added).

CALIFORNIA

Special Text or Address Requirements

☛ No debt collector shall collect or attempt to collect a consumer debt by means of the following practices:

(d)   Communicating with the debtor by means of a written communication that displays or conveys any information about the consumer debt or the debtor other than the name, address, and telephone number of the debtor and the debt collector and which is intended both to be seen by any other person and also to embarrass the debtor. Cal. Civ. Code § 1788.12(d) (West, WEST-LAW current through 1999 portion of 1999-2000 Regular Session and First Extra Session).

☛A creditor [or agent or assignee of a creditor, including an agent engaged in administering or collecting the creditor's accounts] may submit negative credit information concerning a consumer to a consumer credit reporting agency, only if the creditor notifies the consumer affected. After providing this notice, a creditor may submit additional information to a credit-reporting agency respecting the same transaction or extension of credit that gave rise to the original negative credit information without providing additional notice.

(c) The notice shall be in writing and shall be delivered in person or mailed first class, postage prepaid, to the party's last known address, prior to or within 30 days after the transmission of the negative credit information.

(1)   The notice may be part of any notice of default, billing statement, or other correspondence, and may be included as preprinted or standard form language in any of these from the creditor to the consumer.

(2)   The notice is sufficient if it is in substantially the following form:

"As required by law, you are hereby notified that a negative credit report reflecting on your credit record may be submitted to a credit reporting agency if you fail to fulfill the terms of your credit obligations."

(3)   The notice may, in the creditor's discretion, be more specific than the form given in paragraph (2). The notice may include, but shall not be limited to, particular information regarding an account or information respecting the approximate date on which the creditor submitted or intends to submit a negative credit report.

(4)   The giving of notice by a creditor as provided in this subdivision does not create any requirement for the creditor to actually submit negative credit information to a consumer credit reporting agency. However, this section shall not be construed to authorize the use of notice as provided in this subdivision in violation of the Federal Fair Debt Collection Practices Act (15 U.S.C., Sec. 1692 *et seq.*). Cal. Civ. Code § 1785.26 (West, WESTLAW current through 1999 portion of 1999-2000 Regular Session and First Extra Session).

COLORADO

SPECIAL TEXT OR ADDRESS REQUIREMENTS

☛ (1) Within five days after the initial communication with a consumer in connection with the collection of any debt, a debt collector or collection agency shall, unless the following information is contained in the initial written communication or the consumer has paid the debt, send the consumer a written notice with the disclosures specified in paragraphs (a) to (g) of this subsection (1). If such disclosures are placed on the back of the notice, the front of the notice shall contain a statement notifying consumers of that fact.
Such disclosures shall state:

(a)   **The amount of the debt;**

(b)   **The name of the creditor to whom the debt is owed;**

(c)   **That, unless the consumer, within thirty days after receipt of the notice, disputes the validity of the debt, or any portion thereof, the debt will be assumed to be valid by the debt collector or collection agency;**

(d)   **That, if the consumer notifies the debt collector or collection agency in writing within the thirty-day period that the debt, or any portion thereof, is disputed, the debt collector or collection agency will obtain verification of the debt or a copy of a judgment against the consumer and a copy of such verification or judgment will be mailed to the consumer by the debt collector or collection agency;**

(e)   **That upon the consumer's written request within the thirty-day period, the debt collector or collection agency will provide the consumer with the name and address of the original creditor, if different from the current creditor;**

(f)   **That collection agencies are licensed by the collection agency board. The address of the board shall also be disclosed.** If, however, the debt collector is a person employed by the department of personnel for the purpose of collecting debts due to the state on behalf of another state agency, the disclosure required under this paragraph (f) shall state that the activities of such debt collector are subject to sections 12-14-104 to 12-14-109, Colorado Revised Statutes, as contained in the "Colorado Fair Debt Collection Practices Act," that complaints may be filed with the executive director of the department of personnel, and that disciplinary actions will be subject to the rules and regulations of the state personnel system.

(g) That consumers shall not send payments to the collection agency board. Colo. Rev. Stat. Ann. §12-14-109 (West, WESTLAW current through End of 1999 First Regular Session.) (Emphasis added.)

☛ (3)(a) If a consumer notifies a debt collector or collection agency in writing that:

(I) The consumer wishes the collection agency to cease contact by telephone at the consumer's residence or place of employment, then no such further contact by telephone shall be made;

(II) The consumer refuses to pay a debt or the consumer wishes the collection agency to cease further communication with the consumer, then the debt collector or collection agency shall not communicate further with the consumer with respect to such debt, except for a written communication:

(A) To advise the consumer that the collection agency's further efforts are being terminated;

(B) To notify the consumer that the collection agency or creditor may invoke specified remedies which are ordinarily invoked by such collection agency or creditor; or

(C) Where applicable, to notify the consumer that the collection agency or creditor intends to invoke a specified remedy permitted by law.

(b) If such notice from the consumer is made by mail, notification shall be complete upon receipt.

(c) In its initial written communication to a consumer, a collection agency shall include notification of the consumer's rights under this subsection (3). If such notification is placed on the back of the written communication, there shall be a statement on the front notifying the consumer of such fact.

(d) If a consumer orally informs a debt collector or collection agency of any of the matters specified in paragraph (a) of this subsection (3), the debt collector or collection agency shall advise the consumer that such communication must be made in writing. Colo. Rev. Stat. Ann. § 12-14-105 (West, WESTLAW, Current through End of 1999 First Regular Session, Amended by H.B. 00-1182, CO LEGIS 218 (2000), Changes effective July 1, 2000).)

☛ The size and style of information required to be in the initial written communication and the validation of debts notice must comply with the Federal Fair Debt Collection Practices Act. Colorado Collection Agency Board Rule 2.01(2), Available at http://www.ago.state.co.us/cab/cabrules.htm, (Effective date, January 1, 1996. Text of website last modified November 2, 1998).

☛ **Every collection notice mailed or delivered by a collection agency must contain the collection agency's name, mailing address, and telephone number.** The collection agency's address may not be printed on the same line listing the Collection Agency Board's current address required by § *12-14-109(1)(f)* of the validation of debts notice. Colorado Collection Agency Board Rule 2.01(3), Available at http://www.ago.state.co.us/cab/cabrules.htm Effective date, January 1, 1996. Text of website last modified November 2,1998). (Emphasis added.)

CONNECTICUT

SPECIAL TEXT OR ADDRESS REQUIREMENTS

☞ No consumer collection agency shall:

(14) use or attempt to use or make reference to the term "bonded by the state of Connecticut," "bonded," or "bonded collection agency," or any combination of such terms or words, except that the word "bonded" may be used on the stationery of any such agency in type not larger than 12-point. Conn. Gen. Stat. Ann. § 36a-805(14) (West, WESTLAW current through January 1, 2000).

☞ A consumer collection agency may not use unfair or unconscionable means to collect or attempt to collect a debt. Without limiting the general application of the foregoing, the following conduct is a violation of this section:

(8) Using any language or symbol, other than the consumer collection agency's address, on any envelope when communicating with a consumer debtor by use of the mails or by telegram, except that a consumer collection agency may use its business name if such name does not indicate that it is in the debt collection business. Conn. Agencies Regs. § 36a-809-3(g)(8) (West, WESTLAW current with material published in *Connecticut Law Journal* through March 21, 2000).

☞ A consumer collection agency may not use any false, deceptive, or misleading representation or means in connection with the collection of any debt. Without limiting the general application of the foregoing, the following conduct is a violation of this subsection:

(11) Except as otherwise provided in subsection (c) of this section, **the failure to disclose clearly, in *all* communications made to collect a debt or to obtain information about a consumer debtor, that the consumer collection agency is attempting to collect a debt and that any information obtained will be used for that purpose.** (Conn. Agencies Regs., § 36a-809-3(f)11 (West, WESTLAW current with material published in *Connecticut Law Journal* through March 21, 2000). (Emphasis added.)

DISTRICT OF COLUMBIA

SPECIAL TEXT OR ADDRESS REQUIREMENTS

☞ No debt collector shall unreasonably publicize information relating to any alleged indebtedness or debtor in any of the following ways:

4) the use of any form of communication to the consumer, which ordinarily may be seen by any other persons, that displays or conveys any information

about the alleged claim other than the name, address, and phone number of the debt collector. D.C. Code Ann. § 28-3814(e)(4) (West, WESTLAW current through end of 1997-98 District Council Session).

☛ No debt collector shall use any fraudulent, deceptive, or misleading representation or means to collect or attempt to collect claims or to obtain information concerning consumers in any of the following ways:

> (2) **the failure to clearly disclose in *all written* communications made to collect, or attempt to collect, a claim or to obtain, or attempt to obtain, information about a consumer, that the debt collector is attempting to collect a claim and that any information obtained will be used for that purpose.** D.C. Code Ann. § 28-3814(f)(2)(West, WESTLAW current through end of 1997-98 District Council Session). (Emphasis added).

FLORIDA

SPECIAL TEXT OR ADDRESS REQUIREMENTS

☛ In collecting consumer debts, no person shall:

> (16) Mail any communication to a debtor in an envelope or postcard with words typed, written, or printed on the outside of the envelope or postcard calculated to embarrass the debtor. An example of this would be an envelope addressed to "Deadbeat, Jane Doe" or "Deadbeat, John Doe." Fla. Stat. Ann. § 559.72(16) (West, WESTLAW current through End of 1999 First Regular Session.)

HAWAII

SPECIAL TEXT OR ADDRESS REQUIREMENTS

☛ No collection agency shall unreasonably publicize information relating to any alleged indebtedness or debtor, in any of the following ways:

> (4) The use of any form of communication by a collection agency to the debtor or alleged debtor, which ordinarily may be seen by any other person, that displays or conveys any information about the alleged claim other than the name, address, and phone number of the collection agency. Haw. Rev. Stat. § 443B-17(4) (West, WESTLAW current through 1999 Regular Session).

☛ No collection agency shall use any fraudulent, deceptive, or misleading representation or means to collect, or attempt to collect, claims or to obtain information concerning a debtor or alleged debtor, including any conduct which is described as follows:

> (2) The **failure to disclose clearly in *all written* communication made to collect, or attempt to collect, a claim or to obtain, or attempt to obtain, information about a debtor or alleged debtor that the collection agency is**

attempting to collect a claim and that any information obtained will be used for that purpose. Haw. Rev. Stat. § 443B-18(2)(West, WESTLAW current through 1999 Regular Session). (Emphasis added).

☞ No collection agency shall use any fraudulent, deceptive, or misleading representation or means to collect, or attempt to collect, claims or to obtain information concerning a debtor or alleged debtor, including any conduct which is described as follows:

(4) The failure to disclose clearly the name and full business address of the person to whom the claim has been assigned for collection or to whom the claim is owed at the time of making any demand for money. Haw. Rev. Stat. § 443B-18(4)(West, WESTLAW current through 1999 Regular Session).

IDAHO

Special Text or Address Requirements

☞ (1) Every permittee, foreign permittee, and agent shall deal openly, fairly, and honestly without deception in the conduct of the collection agency business. When not inconsistent with the statutes of this state, the provisions of the Federal Fair Debt Collection Practices Act, 15 U.S.C. section 1692, et seq., as amended, may be enforced by the director against agents, permittees, and foreign permittees under the provisions of this chapter.

(2) In any and every instance where the permittee has a managerial or financial interest in the creditor, or where the creditor has a managerial or financial interest in the permittee, disclosure of such interest must be made on each and every contact with a debtor in seeking to make a collection of any account, claim, or other indebtedness where such interest or relationship exists between creditor and permittee. Idaho Code § 26-2229A(1-2) (West, WESTLAW current through end of 1999 Regular Session).

☞ Every permittee under this chapter must maintain an office in the state of Idaho, staffed with at least one (1) natural person who passed the examination required in section 26-2229, Idaho Code, or is exempt from the provisions of this chapter pursuant to section 26-2239(1), Idaho Code, at each branch or facility. Each permittee must have a listed Idaho telephone number and must be open to the public during normal business hours on each business day, provided, however, that the director may in his discretion approve a request for opening at hours other than normal business hours or a portion of a business day. A business day within the meaning of this section does not include Saturdays, Sundays, or legal holidays. Each permittee under this chapter must designate a natural person, who need not be a resident of the state of Idaho, to be responsible for the business carried on at the office and who has passed the examination for a permit required by section 26-2229, Idaho Code. If the person designated by the permittee to be responsible for business carried on at the office is not normally available in the Idaho office, then the **permittee's collection activities with debtors must begin with a written notice to each debtor setting forth a mailing address and a toll-free telephone number whereby a debtor may contact the designated responsible person during normal business hours.** Idaho Code § 26-2223A (West, WESTLAW current through end of 1999 Regular Session).(Emphasis added). Editor's Note: For information on how this statute has been interpreted, please see Dun & Bradstreet Inc. v. McEldowney, 564 F. Supp. 257 (D. Idaho 1983).

ILLINOIS

Sᴘᴇᴄɪᴀʟ Tᴇxᴛ ᴏʀ Aᴅᴅʀᴇss Rᴇǫᴜɪʀᴇᴍᴇɴᴛs

☛ A collection agency as defined in the "Collection Agency Act" [225 ILCS 425/1 et seq.] or any employee of such collection agency commits a deceptive collection practice when, with the intent to collect a debt owed to a person, corporation, or other entity, he:

(a)   represents falsely that he is an attorney, a policeman, a sheriff or deputy sheriff, a bailiff, a county clerk or employee of a county clerk's office, or any other person who by statute is authorized to enforce the law or any order of a court; or

(b)   while attempting to collect an alleged debt, misrepresents to the alleged debtor or to his immediate family the corporate, partnership or proprietary name or other trade or business name under which the debt collector is engaging in debt collections and which he is legally authorized to use; or

(c)   while attempting to collect an alleged debt, adds to the debt any service charge, interest, or penalty which he is not entitled by law to add; or

(d)   threatens to ruin, destroy, or otherwise adversely affect an alleged debtor's credit rating unless, at the same time, a disclosure is made in accordance with federal law that the alleged debtor has a right to inspect his credit rating; or

(e)   accepts from an alleged debtor the payment which he knows is not owed.

The commission of a deceptive collection practice is a Business Offense punishable by a fine not to exceed $3,000. Ill. Ann. Stat. Ch. 720, para. 5/17-5 (West, WESTLAW current through P.A. 91-703, approved May 16, 2000). (Editor's Note: Subsection d of the above section may be preempted by the Federal Fair Credit Reporting Act 15 U.S.C. § 1681t(b)(1)(F)).

a)   ☛ A collection agency shall use only the agency name or tradestyle exactly as it appears on the agency's certificate of registration (the certificate) issued by the Department in all communications, (e.g., ABC Collection Agency cannot use a name such as ABC Acceptance Company) except for skiptracing and envelopes as prohibited by 15 U.S.C. 1692b.(5).

b) **When an agency communicates with a debtor, the agency must state in a written or telephone communication the specific reason for the communication, the name of the creditor, the registered name of the agency, the date of communication in written communication;** and in oral communication, the identity of the collector making the contact. Ill. Admin. Code tit. 68, § 1210.60 (West, WESTLAW current with amendments received through May 26, 2000.) (Emphasis added).

MAINE

Special Text or Address Requirements

☛ A debt collector may not use unfair or unconscionable means to collect, or attempt to collect any debt. Without limiting the general application of this subsection, the following conduct is a violation of this section:

> H. Using any language or symbol, other than the debt collector's address, on any envelope when communicating with a consumer by use of the mails or by telegram, except that a debt collector may use his business name if that name does not indicate that he is in the debt collection business. Me. Rev. Stat. Ann. tit. 32, § 11013(3)(H) (West, WESTLAW current through 1999 First Regular Session).

☛ A licensee shall be available a minimum of 20 hours a week with sufficient personnel to provide information, personally or telephonically, concerning a debtor's account. **Such hours shall appear on all communications sent to Maine debtors.** Code Me. R. Chap. 300, § 2(C)(3) Available at http://www.state.me.us/sos/cec/rcn/apa/02/chaps02 .htm.(Rules Effective March 5, 1985. Text of website last updated April 13, 2000). (Emphasis added).

☛ **A licensee shall disclose the telephone number of its licensed location on the letterhead of all communications sent to Maine debtors.** Code Me. R. Chap. 300, §2(C)(4) Available at http://www.state.me.us/sos/cec/rcn/apa/02/ chaps02.htm. (Rules Effective March 5, 1985. Text of website last updated April 13, 2000). (Emphasis added).

MASSACHUSETTS

Special Text or Address Requirements

☛ An envelope sent through the mails to a consumer debtor by a collection agency engaged in the collection of debt of consumer debtors shall not contain as part of a return address the name of the collection agency or any signification that the communication is related to a debt allegedly overdue. A communication in an envelope to a debtor by a collection agency shall disclose the business address of the agency as stated on the license. **A collection agency engaged in the collection of debt of consumer debtors shall disclose its telephone number and office**

hours on all communication to the consumer debtor. In communicating with debtors, the collection agency shall use only the exact name in which the Commissioner has granted the license. Mass. Regs. Code Tit. 209 § 18.13 (West, WESTLAW current through Register #893, dated April 14, 2000). (Emphasis added).

☛ **It shall constitute an unfair or deceptive act or practice for a collection agency to omit to disclose to a debtor in writing, by delivering or mailing, within five days after the first contact by the collection agency with a debtor, the following information:**

(a)   **The name and mailing address of the collection agency and proper identification of the creditor or the assignee of the creditor on whose behalf the collection agency is communicating;**

(b)   **Identification of the debt;**

(c)   **A brief description of the nature of the default;**

(d)   **A statement of the action required to cure the default;**

(e)   **The name, address, and telephone number of the person to be contacted for additional information concerning the debt and default.**

Whenever a debtor is other than a natural person, only one set of the disclosures outlined in 209 CMR 18.19(1) need be given. Mass. Regs. Code Tit. 209 § 18.19 (West, WESTLAW current through Register #893, dated April 14, 2000). (Emphasis added).

☛ It shall constitute an unfair or deceptive act or practice for a collection agency to contact a debtor in any of the following ways:

(i) Failing to send the debtor the following notice in writing within 30 days after the first communication to a debtor at his place of employment regarding any debt, provided that a copy of the notice shall be sent every six months thereafter so long as collection activity by the collection agency on the debt continues and the debtor has not made a written request as described in 209 CMR 18.15(1)(h):

NOTICE OF IMPORTANT RIGHTS

YOU HAVE THE RIGHT TO MAKE A WRITTEN OR ORAL REQUEST THAT TELEPHONE CALLS REGARDING YOUR DEBT NOT BE MADE TO YOU AT YOUR PLACE OF EMPLOYMENT. ANY SUCH ORAL REQUEST WILL BE VALID FOR ONLY TEN DAYS UNLESS YOU PROVIDE WRITTEN CONFIRMATION OF THE REQUEST POSTMARKED OR DELIVERED WITHIN SEVEN DAYS OF SUCH REQUEST. YOU MAY TERMINATE THIS REQUEST BY WRITING TO THE COLLECTION AGENCY. Mass. Regs. Code Tit. 209 § 18.15 (West, WESTLAW current through Register #893, dated April 14, 2000). (Emphasis added).

MINNESOTA

SPECIAL TEXT OR ADDRESS REQUIREMENTS

☛ No collection agency or collectors shall:

(1) in collection letters or publications, or in any communication, oral or written, threaten wage garnishment or legal suit by a particular lawyer, unless it has actually retained the lawyer. Minn. Stat. Ann. § 332.37(1) (West, WESTLAW current through end of 1999 Regular Session).

☛ No collection agency or collectors shall:

(21) when initially contacting a Minnesota debtor by mail, fail to include a disclosure on the contact notice, in a type size or font which is equal to or larger than the largest other type of type size or font used in the text of the notice. The disclosure must state: **"This collection agency is licensed by the Minnesota Department of Commerce."** Minn. Stat. Ann. § 332.37(21) (West, WESTLAW current through end of 1999 Regular Session). (Emphasis added).

NEW YORK
(Including the Cities of Buffalo and New York City)

SPECIAL TEXT OR ADDRESS REQUIREMENTS

New York State: No requirements in state law, which are more restrictive than the FDCPA.

City of Buffalo: No requirements in city ordinance, which are more restrictive than the FDCPA.

New York City: Any advertisement, letterhead, receipt, or other printed matter of a licensee must contain the license number assigned to the licensee by the New York City Department of Consumer Affairs. The license number must be clearly identified as a New York City Department of Consumer Affairs license number and must be disclosed and disseminated in a lawful manner. Any telephone listing consisting solely of the name, address, and telephone number of the licensee need not specify the licensee's license number.

Licensees holding licenses for more than one location must also include their respective license number(s) clearly identified as New York City Department of Consumer Affairs' license number(s) on all correspondence and other printed matter which contains or makes reference to one or more of such licensees' licensed location(s). New York City, N.Y., Rules, tit. 6, § 1-05 (West, WESTLAW, New York City Rules and Regulations current through December 31, 1999.) (Emphasis added).

☛ Any debt collector communicating with any person other than the consumer for the purpose of acquiring location information about the consumer in order to collect a debt, after the institution of debt collection procedures shall:

(4) not use any language or symbol on any envelope or in the contents of any communication effected by the mails or telegram that indicates that the debt collector is in the debt collection business or that the communication relates to the collection of a debt; provided that a debt collector may use his or her business name or the name of a department within his or her organization as long as any name used does not connote debt collection. New York City, N.Y., Rules, Tit. 6, § 5-77(a)(4) (West, WESTLAW, New York City Rules and Regulations current through December 31, 1999).

☛ A debt collector, in connection with the collection of a debt shall not make any false, deceptive, or misleading representation. Such representations include:

(15) except as otherwise provided under s 5-77(a) and except for any communication which is required by law or chosen from among alternatives of which one is required by law, **the failure to disclose clearly in all communications made to collect a debt or to obtain information about a consumer, that the debt collector is attempting to collect a debt and that any information obtained will be used for that purpose.** New York City, N.Y., Rules, Tit. 6, § 5-77(d)(15) (West, WESTLAW, New York City Rules and Regulations current through December 31, 1999).(Emphasis added).

☛ A debt collector may not use any unfair or unconscionable means to collect, or attempt to collect, a debt. Such conduct includes:

(5) after institution of debt collection procedures, when communicating with a consumer by use of the mails or telegram, using any language or symbol other than the debt collector's address on any envelope, or using any language or symbol that indicates the debt collector is in the debt collection business or that the communication relates to the collection of a debt on a postcard, except that a debt collector may use his or her business name or the name of a department within his or her organization as long as any name used does not connote debt collection. New York City, N.Y., Rules, tit. 6, § 5-77(e)(5)(West, WESTLAW, The New York City Rules and Regulations current through December 31, 1999).

NORTH CAROLINA

SPECIAL TEXT OR ADDRESS REQUIREMENTS

☛ No debt collector shall collect, or attempt to collect, a debt or obtain information concerning a consumer by any fraudulent, deceptive, or misleading representation. Such representations include, but are not limited to, the following:

(2) **Failing to disclose in *all* communications attempting to collect a debt that the purpose of such communication is to collect a debt.** N.C. Gen. Stat. § 75-54 (West, WESTLAW current through 1999 Extra Session).(Emphasis added). Editor's Note: This provision is repeated in N.C. Gen. Stat. § 58-70-110.

☛ **All collection agencies licensed under this Part to do the business of a collection agency in this State, shall in** *all* **correspondence with debtors use stationery or forms which contain the permit number and the true name and address of such collection agency.** N.C. Gen. Stat. § 58-70-50 (West, WESTLAW current through 1999 Extra Session). (Emphasis added).

PUERTO RICO

Special Text or Address Requirements

☛ Puerto Rico does not have a special text requirement, however, a 1984 FTC Consent Decree required a consumer finance company to provide notices in Spanish when collecting debts from consumers in Puerto Rico. (*AVCO Financial Services, Inc.*, 104 F.T.C. 485 (1984)). Collection agencies may want to keep this consent decree in consideration when collecting debts from Puerto Rico residents.

TENNESSEE

Special Text or Address Requirements

☛ In order to protect the rights of debtors, **all letters of collection or notices of collection from a collection agency to a debtor shall contain the following language:**

> **"This collection agency is licensed by the Collection Service Board, State Department of Commerce and Insurance, 500 James Robertson Parkway, Nashville, Tennessee 37243."** Tenn. Code. Ann § 62-20-111(b) (West, WESTLAW current through end of 1999 Regular Session). (Emphasis added).

TEXAS

Special Text or Address Requirements

☛ Except as otherwise provided by this section, in debt collection or obtaining information concerning a consumer, a debt collector may not use a fraudulent, deceptive, or misleading representation that employs the following practices:

(1) using a name other than the:

  (A) true business or professional name or the true personal or legal name of the debt collector while engaged in debt collection; or

  (B) name appearing on the face of the credit card while engaged in the collection of a credit card debt. Tex. Fin. Code Ann. § 392.304(a)(1) (West, WESTLAW current through end of 1999 Regular Session).

☛ Except as otherwise provided by this section, in debt collection or obtaining information concerning a consumer, a debt collector may not use a fraudulent, deceptive, or misleading representation that employs the following practices:

(7) using a written communication that demands a response to a place other than the debt collector's or creditor's street address or post office box. Tex. Fin. Code Ann. § 392.304(a)(7) (West, WESTLAW current through end of 1999 Regular Session).

☞ Except as otherwise provided by this section, in debt collection or obtaining information concerning a consumer, a debt collector may not use a fraudulent, deceptive, or misleading representation that employs the following practices:

(5) **failing to disclose clearly in *any* communication with the debtor that the debt collector is attempting to collect a consumer debt** unless the communication is for the purpose of discovering the location of the debtor. Tex. Fin. Code Ann. § 392.304(a)(5)(West, WESTLAW current through end of 1999 Regular Session). (Emphasis added).

UTAH

Special Text or Address Requirements

☞ A creditor [or collection agency] may submit a negative credit report to a credit reporting agency only if the creditor notifies the party whose credit record is the subject of the negative report. After providing this notice, a creditor may submit additional information to a credit-reporting agency respecting the same transaction or extension of credit that gave rise to the original negative credit report without providing any additional notice.

(3) (a) Notice shall be in writing and shall be delivered in person or mailed first class, postage prepaid, to the party's last-known address prior to or within 30 days after the transmission of the report.

(b) The notice may be part of any notice of default, billing statement, or other correspondence from the creditor to the party.

(c) The notice is sufficient if it takes substantially the following form:

"As required by Utah law, you are hereby notified that a negative credit report reflecting on your credit record may be submitted to a credit reporting agency if you fail to fulfill the terms of your credit obligations."

(d) The notice may, in the creditor's discretion, be more specific than the form given in Subsection (c). For example, the notice may provide particular information regarding an account or list the approximate date on which the creditor submitted or intends to submit a negative credit report. Utah Code Ann. § 70c-7-107 (West, WESTLAW, Current through End of 1999 General Session). *Editor's Note: This provision may be preempted by the Federal Fair Credit Reporting Act 15 U.S.C. § 1681t(b)(1)(F)).*

VERMONT

SPECIAL TEXT OR ADDRESS REQUIREMENTS

☞ The use of any conduct or means which would unreasonably publicize information relating to any debt arising out of a consumer transaction constitutes an unfair act and practice in commerce under 9 V.S.A. Section 2453(a). Such unfair acts include (but shall not be limited to) the following:

> (d) The use of any form of communication to the debtor which ordinarily would be seen by any other person, except telegrams, that displays or conveys any information about the alleged claim other than the name, address, and phone number of the debt collector. Rule CF 104.03 (d) Rule taken from: http://www.state.vt.us/atg/Rule%20CF104.htm. Text of website last updated on July 14, 2000).

☞ The use of any false, fraudulent, deceptive, or misleading representation or means to collect, or attempt to collect, any debt arising out of a consumer transaction or to obtain information concerning debtors constitutes an unfair and deceptive trade act and practice in commerce under 9 V.S.A. Section 2453(a). Such unfair and deceptive acts include (but shall not be limited to) the following:

> (a) The use of any business, company, or organization name while engaged in the collection of claims, other than the true name of the debt collector's business, company, or organization;

> (b) The **failure to clearly disclose in** *all written* **communications made to the debtor or to members of the debtor's family in order to collect, or attempt to collect, a claim or to obtain information about a debtor that the debt collector is attempting to collect a claim and any information obtained will be used for that purpose;**

> (c) Any false representation that the debt collector has information in his possession or something of value for the debtor;

> (d) The failure to clearly disclose the name and full business address of the person to whom the claim has been assigned at the time of communicating the first demand for money after the date of the assignment. **It is an unfair practice if a collector fails to disclose in** *all written* **communications made to a debtor or the debtor's family, that the collector is attempting to collect a debt and that any information obtained will be used for that purpose** RULE CF 104.04(a-d) Rule taken from: http://www.state.vt.us/atg/Rule%20CF104.htm. Text of website last updated on July 14, 2000). (Emphasis added).

WASHINGTON

SPECIAL TEXT OR ADDRESS REQUIREMENTS

☛ No licensee [licensed collection agency] or employee of a licensee [licensed collection agency] shall give or send to any debtor or cause to be given or sent to any debtor any notice, letter, message, or form which represents or implies that a claim exists unless it shall indicate in clear and legible type:

a. The name of the licensee [licensed collection agency] and the city, street, and number at which he is licensed to do business;

b. The name of the original creditor to whom the debtor is owed the claim if such name is known to the licensee [licensed collection agency] or employee: PROVIDED, That upon written request of the debtor, the collector shall make a reasonable effort to obtain the name of such person and provide the name to the debtor;

c. If the notice, letter, message, or form is the first notice to the debtor or if the licensee [licensed collection agency] is attempting to collect a different amount than indicated in his or her first notice to the debtor, an itemization of the claim asserted must be made including:

(i) Amount owing on the original obligation at the time it was received by the licensee for collection or by assignment:

(ii) Interest or service charge, collection costs or late payment charges, if any, added to the original obligation by the original creditor, customer or assignor before it was received by the licensee for collection, if such information is known by the licensee or employee: PROVIDED, That upon written request of the debtor, the licensee shall make a reasonable effort to obtain information on such items and provide this information to the debtor;

(iii) Interest or service charge, if any, added by the licensee or customer or assignor after the obligation was received by the licensee for collection;

(iv) Collection costs, if any, that the licensee is attempting to collect;

(v) Attorneys' fees, if any, that the licensee is attempting to collect on his or her behalf or on the behalf of a customer or assignor;

(vi) Any other charge or fee that the licensee is attempting to collect on his or its own behalf or on the behalf of a customer or assignor.

Wash. Rev. Code Ann. § 19.16.250(8) (West, WESTLAW current through End of 1999 Special Session 1999). (Emphasis added).

☛ Whenever a collection agency is required pursuant to RCW 19.16.250 (8)(c) to disclose to the debtor that interest charges are being added to the original obligation, **the collection agency must also disclose to the debtor the rate of interest**; said rate of interest not to exceed the legal maximum rate pursuant to chapter 19.52 RCW. Wash. Admin. Code § 308-29-070 (West, WESTLAW current with amendments adopted through May 3, 2000). (Emphasis added).

☛ No licensed collection agency shall use any name other than the name set out in its current license when making demand for payment. Wash. Rev. Code Ann. § 19.16.250(7)(West, WESTLAW current through End of 1999 Special Session 1999).

WISCONSIN

Special Text or Address Requirements

☛ (1) Within 5 days after the initial communication with a debtor, **a licensee shall, unless the initial communication is written and contains the following notice or the debtor has paid the debt, send the debtor the following notice in not less than 8 point boldface type:**

> **"This collection agency is licensed by the Office of the Administrator of the Division of Banking, P.O. Box 7876, Madison, Wisconsin 53707."**

This notice shall be typed or printed on either a collection notice or on the validation of any debt directed to the debtor by the licensee pursuant to Section 809 of the Federal Fair Debt Collection Practices Act.

(2) **Where the notice** required by sub. (1) **is printed on the reverse side of any collection notice or validation sent by the licensee, the front of** such notice **shall bear the following statement in not less than 8 point boldface type:**

> **"Notice: See Reverse Side for Important Information."**

Wis. Admin. Code § 74.11 (West, WESTLAW current through Reg. No. 533 (May 2000).(Emphasis added).

WYOMING

Special Text or Address Requirements

☛ A debt collector may not use any false, deceptive, or misleading representation or means in connection with the collection of any debt. Without limiting the general application of the foregoing, the following conduct is a violation of this section:

> (k) Except as otherwise provided for communications to acquire location information under Section 7, the **failure to disclose clearly in** *all* **communications made to collect a debt or to obtain information about a consumer, that the debt collector is attempting to collect a debt and that any information obtained will be used for that purpose.** Wyoming Rules & Regulations, Department of Commerce, Collection Agency Board, Ch. 4, § 10(k) (West, WESTLAW current through End of 2000 Budget Session). (Emphasis added).

☛ A debt collector may not use unfair or unconscionable means to collect, or attempt to collect, any debt. Without limiting the general application of the foregoing, the following conduct is a violation of this section:

(h) Using any language or symbol, other than the debt collector's address, on any envelope when communicating with a consumer by use of the mails or by telegram, except that a debt collector may use his business name if such name does not indicate that he is in the debt collection business. Wyoming Rules & Regulations, Department of Commerce, Collection Agency Board, Ch. 4, § 11(h) (West, WESTLAW current through End of 2000 Budget Session).

CHAPTER 12

Truth in Lending Regulation Z

COST OF DOING BUSINESS

Charges absorbed by the creditor as a cost of doing business are not finance charges, even though the creditor may take such costs into consideration in determining the interest rate to be charged or the cash price of the property or services sold. However, if the creditor separately imposes a charge on the consumer to cover certain costs, the charge is a finance charge if it otherwise meets the definition.

A discount imposed on a credit obligation when it is assigned by a creditor to another party is not a finance charge as long as the discount is not separately imposed on the consumer. The purpose of the TILA, Truth in Lending Act, is to assure a meaningful disclosure of credit terms so that the consumer will be able to compare more readily the various credit terms available to the consumer and to protect the consumer against inaccurate and unfair billing in credit card practices. The TILA requires lenders to clearly disclose any finance charges that a consumer would bear under a credit transaction. A finance charge is defined as a sum of all charges payable directly or indirectly by the person to whom the credit is extended and imposed directly or indirectly by the creditor as an incident to the extension of credit.

If the lender did not charge the cash price customers a different price for the same vehicle than credit customers, then the discount is not considered a finance charge. The hidden finance charge does not constitute a finance charge under the TILA since the discount represents a common practice of buying commercial paper at a price less than its face value and such discounts are not finance charges.[1]

TILA—CLASS ACTION

Efforts by consumers to avoid mandatory arbitration continue to occupy the legal system. Some consumer attorneys attempted to distinguish claims under the Truth and Lending Act as different from other types of claims and therefore mandatory arbitration clauses in agreements covered by TILA should be unenforceable.

A recent case in Texas discussed various attacks on the mandatory arbitration clause. The final conclusion was that there was nothing in the Truth in Lending Act that indicates Congress intended to create a statutory right to class action relief or preferred a class action as the mechanism by which to effect the remedial purposes of the statute.

Citing another case, the Texas Tribunal quoted as follows:

> "So long as the prospective litigant may vindicate his or her statutory cause of action in the arbitrial form, the statute will continue to serve both its remedial and deterrent function."

Consumers retain all of their statutory rights under TILA and there is no language in the arbitration provision suggesting a limitation of the substantive rights. The arbitrator may order injunctive relief if allowed to do so under the terms of an arbitration agreement.

The consumer attorney in this instance lost. (See Chapter 4—Arbitration.)[2]

The consumer contended that the Truth in Lending Act provided a statutory right to bring class actions. The court upheld the arbitration clause under the Federal Arbitration Act and stated that the amendments to the TILA in its accompanying legislative history indicated that Congress recognized class actions as a useful way to enforce the TILA. The TILA does not provide a basic right to bring the class action, nor does it

---

[1] *Balderos v. City Chevrolet, Buick & Geo, Inc.,* No. 97 C 2084, 1998 W.L. 155912 (N.D. Ill. Mar. 31, 1998), aff'd in part, rev'd in part 214 F. 3d 849 (7th. Cir. 2000).

[2] *March v. First USA Bank, N.A.,* 103 F. Supp. 2d 909 (N.D. Tex. 2000).

rely exclusively on class actions as an enforcement mechanism, and the consumer failed to demonstrate that Congress intended to override the Federal Arbitration Act's strong presumption in favor of arbitration in cases involving TILA claims.[3]

LIABILITY OF ASSIGNEE

Section 1641(a) states as follows:

(a) Except as otherwise specifically provided in this title, any civil action for a violation of this title or proceeding under section 108 which may be brought against a creditor may be maintained against any assignee of such creditor only if the violation for which such action or proceeding is brought is apparent on the face of the disclosure statement, except where the assignment was involuntary. For the purpose of this section, a violation apparent on the face of the disclosure statement includes, but is not limited to (1) a disclosure which can be determined to be incomplete or inaccurate from the face of the disclosure statement or other documents assigned, or (2) a disclosure which does not use the terms required to be used by this title.

(b) Except as provided in Section 125(c), in any action or proceeding by or against any subsequent assignee of the original creditor without knowledge to the contrary by the assignee when he acquires the obligation, written acknowledgment of receipt by a person to whom a statement is required to be given pursuant to this title shall be conclusive proof of the delivery thereof and, except as provided in subsection (a), of compliance with this chapter. This section does not affect the rights of the obligor in any action against the original creditor.

(c) Any consumer who has the right to rescind a transaction under Section 125 may rescind the transaction as against any assignee of the obligation.

The courts have uniformly held that "apparent on the face" means exactly that—for an assignee to be liable under TILA, the violation must be apparent on the face of the assigned disclosure documents. The courts have rejected the concept that even though the violation is not apparent on the face, that the assignee owes a duty of diligent inquiry. Even in the situation where there were related loan documents or checks and credits that may have revealed the true cost of the warranty as well as the amount paid to the parties, the court held that the violation was not reflected on the face of the documents and it required the court to resort to evidence or documents extraneous to the disclosure statement.

---

[3]*Sagal v. First USA Bank,* 69 F. Supp 2d 627 (D. Dela. 1999).

A Circuit Court of Appeals also concluded that it would look only at assigned documents to determine liability, even though the additional information to determine the violation was publicly available in the form of state licensing fee tables. The court stated that even though the fee tables may be available to the public, those tables do not constitute an assigned document.

In a recent Court of Appeals decision in the 3rd Circuit, the court analyzed the prior decisions in other circuits and continued to apply the same strict, narrow interpretation applied to this particular section.

In this case, the plaintiff conceded at oral argument that liability cannot be created by knowledge. Plaintiff attempted to draw a distinction between constructive knowledge, which she contended would be insufficient, and actual knowledge, which she asserted was sufficient to support assignee liability. The court disagreed and stated that there was nothing in the history of the text to support such a premise.

The FTC required holder notice was included in the retail installment contract and this provided for assignee liability with regard to "all claims and defenses which the debtor could assert against the seller." The plaintiff then asserted that the retail installment contract should be enforced as written. But several courts, in addition to this court, have already held that the holder notice language standing alone does not suffice to subject an assignee to liability. The notice could not have such an affect, because inclusion of the required language did not result from bargaining or agreement by the parties to reflect a voluntary and intentional assumption of liability. It cannot be considered voluntarily when the statute requires that a failure to include the holder notice is an unfair and deceptive act. Thus, the holder notice is a mandatory clause that must be included because of the actual law. One cannot assume that the holder notice was included voluntarily. (See article in Appendix I.)[4]

INCONSISTENT LOAN DISCLOSURES

The lender tried to provide the debtor with a more favorable type of a notice.

The lender offered in his disclosure statement both a one-day recission period provided under Pennsylvania law and the three-day recission period provided under TILA. The first question the court considered is

---

[4]*Green v. Levis Motors, Inc.*, 179 F. 3d 286 (5th Cir. 1999); *Ellis v. General Motors Acceptance Corp.*, 160 F. 3d 703 (11th Cir. 1998); *Taylor v. Quality Hyundai, Inc.*, 150 F. 3d 689 (7th Cir. 1998); *Ramadan v. Chase Manhattan Corp.*, 229 F. 3d 194 (3rd Cir. 2000).

whether the lender was obligated to include the one-day notice in the financing agreement, because the Board of Governors of the Federal Reserve System had not as yet decided that the one-day notice was preempted by the TILA.

The court found that having the one-day notice and the three-day notice was confusing to the consumer, and therefore the consumer had a period of three years to rescind from the date of the transaction. The lender was not justified in including in the financing statement a notice of plaintiff's right to recission which is required under Pennsylvania law, but which is inconsistent with the TILA, on the ground that the Board of Governors had not yet determined that Pennsylvania law requiring the inclusion is preempted by TILA.

Based on the fact that creditors now had the ability to request an advance ruling from the Board of Governors on whether a state disclosure requirement was preempted by TILA, the Board of Governors deleted the provisions of Regulation Z permitting creditors to include inconsistent state disclosures.

Creditors are no longer free to include inconsistent state disclosures in their loan documents and in this case the defendant was not justified in including the one-day notice required under Pennsylvania law in the financing agreement until the Board had determined that the one-day notice was preempted by TILA.[5]

DISPUTED DEBTS

It is generally suggested that when a suit is started on a credit card, the complaint contain not only a count for breach of contract but also a count for monies loaned as well as account stated. The reason for the count for monies loaned is that sometimes the original credit card agreement is not available or the debtor never signed a credit card agreement because the debtor merely responded to a solicitation to use a credit card. In those cases, a contract action would not be appropriate and the complaint should be confined to a count for monies loaned and an account stated. Monies loaned alleges that the debtor made purchases on credit or obtained cash advances by using his credit card to be repaid in installments depending upon the terms of the credit card agreement.

In some states, this type of pleading enables a creditor (a lender) to be successful without producing a copy of the signed agreement, because it is not an essential piece of evidence to prove your case. Reliance is

---

[5]*Williams v. Empire Funding Corp.*, 109 F. Supp. 2d 352 (E.D. Pa. 2000).

placed on the debtor's course of conduct which is the act of signing for the charges and repaying the monies.

As to the account stated, the creditor must allege that it was their normal business practice to mail itemized monthly billing statements to its cardholders and that the debtor retained the statements without objection, in writing, for over 60 days from the date of the disputed statements. The debtor's acceptance of the charges can be inferred from the fact that the debtor continued to use the credit card, made partial payments, and never attempted to cancel the agreement during the period despite having received the statements for several months.

Under Section 15 U.S.C Section 1666 and Regulation Z Subsection 226-13(b)(1)-1 of the Truth in Lending Act, a debtor has 60 days from receipt of disputed charges to notify the creditor in writing of a billing error to preserve his rights. If the defendant fails to object in writing pursuant to their rights to dispute the bill, the debtor has waived the right to dispute the balance. The case of *Minskoff v. American Express Travel Related Servs. Co.*, 98 F. 3d 703 (2d Cir. 1996) stated as follows:

> "Once a cardholder has established a credit card account, and provided that the card issuer is in compliance with the billing statement disclosure requirements of 15 U.S.C 1637, the cardholder is in a superior position to determine whether the charges reflected on his regular billing statements are legitimate. A cardholder's failure to examine credit card statement, that would reveal fraudulent use of the card, constitutes a negligent omission that creates apparent authority for charges that would otherwise be considered unauthorized under TILA. See TransAmerica 325 N.W. 2nd at 215."

The negligent omission to dispute any charges in a timely manner prevents the debtor from disputing the charges at a later date. Defendant's course of performance in using the card and/or making partial payments demonstrated a willingness to repay the obligation. This duty to review the terms and conditions are set forth in every credit card agreement. The creditor need not produce signed charge receipts if the debtor did not timely dispute the charge. In today's economy, many charges take place without a signed receipt, such as on-line purchases for airline tickets and telephone purchases.

DISCLOSURE OF FEES

The bank contended that they disclosed to the debtor the fax fee and recording charges five weeks prior to the closing and the case fell within the rule that consumer fraud claims may not be predicated upon fully disclosed facts. While full disclosure of the fees was made in advance and no compulsion was exerted upon the debtor to proceed with the transaction, and the debtor had the option to reject the entire transaction and thus the charge for the recording fees and the fax, the court was not impressed. The court felt that the debtor had no choice but to pay the $23.50 for the fax and recording fee. Any reasonable debtor would conclude that the only sane thing to do was to pay the charges rather than jeopardize the closing and the sale of a condominium. The typical act of consumer fraud involves an individual consumer who falls victim to a commercial entity which enjoys "disparity of bargaining power." This was a classic example of consumer fraud and an adhesion contract (where one party to the contract has no choice because of the bargaining power of the other party) and the court found that the bank had violated New York General Business Law Section 349, in that the defendant engaged in a consumer-oriented, misleading practice injuring the plaintiff.[6]

Whether other courts would follow this decision would probably depend upon whether the judge was consumer friendly or creditor friendly, for cases of this nature often go either way. Nevertheless, the prudent lender must understand that using this device to extract a few extra dollars from consumers may expose the lender to liability.

RIGHT OF RESCISSION

Under the Truth in Lending Act, when a loan is granted in a consumer credit transaction secured by the borrower's principal dwelling, the borrower may rescind the loan agreement if the lender fails to deliver certain forms or disclose important terms accurately. This right of rescission expires in the usual case three years after the loan closes or upon the sale of the secured property, whichever date is earlier. The issue presented is whether a borrower may assert this right to rescind as an affirmative defense in a foreclosure action brought by a lender more than three years after the consummation of the transaction.

An important issue is whether a borrower is entitled to rescind a loan transaction due to the failure to make disclosures. The time period is three years and the United States Supreme Court has treated this rule as law in *Beach v. Owen Federal Bank*, 118 S.Ct. 1408 (1998). The consumer alleged rescission and recoupment after suit was instituted against the consumer.

---

[6]*Negrin v. Norwest Mortg., Inc.*, 700 N.Y.S. 2d 184 (App. Div., 2d Dep't 1999).

Plaintiff relied on the Supreme Court decision for its proposition that the consumer's rescission claims are time barred due to the three-year period.

It isn't often that the Supreme Court reviews a section of the Truth in Lending Act and especially one on recoupment. Recoupment has always been allowed in the framework of consumer matters and survives the expiration of the period provided by a statute of limitations that would otherwise bar recoupment as an independent action. The courts usually held that when the plaintiff's action is timely, a defendant may always raise a claim in recoupment even if it can no longer be brought independently. The purpose of the statute of limitations is to keep stale litigation out of the courts, but if the statute would apply and bar an otherwise legitimate defense to a timely lawsuit, the result would be unfair to the consumer. Unfortunately, the issue was whether the time limitation was a statute of limitation and whether it operates, with the lapse of time, to extinguish the right, which is the foundation of the claim, or merely to bar the remedy for its enforcement. Normally, a statute of limitations provides that an action may or must be brought within a certain period of time.

The Court held that a statutory right of rescission could cloud a bank's title on a foreclosure and that the three-year time limit on rescission was not in the nature of the statute of limitations, but was a total bar to the claim itself. The court held that the Act permits no right to rescind, defensively or otherwise, after the three-year period has expired. If the creditor has not complied with the Truth in Lending Act, and the consumer had not asserted his right to rescission within the three years under the Truth in Lending Act, the consumer forfeits his right to rescind, whether he is being sued for foreclosure or otherwise.

The Supreme Court apparently took this definitive action because the right to rescind was such a powerful weapon of the consumer and a three-year period to assert that right is more than sufficient. Furthermore, no evidence appeared in the Congressional Record indicating the nature of the statute of limitations, as opposed to the fact that the right itself will be taken away at the expiration of the three-year period.[7]

---

[7]*Fidler v. Central Coop. Bank (In re Fidler)*, 226 B.R. 734 (Bankr. D. Mass. 1998).

Appendix I

ASSIGNEE LIABILITY FOR TRUTH IN LENDING ACT VIOLATIONS

Donald Maurice

Since its passage in 1968, a violation of the Truth in Lending Act ("TILA"), 15 U.S.C. 1601, et seq., has been a substantial bar to collection of retail consumer accounts. In addition to the statutory requirements found in the TILA statute, TILA authorizes the Federal Reserve Board to promulgate regulations for consumer credit transactions (15 U.S.C. 1604). From this has arisen what is known as "Regulation Z" ("Reg. Z") 12 C.F.R. 226. Together TILA and Reg. Z have placed nearly all facets of consumer credit under Federal regulation. This article is limited to the issue of assignee liability for violation of TILA disclosures.

Whether a consumer transaction is subject to TILA or Reg. Z is an entire subject itself.

DISCLOSURE REQUIREMENTS

One disclosure requirement in Reg. Z provides that in the itemization of the amount being financed by the consumer, the creditor must disclose "any amounts paid to other persons by the creditor on the consumer's behalf" (12 C.F.R. 226.18(c)(iii)). In the case of consumer motor vehicle transactions, dealers would list the price charged to consumers for service contracts, extended warranties, and other similar "protection plans," under "amounts paid to others." Consumers claimed this was a TILA violation because the amount listed by the dealer for the service contract was not really being "paid to others." In fact, the seller retained a substantial portion of the charge as profit (*Shields v. Lefta Inc.,* 888 F. Supp. 894 (N.D. Ill. 1995).

Reprinted with the permission of Donald Maurice.

TILA allows the successful consumer to recover attorney fees, actual damages, and class action statutory damages of the lesser of $500,000, or one percent of the net worth of creditor. As was the case in the 1990s, a string of class actions developed around "the amount paid to others" disclosure requirement to Reg. Z.

TILA does not preempt state laws that do not conflict with its requirements and does not prohibit recovery under state law for the same violation. With this in mind, consumers plead that the TILA violations also resulted in violations of their state's consumer protection laws (National Consumer Law Center, *Truth in Lending* (4th Ed., 1999), §8.64).

The credit agreements, often known as Retail Installment Contracts (RICs), are routinely assigned by dealers to finance companies and banks. In representing the interests of the assignees, it is likely counsel will be faced with a TILA claim. Most likely, it will be an alleged violation of the "amount paid to others" disclosure requirements of 12 C.F.R. 226.18(c)(iii).

ASSIGNEES ARE NOT TILA CREDITORS

The definition of a creditor subject to TILA has evolved favorably over the past 20 years. Prior to 1982, the term "creditor" included all parties to a transaction who regularly extended credit, thereby making an assignee responsible for the TILA disclosures (e.g., *Ford Motor Credit Co. v. Cenance,* 452 U.S. 155, 101 S.Ct. 2239, 2240-41, 68 L. Ed. 2d 744 (1981)). In 1982, however, Congress revised the definition of "creditor" to simplify the TILA's disclosure requirements in the multiple creditor context. Now, in the case of assigned consumer loans, the original creditor is the "creditor" and assignees are not (15 U.S.C. 1602(f)).

Consumers seeking to hold assignees liable for TILA violations often invoke what is known as the FTC Holder Rule. The rule provides that RICs must contain a notice to the consumer that the assignee is subject to all claims and defenses that the debtor could assert against the seller of goods or services (16 C.F.R. 433.2(a)). As part of the 1982 TILA amendments, assignee liability under the FTC Holder Rule was limited to a "violation for which such action or proceeding is brought is apparent on the face of the disclosure statement" (15 U.S.C. 1641(a); *Brister v. Star Chevrolet, Inc.,* 986 F. Supp. 1003, 1008-09 (E.D.La. 1997)).

While the TILA amendments have been in place for nearly 20 years, plaintiffs have continued with their attempts to hold assignees liable as TILA creditors, although these efforts have not proved successful. (See *Kinzel v. Southview Chevrolet Co.,* 892 F. Supp. 1211, 1216 (D.Minn. 1995); *Mayfield v. GE Capital Corp.,* 1999 U.S. Dist. Lexis 4048, RICO Bus. Disp. Guide P9728 (S.D.N.Y. Mar. 31, 1999)).

ASSIGNEE LIABILITY AND THE ART OF "APPARENT ON ITS FACE"

By 1995, the issue of assignee liability under the "apparent on its face" requirement had left many federal district courts divided when considering "upcharges" that were not disclosed in the "amount paid to others" under the disclosure requirements of 12 C.F.R. 226.18(c)(1)(iii). Since the "upcharge," or profit, a dealer retained was not actually being paid to the provider of the extended warranty or service contract, many successfully argued that the non-disclosure was a TILA violation (*Gibson v. Bob Watson Chevrolet/Geo, Inc.*, 1996 WL 316975, rev'd 112 F. 3d 283 (7th Cir. 1997)).

In 1996, an Official Staff Commentary to Reg. Z by the Federal Reserve Board addressed this issue by stating that a creditor "in such cases may reflect (in the RIC) that a creditor has retained a portion of the amount paid to others" (Official Staff Commentary §226.18(c)(1)(iii)-2, 61 Fed. Reg. 14956 (April 4, 1996)).

Of course, the Commentary's use of the word "may" raised questions whether this amended disclosure was mandatory. If it were mandatory, then when a dealer retained profit from "the amount paid to others" and did not disclose it, there should be an "apparent" violation (National Consumer Law Center, Truth in Lending (4th Ed., 1999), §4.7.3.4).

The issue was not decided by any Circuit Court of Appeals until 1998 in *Taylor v. Quality Hyundai, Inc.*, 150 F. 3d 689 (Ct. App. 7th Cir. 1998), reh'g den. 1998 U.S. App. Lexis 21348 (7th Cir. Ill. Aug. 21, 1998), cert. den. 525 U.S. 1141, 143 L. Ed. 2d 41, 119 S. Ct. 1032, 1999 U.S. Lexis 1066, 67 U.S.L.W. 3525 (1999). The language of the RICs in *Taylor* did not state that the dealer had retained a portion of the amount paid to others and plaintiff argued that the non-disclosure was an "apparent" violation. The *Taylor* court rejected the argument, without mention of 1996 Official Staff Commentary. Rather, *Taylor* ignored Reg. Z altogether and focused on the language of the statutory requirements of TILA.

"Apparent on its face" can take two forms; first, "a disclosure that can be determined to be incomplete or inaccurate from the face of the disclosure statement or other documents assigned"; and, second "a disclosure that does not use the terms required to be used by [TILA]." 15 U.S.C. 1641(a). "Apparent," reasoned the *Taylor* court, meant that the TILA violation must appear on the loan documents themselves. An assignee's "awareness" that some seller's practices may violate TILA, even 90% of the time, would not "...be equated to knowledge that a particular disclosure on a particular TILA form is inaccurate or incomplete." (*Taylor*, supra at 694). Thus, the absence of the disclosure recommended by the 1996 Official Commentary would not be apparent because, from the face of the RIC, an assignee would not know whether there is an upcharge in a service contract, even if that were the prevailing practice among dealers from whom the assignee took its assignments. There is no duty of inquiry on the part of the assignee. "Only violations that a reasonable person can spot on the face of the disclosure statement or other assigned documents will make the assignee liable under the TILA." (*Id.*)

More recently, the Third Circuit Court of Appeals refused to allow a consumer to make a case for a TILA violation where one of the "other documents" transferred to the assignee would disclose a violation (such as the price the dealer paid for the service contract). The "other document," an accounting of the transaction, was not part of the TILA disclosure nor was it a specifically "assigned" document; it was merely transferred as part of the loan assignment

(*Ramadan v. Chase Manhattan Corp,* 2000 U.S. App. Lexis 24944 (3d Cir. N.J. Oct. 6, 2000)). The Third Circuit reasoned that §1641(a) of TILA limited the "apparent on its face" inquiry to the TILA disclosure or "other documents assigned" and not all "other documents" that might be transferred to the assignee.

Taylor has been followed by the Third, Fifth, and Eleventh Circuit Courts of Appeals (*Ramadan v. Chase Manhattan Corp.,* supra (3d Cir. N.J. Oct. 6, 2000); *Riviere v. Banner Chevrolet, Inc.,* 184 F. 3d 457, 1999 U.S. App. Lexis 18291 (5th Cir. La. 1999); *Ellis v. GMAC,* 160 F. 3d 703, 1998 U.S. App. Lexis 28456 (11th Cir. Ala. 1998)). District Courts have followed it in the Second Circuit (*Mayfield v. GE Capital Corp.,* supra), Fourth Circuit (*Irby-Greene v. M.O.R., Inc.,* 79 F. Supp. 2d 630, 2000 U.S. Dist. Lexis 60 (E.D. Va. 2000)), Sixth Circuit (*Lozada v. Dale Baker Oldsmobile, Inc.,* 91 F. Supp. 2d 1087, 2000 U.S. Dist. Lexis 4122 (W.D. Mich. 2000)), and Eighth Circuit (*Fielder v. Credit Acceptance Corp.,* 98 F. Supp. 2d 1104, 2000 U.S. Dist. Lexis 7705 (W.D. Mo. 2000)). Only the First and Ninth Circuits have failed to weigh in, but neither Circuit has criticized or refused to follow *Taylor.*

CHAPTER 13

Equal Credit Opportunity Act

No new material.

CHAPTER 13
APPENDIX I

OFFICIAL STAFF COMMENTARY ON REGULATION B EQUAL CREDIT OPPORTUNITY

As amended effective April 1, 1990

Any inquiry relating to Regulation B should be addressed to the Federal Reserve Bank of the Federal Reserve District in which the inquiry arises.

May 1990

CONTENTS

OFFICIAL STAFF COMMENTARY ON REGULATION B

As amended effective April 1, 1990

Following is an official staff interpretation of Regulation B issued under authority delegated by the Federal Reserve Board to officials in the Division of Consumer and Community Affairs. References are to sections of the regulation or the Equal Credit Opportunity Act (15 USC 1601 et seq.).

INTRODUCTION

1. *Official status.* Section 706(e) of the Equal Credit Opportunity Act protects a creditor from civil liability for any act done or omitted in good faith in conformity with an interpretation issued by a duly authorized official of the Federal Reserve Board. This commentary is the means by which the Division of Consumer and Community Affairs of the Federal Reserve Board issues official staff interpretations of Regulation B. Good faith compliance with this commentary affords a creditor protection under section 706(e) of the act.

2. *Issuance of interpretations.* Under appendix D to the regulation, any person may request an official staff interpretation. Interpretations will be issued at the discretion of designated officials and incorporated in this commentary following publication for comment in the *Federal Register.* Except in unusual circumstances, official staff interpretations will be issued only by means of this commentary.

3. *Status of previous interpretations.* Interpretations of Regulation B previously issued by the Federal Reserve Board and its staff have been incorporated into this commentary as appropriate. All other previous Board and staff interpretations, official and unofficial, are superseded by this commentary.

4. *Footnotes.* Footnotes in the regulation have the same legal effect as the text of the regulation, whether they are explanatory or illustrative in nature.

5. *Comment designations.* The comments are designated with as much specificity as possible according to the particular regulatory provision addressed. Each comment in the commentary is identified by a number and the regulatory section or paragraph that it interprets. For example, comments to section 202.2(c) are further divided by subparagraph, such as comment 2(c) (1) (ii)–1 and comment 2(c) (2) (ii)–1.

SECTION 202.1—AUTHORITY, SCOPE, AND PURPOSE

1(a) Authority and Scope

1. *Scope.* The Equal Credit Opportunity Act and Regulation B apply to all credit—commercial as well as personal—without regard to the nature or type of the credit or the creditor. If a transaction provides for the deferral of the payment of a debt, it is credit covered by Regulation B even though it may not be a credit transaction covered by Regulation Z (Truth in Lending). Further, the definition of

creditor is not restricted to the party or person to whom the obligation is initially payable, as is the case under Regulation Z. Moreover, the act and regulation apply to all methods of credit evaluation, whether performed judgmentally or by use of a credit scoring system.

2. *Foreign applicability.* Regulation B generally does not apply to lending activities that occur outside the United States. The regulation does apply to lending activities that take place within the United States (as well as the Commonwealth of Puerto Rico and any territory or possession of the United States), whether or not the applicant is a citizen.

3. *Board.* The term "Board," as used in this regulation, means the Board of Governors of the Federal Reserve System.

Section 202.2—Definitions
2(c) Adverse Action

Paragraph 2(c)(1)(ii)

1. *Move from service area.* If a credit card issuer terminates the open-end account of a customer because the customer has moved out of the card issuer's service area, the termination is "adverse action" for purposes of the regulation unless termination on this ground was explicitly provided for in the credit agreement between the parties. In cases where termination is adverse action, notification is required under section 202.9.

2. *Termination based on credit limit.* If a creditor terminates credit accounts that have low credit limits (for example, under $400) but keeps open accounts with higher credit limits, the termination is adverse action and notification is required under section 202.9.

Paragraph 2(c) (2) (ii)

1. *Default—exercise of due-on-sale clause.* If a mortgagor sells or transfers mortgaged property without the consent of the mortgagee, and the mortgagee exercises its contractual right to accelerate the mortgage loan, the mortgagee may treat the mortgagor as being in default. An adverse-action notice need not be given to the mortgagor or the transferee. (See comment 2(e)–l for treatment of a purchaser who requests to assume the loan.)

Paragraph 2(c) (2) (iii)

1. *Point-of-sale transactions.* Denial of credit at point of sale is not adverse action except under those circumstances specified in the regulation. For example, denial at point of sale is not adverse action in the following situations:

• A credit cardholder presents an expired card or a card that has been reported to the card issuer as lost or stolen.

• The amount of a transaction exceeds a cash advance or credit limit.

- The circumstances (such as excessive use of a credit card in a short period of time) suggest that fraud is involved.

- The authorization facilities are not functioning.

- Billing statements have been returned to the creditor for lack of a forwarding address.

Paragraph 2(c)(2)(v)

1. *Terms of credit versus type of credit offered.* When an applicant applies for credit and the creditor does not offer the credit terms requested by the applicant (for example, the interest rate, length of maturity, collateral, or amount of downpayment), a denial of the application for that reason is adverse action (unless the creditor makes a counteroffer that is accepted by the applicant) and the applicant is entitled to notification under section 202.9.

2(e) Applicant

1. *Request to assume loan.* If a mortgagor sells or transfers the mortgaged property and the buyer makes an application to the creditor to assume the mortgage loan, the mortgagee must treat the buyer as an applicant unless its policy is not to permit assumptions.

2(f) Application

1. *General.* A creditor has the latitude under the regulation to establish its own application process and to decide the type and amount of information it will require from credit applicants.

2. *"Procedures established."* The term refers to the actual practices followed by a creditor for making credit decisions as well as its stated application procedures. For example, if a creditor's stated policy is to require all applications to be in writing on the creditor's application form, but the creditor also makes credit decisions based on oral requests, the creditor's established procedures are to accept both oral and written applications.

3. *When an inquiry becomes an application.* A creditor is encouraged to provide consumers with information about loan terms. However, if in giving information to the consumer the creditor also evaluates information about the applicant, decides to decline the request, and communicates this to the applicant, the creditor has treated the inquiry as an application and must then comply with the notification requirements under section 202.9. Whether the inquiry becomes an application depends on how the creditor responds to the applicant, not on what the applicant says or asks.

4. *Examples of inquiries that are not applications.* The following examples illustrate situations in which only an inquiry has taken place:

- When a consumer calls to ask about loan terms and an employee explains the creditor's basic loan terms, such as interest rates, loan-to-value ratio, and debt-to-income ratio.

- When a consumer calls to ask about interest rates for car loans, and, in order to quote the appropriate rate, the loan officer asks for the make and sales price of the car and the amount of the downpayment, then gives the consumer the rate.

- When a consumer asks about terms for a loan to purchase a home and tells the loan officer her income and intended downpayment, but the loan officer only explains the creditor's loan-to-value ratio policy and other basic lending policies, without telling the consumer whether she qualifies for the loan.

- When a consumer calls to ask about terms for a loan to purchase vacant land and states his income and the sale price of the property to be financed, and asks whether he qualifies for a loan, and the employee responds by describing the general lending policies, explaining that he would need to look at all of the applicant's qualifications before making a decision, and offering to send an application form to the consumer.

5. *Completed application—diligence requirement.* The regulation defines a completed application in terms that give a creditor the latitude to establish its own information requirements. Nevertheless, the creditor must act with reasonable diligence to collect information needed to complete the application. For example, the creditor should request information from third parties, such as a credit report, promptly after receiving the application. If additional information is needed from the applicant, such as an address or telephone number needed to verify employment, the creditor should contact the applicant promptly. (But see comment 9(a)(l)–3, which discusses the creditor's option to deny an application on the basis of incompleteness.)

2(g) Business Credit

1. *Definition.* The test for deciding whether a transaction qualifies as business credit is one of primary purpose. For example, an open-end credit account used for both personal and business purposes is not business credit unless the primary purpose of the account is business-related. A creditor may rely on an applicant's statement of the purpose for the credit requested.

2(j) Credit

1. *General.* Regulation B covers a wider range of credit transactions than Regulation Z (Truth in Lending). For purposes of Regulation B, a transaction is credit if there is a right to defer payment of a debt—regardless of whether the credit is for personal or commercial purposes, the number of installments required for repayment, or whether the transaction is subject to a finance charge.

2(l) Creditor

1. *Assignees.* The term "creditor" includes all persons participating in the credit decision. This may include an assignee or a potential purchaser of the obligation who influences the credit decision by indicating whether or not it will purchase the obligation if the transaction is consummated.

2. *Referrals to creditors.* For certain purposes, the term "creditor" includes persons such as real estate brokers who do not participate in credit decisions but who regularly refer applicants to creditors or who select, or offer to select, creditors to whom credit requests can be made. These persons must comply with section 202.4, the general rule prohibiting discrimination, and with section 202.5(a), on discouraging applications.

2(p) Empirically Derived and Other Credit Systems

1. *Purpose of definition.* The definition under section 202.2(p) (1) (i) through (iv) sets the criteria that a credit system must meet in order for the system to use age as a predictive factor. Credit systems that do not meet these criteria are judgmental systems and may consider age only for the purpose of determining a "pertinent element of creditworthiness." (Both types of systems may favor an elderly applicant. See section 202.6(b)(2).)

2. *Periodic revalidation.* The regulation does not specify how often credit scoring systems must be revalidated. To meet the requirements for statistical soundness, the credit scoring system must be revalidated frequently enough to ensure that it continues to meet recognized professional statistical standards.

2(w) Open-End Credit

1. *Open-end real estate mortgages.* The term "open-end credit" does not include negotiated advances under an open-end real estate mortgage or a letter of credit.

2(z) Prohibited Basis

1. *Persons associated with applicant.* "Prohibited basis" as used in this regulation refers not only to characteristics—the race, color, religion, national origin, sex, marital status, or age—of an applicant (or officers of an applicant in the case of a corporation) but also to the characteristics of individuals with whom an applicant is affiliated or with whom the applicant associates. This means, for example, that under the general rule stated in section 202.4, a creditor may not discriminate against an applicant because of that person's personal or business dealings with members of a certain religion, because of the national origin of any persons associated with the extension of credit (such as the tenants in the apartment complex being financed), or because of the race of other residents in the neighborhood where the property offered as collateral is located

2. *National origin.* A creditor may not refuse to grant credit because an applicant comes from a particular country but may take the applicant's immigration status into account. A creditor may also take into account any applicable law, regulation, or executive order restricting dealings with citizens (or the government) of a particular country or imposing limitations regarding credit extended for their use.

3. *Public assistance program.* Any federal, state, or local governmental assistance program that provides a continuing, periodic income supplement, whether premised on entitlement or need, is "public assistance" for purposes of the regulation. The term includes (but is not limited to) Aid to Families with Dependent

Children, food stamps, rent and mortgage supplement or assistance programs, Social Security and Supplemental Security Income, and unemployment compensation. Only physicians, hospitals, and others to whom the benefits are payable need consider Medicare and Medicaid as public assistance.

SECTION 202.3—LIMITED EXCEPTIONS FOR CERTAIN CLASSES OF TRANSACTIONS

1. *Scope.* This section relieves burdens with regard to certain types of credit for which full application of the procedural requirements of the regulation is not needed. All classes of transactions remain subject to the general rule given in section 202.4, barring discrimination on a prohibited basis, and to any other provision not specifically excepted.

3(a) Public-Utilities Credit

1. *Definition.* This definition applies only to credit for the purchase of a utility service, such as electricity, gas, or telephone service. Credit provided or offered by a public utility for some other purpose—such as for financing the purchase of a gas dryer, telephone equipment, or other durable goods, or for insulation or other home improvements—is not excepted.

2. *Security deposits.* A utility company is a creditor when it supplies utility service and bills the user after the service has been provided. Thus, any credit term (such as a requirement for a security deposit) is subject to the regulation.

3. *Telephone companies.* A telephone company's credit transactions qualify for the exceptions provided in section 202.3(a) (2) only if the company is regulated by a government unit or files the charges for service, delayed payment, or any discount for prompt payment with a government unit.

3(c) Incidental Credit

1. *Examples.* If a service provider (such as a hospital, doctor, lawyer, or retailer) allows the client or customer to defer the payment of a bill, this deferral of a debt is credit for purposes of the regulation, even though there is no finance charge and no agreement for payment in installments. Because of the exceptions provided by this section, however, these particular credit extensions are excepted from compliance with certain procedural requirements as specified in the regulation.

3(d) Government Credit

1. *Credit to governments.* The exception relates to credit extended to (not by) governmental entities. For example, credit extended to a local government by a creditor in the private sector is covered by this exception, but credit extended to consumers by a federal or state housing agency does not qualify for special treatment under this category.

SECTION 202.4—GENERAL RULE PROHIBITING DISCRIMINATION

1. *Scope of section.* The general rule stated in section 202.4 covers all dealings, without exception, between an applicant and a creditor, whether or not addressed

by other provisions of the regulation. Other sections of the regulation identify specific practices that the Board has decided are impermissible because they could result in credit discrimination on a basis prohibited by the act. The general rule covers, for example, application procedures, criteria used to evaluate credit-worthiness, administration of accounts, and treatment of delinquent or slow accounts. Thus, whether or not specifically prohibited elsewhere in the regulation, a credit practice that treats applicants differently on a prohibited basis violates the law because it violates the general rule.

Section 202.5—Rules Concerning Taking of Applications

5(a) Discouraging Applications

1. *Potential applicants.* Generally, the regulation's protections apply only to persons who have requested or received an extension of credit. In keeping with the purpose of the act—to promote the availability of credit on a nondiscriminatory basis—section 202.5 (a) covers acts or practices directed at potential applicants. Practices prohibited by this section include—

- a statement that the applicant should not bother to apply after the applicant states that he is retired

- use of words, symbols, models, or other forms of communication in advertising that express, imply, or suggest a discriminatory preference or a policy of exclusion in violation of the act

- use of interview scripts that discourage applications on a prohibited basis.

2. *Affirmative advertising.* A creditor may affirmatively solicit or encourage members of traditionally disadvantaged groups to apply for credit, especially groups that might not normally seek credit from that creditor.

5(b) General Rules Concerning Requests for Information

1. *Requests for information.* This section governs the types of information that a creditor may gather. Section 202.6 governs how information may be used.

Paragraph 5(b)(2)

1. *Local laws.* Information that a creditor is allowed to collect pursuant to a "state" statute or regulation includes information required by a local statute, regulation, or ordinance.

2. *Information required by Regulation C.* Regulation C generally requires creditors covered by the Home Mortgage Disclosure Act (HMDA) to collect and report information about the race or national origin and sex of applicants for home-improvement loans and home-purchase loans, including some types of loans not covered by section 202.13. Certain creditors with assets under $30 million, though covered by HMDA, are not required to collect and report these data; but they may do so at their option under HMDA, without violating the ECOA or Regulation B.

5(d) Other Limitations on Information Requests

Paragraph 5(d)(1)

1. *Indirect disclosure of prohibited information.* The fact that certain credit-related information may indirectly disclose marital status does not bar a creditor from seeking such information. For example, the creditor may ask about—

- the applicant's obligation to pay alimony, child support, or separate maintenance

- the source of income to be used as the basis for repaying the credit requested, which could disclose that it is the income of a spouse

- whether any obligation disclosed by the applicant has a co-obligor, which could disclose that the co-obligor is a spouse or former spouse

- the ownership of assets, which could disclose the interest of a spouse

Paragraph 5(d)(2)

1. *Disclosure about income.* The sample application forms in appendix B to the regulation illustrate how a creditor may inform an applicant of the right not to disclose alimony, child support, or separate maintenance income.

2. *General inquiry about source of income.* Since a general inquiry about the source of income may lead an applicant to disclose alimony, child support, or separate maintenance, a creditor may not make such an inquiry on an application form without prefacing the request with the disclosure required by this paragraph.

3. *Specific inquiry about sources of income.* A creditor need not give the disclosure if the inquiry about income is specific and worded in a way that is unlikely to lead the applicant to disclose the fact that income is derived from alimony, child support, or separate maintenance payments. For example, an application form that asks about specific types of income such as salary, wages, or investment income need not include the disclosure.

5(e) Written Applications

1. *Requirement for written applications.* The requirement of written applications for certain types of dwelling-related loans is intended to assist the federal supervisory agencies in monitoring compliance with the ECOA and the Fair Housing Act. Model application forms are provided in appendix B to the regulation, although use of a printed form of any kind is not required. A creditor will satisfy the requirement by writing down the information that it normally considers in making a credit decision. The creditor may complete the application on behalf of an applicant and need not require the applicant to sign the application.

2. *Telephone applications.* A creditor that accepts applications by telephone for dwelling-related credit covered by section 202.13 can meet the requirements for written applications by writing down pertinent information that is provided by the applicant(s).

3. *Computerized entry.* Information entered directly into and retained by a computerized system qualifies as a written application under this paragraph. (See the commentary to section 202.13(b).)

Section 202.6—Rules Concerning Evaluation of Applications

6(a) General Rule Concerning Use of Information

1. *General.* When evaluating an application for credit, a creditor generally may consider any information obtained. However, a creditor may not consider in its evaluation of creditworthiness any information that it is barred by section 202.5 from obtaining.

2. *Effects test.* The effects test is a judicial doctrine that was developed in a series of employment cases decided by the Supreme Court under title VII of the Civil Rights Act of 1964 (42 USC 2000e et seq.). Congressional intent that this doctrine apply to the credit area is documented in the Senate Report that accompanied H.R. 6516, No. 94-589, pp. 4-5; and in the House Report that accompanied H.R. 6516, No. 94-210, p. 5. The act and regulation may prohibit a creditor practice that is discriminatory in effect because it has a disproportionately negative impact on a prohibited basis, even though the creditor has no intent to discriminate and the practice appears neutral on its face, unless the creditor practice meets a legitimate business need that cannot reasonably be achieved as well by means that are less disparate in their impact. For example, requiring that applicants have incomes in excess of a certain amount to qualify for an overdraft line of credit could mean that women and minority applicants will be rejected at a higher rate than men and nonminority applicants. If there is a demonstrable relationship between the income requirement and creditworthiness for the level of credit involved, however, use of the income standard would likely be permissible.

6(b) Specific Rules Concerning Use of Information

Paragraph 6(b)(1)

1. *Prohibited basis—marital status.* A creditor may not use marital status as a basis for determining the applicant's creditworthiness. However, a creditor may consider an applicant's marital status for the purpose of ascertaining the creditor's rights and remedies applicable to the particular extension of credit. For example, in a secured transaction involving real property, a creditor could take into account whether state law gives the applicant's spouse an interest in the property being offered as collateral.

2. *Prohibited basis—special-purpose credit.* In a special-purpose credit program, a creditor may consider a prohibited basis to determine whether the applicant possesses a characteristic needed for eligibility. (See section 202.8.)

Paragraph 6(b)(2)

1. *Favoring the elderly.* Any system of evaluating creditworthiness may favor a credit applicant who is age 62 or older. A credit program that offers more favor-

able credit terms to applicants age 62 or older is also permissible; a program that offers more favorable credit terms to applicants at an age lower than 62 is permissible only if it meets the special-purpose credit requirements of section 202.8.

2. *Consideration of age in a credit scoring system.* Age may be taken directly into account in a credit scoring system that is "demonstrably and statistically sound," as defined in section 202.2(p), with one limitation: an applicant who is 62 years old or older must be treated at least as favorably as anyone who is under age 62.

3. *Consideration of age in a judgmental system.* In a judgmental system, defined in section 202.2(t), a creditor may not take age directly into account in any aspect of the credit transaction. For example, the creditor may not reject an application or terminate an account because the applicant is 60 years old. But a creditor that uses a judgmental system may relate the applicant's age to other information about the applicant that the creditor considers in evaluating creditworthiness. For example:

- A creditor may consider the applicant's occupation and length of time to retirement to ascertain whether the applicant's income (including retirement income) will support the extension of credit to its maturity.

- A creditor may consider the adequacy of any security offered when the term of the credit extension exceeds the life expectancy of the applicant and the cost of realizing on the collateral could exceed the applicant's equity. (An elderly applicant might not qualify for a 5 percent down, 30-year mortgage loan but might qualify with a larger downpayment or a shorter loan maturity.)

- A creditor may consider the applicant's age to assess the significance of the length of the applicant's employment (a young applicant may have just entered the job market) or length of time at an address (an elderly applicant may recently have retired and moved from a long-term residence).

As the examples above illustrate, the evaluation must be made in an individualized, case-by-case manner; and it is impermissible for a creditor, in deciding whether to extend credit or in setting the terms and conditions, to base its decision on age or information related exclusively to age. Age or age-related information may be considered only in evaluating other "pertinent elements of creditworthiness" that are drawn from the particular facts and circumstances concerning the applicant.

4. *Consideration of age in a combined system.* A creditor using a credit scoring system that qualifies as "empirically derived" under section 202.2(p) may consider other factors (such as a credit report or the applicant's cash flow) on a judgmental basis. Doing so will not negate the classification of the credit scoring component of the combined system as "demonstrably and statistically sound." While age could be used in the credit scoring portion, however, in the judgmental portion, age may not be considered directly. It may be used only for the purpose of determining a "pertinent element of creditworthiness." (See comment 6(b)(2)–3.)

5. *Consideration of public assistance.* When considering income derived from a public assistance program, a creditor may take into account, for example—

- the length of time an applicant will likely remain eligible to receive such income

- whether the applicant will continue to qualify for benefits based on the status of the applicant's dependents (such as Aid to Families with Dependent Children or Social Security payments to a minor)

- whether the creditor can attach or garnish the income to assure payment of the debt in the event of default

Paragraph 6(b)(5)

1. *Consideration of an individual applicant.* A creditor must evaluate income derived from part-time employment, alimony, child support, separate maintenance, retirement benefits, or public assistance (all referred to as "protected income") on an individual basis, not on the basis of aggregate statistics, and must assess its reliability or unreliability by analyzing the applicant's actual circumstances, not by analyzing statistical measures derived from a group.

2. *Payments consistently made.* In determining the likelihood of consistent payments of alimony, child support, or separate maintenance, a creditor may consider factors such as whether payments are received pursuant to a written agreement or court decree; the length of time that the payments have been received; whether the payments are regularly received by the applicant; the availability of court or other procedures to compel payment; and the creditworthiness of the payor, including the credit history of the payor when it is available to the creditor.

3. *Consideration of income.* A creditor need not consider income at all in evaluating creditworthiness. If a creditor does consider income, there are several acceptable methods, whether in a credit scoring or a judgmental system:

- A creditor may score or take into account the total sum of all income stated by the applicant without taking steps to evaluate the income.

- A creditor may evaluate each component of the applicant's income, and then score or take into account reliable income separately from income that is not reliable, or the creditor may disregard that portion of income that is not reliable before aggregating it with reliable income.

- A creditor that does not evaluate all income components for reliability must treat as reliable any component of protected income that is not evaluated.

In considering the separate components of an applicant's income, the creditor may not automatically discount or exclude from consideration any protected income. Any discounting or exclusion must be based on the applicant's actual circumstances.

4. *Part-time employment, sources of income.*

A creditor may score or take into account the fact that an individual applicant has more than one source of earned income—a full-time and a part-time job or two part-time jobs. A creditor may also score or treat earned income from a secondary source differently than earned income from a primary source. However, the creditor may not score or otherwise take into account the number of sources for protected income—for example, retirement income, Social Security, alimony. Nor may the creditor treat negatively the fact that an applicant's only earned income is derived from a part-time job.

Paragraph 6(b)(6)

1. *Types of credit references.* A creditor may restrict the types of credit history and credit references that it will consider, provided that the restrictions are applied to all credit applicants without regard to sex, marital status, or any other prohibited basis. However, on the applicant's request, a creditor must consider credit information not reported through a credit bureau when the information relates to the same types of credit references and history that the creditor would consider if reported through a credit bureau.

Paragraph 6(b)(7)

1. *National origin—immigration status.* The applicant's immigration status and ties to the community (such as employment and continued residence in the area) could have a bearing on a creditor's ability to obtain repayment.

Accordingly, the creditor may consider and differentiate, for example, between a noncitizen who is a long-time resident with permanent resident status and a noncitizen who is temporarily in this country on a student visa.

2. *National origin—citizenship.* Under the regulation, a denial of credit on the grounds that an applicant is not a United States citizen is not per se discrimination based on national origin.

Section 202.7—Rules Concerning Extensions of Credit

7(a) Individual Accounts

1. *Open-end credit—authorized user.* A creditor may not require a creditworthy applicant seeking an individual credit account to provide additional signatures. However, the creditor may condition the designation of an authorized user by the account holder on the authorized user's becoming contractually liable for the account, as long as the creditor does not differentiate on any prohibited basis in imposing this requirement.

2. *Open-end credit—choice of authorized user.* A creditor that permits an account holder to designate an authorized user may not restrict this designation on a prohibited basis. For example, if the creditor allows the designation of spouses as authorized users, the creditor may not refuse to accept a nonspouse as an authorized user.

3. *Overdraft authority on transaction accounts.* If a transaction account (such as a checking account or NOW account) includes an overdraft line of credit, the creditor may require that all persons authorized to draw on the transaction account assume liability for any overdraft.

7(b) Designation of Name

1. *Single name on account.* A creditor may require that joint applicants on an account designate a single name for purposes of administering the account and that a single name be embossed on any credit card(s) issued on the account. But the creditor may not require that the name be the husband's name. (See section 202.10 for rules governing the furnishing of credit history on accounts held by spouses.)

7(c) Action Concerning Existing Open-end Accounts

Paragraph 7(c)(1)

1. *Termination coincidental with marital status change.* When an account holder's marital status changes, a creditor generally may not terminate the account unless it has evidence that the account holder is unable or unwilling to repay. But the creditor may terminate an account on which both spouses are jointly liable, even if the action coincides with a change in marital status, when one or both spouses—

• repudiate responsibility for future charges on the joint account

• request separate accounts in their own names

• request that the joint account be closed

2. *Updating information.* A creditor may periodically request updated information from applicants but may not use events related to a prohibited basis—such as an applicant's retirement, reaching a particular age, or change in name or marital status—to trigger such a request.

Paragraph 7(c)(2)

1. *Procedure pending reapplication.* A creditor may require a reapplication from a contractually liable party, even when there is no evidence of unwillingness or inability to repay, if (1) the credit was based on the qualifications of a person who is no longer available to support the credit and (2) the creditor has information indicating that the account holder's income by itself may be insufficient to support the credit. While a reapplication is pending, the creditor must allow the account holder full access to the account under the existing contract terms. The creditor may specify a reasonable time period within which the account holder must submit the required information.

7(d) Signature of Spouse or Other Person

1. *Qualified applicant.* The signature rules ensure that qualified applicants are able to obtain credit in their own names. Thus, when an applicant requests individual credit, a creditor generally may not require the signature of another person unless the creditor has first determined that the applicant alone does not qualify for the credit requested.

2. *Unqualified applicant.* When an applicant applies for individual credit but does not alone meet a creditor's standards, the creditor may require a co-signer, guar-

antor or the like—but cannot require that it be the spouse. (See commentary to section 202.7(d) (5) and (6).)

Paragraph 7(d)(1)

1. *Joint applicant.* The term "joint applicant" refers to someone who applies contemporaneously with the applicant for shared or joint credit. It does not refer to someone whose signature is required by the creditor as a condition for granting the credit requested.

Paragraph 7(d)(2)

1. *Jointly owned property.* In determining the value of the applicant's interest in jointly owned property, a creditor may consider factors such as the form of ownership and the property's susceptibility to attachment, execution, severance, or partition and the cost of such action. If the applicant's interest in the property does not support the amount and terms of credit sought, the creditor may give the applicant some other option of providing additional support for the extension of credit, for example—

- requiring an additional party under section 202.7(d)(5)

- offering to grant the applicant's request on a secured credit basis

- asking for the signature of the co-owner of the property on an instrument that ensures access to the property but does not impose personal liability unless necessary under state law

2. *Need for signature—reasonable belief.* A creditor's reasonable belief as to what instruments need to be signed by a person other than the applicant should be supported by a thorough review of pertinent statutory and decisional law or an opinion of the state attorney general.

Paragraph 7(d)(3)

1. *Residency.* In assessing the creditworthiness of a person who applies for credit in a community property state, a creditor may assume that the applicant is a resident of the state unless the applicant indicates otherwise.

Paragraph 7(d)(4)

1. *Creation of enforceable lien.* Some state laws require that both spouses join in executing any instrument by which real property is encumbered. If an applicant offers such property as security for credit, a creditor may require the applicant's spouse to sign the instruments necessary to create a valid security interest in the property. The creditor may not require the spouse to sign the note evidencing the credit obligation if signing only the mortgage or other security agreement is sufficient to make the property available to satisfy the debt in the event of default. However, if under state law both spouses must sign the note to create an enforceable lien, the creditor may require them to do so.

2. *Need for signature—reasonable belief.* Generally, a signature to make the secured property available will only be needed on a security agreement. A creditor's rea-

sonable belief that, to ensure access to the property, the spouse's signature is needed on an instrument that imposes personal liability should be supported by a thorough review of pertinent statutory and decisional law or an opinion of the state attorney general.

3. *Integrated instruments.* When a creditor uses an integrated instrument that combines the note and the security agreement, the spouse cannot be required to sign the integrated instrument if the signature is only needed to grant a security interest. But the spouse could be asked to sign an integrated instrument that makes clear—for example, by a legend placed next to the spouse's signature—that the spouse's signature is only to grant a security interest and that signing the instrument does not impose personal liability.

Paragraph 7(d)(5)

1. *Qualifications of additional parties.* In establishing guidelines for eligibility of guarantors, co-signers, or similar additional parties, a creditor may restrict the applicant's choice of additional parties buy may not discriminate on the basis of sex, marital status or any other prohibited basis. For example, the creditor could require that the additional party live in the creditor's market area.

2. *Reliance on income of another person—individual credit.* An applicant who requests individual credit relying on the income of another person (including a spouse in a non-community property state) may be required to provide the signature of the other person to make the income available to pay the debt. In community property states, the signature of a spouse may be required if the applicant relies on the spouse's separate income. If the applicant relies on the spouse's future earnings that, as a matter of state law, cannot be characterized as community property until earned, the creditor may require the spouse's signature, but need not do so—even if it is the creditor's practice to require the signature when an applicant relies on the future earnings of a person other than a spouse. (See section 202.6(c) on consideration of state property laws.)

3. *Renewals.* If the borrower's creditworthiness is reevaluated when a credit obligation is renewed, the creditor must determine whether an additional party is still warranted and, if not, release the additional party.

Paragraph 7(d)(6)

1. *Guarantees.* A guarantee on an extension of credit is part of a credit transaction and, therefore, subject to the regulation. The rules in section 202.7(d) bar a creditor from requiring the signature of a *guarantor's spouse* just as they bar the creditor from requiring the signature of an *applicant's spouse.* For example, when all officers of a closely held corporation are required to personally guarantee a corporate loan, the creditor may not automatically require that spouses of married officers also sign. However, an evaluation of the financial circumstances of an officer may indicate that an additional signature is necessary, and this may be the signature of a spouse in appropriate circumstances.

7(e) Insurance

1. *Differences in terms.* Differences in the availability, rates, and other terms on which credit-related casualty insurance or credit life, health, accident, or disability insurance is offered or provided to an applicant does not violate Regulation B.

2. *Insurance information.* A creditor may obtain information about an applicant's age, sex, or marital status for insurance purposes. The information may only be used, however, for determining eligibility and premium rates for insurance, and not in making the credit decision.

SECTION 202.8—SPECIAL-PURPOSE CREDIT PROGRAMS

8(a) Standards for Programs

1. *Determining qualified programs.* The Board does not determine whether individual programs qualify for special-purpose credit status, or whether a particular program benefits an "economically disadvantaged class of persons." The agency or creditor administering or offering the loan program must make these decisions regarding the status of its program.

2. *Compliance with a program authorized by federal or state law.* A creditor does not violate Regulation B when it complies in good faith with a regulation promulgated by a government agency implementing a special-purpose credit program under section 202.8(a) (1). It is the agency's responsibility to promulgate a regulation that is consistent with federal and state law.

3. *Expressly authorized.* Credit programs authorized by federal or state law include programs offered pursuant to federal, state, or local statute, regulation or ordinance, or by judicial or administrative order.

4. *Creditor liability.* A refusal to grant credit to an applicant is not a violation of the act or regulation if the applicant does not meet the eligibility requirements under a special-purpose credit program.

8(b) Rules in Other Sections

1. *Applicability of rules.* A creditor that rejects an application because the applicant does not meet the eligibility requirements (common characteristic or financial need, for example) must nevertheless notify the applicant of action taken as required by section 202.9.

8(c) Special Rule Concerning Requests and Use of Information

1. *Request of prohibited information.* This section permits a creditor to request and consider certain information that would otherwise be prohibited by sections 202.5 and 202.6 to determine an applicant's eligibility for a particular program.

2. *Examples.* Examples of programs under which the creditor can ask for and consider information related to a prohibited basis are—

- energy conservation programs to assist the elderly, for which the creditor must consider the applicant's age

- programs under a Minority Enterprise Small Business Investment Corporation, for which a creditor must consider the applicant's minority status

8(d) Special Rule in the Case of Financial Need

1. *Request of prohibited information.* This section permits a creditor to request and consider certain information that would otherwise be prohibited by sections 202.5 and 202.6, and to require signatures that would otherwise be prohibited by section 202.7(d).

2. *Examples.* Examples of programs in which financial need is a criterion are—

- subsidized housing programs for low- to moderate-income households, for which a creditor may have to consider the applicant's receipt of alimony or child support, the spouse's or parents' income, etc.

- student loan programs based on the family's financial need, for which a creditor may have to consider the spouse's or parents' financial resources

3. *Student loans.* In a guaranteed student loan program, a creditor may obtain the signature of a parent as a guarantor when required by federal or state law or agency regulation, or when the student does not meet the creditor's standards of creditworthiness. (See sections 202.7(d)(1) and (5).) The creditor may not require an additional signature when a student has a work or credit history that satisfies the creditor's standards.

SECTION 202.9—NOTIFICATIONS

1. *Use of the term "adverse action".* The regulation does not require that a creditor use the term "adverse action" in communicating to an applicant that a request for an extension of credit has not been approved. In notifying an applicant of adverse action as defined by section 202.2(c)(1), a creditor may use any words or phrases that describe the action taken on the application.

2. *Expressly withdrawn applications.* When an applicant expressly withdraws a credit application, the creditor is not required to comply with the notification requirements under section 202.9. (The creditor must, however, comply with the record-retention requirements of the regulation. See section 202.12(b)(3).)

3. *When notification occurs.* Notification occurs when a creditor delivers or mails a notice to the applicant's last known address or, in the case of an oral notification, when the creditor communicates the credit decision to the applicant.

4. *Location of notice.* The notifications required under section 202.9 may appear on either or both sides of a form or letter.

9(a) Notification of Action Taken, ECOA Notice, and Statement of Specific Reasons

Paragraph 9(a)(1)

1. *Timing of notice—when an application is complete.* Once a creditor has obtained all the information it normally considers in making a credit decision, the application

is complete and the creditor has 30 days in which to notify the applicant of the credit decision. (See also comment 2(f)-5.)

2. *Notification of approval.* Notification of approval may be express or by implication. For example, the creditor will satisfy the notification requirement when it gives the applicant the credit card, money, property, or services requested.

3. *Incompletion application—denial for incompleteness.* When an application is incomplete regarding matters that the applicant can complete and the creditor lacks sufficient data for a credit decision, the creditor may deny the application giving as the reason for denial that the application is incomplete. The creditor has the option, alternatively, of providing a notice of incompleteness under section 202.9(c).

4. *Incomplete application—denial for reasons other than incompleteness.* When an application is missing information but provides sufficient data for a credit decision, the creditor may evaluate the application and notify the applicant under this section as appropriate. If credit is denied, the applicant must be given the specific reasons for the credit denial (or notice of the right to receive the reasons); in this instance, the incompleteness of the application cannot be given as the reason for the denial.

5. *Length of counteroffer.* Section 202.9(a) (1) (iv) does not require a creditor to hold a counteroffer open for 90 days or any other particular length of time.

6. *Counteroffer combined with adverse-action notice.* A creditor that gives the applicant a combined counteroffer and adverse-action notice that complies with section 202.9(a) (2) need not send a second adverse-action notice if the applicant does not accept the counteroffer. A sample of a combined notice is contained in form C-4 of appendix C to the regulation.

7. *Denial of a telephone application.* When an application is conveyed by means of telephone and adverse action is taken, the creditor must request the applicant's name and address in order to provide written notification under this section. If the applicant declines to provide that information, then the creditor has no further notification responsibility.

Paragraph 9(a)(3)

1. *Coverage.* In determining the rules in this paragraph that apply to a given business-credit application, a creditor may rely on the applicant's assertion about the revenue size of the business. (Applications to start a business are governed by the rules in section 202.9(a)(3)(i).) If an applicant applies for credit as a sole proprietor, the revenues of the sole proprietorship will determine which rules in the paragraph govern the application. However, if an applicant applies for business-purpose credit as an individual, the rules in paragraph 9(a) (3) (i) apply unless the application is for trade or similar credit.

2. *Trade credit.* The term "trade credit" generally is limited to a financing arrangement that involves a buyer and a seller—such as a supplier who finances the sale

of equipment, supplies, or inventory; it does not apply to an extension of credit by a bank or other financial institution for the financing of such items.

3. *Factoring.* Factoring refers to a purchase of accounts receivable and thus is not subject to the act or regulation. If there is a credit extension incident to the factoring arrangement, the notification rules in section 202.9(a) (3) (ii) apply, as do other relevant sections of the act and regulation.

4. *Manner of compliance.* In complying with the notice provisions of the act and regulation, creditors offering business credit may follow the rules governing consumer credit. Similarly, creditors may elect to treat all business credit the same (irrespective of revenue size) by providing notice in accordance with section 202.9(a) (3)(i).

5. *Timing of notification.* A creditor subject to section 202.9(a) (3)(ii) (A) is required to notify a business credit applicant, orally or in writing, of action taken on an application within a reasonable time of receiving a completed application. Notice provided in accordance with the timing requirements of section 202.9 (a) (1) is deemed reasonable in all instances.

9(b) Form of ECOA Notice and Statement of Specific Reasons

Paragraph 9(b)(1)

1. *Substantially similar notice.* The ECOA notice sent with a notification of a credit denial or other adverse action will comply with the regulation if it is "substantially similar" to the notice contained in section 202.9(b) (1). For example, a creditor may add a reference to the fact that the ECOA permits age to be considered in certain credit scoring systems, or add a reference to a similar state statute or regulation and to a state enforcement agency.

Paragraph 9(b)(2)

1. *Number of specific reasons.* A creditor must disclose the principal reasons for denying an application or taking other adverse action. The regulation does not mandate that a specific number of reasons be disclosed, but disclosure of more than four reasons is not likely to be helpful to the applicant.

2. *Source of specific reasons.* The specific reasons disclosed under section 202.9(a) (2) and (b) (2) must relate to and accurately describe the factors actually considered or scored by a creditor.

3. *Description of reasons.* A creditor need not describe how or why a factor adversely affected an applicant. For example, the notice may say "length of residence" rather than "too short a period of residence."

4. *Credit scoring system.* If a creditor bases the denial or other adverse action on a credit scoring system, the reasons disclosed must relate only to those factors actually scored in the system. Moreover, no factor that was a principal reason for adverse action may be excluded from disclosure. The creditor must disclose the actual reasons for denial (for example, "age of automobile") even if the relation-

ship of that factor to predicting creditworthiness may not be clear to the applicant.

5. *Credit scoring—method for selecting reasons.* The regulation does not require that any one method be used for selecting reasons for a credit denial or other adverse action that is based on a credit scoring system. Various methods will meet the requirements of the regulation. One method is to identify the factors for which the applicant's score fell furthest below the average score for each of those factors achieved by applicants whose total score was at or slightly above the minimum passing score. Another method is to identify the factors for which the applicant's score fell furthest below the average score for each of those factors achieved by all applicants. These average scores could be calculated during the development or use of the system. Any other method that produces results substantially similar to either of these methods is also acceptable under the regulation.

6. *Judgmental system.* If a creditor uses a judgmental system, the reasons for the denial or other adverse action must relate to those factors in the applicant's record actually reviewed by the person making the decision.

7. *Combined credit scoring and judgmental system.* If a creditor denies an application based on a credit evaluation system that employs both credit scoring and judgmental components, the reasons for the denial must come from the component of the system that the applicant failed. For example, if a creditor initially credit scores an application and denies the credit request as a result of that scoring, the reasons disclosed to the applicant must relate to the factors scored in the system. If the application passes the credit scoring stage but the creditor then denies the credit request based on a judgmental assessment of the applicant's record, the reasons disclosed must relate to the factors reviewed judgmentally, even if the factors were also considered in the credit scoring component.

8. *Automatic denial.* Some credit-decision methods contain features that call for automatic denial because of one or more negative factors in the applicant's record (such as the applicant's previous bad credit history with that creditor, the applicant's declaration of bankruptcy, or the fact that the applicant is a minor). When a creditor denies the credit request because of an automatic-denial factor, the creditor must disclose that specific factor.

9. *Combined ECOA-FCRA disclosures.* The ECOA requires disclosure of the principal reasons for denying or taking other adverse action on an application for an extension of credit. The Fair Credit Reporting Act requires a creditor to disclose when it has based its decision in whole or in part on information from a source other than the applicant or from its own files. Disclosing that a credit report was obtained and used to deny the application, as the FCRA requires, does not satisfy the ECOA requirement to disclose specific reasons. For example, if the applicant's credit history reveals delinquent credit obligations and the application is denied for that reason, to satisfy section 202.9(b) (2), the creditor must disclose that the application was denied because of the applicant's delinquent credit obligations. To satisfy the FCRA requirement, the creditor must also disclose that a

credit report was obtained and used to deny credit. Sample forms C-1 through C-5 of appendix C of the regulation provide for the two disclosures.

9(c) Incomplete Applications

Paragraph 9(c)(2)

1. *Reapplication.* If information requested by a creditor is submitted by an applicant after the expiration of the time period designated by the creditor, the creditor may require the applicant to make a new application.

Paragraph 9(c)(3)

1. *Oral inquiries for additional information.* If the applicant fails to provide the information in response to an oral request, a creditor must send a written notice to the applicant within the 30-day period specified in section 202.9(c)(1) and (c)(2). If the applicant does provide the information, the creditor shall take action on the application and notify the applicant in accordance with section 202.9(a).

9(g) Applications Submitted Through a Third Party

1. *Third parties.* The notification of adverse action may be given by one of the creditors to whom an application was submitted. Alternatively, the third party may be a noncreditor.

2. *Third-party notice—enforcement agency.* If a single adverse action notice is being provided to an applicant on behalf of several creditors and they are under the jurisdiction of different federal enforcement agencies, the notice need not name each agency; disclosure of any one of them will suffice.

3. *Third-party notice—liability.* When a notice is to be provided through a third party, a creditor is not liable for an act or omission of the third party that constitutes a violation of the regulation if the creditor accurately and in a timely manner provided the third party with the information necessary for the notification and maintains reasonable procedures adapted to prevent such violations.

Section 202.10—Furnishing of Credit Information

1. *Scope.* The requirements of section 202.10 for designating and reporting credit information apply only to creditors that furnish credit information to credit bureaus or to other creditors. There is no requirement that a creditor furnish credit information on its accounts.

2. *Reporting on all accounts.* The requirements of section 202.10 apply only to accounts held or used by spouses. However, a creditor has the option to designate all joint accounts (or all accounts with an authorized user) to reflect the participation of both parties, whether or not the accounts are held by persons married to each other.

3. *Designating accounts.* In designating accounts and reporting credit information, a creditor need not distinguish between accounts on which the spouse is an authorized user and accounts on which the spouse is a contractually liable party.

4. *File and index systems.* The regulation does not require the creation or maintenance of separate files in the name of each participant on a joint or user account, or require any other particular system of recordkeeping or indexing. It requires only that a creditor be able to report information in the name of each spouse on accounts covered by section 202.10. Thus, if a creditor receives a credit inquiry about the wife, it should be able to locate her credit file without asking the husband's name.

10(a) Designation of Accounts

1. *New parties.* When new parties who are spouses undertake a legal obligation on an account, as in the case of a mortgage-loan assumption, the creditor should change the designation on the account to reflect the new parties and should furnish subsequent credit information on the account in the new names.

2. *Request to change designation of account.* A request to change the manner in which information concerning an account is furnished does not alter the legal liability of either spouse upon the account and does not require a creditor to change the name in which the account is maintained.

Section 202.11—Relation to State Law

11(a) Inconsistent State Laws

1. *Preemption determination—New York.* Effective November 11, 1988, the Board has determined that the following provisions in the state law of New York are preempted by the federal law:

- Article 15, Section 296a(1)(b)—Unlawful discriminatory practices in relation to credit on the basis of race, creed, color, national origin, age, sex, marital status, or disability. This provision is preempted to the extent that it bars taking a prohibited basis into account when establishing eligibility for certain special-purpose credit programs.

- Article 15, Section 296a(1)(c)—Unlawful discriminatory practice to make any record or inquiry based on race, creed, color, national origin, age, sex, marital status, or disability. This provision is preempted to the extent that it bars a creditor from requesting and considering information regarding the particular characteristics (for example, race, national origin, or sex) required for eligibility for special-purpose credit programs.

Section 202.12—Record Retention

12(a) Retention of Prohibited Information

1. *Receipt of prohibited information.* Unless the creditor specifically requested such information, a creditor does not violate this section when it receives prohibited information from a consumer reporting agency.

2. *Use of retained information.* Although a creditor may keep in its files prohibited information as provided in section 202.12(a), the creditor may use the information in evaluating credit applications only if permitted to do so by section 202.6.

12(b) Preservation of Records

1. *Copies.* A copy of the original record includes carbon copies, photocopies, microfilm or microfiche copies, or copies produced by any other accurate retrieval system, such as documents stored and reproduced by computer. A creditor that uses a computerized or mechanized system need not keep a written copy of a document (for example, an adverse action notice) if it can regenerate all pertinent information in a timely manner for examination or other purposes.

2. *Computerized decisions.* A creditor that enters information items from a written application into a computerized or mechanized system and makes the credit decision mechanically, based only on the items of information entered into the system, may comply with section 202.12(b) by retaining the information actually entered. It is not required to store the complete written application, nor is it required to enter the remaining items of information into the system. If the transaction is subject to section 202.13, however, the creditor is required to enter and retain the data on personal characteristics in order to comply with the requirements of that section.

Paragraph 12(b)(3)

1. *Withdrawn and brokered applications.* In most cases, the 25-month retention period for applications runs from the date a notification is sent to the applicant granting or denying the credit requested. In certain transactions, a creditor is not obligated to provide a notice of the action taken. (See, for example, comment 9-2.) In such cases, the 25-month requirement runs from the date of application, as when—

- an application is withdrawn by the applicant

- an application is submitted to more than one creditor on behalf of the applicant, and the application is approved by one of the other creditors

Section 202.13—Information for Monitoring Purposes

13(a) Information to Be Requested

1. *Natural person.* Section 202.13 applies only to applications from natural persons.

2. *Principal residence.* The requirements of section 202.13 apply only if an application relates to a dwelling that is or will be occupied by the applicant as the principal residence. A credit application related to a vacation home or a rental unit is not covered. In the case of a two- to four-unit dwelling, the application is covered if the applicant intends to occupy one of the units as a principal residence.

3. *Temporary financing.* An application for temporary financing to construct a dwelling is not subject to section 202.13. But an application for both a temporary loan to finance construction of a dwelling and a permanent mortgage loan to take effect upon the completion of construction is subject to section 202.13.

4. *New principal residence.* A person can have only one principal residence at a time. However, if a person buys or builds a new dwelling that will become that person's principal residence within a year or upon completion of construction,

the new dwelling is considered the principal residence for purposes of section 202.13.

5. *Transactions not covered.* The information-collection requirements of this section apply to applications for credit primarily for the purchase or refinancing of a dwelling that is or will become the applicant's principal residence. Therefore, applications for credit secured by the applicant's principal residence but made primarily for a purpose other than the purchase or refinancing of the principal residence (such as loans for home improvement and debt consolidation) are not subject to the information-collection requirements. An application for an open-end home equity line of credit is not subject to this section unless it is readily apparent to the creditor when the application is taken that the primary purpose of the line is for the purchase or refinancing of a principal dwelling.

6. *Refinancings.* A creditor who receives an application to change the terms and conditions of an existing extension of credit made by that creditor for the purchase of the applicant's dwelling may request the monitoring information again but is not required to do so if it was obtained in the earlier transaction.

7. *Data collection under Regulation C.* See comment 5(b)(2)–2.

13(b) Obtaining of Information

1. *Forms for collecting data.* A creditor may collect the information specified in section 202.13(a) either on an application form or on a separate form referring to the application.

2. *Written applications.* The regulation requires written applications for the types of credit covered by section 202.13. A creditor can satisfy this requirement by recording, in writing or by means of computer, the information that the applicant provides orally and that the creditor normally considers in a credit decision.

3. *Telephone, mail applications.* If an applicant does not apply in person for the credit requested, a creditor does not have to complete the monitoring information. For example:

- When a creditor accepts an application by telephone, it does not have to request the monitoring information.

- When a creditor accepts an application by mail, it does not have to make a special request to the applicant if the applicant fails to complete the monitoring information on the application form sent to the creditor.

If it is not evident on the face of the application that it was received by mail or telephone, the creditor should indicate on the form or other application record how the application was received.

4. *Applications through loan-shopping services.* When a creditor accepts an application through an unaffiliated loan-shopping service, it does not have to request the monitoring information.

5. *Inadvertent notation.* If a creditor inadvertently obtains the monitoring information in a dwelling-related transaction not covered by section 202.13, the creditor may process and retain the application without violating the regulation.

13(c) Disclosure to Applicant(s)

1. *Procedures for providing disclosures.* The disclosures to an applicant regarding the monitoring information may be provided in writing. Appendix B contains a sample disclosure. A creditor may devise its own disclosure so long as it is substantially similar. The creditor need not orally request the applicant to provide the monitoring information if it is requested in writing.

13(d) Substitute Monitoring Program

1. *Substitute program.* An enforcement agency may adopt, under its established rulemaking or enforcement procedures, a program requiring creditors under its jurisdiction to collect information in addition to that required by this section.

SECTION 202.14—ENFORCEMENT, PENALTIES, AND LIABILITIES

14(c) Failure of Compliance

1. *Inadvertent errors.* Inadvertent errors include, but are not limited to, clerical mistake, calculation error, computer malfunction, and printing error. An error of legal judgment is not an inadvertent error under the regulation.

2. *Correction of error.* For inadvertent errors that occur under sections 202.12 and 202.13, this section requires that they be corrected prospectively only.

APPENDIX B—MODEL APPLICATION FORMS

1. *FHLMC/FNMA form—residential loan application.* The residential loan application form (FHLMC 65/FNMA 1003), including supplemental form (FHLMC 65A/FNMA 1003A), prepared by the Federal Home Loan Mortgage Corporation and the Federal National Mortgage Association and dated October 1986, complies with the requirements of this regulation in some transactions but not others because of the form's section, "Information for Government Monitoring Purposes." Creditors that are governed by section 202.13(a) of the regulation (which limits collection to applications primarily for the purchase or refinancing of the applicant's principal residence) should delete, strike, or modify the data-collection section on the form when using it for transactions not covered by section 202.13(a) to ensure that they do not collect the information. Creditors that are subject to more extensive collection requirements by a substitute monitoring program under section 202.13(d) may use the form as issued, in compliance with that substitute program.

2. *FHLMC/FNMA form—home-improvement loan application.* The home-improvement and energy loan application form (FHLMC 703/FNMA 1012), prepared by the Federal Home Loan Mortgage Corporation and the Federal National Mort-

gage Association and dated October 1986, complies with the requirements of the regulation for some creditors but not others because of the form's section, "Information for Government Monitoring Purposes." Creditors that are governed by section 202.13(a) of the regulation (which limits collection to applications primarily for the purchase or refinancing of the applicant's principal residence) should delete, strike, or modify the data-collection section on the form when using it for transactions not covered by section 202.13(a) to ensure that they do not collect the information. Creditors that are subject to more extensive collection requirements by a substitute monitoring program under section 202.13(d) may use the form as issued, in compliance with that substitute program.

CHAPTER 14

Fair Credit Reporting Act

PRESCREENING

The pertinent section of the Fair Credit Reporting Act that deals with pre-screening is Section 1615(d) (15 USC 1681(m)) as follows:

Section 615...

(d) Duties of users making written credit or insurance solicitation on the basis of information contained in consumer files:

(1) *In general.* Any person who uses a consumer report on any consumer in connection with any credit or insurance transaction that is not initiated by the consumer, that is provided to that person under section 604(c)(1)(B) (1681(b) shall provide with each written solicitation made to the consumer regarding the transaction a clear and conspicuous statement that

(A) information contained in the consumer's consumer report was used in connection with the transaction;

(B) the consumer received the offer of credit or insurance because the consumer satisfied the criteria for creditworthiness or insurability under which the consumer was selected for the offer;

(C) if applicable, the credit or insurance may not be extended if, after the consumer responds to the offer, the consumer does not meet the criteria used to select the consumer for the offer or any applicable criteria bearing on creditworthiness or insurability or does not furnish any required collateral;

(D) the consumer has a right to prohibit information contained in the consumer's file with any consumer reporting agency from being used in connection with any credit or insurance transaction that is not initiated by the consumer; and

(E) the consumer may exercise the right referred to in subparagraph (D) by notifying a notification system established under section (604)(e) ((16816).

(2) *Disclosure of address and telephone number.* A statement under paragraph (1) shall include the address and toll-free telephone number of the appropriate notification system established under section 604(e). (§1681 b)

(3) *Maintaining criteria on file.* A person who makes an offer of credit or insurance to a consumer under a credit or insurance transaction described in paragraph (1) shall maintain on file the criteria used to select the consumer to receive the offer, all criteria bearing on creditworthiness or insurability, as applicable, that are the basis for determining whether or not to extend credit or insurance pursuant to the offer, and any requirement for the furnishing of collateral as a condition of the extension of credit or insurance, until the expiration of the 3-year period beginning on the date on which the offer is made to the consumer.

(4) *Authority of federal agencies regarding unfair or deceptive acts or practices not affected.* This section is not intended to affect the authority of any Federal or State agency to enforce a prohibition against unfair or deceptive acts or practices, including the making of false or misleading statements in connection with a credit or insurance transaction that is not initiated by the consumer.

The amended Fair Credit Reporting Act looks favorably upon those parties who use prescreening.

The Act requires the marketer to provide the consumer along with each written solicitation a clear and conspicuous statement that the information contained in the consumer's report was used in connection with the transaction, and that the consumer received the offer of credit because the consumer satisfied the criteria of creditworthiness. The consumer must be advised that the consumer was selected for the offer because a certain criteria was met.

Prior to the amendments, the marketer had to make the offer of credit to the consumer unless there was a significant change of circumstances occurred, which was defined in a limited and narrow way. The amendment provides in Subsection (1)(C) that the credit may be withdrawn after the consumer responds to the offer, or there is a change of circumstances wherein the consumer does not meet the criteria that was used to select the consumer or, in the alternative, does not furnish the required collateral. At the same time in Subdivision (3), the marketer must maintain on file for 3 years after the offer the criteria used to select the consumer and any or all criteria bearing on the creditworthiness of the consumer which is the basis for determining whether or not to extend credit as well as the requirement for furnishing of the collateral.

Under Subdivision (2) the consumer must be provided a statement that must have the address and toll-free telephone number of the appropriate notification system provided in Section 604(e) (15 USC 1681(b)(e)), which is the section that provides that a consumer may elect to have his name and address excluded from any list provided by a consumer reporting agency in connection with an extension of credit that is not initiated by the consumer, by notifying the agency that the consumer does not consent to any use of a consumer report in connection with any credit transaction that is not initiated by the consumer (prescreening).

The consumer must be notified of the fact that the credit may be denied if there is a change in circumstances wherein the consumer does not meet the criteria and that the consumer has the right to prohibit information contained in the consumer's file from being used in connection with any prescreening.

Prescreeners may receive only the name and address of the consumer, and any other information must be used solely for the purpose of verifying the consumer's identity.

In the event the offer is withdrawn, the provisions of Section 615 (15 USC 1681(n)(a)(b)) would apply in that the prescreener would be required to deliver notice of the adverse action and would necessarily have to comply with all the terms and conditions of adverse action under the Act. Any withdrawal of the offer must occur between prescreen and acceptance of the offer. Once the offer is accepted, then the offer must be fulfilled. Examples of circumstances that may permit the offer to be terminated include foreclosure of a residence, bankruptcy filing, or entry of a judgment or a lien, providing these items were included in the original criteria to determine who would be selected for the offer. Banks that extend credit to the consumer by use of a prescreen may review the consumer's response form to determine whether the consumer still meets the criteria. The bank may also verify other information to determine if the consumer still meets the criteria, and if the consumer does not, the offer may be withdrawn.

FURNISHERS OF INFORMATION— PRIVATE RIGHT OF ACTION

Furnishers of information have strict criteria set forth in the amended Act. Subdivision A of Section 623 (15 USC 1681 S-2) deals with the duty of furnishers to provide accurate information. Subdivision B provides the duty of furnishers when they have notice of a dispute. Subdivision B sets forth the duties of the furnishers to conduct an investigation, to review all relevant information, to report the results to the consumer reporting agency, and, if the investigation finds the information is incomplete or inaccurate, report those results to all other consumer reporting agencies to which the person furnished the information.

The issue of whether a consumer has a private right of action under the FCRA has come up in several cases and the majority of the cases seem to feel that a private right of action is provided. This premise is exhibited in the controlling Section 623(d) which specifically states as follows:

> (d) "Limitation on Enforcement. Subsection (a) shall be enforced exclusively under Section 621 (15 USC 1681 S) by the Federal agencies and officials and the State officials identified in that section"

The defendants in these cases have indicated that this section covers Subsection (a) of Section 623 and Subdivision (b) of Section 623. Nevertheless, the courts were quick to point out that there was nothing in the language of Subdivision (d) which provides that Subsection (b) is only enforceable by federal and state officials since Section (d) expressly only refers to Subdivision (a), and makes no reference to Subsection (b). Accordingly, the courts have held that a private right of action for consumers to enforce the investigating and reporting duties imposed on furnishers of information does exist as to Subdivision (b) (duties of furnishers of information).

One court has held that the duties created under Section (b) are owed solely to the credit reporting agency and not to a consumer.[1]

JURISDICTION

Another case in the Circuit Court of Appeals of the 9th Circuit recently held that the jurisdiction and venue in a Fair Credit Reporting Act case is

---

[1]*Mandley v. Bank One Dayton,* 2000 U.S. Dist. Lexis 16269 (Arizona, September 18, 2000); *Dornhecker v. Ameritech Corp.,* 99 F. Supp. 2d 918 (N.D. Ill. 2000); *Carney v. Experian Information Solutions, Inc.,* 57 F. Supp. 2d 496 (W.D. Tenn. 1999).

determined by the residence of the consumer. The appellate court disagreed with the district court's conclusion that the injury occurred where one would access the credit reports. The injury was suffered in the state where the plaintiff resided and that is where jurisdiction lies.[2]

IDENTITY THEFT

Identity theft is occurring more frequently than ever before. A social security number and a name and address provide all the information necessary for someone to assume your identity. Articles in the newspapers and magazines recommend that social security numbers not be offered over the telephone or even in person unless it is absolutely necessary. Furnishing your social security number with your address is an invitation to disaster.

The Circuit Court of Appeals addressed this issue of identity theft wherein the court recognized that in many ways persons are required to make their social security numbers available so that they are no longer private or confidential, but open to scrutiny and copying. An application for credit is a perfect example where a social security number becomes available together with your address. The date of your birth or the first name of your parent is used for confirming identification. Thus, one who has access to a credit application has the opportunity to steal your identity.

In a recent case, the impostor was a receptionist in a doctor's office and copied the information that a patient supplied to the doctor. The impostor then applied for credit to four companies subscribing to TRW credit reports. The impostor used the social security number of the plaintiff, but her own address and own telephone number. The only misinformation was the use of the social security number and the date of birth. In each instance, TRW responded to the credit inquiry by treating the application as made by the plaintiff and added the three inquiries to plaintiff's files.

In one case where the credit was approved, the account became delinquent and therefore was referred to a collection agency. The plaintiff became aware of the impostor when she sought to refinance her home and the financing institution saw the report which combined information from TRW and two other reporting agencies. Now aware of the fraud, the consumer contacted TRW and requested deletion from her file. TRW com-

---

[2]*Myers v. Bennett Law Offices*, 238 F. 3d 1068 (9th Cir. 2001); *Bakker v. McKinnon*, 152 F. 3d 1007 (8th Cir. 1998).

plied and thereafter a suit was filed alleging that TRW furnished credit reports without reasonable grounds for believing that she was the consumer whom the credit applications involved, and that TRW had not maintained reasonable procedures required by that statute to assure maximum possible accuracy of the information concerning the individual about whom the report relates.

Under Section 607(b) the Fair Credit Reporting Act provides that whenever a consumer reporting agency prepares a consumer report, it shall follow reasonable procedures to assure maximum possible accuracy of the information. The court, after listening to arguments, decided it was a question for the jury whether identity theft had become common enough for it to be reasonable for a credit reporting agency to disclose credit information "merely because the last name matches a social security number on the file." The reasonableness of TRW's responses should be assessed by a jury with reference to the information TRW had indicating that the impostor was not the plaintiff. TRW argued that people do use nicknames and change addresses, but the plantiff argued "how many people misspell their first name" (in this case, one of the applications had a misspelled first name).

The jury would have to determine whether it is reasonable that a social security number trumps all other information of dissimilarity between the plaintiff and an impostor. A sidelight to the cause of action was that the lower court decided that the statute of limitations runs from the time the credit company issued the reports and the appellate held that the statute of limitations of two years runs from the time of discovery of the fraud and not when the credit reports were issued.

As the databases increase and the opportunities increase, the instances of identity theft will probably increase in direct ratio and the litigation covering identity theft will also increase.[3]

CIVIL LIABILITY

The amended Act has expanded the liability of a consumer reporting agency in Section 616 (15 USC 1681(n)) and Section 617 (1681)(o):

SECTION 616. CIVIL LIABILITY FOR WILLFUL NONCOMPLIANCE

(a) *In general.* Any person who willfully fails to comply with any requirement imposed under this title with respect to any consumer is liable to that consumer in an amount equal to the sum of

---

[3]*Andrews v. TRW, Inc.* 255 F. 3d 1063 (9th Cir. 2000).

(1) (A) any actual damages sustained by the consumer as a result of the failure or damages of not less than $100 and not more than $1,000; or

(B) in the case of liability of a natural person for obtaining a consumer report under false pretenses or knowingly without permissible purpose, actual damages sustained by the consumer as a result of the failure or $1,000, whichever is greater;

(2) such amount of punitive damages as the court may allow; and

(3) in the case of any successful action to enforce any liability under this section, the costs of the action together with reasonable attorney's fees as determined by the court.

(b) *Civil liability for knowing noncompliance.* Any person who obtains a consumer report from a consumer reporting agency under false pretenses or knowingly without a permissible purpose shall be liable to the consumer reporting agency for actual damages sustained by the consumer reporting agency or $1,000, whichever is greater.

(c) *Attorney's fees.* Upon a finding by the court that an unsuccessful pleading, motion, or other paper filed in connection with an action under this section was filed in bad faith or for purposes of harassment, the court shall award to the prevailing party attorney's fees reasonable in relation to the work expended in responding to the pleading, motion, or other paper.

SECTION 617. CIVIL LIABILITY FOR NEGLIGENT NONCOMPLIANCE

(a) *In general.* Any person who is negligent in failing to comply with any requirement imposed under this title with respect to any consumer is liable to that consumer in an amount equal to the sum of

(1) any actual damages sustained by the consumer as a result of the failure;

(2) in the case of any successful action to enforce any liability under this section, the costs of the action together with reasonable attorney's fees as determined by the court.

(b) *Attorney's fees.* On a finding by the court that an unsuccessful pleading, motion, or other paper filed in connection with an action under this section was filed in bad faith or for purposes of harassment, the court shall award to the prevailing party attorney's fees reasonable in relation to the work expended in responding to the pleading, motion, or other paper.

Prior to the amendment the wording in Section 616(a) formerly used in the Act consisted of "any consumer reporting agency or user of the information" which is now changed to "any person who willfully fails to comply with any requirement imposed under this title with respect to any consumer is liable to that consumer in an amount equal to the sum of..."

Prior to the amendment, the next paragraph [Section 616(b)] described the liability as actual damages sustained by the consumer. The amended law repeats "the actual damages" and states that the amount will be not less than $100 and not more than $1,000. The same change is carried over in Section 617, where any consumer reporting agency or user of the information is replaced by "any person." [Section 671(a)]. This section deals with negligent noncompliance. The amended Act also includes attorney's fees. We have not had a considerable amount of litigation on the amended Fair Credit Reporting Act, but it is increasing at a rapid rate.

Another issue of liability arises from the fact that an employee might obtain a report without a permissible purpose and the issue is whether the employer is liable under an agency relationship based on apparent authority. The best protection against this problem is to train your employees properly and be certain that the party who is in charge of obtaining the report is fully aware of the consequences of obtaining a report without a permissible purpose.

> **Credit & Collection Tip:** *When preparing an employment contract (or even as a supplement to an employment application after the party is hired) or in the alternative in the employer handbook that the employee is supposed to examine, set forth the conditions and the procedures to be used to order a credit report. The manual and training may assist you in the event there should be suits for violation.*

UPDATED INFORMATION

Remember that the furnisher of information must notify the credit reporting agency if that furnisher should at a later date determine that the information is inaccurate. This obligation continues even if the furnisher has terminated its contract with the credit reporting agency. The furnisher must act promptly just as if the relationship with the credit reporting agency continued.

FALSE PRETENSES

The Court of Appeals of the 2nd Circuit stated that a report requester who provides a false reason for its request, but has an independent legitimate basis for requesting the report, does not violate the Fair Credit Reporting Act. In summary, the court stated, "a person cannot obtain information to which he has a right under false pretenses" [*Baker v. Bronx-Westchester Investigations, Inc.*, 850 F. Supp. 260 (S.D.N.Y. 1994)].

In the instant case, a real estate broker advised a perspective purchaser that the owner requested a credit check. The purchaser did not wish his credit to be checked until the offer was accepted. Nevertheless, the purchaser told the broker to submit the offer to the owner. The purchaser did not restrict the offer to be on condition that no credit check would be performed. In any event, since the court decided that the offer was made, and there was no condition attached that no credit check would be made, the owner had a legitimate reason to order the credit check even though the broker might have misled the purchaser.[4]

REASONABLE PROCEDURES

The 9th and the 11th Circuits have decided that where a court has found that a disclosure is made for permissible purposes, the inquiry ends and no investigation of the reasonableness of the procedure of the consumer reporting agency procedure is necessary.[5]

In the 7th Circuit, the court endorsed the proposition that once it is shown that the information is relevant and for a permissible purpose, the court need not inquire into the reasonableness of the procedures adopted by the agency to assure that the information will be furnished for purposes defined as permissible under the Act [*Middlebrooks v. Retail Credit Co.*, 416 F. Supp. 1013 (N.D. Ga. 1976)]. We now have a case in the 5th Circuit that agrees with both of those cases and, hopefully, with three circuits agreeing, the issue will not come up again.[6]

INJUNCTION

We have a decision that states no injunctive relief is available either in the Fair Credit Reporting Act or in the Fair Debt Collection Practices Act.

---

[4]*Scott v. Real Estate Fin. Group*, 183 F. 3d 97 (2d Cir. 1999), citing *Baker v. Bronx-Westchester Investigations, Inc.*, 850 F. Supp. 260 (S.D.N.Y. 1994).

[5]*Andrews v. Trans Union Corp.*, 7 F. Supp. 2d 1056 (C.D. Cal. 1998), aff'd in part, rev'd in part sub nom. *Andrews v. TRW, Inc.*, No. 98-56624, 2000 WL 973260 (9th Cir. July 17, 2000).

[6]*Washington v. CSC Credit Servs., Inc.*, 199 F. 3d 263 (5th Cir. 2000), cert. denied, 68 U.S.L.W. 3789 (U.S. June 26, 2000 (No. 99-1623).

The court lacks jurisdiction to grant injunctive relief since the Fair Credit Reporting Act authorizes district courts to enforce only a credit reporting agency's liability to an individual, which the Fair Credit Reporting Act defines in terms of money damages. Conspicuously absent from the FCRA is the grant of authority to enforce a credit reporting agency's compliance with the FCRA's requirements. A request for an injunction by a plaintiff is an application to the court to enforce compliance, something the Act expressly omits. Some courts do allow injunctive relief to private litigants while others only allow the Federal Trade Commission to pursue this remedy.

The thrust of the Fair Debt Collection Practices Act is prevention of harassment and abuse as well as false or deceptive or misleading practices. The relief sought is money damages. Equitable relief such as an injunction, is not available to an individual under the civil liability section of the FDCPA and the court cited several cases setting forth this philosophy. Congress gave the power to the Federal Trade Commission to enforce the Act.[7]

NOTIFICATION OF ADVERSE ACTION

The Equal Credit Opportunity Act mandates that a creditor notify an applicant of its action on an application within 30 days after receiving a completed credit application and provides that each applicant against whom adverse action is taken is entitled to written notification of both the action and the reasons for the action. Where the lender denied the application but offered the applicant an alternative loan that thereafter was accepted by the debtor, the court concluded that the written notice requirement was not necessary because the debtor had accepted the alternative loan application.[8]

---

[7]*Remway v. Information Dynamic*, 399 F. Supp. 1092 (D. Ariz. 1974); *Mangio v. Equifax, Inc.*, 887 F. Supp. 283 (S.D. Fla. 1995); *Ditty v. CheckRite*, 973 F. Supp. 1320 (D. Utah, 1997); *Washington v. CSC Credit Servs.*, Inc., 199 F. 3d 263 (5th Cir., 2000), cert. denied, 68 U.S.L.W. 3789 (U.S. June 26, 2000) (No. 99-1623).

[8]*Diaz v. Virginia Housing Development Authority*, 117 F. Supp. 2d 500 (E.D. Va. 2000).

APPENDIX I

FEDERAL TRADE COMMISSION FACTS FOR BUSINESS

USING CONSUMER REPORTS: WHAT EMPLOYERS NEED TO KNOW

- *Your advertisement for cashiers nets 100 applications. You want credit reports on each applicant. You plan to eliminate those with poor credit histories. What are your obligations?*

- *You are considering a number of your long-term employees for major promotions. Can you check their credit reports to ensure that only financially responsible individuals are considered?*

- *A job candidate has authorized you to obtain a credit report. The applicant has a poor credit history. Although the credit history is considered a negative factor, it's the applicant's lack of relevant experience that's more important to you. You turn down the application. What procedures must you follow.*

As an employer, you may use consumer reports when you hire new employees and when you evaluate employees for promotion, reassignment, and retention—as long as you comply with the Fair Credit Reporting Act (FCRA). Sections 604, 606, and 615 of the FCRA spell out your responsibilities when using consumer reports for employment purposes.

The FCRA is designed primarily to protect the privacy of consumer report information and to guarantee that the information supplied by consumer reporting agencies is as accurate as possible. Amendments to the FCRA—which went into effect September 30, 1997—significantly increase the legal obligations of employers who use consumer reports. Congress expanded employer responsibilities because of concern that inaccurate or incomplete consumer reports could cause applicants to be denied jobs or cause employees to be denied promotions unjustly. The amendments ensure (1) that individuals are aware that consumer reports may be used for employment purposes and agree to such use, and (2) that individuals are notified promptly if information in a consumer report may result in a negative employment decision.

WHAT IS A CONSUMER REPORT?

A consumer report contains information about your personal and credit characteristics, character, general reputation, and lifestyle. To be covered by the FCRA, a report must be prepared by a consumer reporting agency (CRA)—a business that assembles such reports for other businesses.

Employers often do background checks on applicants and get consumer reports during their employment. Some employers only want an applicant's or employee's credit payment records; others want driving records and criminal histories. For sensitive positions, it's not unusual for employers to order investigative consumer reports—reports that include interviews with an applicant's or employee's friends, neighbors, and associates. All of these types of reports are consumer reports if they are obtained from a CRA.

Applicants are often asked to give references. Whether verifying such references is covered by the FCRA depends on who does the verification. A reference verified by the employer is *not* covered by the Act; a reference verified by an employment or reference checking agency (or other CRA) is covered. Section 603(o) provides special procedures for reference checking; otherwise, checking references may constitute an investigative consumer report subject to additional FCRA requirements.

KEY PROVISIONS OF THE FCRA AMENDMENTS

Written Notice and Authorization.

Before you can get a consumer report for employment purposes, you must notify the individual in *writing*—in a document consisting solely of this notice—that a report may be used. You also must get the person's *written authorization* before you ask a CRA for the report. (Special procedures apply to the trucking industry.)

ADVERSE ACTION PROCEDURES.

If you rely on a consumer report for an "adverse action"—denying a job application, reassigning or terminating an employee, or denying a promotion—be aware that:

- **Step 1: Before** you take the adverse action, you must give the individual a **preadverse action disclosure** that includes a copy of the individual's consumer report and a copy of "A Summary of Your Rights Under the Fair Credit Reporting Act"—a document prescribed by the Federal Trade Commission. The CRA that furnishes the individual's report will give you the summary of consumer rights.

- **Step 2: After** you've taken an adverse action, you must give the individual notice—orally, in writing, or electronically—that the action has been taken in an **adverse action notice**. It must include:
  - the name, address, and phone number of the CRA that supplied the report;
  - a statement that the CRA that supplied the report did not make the decision to take the adverse action and cannot give specific reasons for it; and
  - a notice of the individual's right to dispute the accuracy or completeness of any information the agency furnished, and his or her right to an additional free consumer report from the agency upon request within 60 days.

Certifications to Consumer Reporting Agencies.

Before giving you an individual's consumer report, the CRA will require you to certify that you are in compliance with the FCRA and that you will not misuse any information in the report in violation of federal or state equal employment opportunity laws or regulations.

In 1998, Congress amended the FCRA to provide special procedures for mail, telephone, or electronic employment applications in the trucking industry. Employers do not need to make written disclosures and obtain written permission in the case of applicants who will be subject to state or federal regulation as truckers. Finally, no preadverse action disclosure or Section 6 15(a) disclosure is required. Instead, the employer must, within three days of the decision, provide an oral, written, or electronic adverse action disclosure consisting of: (1) a statement that an adverse action has been taken based on a consumer report; (2) the name, address, and telephone number of the CRA; (3) a statement that the CRA did not make the decision; and (4) a statement that the consumer may obtain a copy of the actual report from the employer if he or she provides identification.

IN PRACTICE...

- *You advertise vacancies for cashiers and receive 100 applications. You want credit reports on each applicant because you plan to eliminate those with poor credit histories. What are your obligations?*

You can get credit reports—one type of consumer report—if you notify each applicant in writing that a credit report may be requested and if you receive the applicant's written consent. Before you reject an applicant based on credit report information, you must make a **preadverse action disclosure** that includes a copy of the credit report and the summary of consumer rights under the FCRA. Once you've rejected an applicant, you must provide an **adverse action notice** if credit report information affected your decision.

- *You are considering a number of your long-term employees for a major promotion. You want to check their consumer reports to ensure that only responsible individuals are considered for the position. What are your obligations?*

You cannot get consumer reports unless the employees have been notified that reports may be obtained and have given their written permission. If the employees gave you written permission in the past, you need only make sure that the employees receive or have received a "separate document" notice that reports may be obtained during the course of their employment—no more notice or permission is required. If your employees have not received notice and given you permission, you must notify the employees and get their written permission before you get their reports.

In each case where information in the report influences your decision to deny promotion, you must provide the employee with a **preadverse action disclosure**. The employee also must receive an **adverse action notice** once you have selected another individual for the job.

- *A job applicant gives you the okay to get a consumer report. Although the credit history is poor and that's a negative factor, the applicant's lack of relevant experience carries more weight in your decision not to hire. What's your responsibility?*

In any case where information in a consumer report is a factor in your decision—even if the report information is not a major consideration—you must follow the procedures mandated by the FCRA. In this case, you would be required to provide the applicant a **preadverse action disclosure** before you reject this or her application. When you formally reject the applicant, you would be required to provide an **adverse action notice.**

- *The applicants for a sensitive financial position have authorized you to obtain credit reports. You reject one applicant, whose credit report shows a debt load that may be too high for the proposed salary, even though the report shows a good repayment history. You turn down another, whose credit report shows only one credit account, because you want someone who has shown more financial responsibility. Are you obliged to provide any notices to these applicants?*

Both applicants are entitled to a **preadverse action disclosure** and an **adverse action notice.** If any information in the credit report influences an adverse decision, the applicant is entitled to the notices—even when the information isn't negative.

NON-COMPLIANCE

There are legal consequences for employers who fail to get an applicant's permission before requesting a consumer report or who fail to provide preadverse action disclosures and adverse action notices to unsuccessful job applicants. The FCRA allows individuals to sue employers for damages in federal court. A person who successfully sues is entitled to recover court costs and reasonable legal fees. The law also allows individuals to seek punitive damages for deliberate violations. In addition, the Federal Trade Commission, other federal agencies, and the states may sue employers for noncompliance and obtain civil penalties.

FOR MORE INFORMATION

For your copy of the FCRA, write: Consumer Response Center, Federal Trade Commission, Washington, D.C. 20580; visit the FTC online at **www.ftc.gov**; or call 202-FTC-HELP.

APPENDIX II

FEDERAL TRADE COMMISSION FACTS FOR BUSINESS

CREDIT REPORTS: WHAT INFORMATION PROVIDERS NEED TO KNOW

The Fair Credit Report Act (FCRA) is designed to protect the privacy of credit report information and to guarantee that information supplied by consumer reporting agencies (CRAs) is as accurate as possible. If you provide information to a CRA, such as a credit bureau, be aware that amendments to the law spell out new legal obligations. These amendments were effective September 30, 1997.

DOES THE FCRA AFFECT ME?

If you report information about consumers to a CRA, you are considered a "furnisher" of information under the FCRA. CRAs include many types of databases—credit bureaus, tenant screening companies, check verification services, and medical information services—that collect information to help businesses evaluate consumers. If you provide information to a CRA regularly, the FCRA requires that the CRA send you a notice of your responsibilities.

WHAT ARE MY RESPONSIBILITIES?

The responsibilities of information providers are found in Section 623 of the FCRA, 15 U.S.C. § 1681s-2, and are explained here. Items 2 and 5 apply only to furnishers who provide information to CRAs "regularly and in the ordinary course of their business." All information providers must comply with the other responsibilities.

Federal Trade Commission, Bureau of Consumer Protection, Office of Consumer & Business Education, 202-FTC-HELP, www.ftc.gov (March 1999).

1. General Prohibition on Reporting Inaccurate Information— Section **623(a)(1)(A)** and Section **623(a)(1)(C)**.

You may not furnish information that you know—or consciously avoid know-ing—is inaccurate. If you "clearly and conspicuously" provide consumers with an address for dispute notices, you are exempt from this obligation but subject to the duties discussed in Item 3.

What does "clear and conspicuous" mean? Reasonably easy to read and understand. For example, a notice buried in a mailing is not clear or conspicuous.

2. Correcting and Updating Information—Section **623(a)(2)**.

If you discover you've supplied one or more CRAs with incomplete or inaccurate information, you must correct it, resubmit to each CRA, and report only the cor-rect information in the future.

3. Responsibilities After Notice of a Consumer Dispute from a Consumer— Sections **623(a)(1)(B)** and **623(a)(3)**.

If a consumer writes to the address you specify for disputes to challenge the accu-racy of any information you furnished, and if the information is, in fact, inaccu-rate, you must report only the correct information to CRAs in the future. If you are a regular furnisher, you also will have to satisfy the duties in Item 2.

Once a consumer has given notice that he or she disputes information, you may not give that information to any CRA without also telling the CRA that the information is in dispute.

4. Responsibilities After Receiving Notice from a Consumer Reporting Agency— Section **623(b)**.

If a CRA notifies you that a consumer disputes information you provided:

- You must investigate the dispute and review all relevant information pro-vided by the CRA about the dispute.
- You must report your findings to the CRA.
- If your investigation shows the information to be incomplete or inaccurate, you must provide corrected information to all national CRAs that received the information.
- You should complete these steps within the time period that the FCRA sets out for the CRA to resolve the dispute—normally 30 days after receipt of a dispute notice from the consumer. If the consumer provides additional rele-vant information during the 30-day period, the CRA has 15 days more. The CRA must give you all relevant information that it gets within five business days of receipt, and must promptly give you additional relevant informa-tion provided from the consumer. If you do not investigate and respond

within the specified time periods, the CRA must delete the disputed information from its files.

5. Reporting Voluntary Account Closings—Section 623(a)(4).

You must notify CRAs when consumers voluntarily close credit accounts. This is important because some information users may interpret a closed account as an indicator of bad credit unless it is clearly disclosed that the consumer—not the creditor—closed the account.

6. Reporting Delinquencies—Section 623(a)(5).

If you report information about a delinquent account that's placed for collection, charged to profit or loss, or subject to any similar action, you must, within 90 days after you report the information, notify the CRA of the month and the year of the commencement of the delinquency that immediately preceded your action. This will ensure that CRAs use the correct date when computing how long derogatory information can be kept in a consumer's file.

How do you report accounts that you have charged off or placed for collection? For example:

- *A consumer becomes delinquent on March 15, 1998. The creditor places the account for collection on October 1, 1998.*

  In this case, the delinquency began on March 15, 1998. The date that the creditor places the account for collection has no significance for calculating how long the account can stay on the consumer's credit report. In this case, the date that must be reported to CRAs within 90 days after you first report the collection action is "March 1998."

- *A consumer falls behind on monthly payments in January 1998, brings the account current in June 1998, pays on time and in full every month through October 1998, and thereafter makes no payments. The creditor charges off the account in December 1999.*

  In this case, the most recent delinquency began when the consumer failed to make the payment due in November 1998. The earlier delinquency is irrelevant. The creditor must report the November 1998 date within 90 days of reporting the charge-off. For example, if the creditor charges off the account in December 1999, and reports this charge-off on December 31, 1999, the creditor must provide the month and year of the delinquency (i.e., "November 1998") within 90 days of December 31, 1999.

- *A consumer's account becomes delinquent on December 15, 1997. The account is first placed for collection on April 1, 1998. Collection is not successful. The merchant places the account with a second collection agency on June 1, 2003.*

The date of the delinquency for reporting purposes is "December 1997." Repeatedly placing an account for collection does not change the date that the delinquency began.

- *A consumer's credit account becomes delinquent on April 15, 1998. The consumer makes partial payments for the next five months but never brings the account current. The merchant places the account for collection in May of 1999.*

Since the account was never brought current during the period that partial payments were made, the delinquency that immediately preceded the collection commenced in April 1998 when the consumer first became delinquent.

FOR MORE INFORMATION

If you have questions about the Fair Credit Reporting Act or want a free copy of the Act, write: Consumer Response Center—FCRA, Federal Trade Commission, Washington, D.C. 20580; visit the FTC online at **www.ftc.gov**; or call 202-FTC-HELP.

APPENDIX III

FTC STAFF OPINION— PERMISSIBLE PURPOSE JULY 6, 2000

Kevin Jay Long, B.S.
Medicolegal Research Company
4572 N. Milwaukee Ave. (#5B)
Chicago, Illinois 60630-3745

Dear Mr. Long:

This is in response to your letter requesting a staff opinion concerning Section 604 of the Fair Credit Reporting Act ("FCRA"). Specifically, you request the Commission staff's view as to whether a landlord's attorney, seeking to collect a disputed debt arising from a month-to-month lease, has a permissible purpose under Section 604 to obtain a consumer report in connection with legal action after the tenant has vacated the apartment. For the reasons set forth below, we believe that no permissible purpose exists under Section 604 in such a case. You also request information as to remedies available to consumers under the FCRA for such violations.

Section 604 of the FCRA provides that a consumer reporting agency ("CRA") may furnish a consumer report only for specified permissible purposes. Only Sections 604(a)(3)(A) and 604(a)(3)(F) are arguably applicable to the factual scenario described in your letter.[1] It is our view that neither of these provisions would provide a landlord or landlord's attorney with a permissible purpose to obtain a consumer report in the situation you present.

Section 604(a)(3)(A) allows a third party to receive a consumer report if the third party "intends to use the information in connection with a credit transaction involving the consumer . . . and involving the extension of credit to, or review or collection of an account, of the consumer." In our view, this provision is inapplicable to the residential lease outlined in your letter. Section 604(a)(3)(A) applies only to the review or collection of a credit account, as well as to an extension of credit to a consumer.[2] As discussed in the enclosed staff opinion letter (*Riddle*, 3/17/99), atypical residential lease does not constitute a credit relationship under the FCRA. Section 604(a)(3)(F) allows a person to obtain a consumer report in connection with non-credit transactions. Section 604(a)(3)(F)(i) provides a permissible purpose on behalf of a party who has a legitimate business need for a report "in connection with a business transaction that is initiated by the consumer." Thus, for example, a merchant may procure a report on a consumer who offers to pay for goods with a personal check. Section 604(a)(3)(F)(ii) provides a permissible purpose for a party who has a legitimate business need in connection with an ongoing relationship "to review an account to determine whether the consumer continues to meet the terms of the account." Thus, a financial institution may obtain a report on an existing checking or savings account customer. For the reasons set forth in the following paragraphs, it is our opinion that Section 604(a)(3)(F) does not provide a permissible purpose for a landlord or landlord's attorney to obtain a consumer report when considering legal action against a former tenant.

Section 604(a)(3)(F)(i) is clearly inapplicable in the fact situation presented, where the tenant has vacated the apartment when the landlord's attorney obtained the report. Certainly, this provision would permit a landlord to procure a consumer report to evaluate a consumer's rental application (that is, when the lease "transaction . . . is initiated by the consumer"). However, it does not give any business the right to obtain a report on a customer long after the transaction commenced. Given that Congress (1) amended the FCRA in 1996 so that this purpose is contingent on the consumer initiating the transaction, and (2) conspicuously omitted the "review" purpose allowed in the case of credit and non-credit accounts by Sections 604(a)(3)(A) and (F)(ii), it would not be consistent with the legislative scheme to interpret Section 604(a)(3)(F)(i) to provide a permissible purpose for a landlord or attorney to obtain a consumer report to consider suing a former tenant.

Section 604(a)(3)(F)(ii) is inapplicable because it permits a report user to obtain a consumer report only "to review an account to determine whether the consumer continues to meet the terms of the account." The legislative history shows the narrow focus of this subsection: "The permissible purpose created by this provision . . . is limited to an account review for the purpose of deciding whether to retain or modify current account terms."[3] When a tenant has vacated an apartment, a landlord (or attorney) has no need for a "review" to see if the former tenant "continues to meet the terms of the account" as required by the subsection, and the "limited . . . purpose of deciding whether to retain or modify current account terms" does not exist.

Civil liability and the amount of redress available for violations of the FCRA depends on the culpability of the violator. Sections 616 and 617 impose liability for willful noncompliance and negligent noncompliance with the FCRA, respectively. Both sections provide for redress in the form of actual damages proven by the consumer, plus costs and attorney's fees. For willful violations of the FCRA, the court may also award punitive damages. A person who obtains a consumer report under false pretenses, or knowingly without a permissible purpose, is liable for the consumer's actual damages or $1000, whichever is greater.

The opinions set forth in this informal staff letter are not binding on the Commission.

Sincerely,

Clarke W. Brinckerhoff
Attorney, Division of Financial Practices

Endnotes:

1. The other permissible purposes set forth in Section 604 are not at issue in the fact situation outlined in your letter. Under that section, a CRA may also furnish a consumer report based on a court order or subpoena, the written instructions of the consumer, in connection with employment, insurance, licenses or benefits, and in some circumstances involving child support. For example, a landlord could arrange for the tenant to authorize a credit report at the time he or she applies to rent the apartment, providing a permissible purpose under Section 604(a)(2).

2. *See* S. Rep. No. 103-209, at 11.

3. S. Rep. No.103-209, at 11.

CHAPTER 14
APPENDIX **IV**

FTC STAFF OPINION—
ADVERSE ACTION

July 14, 2000

Ryan S. Stinneford, Esq.
Pierce Atwood
One Monument Square
Portland, Maine 04101

Re: Section 615(a) of the Fair Credit Reporting Act and Section 202.9(f) of Regulation B, implementing the Equal Credit Opportunity Act.

Dear Mr. Stinneford,

This responds to your inquiry concerning the notice to a consumer required by Section 615(a) of the Fair Credit Reporting Act ("FCRA") and adverse action notices under the Equal Credit Opportunity Act ("ECOA"). Section 701(d) of the ECOA requires that a creditor must notify an applicant of the action taken on an application, including requirements in the event of "adverse action" on the application. 15 U.S.C. 1691(d). Regulation B of the Board of Governors of the Federal Reserve System implements the requirements of the ECOA, including the notice requirements set forth in Section 202.9 of that regulation. 11 C.F.R. § 202.9.

Section 615(a) of the FCRA imposes an independent requirement that a consumer be provided specified information in circumstances where adverse action with respect to that consumer is taken "based in whole or in part on any information contained in a consumer report." As you note in your letter, the Federal Reserve Board has indicated that the information required by Section 615(a) of the FCRA can be made on the same document as an ECOA adverse action notice, where the circumstances of a given applicant so warrant. Appendix C to Regulation B provides model forms that combine the FCRA and ECOA disclosures. Appendix C was amended to conform to the 1996 FCRA amendments. See 63 Fed. Reg. 16392, April 3, 1998, copy enclosed.

Your inquiry correctly notes that when an application involves more than one applicant, Section 202.9(f) of Regulation B permits the creditor to provide adverse action notification to only one applicant.[1] You ask

Is it permissible for a creditor to send a combined ECOA/FCRA adverse action notification (similar to Form C-1) only to the primary applicant, even if the application was denied based on the co-applicant's (or guarantor's) consumer report?

For the reasons set forth below, it is our view that the answer is no with respect to a co-applicant and yes with respect to a guarantor.

Section 615(a) requires that *"any* consumer" with respect to whom adverse action is taken must receive the disclosures mandated by Section 615(a) if that action is based "in whole or in part" on information from a consumer report. (Emphasis added). In our view, the plain language "any consumer" includes a co-applicant. Neither Section 202.9(f) of Regulation B, nor the combined disclosure permitted in Appendix C, remove or modify that requirement with respect to co-applicants. The objective of the combined disclosures permitted by the Federal Reserve Board in Appendix C to Regulation B is only to simplify the paperwork involved in making ECOA and FCRA notifications to a single applicant, where both are required—i.e., the action by the creditor is both adverse to the applicant (ECOA), *and* is based in whole or in part on information from that applicant's consumer report (FCRA).

Because Section 603(k)(1)(A) of the FCRA provides that, in the context of a credit application, "adverse action" shall have the same meaning for purposes of the FCRA as is provided in the ECOA, we look to the definition of "adverse action" set forth in Section 701(d)(6) of the ECOA, 15 U.S.C. § 1691(d)(6), and Section 202.2(c) of Regulation B, 12 C.F.R. § 2022(c). Under these authorities, only an "applicant" can experience "adverse action." Section 202.2(c)(1) of Regulation B, 12 C.F.R. § 202.2(c)(1). They further specify that a co-applicant is an "applicant" but that a guarantor is not. Section 702(b) of the ECOA, 15 U.S.C. § 1691a(b); Section 202.2(e) of Regulation B, 12 C.F.R. § 202.2(e).

Thus, in response to the specific example posed in your letter, when there are two applicants a creditor cannot send a combined ECOA/FCRA adverse action notification to only the primary applicant if the application is denied, even in part, based on information in a co-applicant's consumer report. In that circumstance, the co-applicant has been the subject of "adverse action" and must be provided his or her own separate notification to satisfy the requirement of Section 615(a) of the FCRA. If the creditor has provided the ECOA-required information specified in Section 202.9(a)(2) of Regulation B to the primary applicant, it need not be included in the FCRA notice provided to the co- applicant.

The rule is different for a guarantor, because he or she has not experienced "adverse action" that triggers the notice required by Section 615(a) of the FCRA. As discussed above, Section 603(k)(1)(A) of the FCRA adopts the ECOA definition, which excludes a guarantor. Thus a creditor need not provide guarantor with an FCRA adverse action notice, even if the application is denied in whole or in part based upon information from the consumer report of the guarantor. Under these circumstances, therefore, notification to the applicant is all that is required.

I hope that this information is helpful to you. The views expressed herein are the views of the Commission staff and are advisory in nature. They do not necessarily reflect the views of the Commission or of any individual Commissioner.

Very truly yours,

Christopher W. Keller
Attorney

Endnote

[1]Section 202.9(f) further requires that the notice must be given to the primary applicant where one is readily apparent.

APPENDIX V

FTC STAFF OPINION—RESELLER AUGUST 1, 2000

Ben Cohan, Vice President of Operations
Chase Credit Research Corp.
6350 Laurel Canyon Boulevard
North Hollywood, CA 91606

Dear Mr. Cohan:

This letter responds to your inquiry posing five questions about the applicability of various sections of the Fair Credit Reporting Act (FCRA) to the activities of re-sellers of consumer reports. I summarize each inquiry below, in italics, with my response following.

1. Is a re-seller that has no affiliation with any of the national credit repositories required to comply with Section 612(b), which requires each consumer reporting agency that **maintains a file** *on a consumer to make all disclosures mandated by Section 609, when the re-seller "does not maintain files but rather archives" consumer reports?* (Emphases in original)

Yes, a consumer reporting agency ("CRA"), including a mortgage reporting agency or re-seller, is required to make the consumer disclosures prescribed by Section 609, whether the company designates its records "files" or "archives" or uses any other terminology for the information it retains on a consumer. As your inquiry recognizes, Section 612 of the FCRA requires that "[e]ach consumer reporting agency that maintains a file on a consumer shall make all disclosures pursuant to Section 609 without charge to the consumer" under specified circumstances. Section 609, in turn, provides that every CRA shall disclose to the consumer "[a]ll information in the consumer's file at the time of the request." We reach our conclusion that these provisions require disclosure of all information because of the inclusive definition of "file" in Section 603(g) of the FCRA:

The term "file," when used in connection with information on any consumer, means all of the information on that consumer recorded and *retained* by a consumer reporting agency *regardless of how the information is stored.* (Emphasis added)

The use of words such as "retained" and "stored" suggests that a CRA cannot escape its obligation to make disclosure of information on a consumer simply by placing the information in a category that it considers archival.[1]

2. Can a furnisher of information to CRAs require a re-seller of consumer reports to provide the "written consent of a consumer" before the furnisher complies with Section 623(b) of the FCRA?

No. Section 623(b) requires the furnisher to conduct an investigation of disputed information when it is notified by a CRA pursuant to Section 611(a)(2) that a consumer disputes the completeness or accuracy of the furnisher's information with a consumer reporting agency. The consumer's dispute to the CRA under Section 611(a)(1)(A) triggers the furnisher's responsibility to investigate, and the furnisher cannot frustrate the aims of the obligation (or delay the process) by requiring the consumer to, in effect, double-authorize the investigation in a manner that is more burdensome than required by that provision.[2]

*3. Is a re-seller required to comply with Section 611 (a)(1) when the re-seller is **unable to investigate** the information that a consumer disputed?*[3] (Emphasis in original)

Yes. Section 611(a)(1) requires the consumer reporting agency, upon dispute by the consumer of the completeness or accuracy of any item of information, to "reinvestigate . . . and record the current status of the disputed information, or delete the item from the file" if it cannot be verified within 30 days. Section 611(a)(2) requires prompt notice to the furnisher of information of a consumer dispute. The furnisher's responsibility to conduct an investigation of disputed information, imposed in Section 623, is a discrete requirement, separate from the CRA's obligation to record the current status or delete unverified information. Thus, if the furnisher fails or refuses to conduct an investigation (which may constitute a separate violation of the FCRA by the furnisher), the CRA must still comply with Section 611.

4. If the answer to question 3 is "yes," does Section 611(a)(5)(A) require the re-seller to delete the disputed information?

Yes; if the consumer reporting agency (re-seller) cannot investigate within 30 days (with some qualifications contained in the FCRA), then disputed item(s) must be deleted. As noted above, the CRA's obligation to comply with Section 611 is triggered by a consumer dispute—it is statutorily separate from the furnisher's responsibility to investigate, and it does not require any form of "written consent from the consumer."

5. When a re-seller furnishes a consumer report to a lender, and subsequently both the lender and the consumer claim that the request for the report was initiated in error by the lender, is the national repository that reports the "inquiry" permitted to remove the inquiry from its file at the request of the re-seller?

No. If a CRA supplies a consumer report, it may reflect that event by an inquiry notation. There is no legal or policy requirement to display the inquiry (other than to the consumer in connection with disclosure pursuant to Section 609(a)(3)). The fact that a consumer report was requested "in error" does not nullify the fact that the report was furnished; that information must be retained by the CRA so that it can comply with Sections 609(a)(3) and 611(d), among other reasons.

I hope that this information is useful. The views that are expressed above are views of the Commission's staff and do not necessarily reflect the views of the Commission or of any individual Commissioner.

Sincerely,

Christopher W. Keller
Attorney

Endnotes:

1. If the information is retained by the CRA, it must disclose the information available "at the time of the request." For a CRA that updates the information in a consumer's file, this means that the agency need report only the information in the file at the time of the consumer's request. For a re-seller, it requires the disclosure of the "stored" or "retained" file.

2. Section 611(a)(l)(A) requires no written statements of any kind by the consumer, stating that the CRA's reinvestigation duties are triggered when the consumer "notifies the agency directly" of the dispute.

3. As an example of such inability to investigate, your inquiry suggests "such as when a consumer refuses to provide a written consent to the re-seller for investigating the disputed information." As noted in response to inquiry #2, however, no such written consent is required; the consumer dispute itself gives rise to the obligation (and implicit consumer authorization) to investigate, and the furnisher cannot condition its investigation upon consumer consent.

APPENDIX VI

FTC STAFF OPINION—BUSINESS LOAN

July 26, 2000

Charles Tatelbaum, Esq.
General Counsel
National Association of Credit Management
8840 Columbia 100 Parkway
Columbia, MD 21045-2158

Dear Mr. Tatelbaum:

This responds to your letter asking for the staff's opinion on the application of the Fair Credit Reporting Act ("FCRA") to the extension of credit for commercial purposes. Specifically, you inquire whether a permissible purpose exists under the FCRA for a business credit grantor to obtain a consumer report on an individual who is a principal, owner, or officer of a commercial loan applicant (a sole proprietorship, partnership, or corporation), or who signs a personal guarantee in connection with a commercial credit application by a third party. For the reasons discussed hereafter, we answer in the negative.

1. The report on the individual is a "consumer report" subject to the FCRA

Section 603(d)(1) of the FCRA states:

> The term "consumer report" means any written, oral, or other communication of any information by a consumer reporting agency bearing on a consumer's credit worthiness, credit standing, credit capacity, character, general reputation, personal characteristics, or mode of living, which is used or expected to be used or collected in whole or in part for the purpose of serving as a factor in establishing the consumer's eligibility for (A) credit or insurance to be used primarily for personal, family, or household purposes; (B) employment purposes; or (C) any other purpose under Section 604.

We understand your inquiry to mean that the credit report that the business credit grantor obtains is a report on the *personal* credit and other history of the individual who is a principal, owner, or officer of the entity that is undertaking the commercial loan (or who is serving as a guarantor). Because the information is "collected in whole or in part for the purpose of (assisting evaluation of) the consumer's eligibility for credit (or other authorized purpose)," the overwhelming weight of authority is that such a report is a "consumer report," regardless of the unauthorized purpose to which the information may in fact be used by the party procuring the report. *Yang v. Government Employees Ins. Co.,* 146 F.3d 1320, 1325 (11th Cir. 1998); *Comeaux v. Brown & Williamson Tobacco Co.,* 915 F.2d 1264, 1273-74 (9th Cir. 1990); *St. Paul Guardian Ins. Co. v. Johnson,* 884 F.2d 881, 884-85 (5th Cir. 1989); *Heath v. Credit Bureau of Sheridan, Inc.,* 618 F.2d 693, 696 (10th Cir. 1980); *Hansen v. Morgan,* 582 F.2d 1214, 1218 (9th Cir. 1978); *Pappas v. Calumet City,* 9 F.Supp.2d 943, 947-48 (N.D.Ill. 1998); *Boothe v. TRW Credit Data,* 523 F. Supp. 631, 634 (S.D.N.Y. 1981). The Commission's May 1990 Commentary on the Fair Credit Reporting Act,[1] is in accord.[2] Where the information concerns the subject's *business* history or status (i.e., is collected and provided by a commercial reporting agency for use in *business* transactions), of course, its communication to the user does not constitute a "consumer report" under Section 603(d). *Wrigley v. Dun & Bradstreet, Inc.,* 375 F. Supp. 969 (N.D. Ga. 1974); *Boothe,* 523 F. Supp. at 633.[3]

We recogize there is some authority to the contrary. See *Matthews v. Worthen Bank & Trust Co.,* 741 F.2d 217, 219 (8th Cir. 1984), where the court cites a comment by Representative Sullivan to the effect that the FCRA "does not apply to reports used for business, commercial, or professional purposes."[4] While this piece of legislative history is intriguing, we interpret it to mean that reports to business lenders by commercial reporting services such as Dun & Bradstreet, which compile data and provide reports only for commercial purposes, are not covered by the FCRA. It is highly unlikely that Rep. Sullivan's comments were intended to negate Section 603(d)'s specific application to a report made by a credit bureau that "collected (the information) for the purpose of serving as a factor in establishing the consumer's eligibility" for credit or other purposes authorized by the FCRA, by focusing instead solely on the purpose of the user. Emphasizing only the user's purpose emasculates the statute, as articulated by the court in the *St. Paul* case:

> To illustrate the untenable nature of St. Paul's construction of the FCRA in this context, suppose X secured Y's credit report for the sole purpose of disclosing it to embarrass Y. Under St. Paul's reasoning, focusing solely on X's "use" of the report, the report would not be a credit report under the FCRA and thus Y would not be afforded FCRA protections. Not only would this run contrary to congressional intent, it would render meaningless (Section 604) which allows for the release of credit reports only for certain purposes.

> Under St. Paul's reasoning, credit reports would be releasable under all circumstances. If used for non-FCRA purposes, a credit report would be releasable because it did not fall within the FCRA definition of a consumer report. If used for FCRA purposes, a credit report would likewise be releasable because it would meet the definition of a consumer report. We simply cannot conclude that Congress intended such an illogical result.

884 F.2d at 884-85.

We believe the majority view is clearly the correct one,[5] and that a report by a credit bureau on an individual based on information that was collected for the purpose of reporting on that individual does not lose its character as a consumer report because of an impermissible purpose of the user.

2. A commercial transaction does not provide a "permissible purpose" for a consumer report.

Your letter shows that you clearly understand that the lender may always assure a permissible purpose pursuant to Section 604(a)(2), which authorizes a report to be supplied pursuant to the written instructions of the consumer. We disagree, however, with your position that a permissible purpose exists under Section 604(a)(3)(A) or (F)(i). Those subsections provide such a purpose only where the recipient of the report:

> (A) intends to use the information in connection with a credit transaction involving the consumer on whom the information is to be furnished and involving the extension of credit to ... the *consumer*; or ... (F) otherwise has a legitimate business need for the information (i) in connection with a business transaction that is initiated by the *consumer*. (Emphasis added)

Section 604(c) states, "The term 'consumer' means an individual." Your letter states specifically that the "credit process is initiated by *the company* seeking the business or trade credit." When a corporation, partnership, or other business entity—rather than an individual—applies for commercial credit, there is thus neither an "extension of credit to (a) consumer" or "a business transaction that is initiated by a consumer" to provide a permissible purpose under either Section 604(a)(3)(A) or (3)(F)(i).

Because "extension of credit to ... the *consumer*" (emphasis added) is a prerequisite to the application of Section 604(a)(3)(A), where the application is made by a business entity, the provision does not provide a permissible purpose for a lender to obtain a consumer report on a guarantor or co-signer for—or a principal, owner, or officer of—the commercial credit applicant.

Section 604(a)(3)(F)(i), which provides a permissible purpose only for a "transaction that is initiated by the consumer " is also inapplicable to a credit transaction initiated by a business entity. The provision does not encompass commercial or credit purposes; rather, is designed to provide a permissible purpose to a business that is considering a *consumer* application for a purpose other than credit, employment, or insurance set forth in Sections 604(a)(3)(A), (3)(B), or (3)(C).[6] For example, a landlord to whom a consumer applies to rent an apartment, a bank to which a consumer applies to open a checking or savings account, or a merchant to whom a consumer offers a personal check as payment for goods or services has a "permissible purpose" to obtain a consumer report under this provision.[7] Section

604(a)(3)(F)(i) thus provides no authority for a lender to obtain a consumer report in connection with a credit application for any commercial purpose.

The court authorities are generally in accord. A *"consumer* relationship must exist between the party requesting the report and the subject of the report." *Houghton v. New Jersey Manufacturers Ins. Co.,* 795 F.2d 1144, 1149 (3d Cir. 1986) (emphasis added). Thus, there is no permissible purpose to obtain a consumer report on a corporate principal to evaluate the capacity of the company to pay a judgment. *Mone v. Dranow,* 945 F. 2d 306, 308 (9th Cir. 1991). Similarly, "evaluating prospective franchisees does not fall within one of the consumer purposes set forth in the FCRA." *Ippolito v. WNS, Inc.,* 864 F.2d 440, 452 (7th Cir. 1988). Other courts have held that a city had no permissible purpose to obtain a consumer report on the proprietor of a towing company that removed illegally parked cars on request from the police department, regardless of whether the municipality had a contract with the towing company, *Pappas v. Calumet City,* 9 F.Supp.2d 943, 950 (N.D.Ill. 1998); a company had no legitimate "business need" purpose to obtain a consumer report on a former employee who had suddenly resigned and was suspected of embezzlement, *Russell v. Shelter Financial Services,* 604 F. Supp. 201 (W.D. Mo. 1984); and a manufacturer had no "business need" purpose to obtain a consumer report on an individual who operated a mail order business that sold its products among others, *Boothe v. TRW Credit Data,* 523 F. Supp. 631 (S.D.N.Y. 1981).

Again, we acknowledge that the reported cases are not unanimous on the point. In *Advanced Conservation Systems, Inc. v. Long Island Lighting Co.,* 934 F. Supp 53 (E.D.N.Y. 1996), *aff'd without opinion,* 113 F.2d 1229 (2d Cir. 1997), the court found a permissible "business need" purpose for a consumer report on a corporate principal. If that view had any force at some point, it disappeared with enactment of the Consumer Credit Reporting Reform Act of 1996 ("the 1996 amendments") that revised Section 604 and many other sections of the FCRA.[8] The predecessor to Section 604(a)(3)(F)(i), quoted in the foregoing case,[9] provided a permissible purpose if the party "otherwise has a legitimate business need for the information in connection with a business transaction involving the consumer."[10] Because the 1996 amendments abandoned the "involving the consumer" formulation and replaced it with "initiated by the consumer,"[11] it is now clear that there is no permissible purpose unless a consumer (an individual) rather than a business entity initiates the transaction. Thus, in *Pappas v. Calumet City,* 9 F.Supp.2d 943, 950 (N.D.Ill. 1998), a court applying the amended FCRA found no permissible purpose to obtain a consumer report on the corporate principal based on the report user's dealings with the company operated by that individual.

The opinions set forth in this informal staff letter are not binding on the Commission.

Yours truly,

David Medine
Associate Director, Division of Financial Practices

Endnotes:

1. 16 CFR § 600 Appendix; 55 Fed. Reg. 18804-18828 (May 4, 1990). In this letter, specific sections are cited as "FCRA Commentary, comment..." with the latter part of the citation reflecting the applicable comment.

2. See FCRA Commentary, comment 604(3)(E)-2, revised by the Commission from an earlier draft to clarify this point. 55 Fed. Reg. at 18805, 18816.

3. FCRA Commentary, comments 603(d)-2 and 603(d)-3C, 55 Fed. Reg. at 18810.

4. 116 Cong. Rec. 36572 (1970) (Conf. Report on H.R. 15073). Citations from Rep. Sullivan also were featured in lower court decisions that preceded the *Matthews* decision in taking the minority view. *Henry v. Forbes*, 433 F. Supp. 5, 9 (D. Minn. 1976); *Sizemore v. Bambi Leasing Corp.*, 360 F. Supp. 252, 254 (N.D. Ga. 1973); *Fernandez v. Retail Credit Co.*, 349 F. Supp. 652, 654 (E.D. La. 1972).

5. In fact, it is not clear that even the Eighth Circuit continues to follow the *Matthews* case, which is the linchpin of the minority view cited at the beginning of this paragraph. In *Bakker v. McKinnon*, 152 F.3d 1007, 1012 (8th Cir. 1998), that court ignored *Matthews* and instead quoted *St. Paul* approvingly stating, "Under the FCRA whether a credit report is a consumer report does not depend solely upon the ultimate use (of the report), but instead, it is governed by the purpose for which the information was originally collected in whole or in part by the consumer reporting agency."

6. FCRA Commentary, comment 604-1D; 55 Fed. Reg. at 18814.

7. *Estiverne v. Saks Fifth Avenue*, 9 F.3d 1171, 1173-74 (5th Cir. 1993).

8. Title II, Subtitle D, Chapter 1 of Public Law 104-208, the Omnibus Consolidated Appropriations Act for Fiscal Year 1997.

9. 934 F. Supp. at 55.

10. In the original FCRA, this provision was Section 604(3)(E). Because Subsections (a)(3)(E), (b), (c), (d), (e), (f), and (g) were added to Section 604 by the 1996 amendments that also revised this portion of the FCRA, it was re-designated Section 604(a)(3)(F) at that time.

11. The change "restricts the scope of the business need exception by further defining the circumstances in which it applies." *Duncan v. Handmaker*, 149 F.3d 424, 427n3 (6th Cir. 1998).

CHAPTER 15

Fair Credit Billing

No new material.

CHAPTER 16

Skiptracing

No new material.

APPENDIX I

WHO'S WHO IN SKIPTRACING SERVICES

Company	Location	Website	Description
Affiliated Financial Resources	South Daytona, Fla.	Enterprise.america.com/ ~afrden	Provides background checks, employment, criminal searches, and other hard-to-find information.
BusinessCreditUSA.com	Omaha, Neb.	www.BusinessCreditUSA.com	Provides company profiles on 11million U.S. and Canadian firms in either CD-Rom or printed directory format.
Business Transactions Express (see Riskwise, page 379)	St. Cloud, Minn.	www.risk-wise.com	Provides credit, fraud detection, receivable management solutions, and modeling capabilities.
CDB Infotek	Santa Ana, Calif.	www.cdb.com	Locates debtors, uncovers assets, and obtains background information online.
CG Marketing, Inc., a division of Acxiom Corp.	Phoenix, Ariz.	www.cgmarketing.com	Provides Acollaid database of phone numbers, address changes, bankruptcies and Social Security numbers; plus: debtor locating and deceased services.
Collection Data Systems	Simi Valley, Calif.	www.collectone.com	Skiptracing services available as add-ons for collections software systems.
Columbia Ultimate Business Systems, Inc.	Vancouver, Wash.	www.colubs.com	Produces software systems for the accounts receivable management industry, with skiptracing add-ons.
DAKCS Software Systems, Inc.	Ogden, Utah	www.dakcs.com	Provides software systems for the accounts-receivable management industry.
Data Retrieval Systems, Inc.	New York, N.Y.	www.dataretrieval.com	Offers automated asset-based collections and enforcement programs and portfolio enhancements.

Reproduce with permission of *Collections and Credit Risk Magazine.*

DBT Online, Inc.	Boca Raton, Fla.	www.dbtonline.com	Provides online electronic access to public records for locating debtors.
DebtWatcher, Inc.	Mount Laurel, N.J.	www. debtwatcher. com	Offers on-line interactive computerized debt search-and-alert system.
Excel Investigations, Inc.	Alsip, Ill.	N/A	Offers skiptracing information from public databases and confidential resources.
Executive Marketing Services, Inc.	Naperville, Ill.	www.emsphone.com	Provides electronic directory.
People Locator	Ft. Lauderdale, Fla.	N/A	Provides a solution to finding missing witnesses, defendants, debtors, and insured.
Quick Infonet	Denver, Colo.	www.quickinfo.net	Offers access to motor vehicle, voter registration, businesses, UCC liens and national property judgments, bankruptcies, and lien data on a flat fee basis.
Riskwise LLC	St Cloud, Minn.	www.risk-wise. com	Provides comprehensive credit, fraud detection, consumer information, and modeling capabilities with flexible service delivery options.
SkipMaster, Inc.	Eureka, Mo.	www. skipmaster. com	Publishes the Skipmaster Collection Reference Manual, a 600-page guide for skiptracers and collectors designed to increase efficiency and reduce skiptracing costs.
Tracers International	Albany, N.Y.	www.tracers.com	Conducts assets discovery and locating services on a "no hit-no fee" basis.
Trak America, Inc.	Huntington, N.Y.	N/A	Provides home address and phone locate, verification services, property searches, assets location, and legal placement for judgment and non-judgment accounts.
Trans Union	Chicago, Ill.	www.transunion. com	Provides comprehensive consumer information database including credit reporting, fraud prevention tools, account monitoring, risk management, collections services, prescreening solicitations, predictive modeling products and mailing li lui
Universal Communications	Loveland, Colo.	www com .b.com	Provides Tel-Scan, for national unblockable caller identification, and Telegram Notification mailing service, both designed to increase recoveries and reduce skiptracing costs.
VeriFacts, Inc.	Sterling, Ill.	www.skiptracers.com	Provides skiptracing, asset location, and bad debt tracking services.

CHAPTER 17

E-Commerce Technology

E-COMMERCE—TECHNOLOGY

Despite the fact that Wall Street has not been kind to technology stocks in 2000 and 2001, e-commerce and the Internet, as well as the technology advances of the last 5–10 years, will remain with us and will affect every single industry in the United States. To keep abreast of the changing face of business, a chapter on technology and e-commerce is due, and perhaps overdue!

E-MAIL—COLLECTION

If a consumer consents in writing to the use of e-mail regarding the collection effort, one might say that this written consent should overcome the risk of disclosure to any third party. Specifically, the Fair Debt Collection Practices Act (FDCPA) states in Section 805(b) that it prohibits, without the prior consent of the consumer, a debt collector from communicating with any person other than the consumer in connection with the collection of the debt. A third-party disclosure by e-mail could certainly become an issue before the court. Your author does not recommend e-mail for collection efforts unless the agency, law firm, or creditor wants to be a test case.

One might compare this to mailing a letter that falls into the wrong hands and a third party sees the letter, but the sender of the letter deposited the letter in the postal box under the care of the United States Postal Service. A message by e-mail is a bit different, since e-mail is stored in your computer and the recipient's computer indefinitely in several places and is available for inspection in several places. Where the sender of the e-mail knows the circumstances under which the recipient will receive the e-mail and the likelihood of disclosure, a different issue may be presented to the court.

We've had several cases that have held that wiretap laws do not cover retrieval of a person's e-mail from post-transmission storage. The expectation of privacy significantly diminishes once transmission is complete. While the retrieval of an e-mail might be ethically questionable, the courts have held that it is not legally actionable under the Electronic Communications Privacy Act of 1986.

Wiretap laws are only violated when an e-mail is intercepted from intermediate storage or backup protection storage, both of which automatically occur during the course of transmission, or if the e-mail is viewed before the intended recipient has a chance to open it. Once an e-mail has been viewed by the recipient, Judge Brody in the 3rd Circuit found that none of the laws apply to subsequent viewing by a third party accessing it from some form of computer storage. In the case of *Frasier v. Nationwide Mutual Insurance Company* (98-CV-6726, E.D. Pa. 2001), Judge Brody stated that Congress or the states may in the future delineate the extent of employees' authorization to access e-mail, but for now she says employers will continue to have the legal right to monitor and read workers' e-mail communication after the transmission is complete.

E-MAIL—ATTORNEY-PRIVILEGE

The American Bar Association, in a formal opinion, permits a lawyer to transmit information relating to the representation of a client by unencrypted e-mail sent over the Internet without violating the modern rules of professional conduct, because the mode of transmission affords a reasonable expectation of privacy from a technical, logical, and legal standpoint. With regard to highly sensitive information, lawyers should take more exacting measures to preserve the confidentiality of the communication and certainly should consider other modes of transmission in these circumstances.

The various states have set forth in their rules on professional responsibility variations of the above statement. E-mail stays in the system certainly until the recipient opens up his e-mail and even after he deletes the e-mail, the e-mail still may remain.

Up to now, we have not had a substantial amount of litigation with regard to e-mail. But as attorneys decide to utilize e-mail for evidence at trials, the issue of privilege, the extent of the privilege, and the mode of transmission will be before the court. The definition of unusual sensitive matters and routine confidential matters is certainly one that will present problems.

E-MAIL—VOICE MAIL

With regard to e-mail and voice mail, once the communications are stored in the system, the employer would have access to these stored communications because they would fall under the Stored Wire and Electronic Communication statutes 18 USCA Section 2-701. Of course, this access is limited to the employer's use in the ordinary conduct of business. If a stored communication was publicized to co-workers or other third parties for a reason other than to properly conduct the business, the employer might be open to liability. Violations of the Stored Wire and Electronic Communication statute include fines and imprisonment up to one year for a first offense.

When monitoring, it is advisable to provide telephones for personal calls so that personal calls will not be interrupted. Confine the monitoring to the telephones that are used strictly in the ordinary course of business. A detailed manual on monitoring telephone calls should be prepared and each employee should properly acknowledge in writing that he has read and understood the manual. A warning label on the telephone is appropriate. Where no warning is placed on the telephone, and somebody walks in and uses the telephone, there is no implied consent.[1]

WEBSITE—DEBT COLLECTOR

A collection agency sent out a letter and referred the debtor to its website. The debtor did not even look at the website until after the suit was instituted. Nevertheless, the debt collector was held liable for violation of the

---

[1]*George v. Carusone*, 849 F. Supp. 159 (D. Conn. 1994).

Fair Debt Collection Practices Act under Section 1692E(10) which forbids a collector from using "any false representation or deceptive means to collect or attempt to collect any debt."

The court held that there were many misleading statements on the website. The website represented that the agency had three small satellite offices in the United States and 13 in foreign countries, but no such offices existed. The website also stated that there was a "full-time investigation staff" when in fact only one such investigator was employed. The website also stated that a "doctor served on the company's board of directors," but that was also not true.

The court held that since the letter incorporated the website into the letter, all the false representations on the website constituted a false representation or a deceptive means to collect a debt, and therefore, the debt collector violated the FDCPA.

This decision probably stretched the point since it was brought out that the debtor did not even look at the website. Nevertheless, it certainly is a warning to both agencies and attorneys that if they intend to refer to their website in any collection letter, the agency should review the contents of their website. The agency also could be subject to a suit for false advertising to potential users of the agency because the advertising was not truthful.[2]

WEBSITE—LICENSING

The licensing requirements for collection agencies in most states normally deal with the right of the collection agency to collect debts in the particular state. If a collection agency maintains a website, is it required to be licensed under any particular state? It would appear that maintaining a website is not an effort by the collection agency to collect a debt, but is merely the solicitation of business within the state. Whether this solicitation of business within the state meets any of the criteria set down in any of the licensing statutes of the 30-odd states that require licensing has not been addressed to my knowledge by any courts as yet. It would appear that a website is separate from an effort to collect a debt and should not be covered by any of the licensing statutes.

---

[2]*Van Westriemen v. AmeriContinental Collection Corp.*, 2000 WL 509 421 (D. Or. April 12, 2000).

P2P

Person-to-person payments have now become a part of the landscape. In a P2P transaction, a third party offers to a perspective buyer who is online the opportunity to electronically pay a seller without using the traditional credit card method of payment. A third party facilitates this transaction.

A consumer becomes a member of the service and assigns a specific checking account from which the monies can be drawn. The consumer sends an e-mail to the party who is entitled to payment and the recipient receives the e-mail and designates an account in which the funds are to be deposited. The service is presently used primarily for auction sites and, in some instances, for the purchase of goods.

No reason is evident why a consumer debtor cannot pay directly to a collection agency or law firm by using this method. Presently, the use of checks over the telephone (obtaining the necessary information and electronically creating the check) or the furnishing of a credit card number are the fastest and most effective way of receiving money from a consumer. This third option would probably be much cheaper and more effective and the money conceivably could be in the creditor's account within hours.

P2P—NO SIGNATURE

Assume that the credit card company had authorized the transaction and that the seller could prove that the merchandise was shipped. The consumer stated that she did not order the particular merchandise and the merchant did not have her signature on a sale or delivery sheet, since the merchandise was ordered online. When the consumer refused to pay, the normal procedure for the credit card company is to charge back the amount of the transaction to the merchant. As a general rule, Master-Card's policy is when there is a dispute and the merchant has already been paid, it will usually bill the merchant who has not obtained a signature and a card imprint. American Express states that it will absorb the cost of the merchandise only if the merchant can prove it shipped to the cardholder's billing address and obtained a signature proving the goods were delivered. Unless the merchant was using United Parcel or a type of mail that obtains a receipt, the merchant will find this difficult. While most of the large catalogue companies use United Parcel or an overnight delivery service, smaller merchants continue to use the U.S. Postal Service. VISA says that they make these decisions on a case-by-case basis, but emphasizes the fact that it is difficult for the merchant to prove that the party ordered the merchandise when they are unable to obtain a signature.

CALLER ID

Some agencies are utilizing initials as their official name with local and long-distance carriers, so that the agency name will not appear on the debtor's caller ID screen. A few states prohibit this practice and require collection agencies located in the state to display their full business name on any caller ID box. If the business name of the agency contains the word "collection" and the name of the agency may appear on the caller ID screen, the agency should consider changing the name, especially with predictive dialers.

TELEPHONE NUMBER CALL CAPTURING

The ability to acquire the telephone number of a debtor when the debtor calls the office is invaluable. This type of technology is now available and companies will identify debtor's phone numbers through call-capturing technology. This type of technology has been in use by the police for many years as is evident in the movies and the crime dramas on TV.

Is the agency using a deceptive practice to induce the consumer to make a telephone call to the company utilizing the call-capturing technology? Many agencies have ceased using the device, for it seems to be a prime target for the consumer attorneys when an unpublished phone number is acquired.

CELL PHONES

Section 808 of the FDCPA provides as follows:

> "that a debt collector may not use unfair, unconscionable means to collect or attempt to collect any debt. Without limiting the general application of the foregoing, the following conduct is a violation of this section"
>
> (5) causing charges to be made to any person for communications by concealment of the true purpose of the communications. Such charges include, but are not limited [to], collect telephone calls and telegram fees.

We must add to this section the use of cell phones. When a consumer uses a cell phone, whether he receives the call or makes the call, the cell phone is charged and this charge may become a violation of this section. If the debt collector is making a telephone call to a consumer's cell phone number, the consumer is incurring charges. Therefore, debt collectors should refrain from dialing numbers known to be assigned to a cellular or mobile phone without prior consent from the consumer.

COMPUTER EVIDENCE

Since most of the records of both the collection agencies and law firms involved in collection are contained in computer records, the issue of admissibility of computer records frequently comes before the court.

In one case, the former Vice President and Supervisor of FDIC Operations testified that she personally downloaded information from the computer system onto diskettes at the request of the FDIC. She stated that the day after the firm went into receivership, she tested the data on the diskettes for accuracy and kept them in her exclusive possession. She also testified as to the reliability of the firm's computer system. The court admitted the diskettes as evidence.

The defendants objected on the grounds that there was no way for them to determine what information was contained on the diskettes or to cross examine the Vice President about the information. The FDIC provided the defendants with a computer to visualize the information, but the defendants declined to use the computer.

The court stated that even when properly admitted, such records carry no presumption of accuracy and their credibility remains a question for the trier of fact. But the admissibility of business records should be liberally interpreted in favor of admissibility. The witness introducing the document need not have made the entry himself nor even have been employed by the organization during the relevant time. All that is required is that a qualified witness testify that the records were kept in the regular course of business, entries were made of the transaction at the time of the transaction, and it was business procedure to enter the transaction.

The liberal application is derived from the recognition that the trustworthiness of such documents come from their being used for business purposes and not used for litigation. The proponent must establish that the basic elements of the computer system are reliable. The court does not have to identify with precision what status in a particular company's hierarchy a witness must have to be sufficiently knowledgeable to testify about computer records. The witness may be the person who made the writing or record, or had knowledge of the transaction occurrence or event recorded. Neither the programmer nor the party who made the entry is necessary, but the knowledge of the basic elements that afford reliability and trustworthiness to computer-generated data is the criteria.[3]

DISCOVERY

The new federal rule of Civil Procedure Section 26(a-1) provides that either side must furnish to the other side all relevant material with regard to the lawsuit. This includes e-mail and other electronic documents, and probably also includes billing records. The problem with turning over all electronic instruments is that it is possible that the client may have trade secrets or other privileged data on the same disks as information that is discoverable in the suit. For this reason, care must be exercised when providing this kind of documentation. Use of protective order may be considered.

USING FAX MACHINES

Many debt collectors place bold disclaimers on their fax cover sheets in an attempt to avoid any exposure for an unauthorized disclosure to a third party. Your author knows of no decisions that provide that such a disclaimer might conceivably relieve the debt collector from liability. Using faxes is dangerous not only because of the disclosure to an unauthorized third party, but because that disclosure may be so blatant that the damages the consumer sustains may be substantial. Interestingly, although the debt collector might not have violated Section 803 for an unauthorized disclosure to a third party, under Section 808(5), the debt collector might be liable for causing a charge in excess of the debt to the debtor by using the debtor's fax machine.

INTERNET DOMAIN NAMES—GARNISHMENT

The issue is whether the contractual right to use an Internet domain name can be garnished by a creditor. The creditor obtained a judgment against

---

[3]*F.D.I.C v. Carabetta*, 55 Conn. App. 369, 739 A. 2d 301 (1999).

the debtor and commenced a proceeding against Network Solutions (NSI). Network Solutions is the major company that registers Internet domain names. The plaintiff attempted to garnish 38 Internet domain names that the judgment debtor had registered with NSI and asked NSI to place those names on hold and to deposit control of them into the registry under the creditor's name so that the domain names could be advertised and sold to the highest bidder. NSI answered the garnishment summons by stating that no money or other garnishable property belonging to the judgment debtor was being held. NSI characterized the domain name as "standardized, executory service contracts" or "domain name registration agreements."

NSI argued that a domain name cannot function on the Internet in the absence of certain services being provided by a domain name registrar, such as NSI. NSI performs these domain name services pursuant to a standard domain name registration agreement. The lower court held that the domain names were valuable, intangible property and were subject to garnishment. On appeal to the highest court of the State of Virginia, the court addressed this issue at first impression.

Because Internet users can more readily remember a name as opposed to a lengthy sequence of numbers composing an IP number, each individual computer or network has an alpha numeric name called a "domain name." Each portion of the domain name identifies a more specific area than the Internet, and as with IP numbers, are separated by a "dot." NSI's role in the Internet domain name system is to manage domain name registration. NSI charged an initial registration fee of $70 for each new name and it was valid for two years and may be renewed on a yearly basis for a fee of $35 per year. NSI compared applications with a database of existing domain names to prevent the registration of an identical second-level domain name and then matched a domain name to the corresponding IP number for the desired website. All these services are performed pursuant to a registration agreement. While NSI did not verify the registrant's right to use the name, the registrants must make certain representations and warranties, including certifying that the registrant has the right to use the domain name and it does not interfere with the rights of any other party.

The plaintiff argued that the registrant does have a right to transfer the name by using NSI's "registrants' name change agreement" and that therefore NSI only agrees to associate a particular domain name with an IP number and that this contractual right is an "intangible property." The court felt that not all contractual rights may be levied upon and were not willing to sanction the garnishment of NSI services under the terms of the existing garnishment statute. The court treated the domain name in the same way as a telephone number provided by a telephone company. It is merely a right to use the number and therefore a right to use the name.[4]

---

[4]*Network Solutions, Inc., v. Umbro Intern., Inc.*, 259 Va. 759, 529 S.E. 2d 80 (2000).

CHAPTER 17
APPENDIX I

ELECTRONIC SIGNATURES IN GLOBAL AND NATIONAL COMMERCE

15 USCS § 7001 (2000)

§ 7001. General rule of validity [Caution: This section takes effect on October 1, 2000, subject to certain exceptions, pursuant to § 107 of Act June 30, 2000, P.L. 106-229, which appears as a note to this section.]

(a) In general, Notwithstanding any statute, regulation, or other rule of law (other than this title and title II [15 USCS § 7001 et. seq. and 15 USCS § 7021], with respect to any transaction in or affecting interstate or foreign commerce—

   (1) a signature, contract, or other record relating to such transaction may not be denied legal effect, validity, or enforceability solely because it is in electronic form; and

   (2) a contract relating to such transaction may not be denied legal effect, validity, or enforceability solely because an electronic signature or electronic record was used in its formation.

(b) Preservation of rights and obligations. This title [15 USCS § 7001 et. seq.] does not—

   (1) limit, alter, or otherwise affect any requirement imposed by a statute, regulation, or rule of law relating to the rights and obligations of persons under such statute, regulation, or rule of law other than a requirement that contracts or other records be written, signed, or in nonelectronic form; or

   (2) require any person to agree to use or accept electronic records or electronic signatures, other than a governmental agency with respect to a record other than a contract to which it is a party.

(c) Consumer disclosures.

(1) Consent to electronic records. Notwithstanding subsection (a), if a statute, regulation, or other rule of law requires that information relating to a transaction or transactions in or affecting interstate or foreign commerce be provided or made available to a consumer in writing, the use of an electronic record to provide or make available (whichever is required) such information satisfies the requirement that such information be in writing if—

   (A) the consumer has affirmatively consented to such use and has not withdrawn such consent;

   (B) the consumer, prior to consenting, is provided with a clear and conspicuous statement—

      (i)   informing the consumer of (I) any right or option of the consumer to have the record provided or made available on paper or in nonelectronic form, and (II) the right of the consumer to withdraw the consent to have the record provided or made available in an electronic form and of any conditions, consequences (which may include termination of the parties' relationship), or fees in the event of such withdrawal;

      (ii) informing the consumer of whether the consent applies (I) only to the particular transaction which gave rise to the obligation to provide the record, or (II) to identified categories of records that may be provided or made available during the course of the parties' relationship;

      (iii) describing the procedures the consumer must use to withdraw consent as provided in clause (i) and to update information needed to contact the consumer electronically; and

      (iv) informing the consumer (I) how, after the consent, the consumer may, upon request, obtain a paper copy of an electronic record, and (II) whether any fee will be charged for such copy;

   (C) the consumer—

      (i)   prior to consenting, is provided with a statement of the hardware and software requirements for access to and retention of the electronic records; and

      (ii) consents electronically, or confirms his or her consent electronically, in a manner that reasonably demonstrates that the consumer can access information in the electronic form that will be used to provide the information that is the subject of the consent; and

   (D) after the consent of a consumer in accordance with subparagraph (A), if a change in the hardware or software requirements needed to access or retain electronic records creates a material risk that the consumer will not be able to access or retain a subsequent electronic record that was the subject of the consent, the person providing the electronic record—

   (i) provides the consumer with a statement of (I) the revised hardware and software requirements for access to and retention of the electronic records, and (II) the right to withdraw consent without the imposition of any fees for such withdrawal and without the imposition of any condition or consequence that was not disclosed under subparagraph (B) (i); and

   (ii) again complies with subparagraph (C).

(2) Other rights.

   (A) Preservation of consumer protections. Nothing in this title [15 UCSC § 7001 et seq.] affects the content or timing of any disclosure or other record required to be provided or made available to any consumer under any statute, regulation, or other rule of law.

   (B) Verification or acknowledgment. If a law that was enacted prior to this Act [enacted June 30, 2000] expressly requires a record to be provided or made available by a specified method that requires verification or acknowledgment of receipt, the record may be provided or made available electronically only if the method used provides verification or acknowledgment of receipt (whichever is required).

(3) Effect of failure to obtain electronic consent or confirmation of consent. The legal effectiveness, validity, or enforceability of any contract executed by a consumer shall not be denied solely because of the failure to obtain electronic consent or confirmation of consent by that consumer in accordance with paragraph (1)(C)(ii).

(4) Prospective effect. Withdrawal of consent by a consumer shall not affect the legal effectiveness, validity, or enforceability of electronic records provided or made available to that consumer in accordance with paragraph (1) prior to implementation of the consumer's withdrawal of consent. A consumer's withdrawal of consent shall be effective within a reasonable period of time after receipt of the withdrawal by the provider of the record. Failure to comply with paragraph (1)(D) may, at the election of the consumer, be treated as a withdrawal of consent for purposes of this paragraph.

(5) Prior consent. This subsection does not apply to any records that are provided or made available to a consumer who has consented prior to the effective date of this title to receive such records in electronic form as permitted by any statute, regulation, or other rule of law.

(6) Oral communications. An oral communication or a recording of an oral communication shall not qualify as an electronic record for purposes of this subsection except as otherwise provided under applicable law.

(d) Retention of contracts and records.

(1) Accuracy and accessibility. If a statute, regulation, or other rule of law requires that a contract or other record relating to a transaction in or affecting interstate or foreign commerce be retained, that requirement is met by retaining an electronic record of the information in the contract or other record that—

    (A) accurately reflects the information set forth in the contract or other record; and

    (B) remains accessible to all persons who are entitled to access by statute, regulation, or rule of law, for the period required by such statute, regulation, or rule of law, in a form that is capable of being accurately reproduced for later reference, whether by transmission, printing, or otherwise.

(2) Exception. A requirement to retain a contract or other record in accordance with paragraph (1) does not apply to any information whose sole purpose is to enable the contract or other record to be sent, communicated, or received.

(3) Originals. If a statute, regulation, or other rule of law requires a contract or other record relating to a transaction in or affecting interstate or foreign commerce to be provided, available, or retained in its original form, or provides consequences if the contract or other record is not provided, available, or retained in its original form, that statute, regulation, or rule of law is satisfied by an electronic record that complies with paragraph (1).

(4) Checks. If a statute, regulation, or other rule of law requires the retention of a check, that requirement is satisfied by retention of an electronic record of the information on the front and back of the check in accordance with paragraph (1).

(e) Accuracy and ability to retain contracts and other records. Notwithstanding subsection (a), if a statute, regulation, or other rule of law requires that a contract or other record relating to a transaction in or affecting interstate or foreign commerce be in writing, the legal effect, validity, or enforceability of an electronic record of such contract or other record may be denied if such electronic record is not in a form that is capable of being retained and accurately reproduced for later reference by all parties or persons who are entitled to retain the contract or other record.

(f) Proximity. Nothing in this title [15 USCS § 7001 et seq.] affects the proximity required by any statute, regulation, or other rule of law with respect to any warning, notice, disclosure, or other record required to be posted, displayed, or publicly affixed.

(g) Notarization and acknowledgment. If a statute, regulation, or other rule of law requires a signature of record relating to a transaction in or affecting interstate or foreign commerce to be notarized, acknowledged, verified, or made under oath, that requirement is satisfied if the electronic signature of the person authorized to perform those acts, together with all other information required to be included by other applicable statute, regulation, or rule of law, is attached to or logically associated with the signature or record.

(h) Electronic agents. A contract or other record relating to a transaction in or affecting interstate or foreign commerce may not be denied legal effect, validity, or enforceability solely because its formation, creation, or delivery involved the action of one or more electronic agents so long as the action of any such electronic agent is legally attributable to the person to be bound.

(i) Insurance. It is the specific intent of the Congress that this title and title II [15 USCS § 7001 et. seq. and 15 USCS § 7021] apply to the business of insurance.

(j) Insurance agents and brokers. An insurance agent or broker acting under the direction of a party that enters into a contract by means of an electronic record or electronic signature may not be held liable for any deficiency in the electronic procedures agreed to by the parties under that contract if—

(1) the agent or broker has not engaged in negligent, reckless, or intentional tortious conduct;

(2) the agent or broker was not involved in the development or establishment of such electronic procedures; and

(3) the agent or broker did not deviate from such procedures.

§ 7002. Exemption to preemption [Caution: This section takes effect on October 1, 2000, subject to certain exceptions, pursuant to § 107 of Act June 30, 2000, P.L. 106-229, which appears as 15 USCS § 7001 note.]

(a) In general. A State statute, regulation, or other rule of law may modify, limit, or supersede the provisions of section 101 [15 USCS § 7001] with respect to State law only if such statute, regulation, or rule of law—

(1) constitutes an enactment or adoption of the Uniform Electronic Transactions Act as approved and recommended for enactment in all the States by the National Conference of Commissioners on Uniform State Laws in 1999, except that any exception to the scope of such Act enacted by a State under section 3(b)(4) of such Act shall be preempted to the extent such exception is inconsistent with this title or title II [15 USCS § 7001 et. seq. or 15 USCS § 7021], or would not be permitted under paragraph (2)(A)(ii) of this subsection; or

(2) (A) specifies the alternative procedures or requirements for the use or acceptance (or both) of electronic records or electronic signatures to establish the legal effect, validity, or enforceability of contracts or other records, if—

(i) such alternative procedures or requirements are consistent with this title and title II [15 USCS § 7001 et seq. and 15 USCS § 7021]; and

(ii) such alternative procedures or requirements do not require, or accord greater legal status or effect to, the implementation or application of a specific technology or technical specification for performing the functions of creating, storing, generating, receiving, communicating, or authenticating electronic records or electronic signatures; and

(B) if enacted or adopted after the date of the enactment of this Act [enacted June 30, 2000], makes specific reference to this Act [15 USCS § 7001 et. seq. and 47 USCS § 231 note].

(b) Exceptions for actions by States as market participants. Subsection (a)(2)(A)(ii) shall not apply to the statutes, regulations, or other rules of law governing procurement by any State, or any agency or instrumentality thereof.

(c) Prevention of circumvention. Section (a) does not permit a State to circumvent this title or title II [15 USCS § 7001 et. seq. or 15 USCS § 7021] through the imposition of nonelectronic delivery methods under section 8(b)(2) of the Uniform Electronic Transactions Act.

§ 7003. Specific exceptions [Caution: This section takes effect on October 1, 2000, subject to certain exceptions, pursuant to §107 of Act June 30, 2000, P.L. 106-229, which appears as 15 USCS § 7001 note].

(a) Excepted requirements. The provisions of section 101 [15 USCS § 7001] shall not apply to a contract or other record to the extent it is governed by—

(1) a statute, regulation, or other rule of law governing the creation and execution of wills, codicils, or testamentary trusts;

(2) a State statute, regulation, or other rule of law governing adoption, divorce, or other matters of family law; or

(3) the Uniform Commercial Code, as in effect in any State, other than sections 1-107 and 1-206 and Articles 2 and 2A.

(b) Additional exceptions. The provisions of section [15 USCS § 7001] shall not apply to—

(1) court order or notices, or official court documents (including briefs, pleadings, and other writings) required to be executed in connection with court proceedings;

(2) any notice of—

(A) the cancellation or termination of utility services (including water, heat, and power);

(B) default, acceleration, repossession, foreclosure, or eviction, or the right to cure, under a credit agreement secured by, or a rental agreement for, a primary residence of an individual;

(C) the cancellation or termination of health insurance or benefits or life insurance benefits (excluding annuities); or

(D) recall of a product, or material failure of a product, that risks endangering health or safety; or

(3) any document required to accompany any transportation or handling of hazardous materials, pesticides, or other toxic or dangerous materials.

(c) Review of exceptions.

(1) Evaluation required. The Secretary of Commerce, acting through the Assistant Secretary for Communications and Information, shall review the operation of the exceptions in subsections (a) and (b) to evaluate, over a period of 3 years, whether such exceptions continue to be necessary for the protection of consumers. Within 3 years after the date of enactment of this Act [enacted June 30, 2000], the Assistant Secretary shall submit a report to the Congress on the results of such evaluation.

(2) Determinations. If a Federal regulatory agency, with respect to matter within its jurisdiction, determines after notice and an opportunity for public comment, and publishes a finding, that one or more such exceptions are no longer necessary for the protection of consumers and climinating such exceptions will not increase the material risk of harm to consumers, such agency may extend the application of section 101 [15 USCS § 7001] to the exceptions identified in such finding.

§ 7004. Applicability to Federal and State governments [Caution: This section takes effect on October 1, 2000, subject to certain exceptions, pursuant to § 107 of Act June 30, 2000, P.L. 106-229, which appears as 15 USCS § 7001 note.]

(a) Filing and access requirements. Subject to subsection (c)(2), nothing in this title [15 USCS § 7001 et seq.] limits or supersedes any requirement by a Federal regulatory agency, self-regulatory organization, or State regulatory agency that records be filed with such agency or organization in accordance with specified standards or formats.

(b) Preservation of existing rulemaking authority.

(1) Use of authority to interpret. Subject to paragraph (2) and subsection (c), a Federal regulatory agency or State regulatory agency that is responsible for rulemaking under any other statute may interpret section 101 [15 USCS § 7001] with respect to such statute through—

(A) the issuance of regulations pursuant to a statute, or

(B) to the extent such agency is authorized by statute to issue orders or guidance, the issuance of orders or guidance of general applicability that are publicly available and published (in the Federal Register in the case of an order or guidance issued by a Federal regulatory agency).

This paragraph does not grant any Federal regulatory agency or State regulatory agency authority to issue regulations, orders, or guidance pursuant to any statute that does not authorize such issuance.

(2) Limitations on interpretation authority. Notwithstanding paragraph (1), a Federal regulatory agency shall not adopt any regulation, order, or guidance described in paragraph (1), and a State regulatory agency is preempted by section 101 [15 USCS § 7001] from adopting any regulation, order, or guidance described in paragraph (1), unless—

(A) such regulation, order, or guidance is consistent with section 101 [15 USCS § 7001];

(B) such regulation, order, or guidance does not add to the requirements of such section; and

(C) such agency finds, in connection with the issuance of such regulation, order, or guidance, that—

   (i) there is a substantial justification for the regulation, order, or guidance;

   (ii) the methods selected to carry out that purpose—

      (I) are substantially equivalent to the requirements imposed on records that are not electronic records; and

      (II) will not impose unreasonable costs on the acceptance and use of electronic records; and

   (iii) the methods selected to carry out that purpose do not require, or accord greater legal status or effect to, the implementation or application of a specific technology or technical specification for performing the functions of creating, storing, generating, receiving, communicating, or authenticating electronic records or electronic signatures.

(3) Performance standards.

(A) Accuracy, record integrity, accessibility. Notwithstanding paragraph (2)(C)(iii), a Federal regulatory agency or State regulatory agency may interpret section 101(d) [15 USCS § 7001(d)] to specify performance standards to assure accuracy, record integrity, and accessibility of records that are required to be retained. Such performance standards may be specified in a manner that imposes a requirement in violation of paragraph (2)(c)(iii) if the requirement (i) services an important governmental objective; and (ii) is substantially related to the achievement of that objective. Nothing in this paragraph shall be construed to grant any Federal regulatory agency or State regulatory agency authority to require use of a particular type of software or hardware in order to comply with section 101(d) [15 USCS § 7001(d)].

(B) Paper or printed form. Notwithstanding subsection (c)(1), a Federal regulatory agency or State regulatory agency may interpret section

101(d) [15 USCS § 7001(d)] to require retention of a record in a tangible printed or paper form if—

(i) there is a compelling governmental interest relating to law enforcement or national security for imposing such requirement; and

(ii) imposing such requirement is essential to attaining such interest.

(4) Exceptions for actions by government as market participant. Paragraph (2)(C)(iii) shall not apply to the statutes, regulations, or other rules of law governing procurement by the Federal or any State government, or any agency or instrumentality thereof.

(c) Additional limitations.

(1) Reimposing paper prohibited. Nothing in subsection (b) (other than paragraph (3)(B) thereof) shall be construed to grant any Federal regulatory agency or State regulatory agency authority to impose or reimpose any requirement that a record be in a tangible printed or paper form.

(2) Continuing obligation under Government Paperwork Elimination Act. Nothing in subsection (a) or (b) relieves any Federal regulatory agency of its obligations under the Government Paperwork Elimination Act (title XVII) of Public Law 105-277) [44 USCS § 3504 note].

(d) Authority to exempt from consent provision.

(1) In general. A Federal regulatory agency may, with respect to matter within its jurisdiction, by regulation or order issued after notice and an opportunity for public comment, exempt without condition a specified category or type of record from the requirements relating to consent in section 101(c) [15 USCS § 7001(c)] if such exemption is necessary to eliminate a substantial burden on electronic commerce and will not increase the material risk of harm to consumers.

(2) Prospectuses. Within 30 days after the date of enactment of this Act [enacted June 30, 2000], the Securities and Exchange Commission shall issue a regulation or order pursuant to paragraph (1) exempting from section 101(c) [15 USCS § 7001(c)] any records that are required to be provided in order to allow advertising, sales literature, or other information concerning a security issued by an investment company that is registered under the Investment Company Act of 1940, or concerning the issuer thereof, to be excluded from the definition of a prospectus under section 2(a)(10)(A) of the Securities Act of 1933 [15 USCS § 77b(a)(10)(a)].

(e) Electronic letters of agency. The Federal Communications Commission shall not hold any contract for telecommunications service or letter of agency for a preferred carrier change, that otherwise complies with the Commission's rules, to be legally ineffective, invalid, or unenforceable solely because an electronic record or electronic signature was used in its formation or authorization.

§ 7005. Studies [Caution: This section takes effect on October 1, 2000, subject to certain exceptions, pursuant to §107 of Act June 30, 2000, P.L. 106-229, which appears as [15 USCS § 7001 note.]

   (a) Delivery. Within 12 months after the date of the enactment of this Act [enacted June 30, 2000], the Secretary of Commerce shall conduct an inquiry regarding the effectiveness of the delivery of electronic records to consumers using electronic mail as compared with delivery of written records via the United States Postal Service and private express mail services. The Secretary shall submit a report to the Congress regarding the results of such inquiry by the conclusion of such 12-month period.

   (b) Study of electronic consent. Within 12 months after the date of the enactment of this Act [enacted June 30, 2000], the Secretary of Commerce and the Federal Trade Commission shall submit a report to the Congress evaluating any benefits provided to consumers by the procedure required by section 101(c)(1)(C)(ii) [15 USCS § 7001(c)(1)(C)(ii)]; any burdens imposed on electronic commerce by that provision; whether the benefits outweigh the burdens;; whether the absence of the procedure required by section 101(c)(1)(C)(ii) [15 USCS § 7001(c)(1)(C)(ii)] would increase the incidence of fraud directed against consumers; and suggesting any revisions to the provision deemed appropriate by the Secretary and the Commission. In conducting this evaluation, the Secretary and the Commission shall solicit comment from the general public, consumer representatives, and electronic commerce business.

§ 7006. Definitions [Caution: This section takes effect on October 1, 2000, subject to certain exceptions, pursuant to § 107 of Act June 30, 2000, P.L. 106-229, which appears as [15 USCS § 7001 note.]

For purposes of this title [15 USCS § 7001 et seq.]:

   (1) Consumer. The term "consumer" means an individual who obtains, through a transaction, products or services which are used primarily for personal, family, or household purposes, and also means the legal representative of such an individual.

   (2) Electronic. The term "electronic" means relating to technology having electrical, digital, magnetic, wireless, optical, electromagnetic, or similar capabilities.

   (3) Electronic agent. The term "electronic agent" means a computer program or an electronic or other automated means used independently to initiate an action or respond to electronic records or performances in whole or in part without review or action by an individual at the time of the action or response.

(4) Electronic record. The term "electronic record" means a contract or other record created, generated, sent, communicated, received, or stored by electronic means.

(5) Electronic signature. The term "electronic signature" means an electronic sound, symbol, or process, attached to or logically associated with a contract or other record and executed or adopted by a person with the intent to sign the record.

(6) Federal regulatory agency. The term "Federal regulatory agency" means an agency, as that term is defined in section 552(f) of title 5, United States Code.

(7) Information. The term "information" means data, text, images, sounds, codes, computer programs, software, databases, or the like.

(8) Person. The term "person" means an individual, corporation, business trust, estate, trust, partnership, limited liability company, association, joint venture, governmental agency, public corporation, or any other legal or commercial entity.

(9) Record. The term "record" means information that is inscribed on a tangible medium or that is stored in an electronic or other medium and is retrievable in perceivable form.

(10) Requirement. The term "requirement" includes a prohibition.

(11) Self-regulatory organization. The term "self-regulatory organization" means an organization or entity that is not a Federal regulatory agency or a State, but that is under the supervision of a Federal regulatory agency and is authorized under Federal law to adopt and administer rules applicable to its members that are enforced by such organization or entity, by a Federal regulatory agency, or by another self-regulatory organization.

(12) State. The term "State" includes the District of Columbia and the territories and possessions of the United States.

(13) Transaction. The term "transaction" means an action or set of actions relating to the conduct of business, consumer, or commercial affairs between two or more persons, including any of the following types of conduct—

(A) the sale, lease, exchange, licensing, or other disposition of (i) personal property, including goods and intangibles, (ii) services, and (iii) any combination thereof; and

(B) the sale, lease, exchange, or other disposition of any interest in real property, or any combination thereof.

§ 7021. Transferrable records

(a) Definitions. For purposes of this section:

(1) Transferable record. The term "transferable record" means an electronic record that—

  (A) would be a note under Article 3 of the Uniform Commercial Code if the electronic record were in writing;

  (B) the issuer of the electronic record expressly has agreed is a transferable record; and

  (C) relates to a loan secured by real property.

A transferable record may be executed using an electronic signature.

(2) Other definitions. The terms "electronic record," "electronic signature," and "person" have the same meanings provided in section 106 of this Act [15 USCS § 7006].

(b) Control. A person has control of a transferable record if a system employed for evidencing the transfer of interests in the transferable record reliably establishes that person as the person to which the transferable record was issued or transferred.

(c) Conditions. A system satisfies subsection (b), and a person is deemed to have control of a transferable record, if the transferable record is created, stored, and assigned in such a manner that—

(1) a single authoritative copy of the transferable record exists which is unique, identifiable, and, except as otherwise provided in paragraphs (4), (5), and (6), unalterable;

(2) the authoritative copy identifies the person asserting control as—

  (A) the person to which the transferable record was issued; or

  (B) if the authoritative copy indicates that the transferable record has been transferred, the person to which the transferable record was most recently transferred;

(3) the authoritative copy is communicated to and maintained by the person asserting control or its designated custodian;

(4) copies or revisions that add or change an identified assignee of the authoritative copy can be made only with the consent of the person asserting control;

(5) each copy of the authoritative copy and any copy of a copy is readily identifiable as a copy that is not the authoritative copy; and

(6) any revision of the authoritative copy is readily identifiable as authorized or unauthorized.

(d) Status as holder. Except as otherwise agreed, a person having control of a transferable record is the holder, as defined in section 1-201(20) of the Uniform Commercial Code, of the transferable record and has the same rights and defenses as a holder of an equivalent record or writing under the Uniform Commercial Code, including, if the applicable statutory requirements under section 3-302(a), 9-308, or revised section 9-330 of the Uniform Commercial Code are satisfied, the rights and defenses of a holder in due course or a purchaser, respectively. Delivery, possession, and endorsement are not required to obtain or exercise any of the rights under this section.

(e) Obligor rights. Except as otherwise agreed, an obligor under a transferable record has the same rights and defenses as an equivalent obligor under equivalent records or writings under the Uniform Commercial Code.

(f) Proof of control. If requested by a person against which enforcement is sought, the person seeking to enforce the transferable record shall provide reasonable proof that the person is in control of the transferable record. Proof may include access to the authoritative copy of the transferable record and related business records sufficient to review the terms of the transferable record and to establish the identity of the person having control of the transferable record.

(g) UCC references. For purposes of this subsection, all references to the Uniform Commercial Code are to the Uniform Commercial Code as in effect in the jurisdiction the law of which governs the transferable record.

§ 7031. Principles governing the use of electronic signatures in international transactions.

(a) Promotion of electronic signatures.

   (1) Required actions. The Secretary of Commerce shall promote the acceptance and use, on an international basis, of electronic signatures in accordance with the principles specified in paragraph (2) and in a manner consistent with section 101 of this Act (15 USCS § 7001]. The Secretary of Commerce shall take all actions necessary in a manner consistent with such principles to eliminate or reduce, to the maximum extent possible, the impediments to commerce in electronic signatures, for the purpose of facilitating the development of interstate and foreign commerce.

   (2) Principles. The principles specified in this paragraph are the following:

      (A) Remove paper-based obstacles to electronic transactions by adopting relevant principles from the Model Law on Electronic Commerce adopted in 1996 by the United Nations Commission on International Trade Law.

      (B) Permit parties to a transaction to determine the appropriate authentication technologies and implementation models for their transactions, with assurance that those technologies and implementation models will be recognized and enforced.

      (C) Permit parties to a transaction to have the opportunity to prove in court or other proceedings that their authentication approaches and their transactions are valid.

      (D) Take a nondiscriminatory approach to electronic signatures and authentication methods from other jurisdictions.

(b) Consultation. In conducting the activities required by this section, the Secretary shall consult with users and providers of electronic signature products and services and other interested persons.

(c) Definitions. As used in this section, the terms "electronic record" and "electronic signature" have the same meanings provided in section 106 of this Act [15 USCS § 7006].

Index